W9-BLR-632

ALSO BY MICHAEL KARPIN

Murder in the Name of God: The Plot to Kill Yitzhak Rabin
(with Ina Friedman)

THE BOMB IN THE BASEMENT

HOW ISRAEL WENT NUCLEAR AND WHAT THAT MEANS FOR THE WORLD

MICHAEL KARPIN

SIMON & SCHUSTER

NEW YORK   LONDON   TORONTO   SYDNEY

SIMON & SCHUSTER
Rockefeller Center
1230 Avenue of the Americas
New York, NY 10020

For information about special discounts for bulk purchases,
please contact Simon & Schuster Special Sales at
1-800-456-6798 or business@simonandschuster.com

Manufactured in the United States of America

1   3   5   7   9   10   8   6   4   2

Library of Congress Cataloging-in-Publication Data
Karpin, Michael I.
The bomb in the basement : how Israel went nuclear and
what that means for the world / Michael Karpin.
p.   cm.
Includes bibliographical references and index.
1. Nuclear weapons—Israel. 2. Israel—Military policy. I. Title.
UA853.I8K375 2006
355.02'17'095694—dc22   2005051689
ISBN-13: 978-0-7432-6594-2
ISBN-10: 0-7432-6594-7

ACKNOWLEDGMENTS

MUCH OF THE RESEARCH of this book was done in connection with my documentary *A Bomb in the Basement*, which was the first film to explore the creation of Israel's nuclear program. Since it was released in 2001, the documentary has been screened in many countries. My good friend Abraham Kushnir conceived the film and produced it, and I owe him many thanks. Journalists Larry Kohler in New York and Yoav Toker in Paris did outstanding work as we gathered a broad foundation of data. I am grateful to the many people in many countries who allowed me to pester them for hours in interviews.

Ronnie Hope, chief copy editor of the *Jerusalem Report* magazine, was a steady source of wise counsel. He gave me invaluable advice on both language and content. Yossie Abadi, partner at the Caspi & Co. law firm in Tel Aviv, helped minimize the number and consequences of the deletions executed by the Israeli military censor. Naama Nehushtai drew the maps with consummate skill.

My sister-in-law, Shulamith Bahat, associate executive director of the American Jewish Committee, connected me to literary agent Regina Ryan in New York, who in turn guided me with great patience both before and during the writing and led the way to my publisher, Simon & Schuster. It is doubtful that this book would have been published without Regina's unflagging support, and I am especially grateful to her. My editor, Bob Bender, handled the manuscript with forbearance and professionalism, while working within a tough schedule. I am profoundly appreciative. His assistant, Johanna Li, coordinated the production stages. My appreciation goes to the copy editor, Tom Pitoniak, for his meticulous analysis of the manuscript, and to Executive Director of Publicity Victoria Meyer and Publicity Manager Rebecca Davis for organizing the promotional campaign for the book.

I was sustained throughout this project by the support and encouragement of my family—my wife, Pnina, my daughter, Maya, and my two sons, David and Daniel.

All of these people have been loyal partners in my work, but the responsibility for any flaws in the finished product is mine alone.

Jerusalem, March 2005

CONTENTS

Author's Note   ix

Introduction   1

1   A Dreadful Journey   7

2   The A Team   30

3   A French Window Opens   57

4   An Unprecedented Deal   74

5   First Nuclear Accident   96

6   A Nuclear Complex Grows in the Desert   117

7   Dimona Is Uncovered   146

8   De Gaulle Throws a Monkey Wrench in
     the Works   168

9   The Deception That Worked   178

10   A Mossad Conspiracy   196

11   The Heir   216

12   Cleaning the Stables   242

13   "We Have the Option"   268

14   A Secret Compromise   287

15   The Sadat-Kissinger Axis   322

16   Two Scenarios: War (with Iran) or Peace   337

Notes   361
Bibliography   383
Index   389

AUTHOR'S NOTE

THE MANUSCRIPT OF THIS BOOK was submitted to military censorship for inspection, as Israeli law requires of all Israeli media, foreign journalists in Israel, academic researchers, and authors who intend to publish information about Israel's security or defense matters. The chief censor, an army general, is entitled by law to block publication of anything that might, in the censor's judgment, damage the State of Israel.

The censor's office went over every sentence of this book carefully. A large number of passages, sentences, and words were blue-penciled. I appealed against rulings that seemed groundless to me, and many of my appeals were upheld, but in two places important information had been deleted and in some cases I was compelled to compromise on the wording of certain sentences. Nevertheless, in spite of the censor's scissors, this book contains important information that has not been publicly discussed before. It presents the Israeli nuclear project from a new perspective and gives a comprehensive account of Israel's "bomb in the basement."

I have been engaged in the news industry in Israel for thirty-six years, often handling information related to security that entails working with the censors. I know the regulations that we journalists have to abide by. The Supreme Court of Israel has ruled that censorship is warranted only when publication would create "near certainty of actual damage to the security of the state."[1] Unfortunately, the censors have sometimes confused style with substance and have chosen to quarrel over language rather than to assess, as required, the risk of actual damage to the state. Instead of removing real classified nuclear information, the government maintains a large bureaucracy that frequently spends its time altering harmless expressions that have nothing to do with confidential intelligence. Aluf Benn, the political correspondent of *Ha'aretz*, Israel's most influential daily newspaper, recently complained about this. He wrote:

Diligent workers waste their time erasing the words "nuclear weapons" and substituting "nuclear capability," or forcing the reporters to insert the words "according to foreign sources." In the eyes of the censor, any publication in the Israeli media is seen as official confirmation and exposure of the secret. Perhaps that's the way it was in the days of the [British] mandate, and Ben-Gurion. Today there is no reason for the media to serve as a means of implementing the "nuclear ambiguity policy" or any other governmental decisions.

Benn is right. The state has the legal authority to punish people who disseminate secrets whose publication could truly harm national security. This was apparently demonstrated in the case of Mordechai Vanunu, the technician from Dimona who was the first to blow the whistle on Israel's nuclear program in spite of his oath as a government employee not to reveal official secrets. Instead the bureaucracy wastes its time quibbling with journalists over language. That is why you will not see in this book such phrases as "Israel's nuclear weapons" or "Israel's atomic arsenal" or any of the many equivalents of those phrases.

In accord with its policy of ambiguity, to this day the State of Israel has never confirmed that it possesses nuclear weapons, a subject that I discuss in this book, though without using forbidden phrases. The interpretations of the diary of Munya Mardor, the founder of the state weapons development authority, and of his book *Rafael* by the world media and foreign publications with regard to the nuclear subject were not officially approved by Israel.

THE BOMB IN
THE BASEMENT

INTRODUCTION

SINCE THE EARLY 1970S, Israel has had the ultimate deterrent weapon, and by virtue of this fact there is virtually no one today who is not reconciled to Israel's existence as a sovereign entity in the Middle East. The Arabs can no longer throw the Jews into the sea, as some of their leaders used to threaten. This book recounts the history of this development.

In attaining nuclear capability, the Israelis had to hide what they were up to from the eyes of the world, in order to avoid provoking the curiosity of the international inspection bodies whose task it is to prevent the proliferation of nuclear weaponry. This was no less difficult a task than the actual achievement of the nuclear option.

Once the secret was out, Israel managed to persuade much of the world that its case is a special one, and this too was an achievement whose importance cannot be exaggerated. At the beginning of the third millennium, Israel is the only country outside of the great powers whose right to possess a doomsday weapon is accepted by most of the world. Unlike Pakistan and India, North Korea and Iran, Libya and Iraq, Israel has not been asked to give up its nuclear capability or to bare it to the world's scrutiny; it has not been censured for producing the ultimate weapon, nor has it been threatened with sanctions.

In the changed landscape since 9/11, statesmen in Europe and the United States have not hesitated openly to express their understanding of Israel's special status. British Prime Minister Tony Blair and his foreign secretary, Jack Straw, are among those who have done this.[1] But the clearest confirmation was sounded by the American secretary of defense, Donald Rumsfeld, at a NATO conference in Munich on February 7, 2004. A Palestinian journalist had asked him:

Mr. Secretary, you talked about countries that were trying to produce weapons of mass destruction. You talked about Iran and North

Korea. I have a question, a direct question to you. What are you doing with Israel? As far as Israel is concerned, Israel has more atomic weapons than any other country in the region. Why do you remain silent in regard to Israel? I think it's important to answer this question because this has to do with the world, the strategy that we are pursuing today. I think that if the position towards Israel were different, then the situation would be different in the Near East, and this is a great problem.

Rumsfeld replied in his own unique style, but made things utterly clear:

You know the answer before I give it, I'm sure. The world knows the answer. We take the world like you find it; and Israel is a small state with a small population. It's a democracy and it exists in a neighborhood that in many—over a period of time has opined from time to time that they'd prefer it not be there, and they'd like it to be put in the sea. And Israel has opined that it would prefer not to be put in the sea, and as a result, over a period of decades, it has arranged itself so it hasn't been put in the sea.

It can be assumed that the journalist did not get much satisfaction from this reply. And he probably would have skipped the question altogether had he known that Rumsfeld would use it to send a strong message to Israel's neighbors, especially Egypt and Iran, who had been demanding that Israel give up its nuclear option. Never before had such a senior U.S. official so clearly endorsed in public Israel's right to possess that option.

The practical expression of the position taken by Rumsfeld had come in a Memorandum of Agreement (MOA) that Israel and the United States signed on October 31, 1998. Its purpose was to provide Israel with protection against attacks involving missiles and weapons of mass destruction by other countries in the region. In this MOA, the United States tried to strengthen Israel's "defensive and deterrent capabilities," through assistance "diplomatic or otherwise" in order to defend it from "direct threats to Israel's security arising from the regional deployment of ballistic missiles of intermediate range or greater."

This agreement went further than any prior public document. It is possible that other such agreements existed, but they were kept secret, and so they had no deterrent effect. Although this agreement does not obligate the United States to send its military to help Israel if it is attacked by missiles, neither does it restrict Israel's response. The United States gives Israel permission to take independent preventive action if it is in danger. The original memorandum was signed by President Bill Clinton and Prime Minister Benjamin Netanyahu, and later ratified by President George W. Bush and Prime Ministers Ehud Barak and Ariel Sharon. This understanding, which among other things allows Israel a large degree of freedom in formulating its strategy toward the Iranian nuclear program, came after a long and complicated history that is the main subject of this book.

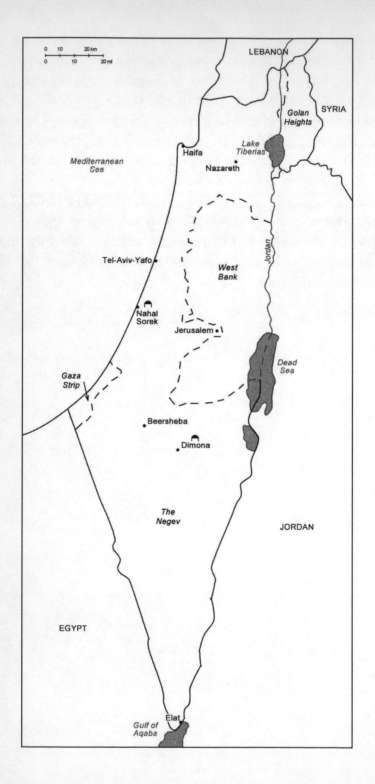

0   10   20 km
0   10   20 ml

LEBANON

SYRIA

Golan
Heights

Mediterranean
Sea

Haifa

Lake
Tiberias

Nazareth

Tel-Aviv-Yafo

Jordan

West
Bank

Nahal
Sorek

Jerusalem

Dead
Sea

Gaza
Strip

Beersheba

Dimona

The
Negev

JORDAN

EGYPT

Elat

Gulf of
Aqaba

THE MIDDLE EAST

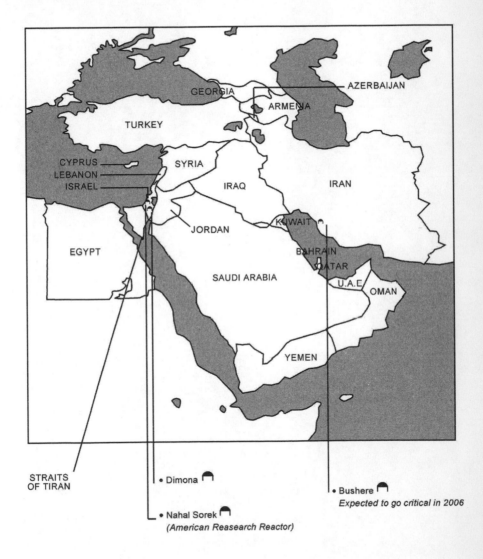

GEORGIA

AZERBAIJAN

ARMENIA

TURKEY

CYPRUS

LEBANON

ISRAEL

SYRIA

IRAQ

IRAN

JORDAN

KUWAIT

EGYPT

BAHRAIN

QATAR

SAUDI ARABIA

U.A.E.

OMAN

YEMEN

STRAITS
OF TIRAN

• Dimona

• Bushere

Expected to go critical in 2006

• Nahal Sorek

(American Reasearch Reactor)

CHAPTER ONE

A Dreadful Journey

BEN-GURION STOOD IN SILENCE at the edge of the mass grave at Bergen-Belsen concentration camp, tears rolling down his cheeks. A British major stood at his side and described the scene of horror he had witnessed when he entered the camp as it was liberated six months before, on April 15, 1945. There were piles of corpses between the long lines of barracks. One of the heaps of bodies was higher than the roof of the barracks. On the pathways lay hundreds of living skeletons. Thousands were dying of starvation and disease inside the huts. In the five days that followed, fourteen thousand inmates died of typhus and dysentery. The British army lacked the means to cope with a disaster of such dimensions. To wipe out the typhus epidemic, they had to burn the barracks. They rounded up German civilians from the vicinity and ordered them to bury the corpses. The Germans picked up the bodies and threw them into the pit. This is where they were buried, said the major, pointing at the roped-off mound of loose earth in front of them.

Ben-Gurion was stunned. A seventeen-year-old camp survivor, Tamar Shpruch, remembers seeing him, a short, sturdy figure in a cloth coat, hunched up and weeping. She remembers that day—the date etched in her memory, October 27, 1945. She had pushed into the circle of Jewish survivors surrounding him because she knew his name. She did not know then that he was the leader of the Jews of Palestine, then under the British mandate.

Years later, Ben-Gurion's closest aide, Yitzhak Navon, who in the late 1970s was to become the fifth president of Israel, related that Ben-

Gurion had never been able to free himself of the scenes he had witnessed in Germany in the autumn of 1945. "When he remembered that
journey, he would emotionally describe what he had experienced, and
tear at his hair and ask, 'How could it happen? Such horrible slaughter.
Such awful atrocities,'" Navon recalled.

David Ben-Gurion traveled to Germany in mid-October 1945, five
months after the Nazis surrendered to the Allies, to get a firsthand impression of the aftermath of the destruction of European Jewry. In the
displaced-persons camps, he met those who had survived the ghettoes
and the death camps, among them distant relatives and acquaintances
from his birthplace in Poland. From them he heard tales that left him in
shock. The scope of the Holocaust was already known across the world;
this is not what astonished Ben-Gurion. But for a Jew who had spent the
war years far from the European inferno, this first human contact with
the living testimonies from hell was stunning, heartbreaking.

Ben-Gurion visited the Dachau concentration camp, outside Munich,
and the extermination camp at Bergen-Belsen, near Hanover. At
Dachau, he paced the length of the barracks that had housed the inmates, and gazed at the narrow, wooden bunks into which they had been
crammed. At one end of the camp, he stood in shock facing the cremato-
rium. The stench of burned flesh still hung in the air. On the vast plateau
where the Bergen-Belsen camp had been built, Ben-Gurion stopped at
the memorial monuments that had just been put up over the mass graves,
and copied into his notebook the epitaphs inscribed on them.

Groups of excited survivors pressed around Ben-Gurion, and he stood
among them, listening patiently to their accounts, and asking questions.
What had they gone through? How had the Nazis abused and tortured
them and murdered their families? Who had rescued them? Diligently,
he recorded their replies in his notebook. Survivors spoke all at once, the
stories of their ordeals tumbling out, and he made no attempt to hush
them, but listened patiently, asking an occasional question in Polish or
Yiddish, sometimes uttering an emotional phrase in Hebrew.

He asked in Polish if they were ready to go to Palestine. Some said
"Yo" in Yiddish, and others "Ken" in Hebrew—yes. Some shouted
"Bravo!" and clapped their hands. He told them the journey was per-
ilous, that the British had imposed a blockade along the Mediterranean

coastlines to prevent Jews from reaching Eretz Yisrael (Hebrew for the Land of Israel, what was then Palestine), beyond the minuscule immigration quota that they had set. Perhaps the survivors who wanted to go would have to break the blockade by force, launch hunger strikes, face dangerous situations. Most responded with enthusiastic cries of "We are ready," and "Give the orders."

Ben-Gurion spoke quietly. He said there was only one solution to the dire condition of the Jewish people: "Eretz Yisrael as a Jewish center, which does not rely on others but builds its strength, its will and its independence."[1] Tamar Shpruch remembers that sentence, which Ben-Gurion would repeat in various versions countless times in the years to come.

Someone began to sing the anthem of the Jewish partisans who had fought the Nazis, and others joined in. They sang all of the verses in Yiddish; some of them wept. Ben-Gurion listened, visibly moved. After the song, there was quiet. Ben-Gurion said it was the first time he had heard it, and asked how many Jewish partisans there had been. "Many," "thousands," came the reply from the crowd. For Ben-Gurion, the fact that thousands of Jews had fought the Nazis was a tremendous revelation. Not all the Jews had surrendered abjectly and gone passively to their deaths, as the world had been led to believe. Many had chosen to fight back. He asked them to dictate the words of the song and he wrote them down, slowly in his notebook:

> *You must not say that you now walk the final way,*
> *Because the darkened heavens hide the blue of day.*
> *The time we've longed for will at last draw near,*
> *And our steps, as drums, will sound that we are here.*

Ben-Gurion's host in Germany was General Walter Bedell Smith, chief of staff to General Dwight D. Eisenhower, the supreme Allied commander. Smith gave Ben-Gurion a military escort and introduced him as head of the Jewish community in Palestine to Eisenhower. According to Ben-Gurion, Eisenhower received him with a "warm welcome" and called him "the moving spirit behind the enterprise of building Palestine." Fifteen years would pass until the two would meet again: In 1960, Eisenhower, as president of the United States, was host to the first-ever visit—albeit not a state visit—to the White House by an Israeli prime minister: David Ben-Gurion. Then Ben-Gurion would plead for arms to meet Israel's defense needs, but now, at Eisenhower's Frankfurt headquarters,[2] there were other matters on the agenda. Ben-Gurion first thanked Eisenhower for the adequate treatment given to the Jewish refugees, then suggested that they all be concentrated in one area, under a form of "self-management," and that they have "physical training, drill exercises and discipline," in order to bolster their confidence in themselves and to "minimize contacts with Germans."

But bolstering the self-confidence of the refugees and boosting their spirits was not what was on Ben-Gurion's mind when he met with the supreme Allied commander. Since the end of the world war, Ben-Gurion's acute political sense had led him to concentrate on building up the military strength of the Jews in Palestine. Ben-Gurion wanted to integrate some of the refugees, at least the younger ones, in his plans to defend against what he was sure was an imminent attack by the Arabs. If conditions could be created within the displaced-persons camps that would make it possible to organize the young Jews in semimilitary formations and even to train them in the use of light arms, they could then be shipped to Palestine and sent into the battlefield immediately after disembarking. The British were still refusing to give up their mandate and remove their army, and so were thereby delaying the declaration of Jewish independence. But to Ben-Gurion that event was visible on the horizon, and he knew that when it came, a bitter struggle with the Arab states would ensue. Ben-Gurion's analysis proved very accurate.

One evening at the end of October 1945, a few days after Ben-Gurion's visit to Bergen-Belsen, emissaries from Palestine loaded Tamar Shpruch's group of *halutzim* onto a military truck that had been stolen from a British army camp not far from Belsen. The truck set out for the port of Le Havre in France, on the English Channel. Two days later, the truck reached its destination and stopped. A handsome young man in an English officer's uniform lifted the canvas cover of the back of the truck, climbed in, and said in perfect German, "My name is Meir Mardor, but everyone calls me Munya. Our people stole this truck from the British army for you. Soon you'll be boarding a cargo ship that we bought in

America and outfitted here. You are part of the quota that the British have set for Jewish immigration into Palestine, and therefore I do not expect you to have any problems. Soon we'll meet in Eretz Yisrael." Minutes later, the group was climbing the ship's gangplank and onto the upper deck.

In those days, Mardor was one of the heads of the underground organization known as "Ha-Mossad l'Aliyah Bet," or the "Institute for Illegal Immigration," which had been set up by the Zionist movement in order to smuggle displaced Jewish refugees from across the continent to European ports, and from there by ship to Palestine. From Ha-Mossad l'Aliyah Bet evolved Ha-Mossad le'Modiin ule-Tafkidim Meyuhadim (Institute for Intelligence and Special Duties), or "the Mossad" in short, founded in 1951, Israel's equivalent to the CIA.

Munya Mardor would later become the director of RAFAEL, the Israeli government's arms development agency. Mardor, according to foreign reports, headed the team of experts who developed Israel's atomic capability.

While Tamar's ship was leaving Le Havre on its way to the Mediterranean, Ben-Gurion was in Paris. There he summoned senior Mossad operatives and ordered them to step up the pace at which they were shipping the refugees out of Europe, despite the British blockade of the Palestinian coast. For months he had concentrated a great deal of effort on enlisting the support of French military and political officials who had fought the Nazis as members of the Maquis. They had emerged from the underground only a short while before, when the Allies had invaded Europe and liberated France. He conferred with some of the heads of *l'armée juive*, the "Jewish army," which had fought as part of the French underground. He also met with commanders of General Charles de Gaulle's Free French forces, who had operated in exile out of London and had now returned and were filling key posts in the interim government in Paris. This network of French support assisted Ben-Gurion in setting up a sophisticated operational headquarters in Paris. Senior French government officials and army officers helped Mossad overcome the obstacles placed by the British in the way of the migration of Jews to Palestine. They enlisted military experts, contributed funds, and even supplied the Mossad operatives with weapons.

Support was forthcoming from the very highest echelons of the French government. The foreign minister, Georges Bidault, quoted de Gaulle to Ben-Gurion. "I have been to Palestine," the French leader said, "and I have seen that the Jews are the only force that is building it." Bidault himself said at the meeting that "the government of France relates with sympathy to Zionism." In 1938, Bidault had led the French opposition to the Munich agreement with Hitler. Immediately after the French capitulation to Germany, the Vichy regime arrested him. He was released on probation, joined the Maquis, and was involved in an underground newspaper, *Combat*, whose editor was the writer Albert Camus. At the end of May 1943, after the legendary underground leader Jean Moulin was captured by the Nazis and killed in prison, Bidault replaced him. Before D-Day in June 1944, he was made responsible for coordination between the invading Allied forces and the Maquis cells. A Catholic, he felt close to Zionism mainly because of the common fate of the Frenchmen and the Jews in Nazi prisons and concentration camps. He was not alone; many of the leaders of the Free French felt remorse over the fact that some French circles had cooperated with the Nazis in the "Final Solution." Some of them declared this openly.

One of these conscience-stricken Frenchmen was Abel Thomas, an officer in the Free French forces, who had returned to Paris with de Gaulle. He had just learned that his younger brother, Pierre Thomas, a lieutenant in the French Resistance, had been tortured by the Gestapo in the Dora-Buchenwald concentration camp in Nazi Germany, where he died of starvation on February 22, 1945, at the age of twenty-three.

Pierre Thomas was not a Jew; he was killed because he fought to liberate his country. Abel heard about the suffering of the Jews in the displaced-persons camps, and felt a commonality of fate. He decided that from then on, he would give as much help as he could to the remnants of the Holocaust. This would become his life's mission.

Ben-Gurion would meet Thomas only in the late 1950s, when the special relationship of the Israelis with the French, whose seeds Ben-Gurion planted in 1945, would reach fruition. At issue when they met was a Soviet threat to launch missiles against Israel, and Thomas was one of the senior French government officials who would move mountains to provide Israel with the means to defend itself. Strange as it is, one could say that the murder of the young Frenchman Pierre Thomas was a crucial early link in a chain of events that years later allowed Ben-Gurion to realize his vision of arming Israel with a nuclear capability.

DAVID BEN-GURION, the man who conceived the idea of the Jewish doomsday weapon, was born in 1886 in Plonsk, a small provincial town in eastern Poland, which earlier in the 19th century had been conquered by the Russian czarist empire. More than 70 percent of the population of Plonsk were Jews. Avigdor and Sheindel Gruen named their fourth son David Yosef. Avigdor Gruen was an educated, well-read man who spoke several languages and made a living from writing petitions and giving legal advice. Although he wasn't a law graduate, the authorities permitted him to appear in court. "My father gave me my love of the Jewish people, for the Land of Israel, and for the Hebrew language," David Ben-Gurion wrote to his family in New York when Avigdor died. Actually, it was his grandfather, Zvi Arieh Gruen, who taught him Hebrew, which he learned to speak and read fluently.

Young David was weak and sickly, and his mother pampered him and favored him over his brothers. He became very attached to her. "My mother died in my childhood, when I was ten," he related many years later. "But I remember her well, as if she were still alive, and I know she was the epitome of purity, love, nobility, humanity, and devotion."

David Gruen was a classic product of the second generation of the Zionist revolution, which had begun in Eastern Europe a few years before he was born. The revolution's primary goal was to free the Jews from Europe, a hostile environment filled with anti-Semitic hatred, and to settle them in their own land. There they would build a sovereign, modern nation with a single language and a rational economic structure. The vision was to establish in this Land of Israel an exemplary society, secular and democratic, and to create a new type of Jew: a free and productive citizen who would shed the long black coat worn by the ghetto Jew, shave off his side-locks and beard, drop the preoccupation with religious studies and devotions, and let go of the belief that the Land of Israel would be redeemed only by divine providence and the coming of the messiah. The Jews, the early Zionists believed, must discard the traits that characterized the Diaspora in Europe: conservatism, provincialism, narrow-mindedness, and blind resignation to the blows of fate.

"From the age of five, it was clear that I would settle in the Land of Israel," Ben-Gurion told his biographer, Michael Bar-Zohar. In those years, most Jewish migrants headed for the New World. Only a few had the courage to make their way to Palestine. There were fewer than eighty thousand Jews living there in the summer of 1906, when the boat carrying the twenty-year-old David Gruen anchored off Jaffa. That day, he wrote in his diary that he was charmed, happy, and "totally intoxicated." In a letter to his father he gushed in poetic Hebrew: "The air was wonderful, full of sweet scents like the air of the Garden of Eden, clean and clear as pure glass; in that air we could see a distance of dozens of miles." He was in love with the Land of Israel. That night, out of sheer excitement, he couldn't sleep a wink. A week later, he contracted a fever, and a physician, Dr. Stein, advised him to go back to Russia. "There is nothing you can do. You simply can not stay here," he told him. David Gruen did not take his advice, of course.

When he was twenty-four and an agricultural laborer, a *halutz* in the Land of Israel, he adopted the ancient Hebrew name Ben-Gurion.[3] He was a Zionist and a socialist: He believed Jews had the right to establish a national home of their own in the Land of Israel, and aspired to set up a cooperative, egalitarian Jewish society there. He had been steeped in Zionism at home, and he believed in it with all his heart, uncompromisingly. His socialism developed in the ideological ferment that spread in Russia after the failed revolution of 1905.

Ben-Gurion had abandoned religion in his youth. In one swoop, he turned secular, giving up the tefillin along with prayer and the precepts of Judaism. When his father learned of this, he slapped his son on the cheek for the first and only time in his life, but David was resolute, and his father gave up.

Ben-Gurion was a stocky man, with dark eyes, curly hair, and a disproportionately large head. From an early age he tended to withdraw into himself. His hunger for learning was insatiable, and his memory phenomenal. Strict with himself and determined, he read books obsessively. For most of his life he kept a diary, in which he documented his life hour by hour, event by event. It is therefore easy to follow his steps and to understand his motives.

From an early age Ben-Gurion knew he was meant for greatness; he was driven by a deep sense of mission. His authority was natural and people felt secure in his presence. However, he would pose difficult objectives for himself and his followers. So it was when he informed his comrades in 1932 of his desire to make the socialist camp the majority in the Zionist movement. "When I presented the concrete challenge for the first time . . . many of the comrades said it was impossible," he wrote to friends three years later. When in November 1929 he announced his decision to bring about a Jewish majority in the land of Israel, his audience thought he was fantasizing. At that time there were five times more Arabs than Jews in the country.

Ben-Gurion could always foresee events that were still a long way over the horizon. Late in 1936 he spoke of "the impending world war." A week after the Wehrmacht invaded Poland, on September 8, 1939, he declared in a speech in Jerusalem that World War I "gave us the Balfour Declaration, this time we must bring about a Jewish state." (In the Balfour Declaration of 1917, the British government promised Palestine as a national homeland for the Jews.) Even before the war in Europe, Ben-Gurion foresaw that it would accelerate the breakup of the British Empire, causing the end of the mandate in Palestine and enabling the establishment of a Jewish state.

Nevertheless, on May 8, 1945, as the war was ending, he walked the streets of London, among the ruined buildings, mingling with the jubilant, excited throng, and was depressed. The same night he wrote this in his diary: "A sad day of victory, very sad."

This was far from the finest hour of the Jewish people, who had paid a great price without even beginning to feel the joy of victory. The Jewish sacrifice appeared to have been utterly pointless, without any profit whatsoever, miserable, and humiliating. Of course, in retrospect it was precisely this great disaster, the greatest in the history of the Jewish people, that marked the beginning of the end of the long Zionist struggle for the establishment of an independent Jewish state in the Land of Israel. As the dimensions of the Holocaust were emerging after the war's end, Ben-

Gurion was convinced that world public opinion would line up behind the underdog and push enlightened leaders to solve the Jewish problem once and for all. The time of trial for all that he had focused his powers on since his youth was fast approaching.

Ben-Gurion came to this historical crossroads fully prepared. In 1945, at age fifty-nine, he was a mature statesman. Since the age of twenty, when he was first elected to a position of leadership, he had planned far ahead.[4] With great skill, he prepared the Jews of Eretz Yisrael for the decisive moment. By the mid-1940s, he had no doubt whatsoever: A brutal military confrontation would soon break out between the Jews and the Arabs in Palestine. If the Arabs lost, they would try again and again and again. If the Jews lost but once, they would be doomed to extinction. The Jews must therefore prepare themselves for a prolonged and determined armed struggle.

This way of looking at the reality of the Middle East seems logical and natural today, with the benefit of hindsight, but it was far from the way the early Zionists saw things. The outlook prevalent among the Jewish Zionist pioneers of the early 20th century was very different. Some were motivated by a desire to shape an ideal, utopian reality, influenced by romantic British and German Orientalism, while others were influenced by European colonialist ideology. The implications of these views would be fateful in the future relationship between Jews and Arabs in Palestine.

Most of the Zionist leadership chose to close its eyes and totally ignore the fact that there were hundreds of thousands of Arabs with deep roots in Palestine. This is why since the creation of the modern Zionist movement approximately 120 years ago, a myth has grown up, according to which the first Zionists settled in a country empty of inhabitants. When Ben-Gurion encountered this conception, he would dismiss it. "The illusion that Eretz Yisrael is an uninhabited land, in which we can do as we wish, without taking the local population into account, has caused us a great deal of damage," he declared at a meeting of the Jewish National Committee in 1921. A small and elitist circle, Brit Shalom (the Peace League), supported by the philosopher Martin Buber and the first president of the Hebrew University, Yehuda Leib Magnes,[5] advocated the establishment of a joint Jewish-Arab government in a binational state in Palestine. But Ben-Gurion mocked the naïveté of the Brit Shalom circle, and called its members "rootless," meaning they had lost their fundamental national consciousness.

Another grouping, to which Ben-Gurion belonged in his early years in Palestine, adopted a romantic-Marxist approach, holding that the ignorant Arab peasants, who were being exploited by the *effendis* (landowners), would welcome the educated and progressive Jews as their saviors. After all, both were members of the working class and as such had a common goal, the overthrow of the capitalists. "We have not come here to steal a country," said Ben-Gurion, "but to build it and revive it"—for the Arabs as well as the Jews. This was Zionism's moral justification. The Arabs "should understand this," primarily because "they are incapable of building the country themselves," and secondly because "they aren't strong enough to eject us." He urged his comrades to display solidarity with the Arab peasant: "The encounter between the Hebrew elite and the Arab laborer should be an encounter of working comrades," he wrote in a 1920 article, "On the Arab Peasant and in His Land," in phraseology reminiscent of a Russian revolutionary, adding: "Only between two free national groups of workers, each of which can stand on its own, will it be possible to establish the harmonious and comradely life which we must place at the foundation of our settlement enterprise in the Land." According to this concept, Ben-Gurion expected two societies to develop in parallel in Palestine, each helping the other. Characteristically, he prepared detailed plans for achieving economic and agricultural cooperation, and he expounded on them to both Jews and Arabs. "The Land of Israel will be for both the Hebrew nation and the Arabs who live in it," he wrote in another article, "The Hebrew Worker and the Arab," in 1926.

Ben-Gurion's optimism was justifiable. During most of the 1920s, the relationship between Jews and Arabs was peaceful. The economy expanded. The British administration in Palestine was successfully governing from day to day, but encountered difficulty in navigating between the competing Arab and Jewish national interests. The complications were a direct result of the conflicting territorial promises that the British government made during World War I.

One promise was made to the Arabs in 1915. On behalf of His Majesty, the British High Commissioner in Egypt, Sir Henry McMahon, had promised the patriarch of the Hashemite family and Sharif of Mecca, Hussein ibn Ali, control of most Arab lands in the Middle East, exclusive of the Mediterranean coast, in exchange for Hussein's commitment to lead a Bedouin armed revolt against the Ottoman Empire. The legendary Lawrence of Arabia (British intelligence officer T. E. Lawrence) guided the successful revolt that ousted the Turks from the entire Arabian Desert, from the Hejaz in the south (which became part of the Kingdom of Saudi Arabia in 1932) to Damascus (Syria) in the north.

Another territorial obligation was made on May 16, 1916, when Britain and France signed the secret Sykes-Picot treaty (the two diplomats who negotiated the treaty were the French François Georges-Picot and the British Mark Sykes), in which the future victorious Allies defined the boundaries of the postwar Middle East. The treaty was in direct contravention of the McMahon-Hussein agreement that had spurred on the Arab Revolt.

A third territorial promise was made to the Jews. On November second 1917, the British foreign minister, Lord Arthur Balfour, issued a declaration announcing his government's support for the establishment of "a Jewish national home in Palestine." The British establishment had a long tradition of supporting the restoration of the Jews in their own land for religious, imperialistic, and even idyllic motives. It has been suggested that the declaration was intended to favor the Jews so that the Jewish communities in the United States and Russia would influence their governments to support the British cause in the war. In any case, this British pledge became the basis for international support for the founding of the modern State of Israel.

Based on the Sykes-Picot treaty, on April 19, 1920, the League of Nations decided to assign Britain the mandate over Palestine and the responsibility for implementing the Balfour Declaration. (France obtained a mandate over Syria, carving out Lebanon as a separate state.)

In 1921, the British divided its mandate in two. East of the Jordan River became the Emirate of Transjordan (today the Kingdom of Jordan) and west of the Jordan River became the Palestine mandate. This was the first time in modern history that Palestine became a unified political entity.

As the '20s drew to an end, the political arena in Palestine began swaying. The rising tide of European Jewish immigration to Palestine (between 1920 and 1930, one hundred thousand Jews came to live in Palestine), Arab land purchases by the Jewish Agency, and the establishment of dozens of new Jewish settlements generated increasing resistance by Arab political leaders. They feared that Jewish expansion would lead to the establishment of a Jewish state.

In 1928, Muslims and Jews in Jerusalem began to clash over their religious rights at the Wailing Wall, the sole remnant of the second Jewish Temple and a holy site to Muslims. The Wailing Wall clashes were tolerable, but tension between the communities had grown and a powerful wave of violence broke out. The grave events that followed caused Ben-Gurion to change his optimistic political outlook in a flash.

On a blazing summer's day—August 23, 1929—thousands of Arabs, headed by the Grand Mufti of Jerusalem, Haj Amin al-Husayni, attacked Jews in downtown Jerusalem. Screaming "Itbah al Yahud" ("Kill the Jews"), the mob fell upon passersby, murdering some of them, and looting and burning Jewish stores. The next day rioting spread to other cities and to dozens of smaller communities. In Hebron, fifty-nine Jews were slaughtered; in Safed, ten.

The mandatory (mandate) government's response was hesitant. Only after two days did the British army go into action and quell the rioting. In a week, 133 Jews had been murdered and 339 wounded. Shock gripped the Jews of Eretz Yisrael and the world. It was the first time that Arabs had attacked Jews in an organized onslaught, and was all the more horrifying because the Jews had created the Zionist movement and come to live in the land precisely to get away from pogroms that Russian anti-Semites had perpetrated in the 1880s.

Ben-Gurion's thinking changed rapidly. He possessed an important attribute for a leader: flexibility. His political outlook was never rigid. So when he had absorbed the new situation, he discarded his romantic naïveté toward the Arabs and adopted a pragmatic, determined realism, an awareness of the harsh truth: Two national liberation movements were fighting for the same country.

Foreseeing the future twenty years hence, he wrote: "When a Jewish state is established, it will be attacked by its neighbors." His conclusions were that Arabs would endanger the Jewish entity in Palestine, that they were the true enemy, and it was therefore necessary to bring more young

Jews from the Diaspora and to set up an effective defense apparatus. These conclusions seem obvious today, but they were far from self-evident in 1929 and even sounded eccentric. "It is inconceivable that we should live in the Land under the protection of foreign bayonets indefinitely," he wrote, and he told a friend: "It is essential that we solve the security problem with our own resources." The origin of the Jewish army was, therefore, rooted in practical necessity: to respond to the riots instigated by the Arabs.

It was not necessary to exactly match the military power of the Arabs, Ben-Gurion believed. It would suffice if there were two trained Jewish youths for every three Arabs. In the terms prevalent in the Zionist movement in the early 1930s, this was revolutionary. According to the British Mandate census, in 1931 there were 860,000 Arabs and 175,000 Jews in Palestine, and in the age group of twenty to forty, only 30,000 Jews and 100,000 Arabs. Ben-Gurion was demanding that another 30–40,000 young Jews be brought to Eretz Yisrael immediately.

The "disturbances" of 1929, and the "Arab Revolt"[6] of 1936 imbued Ben-Gurion with a deep anxiety, which remained with him throughout his life. In December 1936, at a meeting with his close friends in Jerusalem, he said: "The danger we face is not rioting, but extermination. The attackers will not be only the Arabs of Palestine, but also the Iraqis and Saudi Arabians, and they have warplanes and artillery. We have to prepare seriously to constitute a substantial force in this country, capable of standing up to a massive offensive." His friends looked at him as if he had lost his mind. Others attributed his prophesy of doom to a transient mood. But Ben-Gurion meant what he said, and indeed, his forecast was fulfilled almost entirely twelve years later, immediately after he declared the independence of the State of Israel. And this fear of extermination lasted even after the victory in the War of Independence and led Ben-Gurion to his decision to develop the Israeli nuclear option.

AT THE BEGINNING of World War II, the Zionist leadership had no doubt that the British government headed by Winston Churchill, Zionism's greatest friend in Britain, would give the Jews their national home in Palestine. The Jews were allies. There were thousands of Jews in the

British forces. The Palestinian Arabs supported Hitler, and the Mufti of Jerusalem, al-Husayni, had been received as an ally in Nazi Berlin. In 1943, a committee of British cabinet ministers recommended the partition of Palestine between the Jews and the Arabs. Churchill called their report "a very nice piece of work." Zionist leaders were quite confident that immediately after the war, Churchill would force his opinions on the cabinet and Parliament, and the way to Jewish independence would be clear.

Reality proved entirely different. In April 1945, Churchill's foreign secretary, Anthony Eden, persuaded him that the partition of Palestine between Jews and Arabs would harm British interests. First of all, the supply of oil from the Middle East would be gravely threatened. Second, the Jews would encourage the entry of the Soviet Union into the Middle Eastern arena. A month earlier, in March, Eden had assisted in the establishment of the Arab League. The British, in order to demonstrate that they were not about to give up the mandate, closed the shores of Palestine to boats carrying Jewish refugees from Europe. Then in July, the British electorate voted out Churchill's Conservative government. Again Zionist leaders rejoiced; after all, the Labor Party had always taken a clearly pro-Zionist stance and at its annual conference one year earlier, in 1944, had adopted a resolution in favor of a Jewish state in all of western Palestine, with the Arab population transferred to the neighboring Arab countries. Labor's policy was so far-reaching that the Zionist leadership had sought to have the population-transfer proposal kept secret, in order not to antagonize the Arab rulers. Now, with Labor in power, the Zionists were confident that the establishment of the Jewish state was a certainty.

But again, they reaped disappointment. In November, it became clear that Labor would not implement the 1944 resolution. The restrictions on Jewish immigration to Palestine remained in force. At most, the Labor government would be prepared to appoint yet another committee to investigate the possibilities for a solution to the Palestine question.

This was a heavy blow, and the president of the World Zionist Organization, Chaim Weizmann, was stunned. For years, the well-oiled and efficient Zionist diplomatic machine he headed had striven to achieve one goal: the fulfillment of the British promises encapsulated in the Balfour Declaration. Weizmann, who was to become Israel's first president and a staunch opponent of Ben-Gurion's nuclear project, had no doubt that after the war Britain would remain the dominant power in the Middle East and would have the goodwill to declare an end to the mandate and enable the establishment of a Jewish state. Now, in London his associates were speaking of "British treachery."

Ben-Gurion, on the other hand, was not disappointed. He had not believed that Britain would give up Palestine easily and willingly. In order to hurry the British retreat he turned to a plan of armed struggle. Weizmann objected strenuously. His entire career as a Zionist leader had rested on one principle: the achievement of Jewish goals through diplomacy, and never through force. His close friend the philosopher Sir Isaiah Berlin called his policy "patient diplomacy." But Ben-Gurion put it this way at a meeting with Sir Isaiah in Washington, D.C., in December 1941: "Weizmann's patient appeals to history and reason are out-dated weapons. The leaders of the world are listening, but they do not do anything . . . Ultimately, these people will of necessity behave in accordance with the national interests of their countries. They will not be ready to help the Jews on sunny days or on rainy days . . . Only the Jews themselves, only their power concentrated in the United States and in Eretz Yisrael will stand them in good stead in any circumstances."

Ben-Gurion both admired and despised Weizmann. He admired how the Polish-born professor of chemistry had persuaded the British to give the Jews the Balfour Declaration, but he thought Weizmann loved England, and the English people, more than Eretz Yisrael.

In the variegated gallery of the Zionist leadership, there were no persons more different than these two, in their nature and their appearance. Ben-Gurion the pioneer, wearing work clothes of simple khaki cloth, was a working-class leader, a revolutionary, working his way gradually up the hierarchy of the leadership. Weizmann, a Jewish aristocrat, had been born with a silver spoon in his mouth and never knew a moment's poverty or hardship. The one was short and sturdy, incapable of making small talk or exchanging pleasantries; the other tall and aloof, a man of the world who captivated political leaders, generals, and intellectuals with his charm. Ben-Gurion was down-to-earth, energetic, modest to the point of asceticism, and always traveled third-class. Weizmann and his ever-present entourage went first-class; he relished the good life, fine food and wine, and the company of women. The one was an unpolished autodidact, lacking a formal education; the other a world-renowned scientist, who as a faculty member of the University of Manchester during World War I had developed for the British war effort a synthetic acetone for use in explosives, winning him fame and the affection of the nation.

The relationship between the two was complex. They met and corresponded infrequently, but nevertheless for almost the entire first half of the 20th century they trod parallel courses toward a common goal. Both aspired to see the establishment of the Jewish state. Both intended to use moderate, proportionate means to achieve this, and both were repelled by terrorism. Both preferred reaching a territorial compromise with the Arabs. They divided the work: As president of the World Zionist Organization, Weizmann led the worldwide diplomatic effort, and as leader of the workers in Eretz Yisrael, Ben-Gurion set up the infrastructure for the state-to-be. Ben-Gurion guided the practical Zionism that settled and built the Land. Weizmann was at the head of the political Zionism that negotiated in order to gain recognition for Jewish independence in the Land of Israel. As long as the responsibility for the future of Palestine lay with His Majesty's government, agreement usually prevailed between them. Weizmann would do the diplomatic lobbying in London, and Ben-Gurion would fight the British high commissioner in Jerusalem to be allowed another settlement and another immigrant's visa.

When it became clear that Britain was reneging on its commitment to the Zionist movement, Ben-Gurion laid down new guidelines. He launched an open armed struggle against the British mandate, and at the same time sought American sponsorship for the goals of Zionism. This was an expression of a principle that had gathered strength in the wake of the Holocaust and was highly relevant to Ben-Gurion's eventual decision to develop nuclear weapons: The Jews must not rely on gentiles. They must take their fate into their own hands. Moving the focus of the diplomatic struggle to the United States was intended to exploit the power of the American Jewish community and its influence over the administration in Washington.

Weizmann differed with Ben-Gurion on both issues. He argued that an armed struggle against the British would undermine the achievements of Zionism, and he was convinced that the future of Jewish settlement in the Land of Israel would be decided according to the wishes of London, not Washington. Abba Hillel Silver, the energetic leader of American Zionists, lined up with Ben-Gurion. Stephen S. Wise, the leader of American Reform Jewry, supported Weizmann's position. After a bitter struggle, Ben-Gurion came out on top. The result of the confrontation was a decline in Weizmann's stature. At the 22nd Zionist Congress in Basel, Switzerland, in 1946, Weizmann failed to win reelection as president of the World Zionist Organization.[7] Six of the nineteen members of the new Zionist executive were Americans.

The diversion of the Zionist diplomatic effort to the United States was a fateful move, perhaps the most important taken by the Zionist movement after the war. Placing the Zionist eggs in the American basket was a significant step forward in the process of achieving independence. Ben-Gurion, with his acute historical and political sense, had determined that America would now lead the free world and decide the fate of the Middle East. The implications of American involvement were a key factor Ben-Gurion would eventually have to take into account in the development of Israel's nuclear capability.

The conflict over whether Zionism's orientation would be British or American had sharpened the antagonism between the two leaders. Some years later, when Weizmann was filling his largely ceremonial post as first president of the State of Israel, and power was concentrated in Prime Minister Ben-Gurion's hands, the nuclear issue sparked a new dispute. Weizmann the scientist (for whom the country's leading research institution, the Weizmann Institute in Rehovot, which he ran and where he made his residence, had been named) would marshal all of his considerable influence over the Israeli scientific community to try to sabotage Ben-Gurion's plan to develop a nuclear option.

In the second half of 1945, Ben-Gurion pinned all of his hopes on the American Jewish community and its influence over president Harry S. Truman and his administration. Truman's predecessor, Franklin D. Roosevelt, had put Ben-Gurion off, because Roosevelt spoke one language to the Jewish leaders and another to the Arab leaders. But in April 1945, after Roosevelt's sudden death and Truman's swearing in as his successor, Ben-Gurion knew the dice were rolling in his favor. In August, he concluded that Truman would support the Palestine partition plan, and in fact, later that month, immediately after his return from the Allied Big Three's victory summit in Potsdam, Truman announced his wish to see the establishment of a Jewish state. His special emissary Earl G. Harrison, United States representative on the Intergovernmental Committee on Refugees, traveled to the displaced-persons camps to report on their condition and recommended the immediate transfer of 100,000 Jews to Palestine. The British government ignored the recommendation, but Ben-Gurion was confident that the fate of Zionism was now in good hands. That autumn, on the eve of the fast of Yom Kippur, the most solemn day in the Jewish calendar, and after being subjected to an intensive lobbying and softening-up effort by the American Zionist leadership, Truman declared that the United States accepted partition of Palestine. This was the time for Ben-Gurion to launch a huge effort in the United States to prepare for the inevitable military conflict with the Arabs.

Ben-Gurion knew America well. He had lived in New York for three years after the Turks exiled him from Palestine in 1915, and had become fluent in English. In December 1917, he married Paula Monbaz, a New York hospital nurse, and the pair took an apartment in Brooklyn.

Ben-Gurion found similarities between the early American pioneers and the *halutzim* of Eretz Yisrael. He admired the American Constitution, and the sense of liberty prevalent in the country. The pace of life astonished him. Through the 1940s he visited the United States every two years, staying for several weeks and sometimes for months. Ben-Gurion was in New York from November 1941 to September 1942 and witnessed the country's reaction to the surprise Japanese attack on Pearl Harbor.

In May 1942, at a special conference in New York's Biltmore Hotel, Ben-Gurion persuaded the majority of the six hundred delegates of American Jewish organizations to pass a resolution calling for a program of intense activity to increase Jewish immigration to Eretz Yisrael, including the use of violence against the British mandate. In Zionist history, this resolution is known as "the Biltmore program."

With each visit Ben-Gurion developed a deeper relationship with, and greater esteem for, the leaders of the American Jewish community, such as Supreme Court Justices Louis Brandeis and Felix Frankfurter, along with Abba Hillel Silver, Meyer Weisgal, Stephen Wise, Louis Lipsky, and many others. The more he got to know the community and its heads, the more his esteem for them grew. Although most American Jews were at that time not Zionists, he wrote to a friend, "That's where the masses are, that's where the power is, that's where the money is. If we want to do great things, it would be hopeless without America."

In June 1945, Ben-Gurion traveled to New York to raise money for armaments. On his arrival he summoned Weisgal, a Zionist activist, a talented impresario, and a close associate of Weizmann. For hours Ben-Gurion spoke of what was going to happen in Palestine. The Arabs will attack, Ben-Gurion warned, and so there was an urgent need to raise money, acquire arms, and mobilize professional manpower. "He told me at great length what he wanted," Weisgal related in his memoirs. "The main thing was: Can you locate 30 Jews who will follow me blindly, who will do what I ask without asking questions?"

A day later, Henry Montor reported to Ben-Gurion. He was the executive director of the United Palestine Appeal. Weisgal described him as follows: "He had a genius for fundraising, and he knew everybody worth knowing." Montor gave Ben-Gurion a list of seventeen Jews, all of whom, he said, were "men of means, whose dedication to the security of the *yishuv* could be relied upon." (*Ha'yishuv*, Hebrew for "the community," was the word used for the Jewish population of Palestine before the establishment of the State of Israel.) Everyone on the list was invited to a secret conclave to be held at 9:30 on the morning of Sunday, July 1, at the home of the millionaire Rudolf S. Sonneborn on 57th Street.

Ben-Gurion opened the meeting: "We are soon about to face the armies of all the Arab states, when the British leave the country. We can stand up to them, if we have the weapons that we need. In the ruins and confusion of Europe, there is no certainty that we will be able to get what we thought we would. Most importantly, the weapons that the Haganah[8] has already acquired were adequate to cope with the local Arab gangs, but not regular armies, mostly armed by Britain. It is essential that in due course we build up a military industry, and when this [second world] war ends[9] it will be possible to purchase the necessary machinery and instruments in the USA . . . Hundreds of thousands of dollars, perhaps millions, will be needed for this. Are you ready to provide the necessary funds?"

The discussion went on for seven and a half hours, and when it was over the participants agreed to finance the acquisition of weapons and equipment that the young state would require. Ben-Gurion wrote in his diary: "This was the best Zionist meeting that I've had in the United States." In the secret papers of the state-in-the-making the seventeen American millionaires were given the code name "the Sonneborn Institute," after their host. In the coming years, its members would contribute millions of dollars to buy munitions, machinery, hospital equipment and medicines, and ships to carry refugees to Eretz Yisrael.[10]

The first consignment of machinery for the production of munitions purchased with money from the Sonneborn Institute left New York for Palestine in February 1946. By January 1947, some 950 shipments of dismantled machinery left the port of New York for Palestine. Chaim Slavin, who later become the director of the Israeli Military Industries, had been sent to New York to organize the shipments. Many years later, Slavin revealed in a press interview that in the consignment documents the crates were described as containing "textile machinery." The British customs officials never suspected anything was amiss, and so the equipment reached its destination and became the foundation of the Israeli military industry.

Fifteen years later, when foreign intelligence operatives and inquisitive journalists discovered that a gigantic construction project was under way in the Negev, near the small immigrant town of Dimona, the Israeli authorities maintained that it was a "textile factory." And in official Israeli documents, "the textile factory" became the code name of the Dimona nuclear project.

The Sonneborn Institute would emerge again in 1956–57, when a nuclear agreement between Israel and France was being discussed. Ben-Gurion once again drew up a list of wealthy Jews, this time to help finance the reactor and related installations. The millionaires of the Sonneborn Institute were the first to receive his appeal.

IN MID-NOVEMBER 1945, Ben-Gurion returned to Jerusalem and summoned the Representative Assembly of the Jews in Palestine to hear his report on his mission to Germany. A recording of his speech is to be found in the archives of Kol Yisrael, the Israeli state radio station. Ben-

Gurion's voice is restrained. From time to time, someone in the audience can be heard sobbing, or emitting a sigh of pain. "I was in Dachau and Belsen. I saw the gas chambers, where every day they poisoned thousands of Jews, men and women, the aged and the elderly, infants and children, led them naked as if they were going to take showers. The gas chambers are really built as if they are shower rooms, and the Nazis would peep in from the outside to see the Jews writhe and struggle in their death throes. I saw the furnaces in which they burned the bodies of hundreds and thousands and millions of Jews from all the countries in Europe (here an outburst of weeping is audible on the recording) . . . I saw the gallows in Belsen, on which they would hang a number of Jews at once for sins such as coming two minutes late for forced labor, and all the other prisoners had to gather and watch the display. I saw the kennels where they bred the savage dogs that were trained to be set on the Jews on their way to work or to be killed. I saw the platforms, on which naked Jewish men and women were laid and the camp commanders would stand and shoot them in their backs, and I saw the few remnants, the survivors of the six million who were slaughtered in the sight of the world, an indifferent world, foreign, cold, cruel . . ."

There, in the death camps of Europe, in the encounters with the remnants of Europe's Jews, only two months after the United States had loosed atom bombs on Hiroshima and Nagasaki, leading to the unconditional surrender of Japan, Ben-Gurion reached his first understanding of the deterrent advantage inherent in nuclear capability. True, at that time, when the Jewish nation was at one of the lowest points in its history, before the establishment of Israel as an independent state had been ensured, the very idea of developing a Jewish nuclear option seemed totally fanciful. Nevertheless, the lessons drawn by Ben-Gurion from the death camps meshed naturally with his understanding of the new reality that had been created in the world: There was now a new kind of absolute deterrence, and if the Jews got it no one would dare to contemplate their extermination. Ben-Gurion never publicly expressed the idea in such clear terms, because he was loyal to the rules of secrecy, as were most members of his generation. But a careful reading of his diaries and other writings suggests that the connection between the Holocaust and the ultimate weapon was etched into his consciousness during his visit to the killing fields.

In Israel's War of Independence in 1948–49, Tamar Shpruch fought in the infantry. Then she married Hans Freund, who had been hidden along with his mother by good Germans in Berlin; she left her kibbutz and embarked on a career in special education. In recent years, she has been a tour guide. Although she experienced the Nazi horrors as a young and healthy girl, and although six decades have passed, not a day goes by that she does not see in her mind's eye pictures of the tortured, starving victims in the labor camps, of people falling by the wayside in the forced march from Poland to Germany, and getting shot in the head. To most Israelis, born after World War II in an independent Jewish state, Tamar Freund represents the depths of the existential dread that the Holocaust and the extermination of over a third of the Jewish people has carved into Israel's consciousness. This is the dread that was absorbed by Ben-Gurion during that journey to occupied Germany, the dread that gave birth to the idea of arming the Jewish people with an ultimate weapon of defense.

CHAPTER TWO

The A Team

AT PRECISELY TEN O'CLOCK in the morning, on January 22, 1952, Munya Mardor presented himself at the entrance to the Tel-Aviv residence of David Ben-Gurion, Israel's prime minister and minister of defense. The sentry saluted and Ben-Gurion's wife, Paula, met Mardor in the hall and shook hands with him. The prime minister's military secretary led him to the office on the second floor. The door was open and Ben-Gurion waved him in and pointed to a chair.

Mardor was tense. For three months Ben-Gurion had been trying to persuade him to become head of the newly founded division for research and development at the Defense Ministry. Mardor had firmly resisted the offer. In mid-1949 he retired from the military, after serving for fifteen stormy and dangerous years, during which he had carried out many special missions, mostly in the underground. Now, after a difficult period adapting to civilian life, he had set up a private company, fathered a son, Rami, and was beginning to settle down.

The night before, Munya discussed the future with his wife, Lenka. They were an impressive couple. He was a tall, well-built man, meticulous about his attire and his hair. His visage was Aryan, with a high forehead. She was also tall and good-looking, with long blond hair, fine lips, and an aquiline nose. During World War II she was the youngest officer in the British army's women's corps, the Auxiliary Territorial Service, in Egypt. When Israel's War of Independence broke out in 1948, she joined the Israel Defense Forces (IDF). Their talk was charged with tension. Lenka had never interfered in Munya's career, although it was often difficult to restrain herself. He had been away for most of her pregnancy. She knew that if he accepted Ben-Gurion's proposal, he would put everything he had into the job, and the family burden would be entirely hers. If you want to build a business, she told him, time isn't on your side. He knew she was right; in a year's time he'd be forty. It was in the early hours that they decided that he'd say no to the prime minister. During the drive from their home on Haifa's Mount Carmel to Tel Aviv, he rehearsed his rejection speech: "I lack the training for a scientific mission. I have no experience in so complex a field. For years I served as a loyal soldier. Now I want to build an economic basis for my family."

The followers of Ben-Gurion were known as Ben-Gurionists in the same way that Stalin's followers—with all the differences—were called Stalinists. Mardor was no Ben-Gurionist. Once his daughter, Gonnie, asked her father if he venerated Ben-Gurion, and he replied: "I admire him. We shouldn't venerate anyone." Years later, he'd tell Gonnie: "Never serve any person. Serve a cause." What's more, Mardor wasn't politically identified, and although he grew up in a Zionist socialist youth movement, his life wasn't guided by any ideology. He was known as a creative man with a rich imagination, and a supremely practical man, someone who could get things done.

For months, Ben-Gurion had trained his heavy artillery on Mardor: Cabinet ministers, the chief of staff, the heads of the defense establishment, close friends who had shared daring exploits with him, all were sent to try to persuade Munya—as he was known to all—to accept the mission. But he held firm in his refusal.

One of the men who tried to persuade Mardor to work for the Defense Ministry was Professor Ernst Bergmann, Ben-Gurion's scientific adviser. Ernst David Bergmann had been born in Germany in 1903. His father, Judah, was a well-known rabbi and author. Ernst wrote his doctoral thesis in chemistry at Berlin University under Wilhelm Schlenk, famous as the discoverer of lithium. Schlenk and the young Bergmann collaborated on "The Complete Handbook of Organic Chemistry" (*Ausführliches Lehrbuch der Organischen Chemie*), a two-volume work that for decades was considered the basic textbook on chemistry. The first volume came out in 1932, shortly before the Nazis took over the government of Germany.

When the second volume appeared in 1939, Bergmann's name was left off the cover, because he was a Jew.

The Nazis determined the course of Bergmann's life: Soon after they took power, he had the foresight to leave for England. There he was introduced to Chaim Weizmann, then the leader of the Zionist movement and himself a prominent chemistry professor. The two would become close friends and colleagues.

Weizmann offered Bergmann the scientific directorship of the Daniel Sieff Research Institute, then being built in Palestine with donations from the Anglo-Jewish Sieff family; Weizmann was its president.[1] At considerable risk to his career, Bergmann agreed. In the early 1930s, Palestine was a remote, undeveloped backwater with a Jewish population of 175,000 souls. But Weizmann's enthusiasm infected Bergmann. It was Weizmann himself who had planned the institute that would eventually bear his name and was overseeing its construction near Rehovot, a small Jewish town on the coastal plain south of Tel Aviv. To do so, Weizmann traveled to Palestine and took up residence in a rented hut near the building site. His wife, Vera, fell in love with the surrounding sand dunes and orange groves and decided to purchase an eleven-acre plot nearby. "I bought the scenery," she wrote in her memoirs. For the next two years she devoted herself to building a new residence for the leader of world Jewry in the Land of Israel.

The modest research institute was a two-story building with two departments, organic chemistry and biochemistry, as well as Weizmann's personal laboratory. As scientists of Jewish background were forced to flee Germany because of Nazi persecution, the Sieff Institute became a haven for many of them. When Bergmann developed a plan for a massive expansion of the Institute, some of his colleagues accused him of daydreaming. But in retrospect, seventy years later, it is clear that his vision was crucial among all the events and actions that worked together to give Israel the nuclear option. At the Sieff Institute, on January 1, 1934, fourteen years before Ben-Gurion declared an independent State of Israel, Bergmann began training the researchers who would build the scientific infrastructure for the Israeli military industry and, just over thirty years later, would build Israel's secret weapon.

In 1937, the Weizmanns left their home in Kensington, London, for the magnificent villa that German-Jewish architect Erich Mendelsohn had designed on the plot near the Institute. The Jews of Palestine called the villa "the White House." That same year, Bergmann's wife, Otilia, died from bone cancer. Vera and Otilia had been close friends.

During World War II, Bergmann was involved in various military projects in Britain, France, and the United States. Working together in London, he and Weizmann helped the Allied war effort by developing a process for the production of monomers, necessary for the manufacture of synthetic rubber from agricultural raw materials.

When Bergmann returned to Palestine in 1946, the Sieff Institute had expanded and become the Weizmann Institute. Bergmann was now famous. His reputation as a chemist and the fact that he was Weizmann's protégé aroused Ben-Gurion's curiosity. The two began meeting frequently, and Ben-Gurion expounded his doctrine: When a Jewish state arose, the secret of its existence would be based on its technological and scientific superiority. If a considerable technological gap could be opened up between it and the Arabs, its survival would be assured. Bergmann was excited. Political activity and intimacy with those at the controlling core of the state-in-the-making was preferable to the relative anonymity of the ivory tower.

Ben-Gurion's magic worked so well on Bergmann that he was persuaded to mobilize the Weizmann Institute on behalf of the security of the embryonic state. By 1949, after the declaration of independence and the ensuing war, there were sixty laboratories operating at the Institute, in nine scientific fields: organic and inorganic chemistry; biochemistry; bacteriology; optics; electronics; polymer research; isotope research; applied mathematics, including geophysics; and biophysics. An experimental-biology laboratory was under construction.

Ben-Gurion and Bergmann aimed to put the Institute's labs at the disposal of the defense establishment, but Weizmann, for whom diplomacy rather than military power was paramount and who believed science should be free of governmental control, stood in their way. He feared that through Bergmann, Ben-Gurion would take control of the Institute and impinge on its independence. Indeed, from the very beginnings of the Institute, its scientists had been involved in clandestine security research. The development of a recoilless gun, for example, was carried out in a doubly secret operation, as the scientists had to conceal their activities not only from the British mandatory authorities, but also from the president of their own institute. He was either unaware of the underground projects or pretended to be so, and at every opportunity he deplored the mixing of pure research and political matters. When the War of Independence was over, Weizmann believed that investing substantial scientific efforts in defense research would impair civilian scientific progress, and would encourage hawkish politicians to perpetuate the conflict with the Arabs. "I told him," Bergmann related, "that to my mind all our lives we would be in a situation that would require military research." This statement is testimony of the extent to which Ben-Gurion's outlook had influenced Bergmann.

No less than Ben-Gurion, Bergmann was convinced that after the Holocaust the Jewish people would be fully justified in building an ultimate weapon for their defense. Years later, when a left-wing political leader questioned Ben-Gurion's wisdom in the matter of nuclear development, Bergmann wrote to him: "There is no one in the country who does not fear nuclear war, and there is no one who does not hope that despite everything reason will prevail in tomorrow's world. But we have no right to substitute hopes and illusions for exact knowledge and cold evaluation of the real situation. I am unable to forget that the Holocaust took the Jewish people by surprise. This nation can not permit itself to be so deluded once again."

Both Ben-Gurion and Weizmann demanded exclusive loyalty from Bergmann. Many years later, in 1973, Bergmann described the compromise that he proposed to Weizmann: to make the Weizmann Institute the central scientific institution of the State of Israel, "with both a civilian and a military nature." Weizmann objected strenuously, but Ben-Gurion, as usual, won. Weizmann's refusal to allow Bergmann to integrate pure scientific research and military research forced Bergmann to choose. "After eighteen years of working together, a split opened up between us," he ruefully said in describing how he was made to abandon the man who had nurtured him since his youth. Weizmann's close associate Meyer Weisgal wrote: "The intimacy, and the honest understanding, the complete trust that existed between them for many years, gradually dimmed and eventually vanished. It was torture for everyone concerned."

There was another, personal, reason for the rift. After his wife died Bergmann fell in love with Weizmann's secretary, the beautiful Hani Itin, and married her. Prior to that, while his wife was still alive, Bergmann had been rumored to have had affairs. Vera Weizmann who had been very close to Bergmann's wife, and who had herself been the victim of her husband's affairs, broke off her friendship with Bergmann. So did her husband.

Bergmann's remarriage and the Weizmanns boycott of him were grist for the gossip mills of the political and scientific communities. Eventually the two men negotiated through the mediation of Meyer Weisgal, and it was decided that Bergmann would cease to be director of the Institute and a member of the governing body, and would go on a year's sabbatical. There was no mention of the dispute in any of the newspapers in Palestine. In those years, there was no public discussion of the personal affairs of the nation's leaders.

In July 1951, Bergmann finally crossed over. From now on he would hold the civilian title of scientific adviser to the defense minister, and he would unofficially direct the operations of the IDF's Science Corps, known by its Hebrew acronym HEMED. "Ben-Gurion insisted that I get a military rank," Bergmann related. "I told him 'no'. . . My reasoning was that because I assumed that we would have to get much information from abroad it would be better when I was on overseas missions if I came as a civilian and not a soldier. I know many professors in Europe and America who would stop relating to me as a man of science, if I were an army officer." Ben-Gurion conceded. In addition to his work in the defense establishment, Bergmann continued researching and teaching in the labs of the Israel Institute of Technology, or Technion, in Haifa, and at the Hebrew University in Jerusalem. But he no longer had any access to the Weizmann Institute. The boycott Weizmann had imposed on him was absolute.

The Science Corps had been set up in 1948, at the same time as the State of Israel and the IDF. It incorporated all the cells of the primitive military industries that had operated in Palestine, most under the auspices of the Haganah, the mainstream underground organization. In these cells, hundreds of people—university researchers, engineers employed by the mandate administration or private firms, technicians, metal workers—had manufactured and assembled light arms, mines and grenades; improvised explosive materials; and developed flamethrowers, smoke grenades, and armor-piercing munitions. Some engineers and technicians had been mobilized during World War II into British army weapons-development units, where they acquired valuable expertise. While still in the underground, several months before the British left, the Haganah enlisted twenty chemistry students, and then a group of physics students. Laboratories and workshops were established, and at the start of the War of Independence, production of light arms and ammunition began.

When the war ended, it turned out that the Israeli victory alone would not ensure the continued existence of the state. The humiliated Arabs were planning further attacks, and were swearing to throw the Jews into the sea. Israel's chances of surviving depended upon its ability to win the arms race. "Time is pressing," Mardor wrote in his diary. "How can we obtain those modern and sophisticated weapons so necessary for the long-term requirements of the state, and which our purchasing arms cannot reach?"

Israel's greatest difficulty was the embargo on the sale of arms to the Middle East instituted by the United States, Britain, and France in 1952. At that time, the French and the British governments acted in full coordination with the American administration in matters concerning the Middle East, and the embargo was meticulously observed. Israel could not even import rifles. A consignment of pistols sent from the United States to Israel had to be labeled "sporting equipment." The Israeli Air Force was equipped only with old models of aircraft. It could not buy even one modern bomber. Jet aircraft had not yet flown in Israeli skies.

Israeli diplomats trying to persuade Washington and London to supply the new state with defensive weapons were bluntly refused. Britain would not even undertake to stop selling arms to Egypt. The U.S. secretary of state, John Foster Dulles, told the Israelis that there was no proof that the balance of power in the Middle East had been upset, or that it would be in the future. In the light of the especially close relationship between the United States and Israel early in the 21st century, it is difficult to grasp the coolness, the distance that prevailed in the relationship a half century ago. The circumstances that in later decades brought the two nations together were nonexistent in the 1950s: The identity of interests in terms of the Cold War was not yet evident; the Jewish lobby in the United States was still in its infancy; the impact of the Holocaust had not emerged to the extent that it did later; and the pattern of shared Judeo-Christian values did not dominate American public discourse as they would when Islamic terror became a major threat.

It was only toward the end of the 1950s, against a background of political instability in the Middle East—exemplified by the coup that toppled the pro-Western regime in Iraq and the teetering of both the Lebanese government and the Jordanian monarchy—that the United States first recognized Israel's potential as a pro-Western bastion in the region. Before that, with the Eisenhower administration's foreign policy dominated by the confrontation with the Soviet bloc, the goal in the Middle East had been to establish an alliance of Arab states to face the threat of a communist takeover of the region. To achieve this, the United States was willing to supply arms to states that would line up with its policies, and refrained adamantly from providing weapons to Israel.

Israel was therefore compelled to develop its own armaments. This required large-scale investment of resources in the construction of the scientific and technical infrastructure for a modern, sophisticated defense industry. Ben-Gurion, having reached the conclusion that the military was the only organization in the country that could take on this task rapidly and efficiently, decided that all military research and development would be carried out within the IDF. In the early days of the Science Corps or HEMED, almost all the research was done at the Weizmann Institute, which was in fact its base, despite Chaim Weizmann's objections.

Although nuclear research was at an elementary level, both Ben-Gurion and Bergmann attributed supreme importance to it. The unit that handled nuclear physics was known as HEMED C. It was set up by a thirty-year-old Russian-born researcher named Israel Dostrovsky, who had obtained a doctorate in physical chemistry at University College, London. In 1948, Dostrovsky established both the isotopes department at the Weizmann Institute and HEMED C. He was given the rank of major. Israeli physicist Yuval Neeman, who in the 1950s was deputy chief of military intelligence, says that Ben-Gurion co-opted Bergmann into the Defense Ministry and put Dostrovsky in charge of HEMED C for the simple reason that he already aspired to develop a nuclear option.

Toward the end of the mandate, Haganah intelligence reported that the British had found oil and phosphate deposits in the northern Negev.[2] The report said the British were maintaining total secrecy about these geological findings, but on the desk of the district commissioner in his Beersheba office there were pieces of black rock quarried at the site of the phosphate deposits. Nothing more was heard of the oil, but phosphates are a source of uranium, and late in 1948, in the midst of the War of Independence, Bergmann suggested to Ben-Gurion that a scientific mission be sent to the northern Negev to find the phosphate deposits and check the amount of uranium they contained. The task was entrusted to Dostrovsky, the only scientist in Israel at the time with knowledge of the process for producing the required uranium-235 isotope, extracted from natural uranium.[3] Dostrovsky's team found phosphates from which it was possible to extract uranium.

The task for Dostrovsky and his team was made difficult by the fact that the Negev was under siege. The Egyptian forces that had invaded Israeli territory from the Sinai peninsula, had cut off the Negev from the rest of the country. Yuval Neeman believes that the urgency with which the team was dispatched illustrates just how determined Ben-Gurion and Bergmann were on the nuclear issue.

The confusion between the military and academic spheres was one of the reasons for the eventual failure of the idea to incorporate a research and development unit inside the IDF. The military found it difficult to absorb a scientific community accustomed to academic freedom. HEMED was a foreign body in the armed forces. Bergmann suggested to Ben-Gurion that HEMED be made into a civilian body and incorporated into the Defense Ministry, under the direct supervision of the minister himself. Ben-Gurion agreed, and began searching for the right person to head the new division for research and development—someone efficient, creative, and loyal.

To Ben-Gurion, Munya Mardor seemed the right man. As one of the top figures in the gigantic enterprise, which in the mythology of the Zionist revolution was known as the *rekhesh*, Hebrew for "acquisition" or "purchasing," Mardor proved his limitless dedication to the Zionist purpose. His network effectively exploited the profoundly chaotic situation that prevailed across the continent in the wake of the war to steal light arms, ammunition, explosives, and other material from the British army's arsenals, in order to equip the Jewish army in Palestine for its war against the Arabs. Trucks, fuel, and equipment were taken from the military. They produced counterfeit documents of all kinds, including travel passes and visas. The network bribed officials and soldiers and collaborated with smugglers. It moved convoys of trucks loaded with stolen weapons and equipment across Europe, to the coasts of France or Italy. It acquired cargo ships, provided them with crews, and sailed them to Palestine. This well-oiled machine functioned for three years, staffed by hundreds of men and women totally dedicated and committed to the cause. In April 1948, a month before the Declaration of Independence of the new State of Israel, Mardor directed the airlift from Czechoslovakia to Israel of arms that are credited with playing a decisive role in the war. Ben-Gurion was eager to harness the practical experience and the creative ability of the man who had run complicated operations in such difficult conditions.

The prime minister turned to Bergmann to persuade Mardor. But Bergmann was concerned about his own status. He was ready to forgo administrative responsibilities, but he wanted to be in charge of the scientific research and development. He sent the reluctant Mardor a written plan, detailing the structure of the division and his suggestions for sharing responsibilities between them. However, Mardor, in addition to his personal reservations about taking the job, was not a man who liked sharing power, and he made it known that he wouldn't even consider the position unless he was in sole charge of the entire division. Ben-Gurion's associates prevailed upon Bergmann to reconsider, and he cabled Mardor: "I have been told of your reservations, and it seems to me that they are based on a misapprehension. Please accept the position. I assure you that everything will sort itself out for the best, in full cooperation and fruitfulness." But even with this hurdle removed, Lenka Mardor's objections remained an obstacle. And although he had insisted on full control of the division, Mardor now argued that he lacked the scientific expertise necessary to head it.

On that winter's morning of 1952 in Ben-Gurion's office, Mardor tried to make it clear that he was professionally unqualified. I have no scientific training, he told Ben-Gurion, and it would be presumptuous for me to take charge of a select team of scientists. The prime minister, however, was unimpressed. No one is an expert at everything, he said, repeating one of his most frequently used slogans. In this job, we need an expert at mobilizing people. Use your common sense, and you will become an "expert on experts," he said with a laugh. Mardor then played the family card, saying that taking the job would cause great difficulties in that sphere. But Ben-Gurion trumped that by appealing to Mardor's patriotism. This is a national mission, he told Mardor, and you must accept it. Like many others of his generation, Mardor lived with a deep sense of responsibility toward his people, one that could be fulfilled, he wrote in his diary, "only by the feeling that I am performing a mission."

One reason for this was rooted in his responsibility for a grave tragedy that had plagued his conscience ever since it happened. In the annals of the operations of the Jewish underground against the British, this affair was known as the sinking of the refugee ship *Patria*.

In November 1940, three ships carrying 1,800 Jewish refugees from Nazi Germany, Austria, and Czechoslovakia were riding at anchor in Haifa Bay. Emissaries from the Jewish community in Palestine—the *yishuv*—had brought them as part of the "illegal" immigration effort, despite the blockade of the country's shores imposed by the mandate authorities. British paratroops seized the ships and prevented their human cargo from disembarking. Acting on orders from London, the mandatory government was preparing to deport the refugees. They were all transferred to the *Patria*, which the Royal Navy had provided for that purpose.

The leaders of the *yishuv* were stunned. Deportation of immigrants would sabotage the most important of the goals of Zionism: to increase the Jewish population of the Land of Israel, prior to the decisive struggle with the Arabs over its future. At first, emissaries from Ben-Gurion attempted to persuade the British to cancel their harsh decision, but when the negotiations failed, it was decided to disable the *Patria* and prevent it from sailing. An order was issued to place a bomb on the ship, big enough to blow a small hole in the hull and cause the ship to list to one side. The actual sabotage mission was entrusted to Munya Mardor, the commander of the Haganah's special operations company in the north.

Mardor had joined the Haganah's permanent cadre shortly after arriving in Palestine in the early 1930s. He was born in 1913 in the Western Ukrainian district capital of Poltava, halfway between Kharkov and Kiev and on the train line between Moscow and Berlin. His family owned a sawmill. Mardor was educated in a Zionist-socialist atmosphere, and absorbed the tenet that the individual should subject his will to Jewish national requirements, but he nonetheless displayed a strongly independent streak. At eighteen, he went to Paris to study architecture at the Sorbonne. Although the teachers noted his remarkable creative talents, his desire to do his duty to his people prevailed over professional ambition and he dropped out of university in order to travel to Palestine as a pioneer. Upon arriving in Haifa, Mardor worked as a stevedore in the port; in letters home he never told the truth about the hardships he encountered. Soon after enlisting in the Haganah, he began to stand out, and was promoted to positions of command.

Mardor's entire family was wiped out in the Holocaust, except for one of his mother's brothers. His mother, Eugenia, was murdered in the Babi Yar forest, outside Kiev. Like most of the pioneers who had left families behind in Europe, Mardor battled with his conscience. The loss of his family cast a shadow over the rest of his life.

In preparation for the sabotage mission, he disguised himself as a manual laborer and found a job with an Arab contractor in the port. In a stroke of luck, the contractor was assigned the task of repairing the oven in the *Patria*'s galley and Mardor was ordered to carry bricks and bags of cement onto the ship, enabling him to study the target from close up. The decks were swarming with British paratroops and policemen. The refugees were crammed into inadequate quarters and there wasn't enough food. "I was shocked and angry at what I saw on board, particularly at the condition of the children, the women and the old people," he wrote. He planned the sabotage operation. He himself would carry the bomb into the port and onto the *Patria*. One of the young refugees would take it down into the bottom of the ship and, at the appointed time, light the fuse.

The plan worked only too well. The blast was powerful, and the hole in the hull was too large. Mardor stood on the quay and watched as the ship keeled over and then began sinking, all in a matter of minutes. Hundreds of refugees were trapped below deck. Port workers tried to cut a way in with their welding equipment. Mardor stood there, stunned. Two hundred Jewish refugees went down in front of his eyes. "Those were nerve-wracking, soul-destroying times," he wrote in his diary, "as each day they extricated more and more victims from the sea." The hull of the *Patria* had been eaten through by rust, making it more vulnerable than it should have been.

The survivors were taken to an internment camp south of Haifa. The order to deport them was rescinded. But Mardor was inconsolable. "Every day since it happened, I have lived with the memory," he wrote.

It is therefore no wonder that Ben-Gurion's appeal to Mardor's sense of national duty worked. Mardor agreed to become head of the new scientific division of the Defense Ministry, but on his own terms: total control, including the setting of research and development priorities. Bergmann would be his subordinate. Mardor was conscious of the burden of responsibility. He would be in charge of the principal body behind the biggest and most expensive projects of the young state.

Mardor's first step was to go up to Jerusalem, to get the blessing of the Katchalsky brothers. After Bergmann, they were the scientists closest to the political establishment. Ephraim Katchalsky (later Katzir) was a physicist, his brother Aharon was a chemist.[4] "We regarded them as totally trustworthy and partners in defense research," Mardor wrote. The brothers had been active in the Haganah's underground military industry, and in the foundation of HEMED. In Israel's scientific community they were the exception, as most of the country's academic researchers opposed Ben-Gurion's integration of a scientific research institute within the military. In years to come, whenever defense research hit a crisis, the brothers would come to Mardor's aid.

Ben-Gurion dubbed the division EMET, the Hebrew word for "truth" and also the acronym for "division of research and planning." He saw importance in the symbolism of language and, according to Mardor, stressed that the unit would have to live up to its name to the fullest extent, both in striving to discover the scientific truth, and in always strictly reporting the truth about its activities. This was EMET's hierarchy: Ben-Gurion, as minister of defense, would set policy; Mardor would be in charge of carrying it out; and Bergmann would head the scientific department and the Atomic Energy Commission that had secretly been established in the Defense Ministry, without any written definition of its sphere of authority. The liaison between the three factors—EMET, the commission, and the minister of defense—would be the youthful director general of the Defense Ministry, Ben-Gurion loyalist Shimon Peres.

In 1943, at the age of twenty, Peres had been chosen to head the labor-oriented youth movement, Hanoar Ha'oved, a post that gave him a degree of public exposure and brought him close to the leadership of the Jewish community in Palestine. This was the gateway to his political career. He met Ben-Gurion for the first time on a winter's day in 1946. Peres had to travel from Tel Aviv to Haifa, and someone arranged a lift for him in the future prime minister's car. The young man was excited. "Do you know what it meant to spend almost two hours in the same car as Ben-Gurion?" Peres recalled longingly, some fifty years later. "I got into the car, and to my disappointment, Ben-Gurion wrapped himself in his coat, turned his back on me and ignored my presence." But as they reached the outskirts of Haifa, "Ben-Gurion suddenly turned to me and said: 'You know, Trotsky was no leader.' I was eager to converse with him, and I immediately asked him why, and he said, 'Why do you ask why? What kind of policy was that? Not peace, and not war? You have either peace and pay the price, or war and take the risks. Otherwise, it's a Jewish concoction, and not a political decision.' Then Ben-Gurion said that Lenin's intellectual ability was inferior to Trotsky's, but Lenin reached the leadership position because he knew how to decide. And that was the first lesson that I learned from Ben-Gurion."

Peres was born in 1923, in the Jewish village of Vishneva, about sixty miles south of Minsk, today the capital of Belarus, and then part of Poland. All of the one thousand families living in Vishneva were Jewish. His original family name was Persky. His mother was a librarian and gave him a love of books. At the age of nine, he read Dostoyevsky's *Crime and Punishment*. Both his father and his grandfather had been born in nearby Volozhin and had studied at the famous yeshiva (religious seminary) there. The grandfather took charge of Shimon's education and each day taught him a page of Talmud. "As a child, I was very religious, and it was only after we came to Palestine, in 1934, that I changed my behavior and the kind of clothing that I wore. It was like passing from one world into

another," he said decades later. In his new world, the boy would be educated in a new ideology: socialism. He was sent to one of the agricultural
schools, where the labor movement elite were trained, and at fifteen he
was one of a group of pioneers that set up a kibbutz in the Galilee. In
1946, he and Moshe Dayan were sent as representatives of the youth
wing of the Labor Party to the Zionist Congress in Vienna. A year later,
he was recruited into the Haganah, and made responsible for manpower
recruitment and arms acquisition. During the War of Independence he
filled various civilian staff positions. The fact that he never wore a uniform or bore arms was often used against him by his opponents. This together with his youth and lack of experience led many to sharply protest
Ben-Gurion's decision to make him director general of the Defense Ministry. But Peres was diligent and ambitious, which made up for his lack of
charisma and of formal education. He didn't know English but was a
quick learner.

Peres was aware that he was the object of criticism: "That's correct. Almost all the people over whose heads I was promoted were older and
richer in experience than I was, and I think that Ben-Gurion chose me
for the job because I was a daring young man and did not fear breaking
the conventions." In Ben-Gurion's eyes, daring was indeed the decisive
quality. He picked Mardor for exactly the same reason. Although Mardor
was more experienced in security matters than Peres, the two found a
common denominator in their shared goals.

"I had no illusions. It was clear that it was incumbent upon us to create
a reality in which Israel would be able to rely upon itself in most spheres,
and especially in weapons systems that there was no chance that foreign
governments would permit us to purchase them because of their power,
quality and sophistication." That was how Mardor defined the challenge
facing the organization he would build and manage. In other words,
EMET would have to develop the same modern, advanced weaponry
that was produced by large powers.

Ben-Gurion told EMET to make strategic projects the first priority.
The military brass ground their teeth in frustration. They would have
preferred a service unit that would fill orders according to their needs.
They wondered why vast resources would be devoted to the research and
development of long-term projects of doubtful feasibility, while the pro-

duction of more basic munitions, simple but necessary, was subordinated. Mardor wrote: "We fought fanatically to avoid becoming a mere service unit with high technological ability, to provide the current needs of the IDF, but to be rather a body that initiates defense R&D, and tackles projects for sophisticated, advanced weapons systems."

Bergmann helped Mardor draw up a work plan. In his imagination, Bergmann was toying with a grandiose scheme: Israel would with its own resources build a nuclear reactor for the production of atomic energy. A team headed by Israel Dostrovsky devised a process for the cheap production of the heavy water needed to operate a nuclear reactor. Fissile material could be extracted from the uranium found in the phosphate deposits in the Negev. Bergmann sketched a plan for the production of ten tons of natural uranium a year. These supplies of heavy water and uranium, Bergmann informed the prime minister, would enable Israel to set up a nuclear reactor and to produce, according to foreign sources, plutonium. "It is within our grasp to build a nuclear reactor and create atomic power," he wrote in a memorandum.

Ben-Gurion adopted Bergmann's positions unquestioningly. At the scientific adviser's recommendation, the cabinet approved the establishment of a plant for the extraction of uranium from phosphates. But there were obstacles to implementation: The concentration of uranium in the Negev phosphates was very low, and the state's coffers were empty. The small team plotting the nuclear project detected a tendency on Bergmann's part to ignore the constraints of reality. Peres used the term "overenthusiastic" in describing Bergmann's plans. Dostrovsky wondered how Ben-Gurion's practical common sense had succumbed to Bergmann's fertile imagination. At the Weizmann Institute, top scientists mocked Bergmann behind his back.

Fifty years later, Peres described a conversation he had with the prime minister: "There was a serious dispute with Bergmann, and I told Ben-Gurion about it. I never hid anything from him. I gave him all the reasoning. What did I have here to hide from him? I simply told Ben-Gurion that in Israel there was no industry that could forge the core of the reactor, the furnace. If Bergmann's stand had been accepted, it wouldn't have happened." Despite Bergmann's tendency to skew his view of reality to suit his needs, it is doubtful that Israel would have achieved its nuclear goals without his vision. Most of the people involved in implementing the project, including Peres and Dostrovsky, came to believe that Bergmann's contribution was essential.

From the start of his career in the defense establishment, Bergmann held that the scientific infrastructure had to be developed from the very foundations. "It is impossible to skip pure research, and to begin from applied research," he advised Mardor. But Mardor had his doubts. "I had the feeling that at the bottom of Prof. Bergmann's outlook there was a belief that a scientist's entire mission was research for the sake of research, in the nature of 'art for art's sake,'" he wrote, expressing the fear that after years of pure research, results would prove irrelevant to the production of armaments and a substantial investment would have gone down the drain. But Bergmann persisted, and convinced Mardor.

To the displeasure of the military command, Mardor and Bergmann stuck to the large-scale, long-term projects whose implementation required a high level of theoretical research. Later, after France supplied Israel with a powerful nuclear reactor and, as foreign sources have reported, a plant for the separation of plutonium, and the building of the nuclear option was stepped up, this pure research would supply solutions for streamlining physical and chemical processes. It is doubtful that without parallel development of both pure and applied research the defense establishment would have been able to build a nuclear option. One of the principal reasons for the delay in the development of the "Islamic bomb" was the absence of a cadre of high-level scientists in the field of pure nuclear research.

Mardor instilled an esprit de corps in his staff. You are the spearhead, he would tell them, the top team in the top league. He recruited graduates by offering similar terms of employment as those prevailing at the Hebrew University, including sabbaticals and special contracts. As the director, he reserved the right to move personnel around, an unusual practice in the socialist economic system prevailing in Israel at that time, when bosses couldn't budge a worker without union approval.

Mardor also inculcated security consciousness among the staff. If there was anyone in the world with secrecy imprinted in his genes, it was him. On the phone, he would speak in code. If he took documents home, he would read them with a pistol at his side. He never spoke a word about his work to his children. "We grew up in the underground, in a reality of secrecy, everything was clandestine," says his daughter, Gonnie; her brother, Rami, nods in agreement. Once Mardor found out that his chauffeur, Uzi, had told his son a secret, and immediately dismissed him.

A firm friendship grew up between Mardor and Bergmann. Mardor gave him almost total scientific freedom, and Bergmann blossomed. He was a born educator, who believed in people unreservedly and gave his young researchers boundless credit. After their first year of joint activity, before Rosh Hashanah, the Jewish New Year, Bergmann wrote to Mardor: "To me, the close cooperation with you was a pleasure and a great help . . . I hope we will be able to work together for many more years, and that we will make EMET one of the most important institutions in the country."

That was in 1953. In September of the same year, Colonel Yuval Neeman returned to Israel, after completing his term as Israeli military attaché in Paris. The IDF chief of staff introduced him to the prime minister as the next head of planning in the General Staff. Ben-Gurion was impressed with the short, bespectacled young man. In his diary, he called Neeman a "genius" and noted that he graduated from high school at age thirteen. Ben-Gurion got it wrong—Neeman had been fifteen—but he certainly had the brain of a genius.

"I spoke to Ben-Gurion, and I got the impression that he had internalized the importance of the nuclear issue," Neeman said fifty years later. "To me it was clear why so much was being invested in the nuclear thing, but I was not yet familiar with the physics." In the course of the next nine years, Neeman would learn about nuclear physics. The doctoral thesis that he submitted in London, in 1961, was written under the supervision of the Pakistan born Nobel laureate Abdus Salam, and it would win Neeman renown in the scientific world. But in 1953, Neeman was still an active officer in the military. As the head of planning of the General Staff, he liaised with the Atomic Energy Commission (AEC). The five other members were scientists.5 The prime minister was intimately involved in the AEC's work. As a rule, Bergmann spoke for him. "Bergmann would say, 'the prime minister requests this,' or 'the cabinet requests that,'" Neeman recalled.

At its first meeting, the AEC discussed the application of a young doctoral student of physics, Amos de Shalit, for a further year's study in Switzerland. This called for an allotment of $100,000 dollars, a hefty sum in those days. De Shalit was one of a group of doctoral students sent abroad by EMET to study various aspects of the structure of the atom, and of nuclear reactors, under renowned physicists. Most of them had completed their master's degrees in theoretical physics under Giulio (Yoel) Racah, who had studied nuclear physics at the University of Florence with the 1938 Nobel laureate Enrico Fermi, one of the builders of the American atomic bomb. There were as yet no doctoral supervisors in Israel. The students worked in laboratories in Switzerland, England, Italy, Holland, and the United States. "We ourselves had to cultivate the professional potential necessary for defense research and development, and bring it up to the required level," Mardor wrote.

Ben-Gurion and Bergmann set aside substantial sums for the training of the young scientists, and the results were good: In less than ten years, a pool of researchers was created in Israel that had acquired expertise from some of the most prominent nuclear scientists in the world, including Victor Weisskopf, Wolfgang Pauli, and Paul Scherrer in Switzerland; Isidore Rabi and Fermi in the United States; and some of Fermi's successors in Italy.

When the young scientists returned to Israel with their Ph.D. degrees, Bergmann made sure that the state fully recouped its investment in them. Some tried to avoid repaying their debt to the nuclear program and to embark on independent academic careers, but Bergmann exerted ruthless pressure, including the threat of academic ostracism.

Amos de Shalit took the lead in the opposition to Bergmann's nuclear initiative in the scientific community.[6] He believed that building a nuclear option, dependent on a powerful reactor, was not appropriate in view of the dimensions of the Israeli economy, and he told Shimon Peres that "it is a thing for the powers, and not for a small, poor country like Israel." De Shalit persuaded Meyer Weisgal, who had taken over from Bergmann as director of the Weizmann Institute, to offer EMET's young scientists positions in the Institute's department of nuclear physics. Bergmann and Mardor put up a tough fight against the move, but at least in the short term, political circumstances favored the Institute.

Early in December 1953, Ben-Gurion, exhausted after decades of continuous political responsibility, decided to take a rest "for a year or two" from his work as prime minister and minister of defense. He settled at Kibbutz Sdeh Boker in the Negev and devoted himself to writing. Before his departure from office, the staff of EMET held a farewell ceremony for him. Dozens of officers and scientists and office staff stood before him, anxious about the future. Mardor foresaw a crisis.

Replacing Ben-Gurion as prime minister was Moshe Sharett, who had served until then as foreign minister and who held dovish positions in the confrontation with the Arabs. The Defense Ministry was taken over by Pinhas Lavon, a leading figure in the labor movement since the 1930s, and a hawk. Mardor and Bergmann escorted Lavon on his first visit to EMET. From the very beginning, he was skeptical. The nuclear program seemed wasteful and impractical to him. The military command took the opportunity to insist on changes in EMET's priorities, to cancel long-term costly projects, including nuclear research, and to expand projects concerned with conventional weapons. De Shalit and Weisgal took advantage of the defense minister change and planned to move all the nuclear research, including scientists and equipment, from EMET to the Weizmann Institute. They needed Lavon's approval.

Mardor was on leave. Ben-Gurion's absence troubled him a lot and Mardor's work relations with Lavon were tenuous. Mardor's deputy, Shalhevet Freier, became acting director at EMET. This man, whose unusual biblical first name means "flame," was a talented and remarkable person. Ben-Gurion had conscripted him into the directorate of EMET because of his unique contribution to the underground. But he soon found himself in a sharp dispute with defense minister Lavon.

In January 1954, Lavon announced that he had decided to close down the physics department of EMET's Institute No. 4. The entire department, including its equipment and instruments, would be transferred to the Weizmann Institute, just as de Shalit and Weisgal had planned. Lavon assigned the ministry director general, Shimon Peres, the task of implementing the transfer.

Mardor was not even consulted. His wife had given birth to their daughter, Gonnie, and he was still on leave. In his diary he quoted rumors that the deal for the transfer of Institute 4 was done over lunch between Weisgal and Lavon. He called this bargain "a general sale," in which the Institute was to pay the state half a million lira ($280,000 at the January 1954 exchange rate). The Weizmann Institute issued a statement saying that the transferred physicists "would not be employed at any tendentious work, but only at completely pure research." In other words, the team of physicists that Bergmann and Mardor had trained would no longer be working at applied science or on defense projects.

Mardor was furious. Removing physics research from EMET spelled the end of nuclear research. Transferring the physicists to the Weizmann Institute would be a fatal blow to the reservoir of scientists that HEMED and EMET had built up. The vast investment in the advanced training abroad of the brilliant young scientists, each of whom had been assigned a specific project, would be a total loss.

At the eleventh hour, Mardor broke his leave in order to meet the physicists and try to persuade them to stay with EMET, but they refused. The Weizmann Institute promised them working conditions and salaries far superior to those at EMET. And all of the country's universities had lined up to inherit the staff and equipment of Institute 4. "In those days, this was the general mood," Mardor wrote. Indeed, most of the academic community in Israel had reservations about the scientific defense projects initiated by Ben-Gurion and Bergmann. Lavon's move was therefore in harmony with the spirit of the times. Atomic research came to a total standstill, and the activities of the Atomic Energy Commission ceased.

But Ben-Gurion would return to the political arena a lot sooner than Mardor had imagined. Only a few months after he moved to Sdeh Boker, Israel was shaken by a security scandal, which became known as the Lavon Affair, or just the Affair.

In July 1954, an underground cell set up in Egypt by Israeli intelligence was discovered by Egyptian police. Local Jewish youths had been recruited for an operation code-named Susanna, and instructed to sabotage American and British cultural institutions. The goal was to create the impression that Egyptian nationalists had carried out the attacks and thereby undermine relations between Egypt and the West and make the British give up their plan to hand over control of the Suez Canal to the Egyptians. In one of the cell's first actions, a primitive incendiary bomb went off in the pocket of one of the agents as he climbed the stairs leading to a movie theater in Alexandria. He was caught and in the wake of his interrogation the Egyptian police rounded up all the others. Two were sentenced to death and six others to long prison terms.

The exposure of the failed operation and the severe sentences stunned the Israeli political establishment and public. In the investigation of the affair, the head of military intelligence claimed that Lavon gave the order to activate the cell. Lavon claimed the intelligence chief controlled the cell himself, at his own discretion. The investigation was inconclusive, but Lavon was compelled to resign. In early 1955, thirteen months after Ben-Gurion withdrew, his successor as prime minister, Sharett, flew to Sdeh Boker and asked him to come back as minister of defense. A week later, Ben-Gurion was cheered by hundreds of citizens as he strode briskly into the Knesset, Israel's parliament, in Jerusalem, clad in khaki and with his wife, Paula, at his side. In Tel Aviv, the staff of the Defense Ministry held a reception in honor of his return. Mardor heaved a sigh of relief and returned to work. "Once more I immersed myself entirely in my work as director of EMET," he wrote.

Lavon's instructions to cease long term scientific research were rescinded and the nuclear project was once more given top priority. "Our circumstances are such that it is worthwhile investing sums of money, even if there is only a hope of achieving this thing. I am certainly in favor of it," Ben-Gurion said at a meeting of the inner leadership of the defense establishment in May 1955. By "our circumstances," he meant the worsening security situation and Israel's need to prepare for a further round of warfare; "this thing" being the nuclear project. Only very rarely did Ben-Gurion use the explicit words "atomic" or "nuclear" or "bomb." His biographer, Michael Bar-Zohar, recalls that Ben-Gurion spoke to him often about the nuclear option, "despite the fact that he was not eager to discuss it, for a simple reason: Ben-Gurion was a man of the old generation, who believed that one does not chat about security; only when he was certain that I would not give anything away was he ready to talk to me about it. Yes, for him it was a most vital thing."

Ben-Gurion invited American scientists who had taken part in the Manhattan Project to visit him in Israel. These were the men who built the atomic bombs that were dropped on Hiroshima and Nagasaki. The first meeting, and the most important one, took place in 1952, when the chief scientist of the Manhattan Project, Robert Oppenheimer, and the "father of the hydrogen bomb," Edward Teller, spent several hours with the prime minister at his home in Tel Aviv. In 1958 Oppenheimer again held lengthy conversations with Ben-Gurion and Bergmann when he came to Israel for the inauguration of the Weizmann Institute's nuclear research division. In the 1960s, Teller met Ben-Gurion, Peres, Bergmann, and Mardor on a number of occasions, as did other nuclear scientists, including Isidore Rabi and Victor Weisskopf. All of these men, incidentally, were Jewish. (To the best of my knowledge, no minutes were taken at these meetings but it is possible that in those of Ben-Gurion's diaries that are still classified, his remarks about them may yet be found.) Fifty years later, Shimon Peres observed: "The foreign scientists fueled our imaginations, as well as our apprehensions that we did not have the capability of achieving it, that it was only for the giants, a luxury attainable only by the great nations of the world, and that a lousy little country like ours could never climb those peaks and reach those heights."

Unlike the American Manhattan Project, Israel's nuclear program evolved in an improvised fashion, without an overall master plan. Ben-Gurion laid down the strategic goal, but the implementation depended upon chance and opportunity. When the opportunity to get hold of information or rare materials arose, it was seized and exploited to the full. Often, beginners' mistakes were made.

In December 1953, President Dwight D. Eisenhower delivered a historic speech in the General Assembly of the United Nations in which he presented a far-reaching program called "Atoms for Peace." At the president's request, Congress amended the 1954 Atomic Energy Act, the fundamental U.S. law on both the civilian and the military uses of nuclear materials. It declared the administration policy: "The development, use, and control of atomic energy shall be directed so as to promote world peace, improve the general welfare, increase the standard of living, and strengthen free competition in private enterprise."

The immediate effect of this act was a removal of limitations on the dissemination of American nuclear expertise, data from nuclear experiments, and the sale of nuclear materials and equipment, including reactors to any state that wished to make use of them for economic development.

As part of that program the United States offered Israel an agreement on nuclear cooperation for peaceful purposes. America would supply Israel with a small reactor for research. When the formulation of a draft agreement was finalized on May 18, 1955, prime minister and foreign minister Sharett consulted his defense minister, Ben-Gurion. "We read the agreement and could find nothing wrong with it. It restricts neither our connections with other powers, nor our use of nuclear power that we produce on our own," Sharett wrote in his diary.

The agreement was signed in July 1955. America would supply Israel with an experimental, low-powered reactor of up to 5,000 kilowatts of the "swimming pool" type (in which uranium rods are immersed in a pool of heavy water that serves mainly to moderate the chain reaction process and as a coolant). The reactor would serve to train scientists and to produce radioactive isotopes for use in medicine and industry. Israel undertook to use it for peaceful purposes only and the United States agreed to finance its construction with a $350,000 grant. The experimental reactor would rise where the Soreq River enters the Mediterranean, a few kilometers south of Tel Aviv, and be named the Nahal (river in Hebrew) Soreq reactor.

A month later, the first conference under United Nations auspices on the peaceful uses of nuclear energy took place in Geneva. Israel was represented by a high-powered team of diplomats and scientists, including Bergmann, Dostrovsky, and de Shalit. After the conference, Bergmann summed up his impressions in a twenty-one-page document classified as top secret. According to this summary, Bergmann had ambitious plans for broadening nuclear research in Israel. In Geneva he wanted to clarify whether the United States would be willing to allow Israel to adapt the experimental reactor by upgrading it so that it would be capable of producing plutonium. The Israelis hoped that in addition to the small amount of uranium that the Americans would supply, they would be permitted to use natural uranium from Israeli sources in the reactor. Dostrovsky had calculated that it would be possible to extract some eight grams of plutonium a month from the Israeli uranium—and that was the amount required, he believed, to carry out the requisite experiments.

In a tense encounter with the chairman of the U.S. Atomic Energy Commission, Admiral Lewis L. Strauss, Bergmann expressed gratitude for Strauss's assistance in reaching the newly signed agreement. According to Bergmann, Strauss replied that "he had not helped on those matters, since he is in a special situation," a hint at his Jewish origins. Bergmann then informed Strauss of Israel's interest in using the reactor to be supplied by the Americans to produce small quantities of plutonium from the uranium discovered in the Negev. Strauss replied unequivocally that Israel would not be permitted to produce even the smallest quantities of plutonium. The United States would be careful to maintain supervision over the reactor. Afterward, "in order to dispel the tension," in Bergmann's words, Strauss asked him when the Jewish high holidays, Rosh Hashanah and Yom Kippur (New Year and the Day of Atonement), which usually fall in September, were being celebrated.

Israel wanted more than the research reactor the United States was willing to sell, if only because that reactor would be subject to American inspection, which would preclude using it to produce plutonium from Israeli uranium. Israel was interested in "a real reactor," as Bergmann put it; not the miniature "swimming pool" variety, but a PWR-type reactor, which it could operate without supervision and use for the extraction of plutonium.[7] American officials in Geneva did not ascribe great importance to Israel's interest in plutonium production. It is doubtful whether Strauss and others believed that at that time Israel was capable of producing plutonium in sufficient quantities.

When the Geneva delegation returned to Israel, Bergmann recommended that the American research reactor be adapted "with improvements that our physicists will propose and the Americans will find to be acceptable." He recommended that twenty tons of heavy water be acquired in America, "on condition that this can be done without American inspection," which is to say that Israel would be able to do whatever it wanted to do with it. He also recommended that Israel stockpile quantities of uranium. Though Bergmann's report on the Geneva conference was cautiously phrased, it revealed his intentions: to exploit the research reactor for the separation of plutonium, in violation of Israel's agreement with the United States.

De Shalit realized what Bergmann was up to, and fired off a letter to Mardor, warning against trying to mislead the Americans. This is what he wrote, in part (with my clarifications added):

You must forget about submitting a plan [to the American AEC] which does not give the true goals [Israel's intention to use it to produce plutonium]. Almost all the people we spoke to [in the American delegation] were very aware of the plutonium issue and it is clear that it is impossible to slip it in under references to fission products, power stations etc. I do not think that there is even one person in the responsible circles in America who will believe that any country which possesses a process for the separation of plutonium from uranium on a large scale, as well as the objective possibility of doing it, will not exploit its knowledge for military purposes, or at least for experiments in that direction.

De Shalit commented that if Israel wanted plutonium, "it would be better to ask for it straight out, rather than try to outsmart ourselves by building a complicated reactor for that purpose." De Shalit's letter also contained a general warning against the Israeli defense establishment's nuclear weapons aspirations:

A small country naturally bears few international obligations, and no matter how great its leaders may be, it is impossible to rely on a small country like this that in an hour of despair, with its back to the wall, it will not use this unearthly weapon.

Compared to the conventional statements of the circle of scientists and politicians involved in the nuclear project, de Shalit's letter was extraordinarily trenchant, and its effect significant: Ben-Gurion forbade using the American reactor to produce plutonium, and ordered that the agreement be adhered to meticulously. Bergmann was warned to be more careful about the way he expressed himself in the future, and for a while de Shalit was ejected from the inner circle of decision makers.

Ben-Gurion never abandoned his nuclear vision, however. On the contrary, mounting anxiety about an Arab offensive merely strengthened his certitude that Israel must possess the ultimate weapon. The Arabs will attack us again and again, and they will retreat again and again, but if they ever win a single victory, that will be the end of us, Ben-Gurion often told the heads of the defense establishment. He rejected all attempts to exploit the American research reactor in violation of the agreement, but he now turned to Europe. War clouds were gathering on the Mideast horizon. Ben-Gurion resumed the office of defense minister in February 1955, and became prime minister again in November after the general elections. He instructed Israel's representatives abroad to mobilize in a special effort to acquire arms. The embargo imposed by the powers was still in force, but in at least one place cracks were appearing. That was where Israel would concentrate its major endeavors.

CHAPTER THREE

A French Window Opens

THE OFFICE OF THE ISRAELI ambassador in Paris, Jacob Tzur, looked out over the Champs d'Élysées and the Arc de Triomphe. On his desk lay Tzur's personal diary. On May 12, 1955, he wrote: "A friend came to me today and told me that concern over Israel's defensive capability is particularly great in the [French] Interior Ministry, headed by the young Radical Party leader, Maurice Bourgès-Maunoury. Two of his senior aides asked my friend to establish a connection between them and the embassy. Although the Interior Ministry does not have a direct influence over armaments issues, there is an assumption that they can help in another way. I asked for their names, and after some hesitation he told me that they were Abel Thomas and Louis Mangin. I called in Joseph Nahmias and tasked him with meeting them."

The naïve ambassador had no idea that for about a year Lieutenant Colonel Nahmias, the Israeli military attaché, had been working with government officials and military officers without Tzur's knowledge. Nahmias had conferred with Thomas only days before and reported back directly to Shimon Peres, the director general of the Defense Ministry in Tel Aviv. The ambassador had been left out of the loop, and so had the Foreign Ministry in Jerusalem. And not only them. Most of the members of the cabinet had been left out too. At that time, Prime Minister and Minister of Defense David Ben-Gurion wanted only his intimate associates—the chief of the General Staff of the Israel Defense Forces (IDF), Lieutenant General Moshe Dayan, Peres, and their closest aides—involved in the task of finding a source of weaponry.

A few days before the ambassador called Nahmias to his office and told him to meet the two Interior Ministry officials, Nahmias had been a guest at a cocktail party attended by right-wing French politicians and army officers who had served in Algeria. For the first time he heard the suggestion that France and Israel join forces against the Arabs. The host introduced Nahmias to Abel Thomas and the two withdrew to a corner for a lengthy conversation. Nahmias was surprised: "I was facing a young man, sloppily dressed, absent-minded, and unimpressive," he related a few months later. Although they had never met before, Thomas lectured him on a detailed plan for cooperation between the two countries.

Nahmias was confused. Because of the negative impression that Thomas had made, the military attaché explored other channels. It took him some months to realize that he had erred. If there was anyone in the French defense establishment who was capable of bypassing the bureaucracy, deceiving the pro-Arab Foreign Ministry, and rapidly organizing consignments of arms to Israel, it was Abel Thomas. This strange philo-Semitic gentile had taken upon himself the mission of ensuring the continued existence of the Jewish state during this fateful period, when its security was in jeopardy. He was driven by purely moral considerations, he subsequently declared many times. In World War II, Thomas joined the Free French Forces, led by Charles de Gaulle. He was a tank officer in the Leclerc division, which landed in Normandy on D-Day, June 6, 1944, and which was the first Allied unit to enter Paris in August. After the war, General Marie-Pierre Koenig awarded the Croix de Guerre to Thomas and, posthumously, to his brother Pierre, who was murdered by the Nazis at Buchenwald.

Out of the Nazi oppression and the Maquis resistance a new regime took shape in postwar France. Thomas was a key figure in setting up the defense establishment. Right after the war he was taken under the wing of the leader of the Radical Socialist Party, Maurice Bourgès-Maunoury, who was minister of the interior in 1955 when the special links with Israel were forged. Thomas was his *chef de bureau*.

At the end of 1954, the security situation along Israel's borders with Egypt, Jordan, and Syria was deteriorating. Jerusalem cabled instructions to all Israeli embassies to urgently seek sources for the acquisition of arms. Ben-Gurion ordered that a special effort be made in France. In

April 1955, Shimon Peres was sent to Paris with instructions to renew the links with the French establishment that had been forged by Ben-Gurion immediately after World War II. But once there he found himself groping in the dark. The young Defense Ministry director general did not know France and couldn't speak a word of the language. He improvised his first contact. An Israeli automobile importer whom he bumped into, Yitzhak Shubinski, told him that the economic adviser to French Prime Minister Edgar Faure was a brilliant Algerian-born Jewish economist by the name of Georges Elgozy. "He helped me and he will help you," the businessman told Peres.

Georges Elgozy was very well connected. A forty-three-year-old intellectual and a friend to André Malraux and Albert Camus, he was close to the political circles that represented the "clean" France, those who had not collaborated with the Germans. In later years, Elgozy was to become renowned as a philosopher who studied ways of humanizing automation and computerization, and promoted the unification of Europe.

Peres was unaware of Elgozy's various intellectual gifts when he followed up on Shubinski's advice in his quest for links within the French governmental establishment. He asked military attaché Nahmias to call Elgozy and request a meeting. Elgozy invited them both to his home in Paris.

"We arrived at Elgozy's home and I had never seen anything like it," says Peres, recalling his visit. "Elgozy was a bachelor. From an early age, he had been an art collector. The walls were covered with the best of French art, Chagalls and Picassos. He had bought them before they were famous. Even, if you'll excuse me, in the bathroom there were wonderful works of art."

The way of life of the Parisian elite awed the young Israeli. In Israel, there was a regime of strict austerity. People wore khakis and needed ration coupons to buy groceries. The restaurants served simple fish slices. Meat was a rarity. At that time, life in young Israel was as drab as that in communist Russia.

"When we entered, Georges said, 'First of all, I need my mother's permission. He took me into the salon, where in an armchair that looked like a royal throne, sat his mother. I approached her, and she said, 'Give me your hand.' She examined it and said, '*Georges, ça va.*' He said, 'Very well. Come and see me tomorrow, at the Hotel Matignon, the residence of the French Prime Minister.'

"We came to Hotel Matignon at 10 o'clock the next morning, and as we went up to the second floor, my heart sank, fearing it was all a bluff. I read the nameplates on the doors, Prime Minister, Diplomatic Adviser, Economic Adviser Georges Elgozy. We enter and Georges says, 'Tell me what it's all about.' I say that we want to buy planes, but there's the problem of the embargo, and he says, 'Well, let's go and see the prime minister.' We go in to the prime minister. Georges says, '*Monsieur le prime ministre*, let me handle this.' 'With pleasure,' says the prime minister. From then on, we sat in Georges' room, phoning all over France. Government offices, Dassault Industries, arms manufacturers. We ran everything from there. It was like a fairy tale."

Phones rang in the bureaus of ministers and senior officials. All replied politely, but usually in the negative. Yes, we sympathize with Israel, Peres was told, but because of the embargo we cannot comply with your request.

Peres's mission was a failure. The French establishment was holding back. Nevertheless, the meeting with Elgozy proved highly fruitful from Peres's point of view. Elgozy's name opened doors. Ministers and generals agreed to hear what the young Israeli had to say as he described the difficulties facing the young state, which had so recently absorbed the survivors of the Holocaust.

Ben-Gurion kept trying, sending Peres to Paris again in early May 1955, this time with an arms shopping list to present to Defense Minister Pierre Koenig. The French reply was still negative. France had no interest in getting into a dispute with Washington and London.

However, in another part of the world a process was under way that would change the picture. The rebellion against French colonial rule in Algeria was gathering momentum. In March 1954, the exiled Algerian leader Ahmed Ben Bella had founded the Algerian National Liberation Front (FLN) in Cairo. In November of that year, the FLN declared war against what it called the French occupation forces and launched a barrage of terrorist attacks on army camps, police stations, and government buildings, first in the Batna-Constantine area, in northeastern Algeria, and then in other districts. France sent in reinforcements. Paris regarded Algeria as an integral part of the republic and was determined to suppress the uprising. Soon the terror operations and the retaliatory measures paralyzed economic activity in Algeria and a tide of blood washed over the land.

The French government suspected that the instigator of the rebellion and its inspiration was President Gamal Abdel Nasser of Egypt. In 1952, Nasser had seized power in the revolution of the "Free Officers" (a secret revolutionary group) and abolished the monarchy. Now, in Algeria, French intelligence discovered arms that the Egyptians had sent to the FLN rebels. The weapons were obsolete, compared to the French army's equipment, but the FLN fighters used them to good effect. In France, the idea took shape that unless something was done to weaken Egypt and its president, it might be impossible to overcome the Algerian rebellion.

In August 1955, first reports reached the West that an arms deal between communist Czechoslovakia and Egypt was being negotiated. Israel suspected that the Soviet Union was behind Czechoslovakia's move, although this was not officially confirmed. Israel's apprehension grew. Government leaders feared that unless Israel could find a source of weaponry soon, the country would be in mortal danger.

Israel needed arms and France needed intelligence about Nasser's role in instigating and promoting the Algerian rebellion. Israel had access to such intelligence and France had weapons. The first to perceive this dovetailing of France's and Israel's interests were French Interior Minister Bourgès-Maunoury, whose ministry was responsible for Algeria, and his close aide, Abel Thomas.

Peres met Thomas for the first time in late September 1955, in a restaurant in Paris's 16th Arrondissement. When Thomas walked in, late, Peres felt disconcerted, just as Nahmias had when he met Thomas. "He made a strange impression on me," Peres related years later. "He didn't stop talking, pouring out ideas, proposals, plans, as if we were old friends." Even before the entrees were served, Thomas had proposed creating a direct link, "without the diplomatic formalities," in his words. He had no difficulty persuading Peres to leave the Foreign Ministry in Jerusalem out of the picture. Peres had reported directly to Ben-Gurion since undertaking his campaign of lobbying in France, and as before, Ambassador Tzur was unaware of the meeting with Thomas. "I am speaking in the name of Minister Maurice Bourgès-Maunoury," Thomas declared, and he invited Peres to go with him to the minister's home, "to make concrete plans." Despite Peres's amazement at the bluntness of the proposal and the undiplomatic language, he agreed. "I had nothing to lose," he explains.

Bourgès-Maunoury received Peres with all due honor. A French artillery officer who had been taken prisoner by the Germans in 1940, he empathized with the lot of the Jewish people. When he was released from a German POW camp in 1942, he had crossed the Pyrenees and eventually joined the Free French forces in London. He had parachuted into France twice, the second time to coordinate between the Maquis and the Allies in preparation for the invasion on D-Day. After taking part in the liberation of the city of Lyon in September 1944, he had headed for Paris and was wounded on the way in a skirmish with the Germans.

Bourgès-Maunoury expounded his strategy to Peres, point-blank: Israel and France have common interests, and they should work together. In Israel, a million Jews were besieged by Arabs, and in Algeria, a million Frenchmen were in the same situation. "Nasser reminds me of Hitler. He is an extremist who employs terrorist tactics and is enthralled by his own speeches," said Bourgès-Maunoury. Peres described Israel's situation in detail. The Arabs were arming, he said, and Israel would have to face them empty-handed. Thomas recalls being shocked: "Peres cited hard facts. He spoke for Dayan and Ben-Gurion. He said, 'Look, this is a difficult time in our history, and it is possible that we will be wiped off the map. If we do not get aircraft, we will not be able to stand up to an offensive by Nasser, and we'll be destroyed. If we do not get serious help to enable us to defend ourselves, we will cease to exist.' In other words, Israel's Jews would once again become wanderers."

"How is it that I took such an interest in Israel that it became my life's concern?" Thomas asked, years later, and immediately replied: "I became interested in Israel's fate from the moment that I learned that my brother, Pierre Thomas, had been arrested by the Gestapo as a member of the Maquis and an officer cadet, and was tortured and died in a concentration camp, in the crematoria, despite the fact that he was not a Jew."[1]

Peres recalls sensing in those days that many Frenchmen harbored deep feelings of identification with the Jewish victims of the Nazis. "It was a matter of great shame that gripped the French after the defeat at the hands of the Nazis," he told me. "Some of them were in the death camps. I shall never forget that the chief of the general staff of the French armed forces, his name was General Paul Ely, invited me to dinner. He was tall and slim and his hand was paralyzed. I was seated next to his wife, and she said to me: 'Monsieur Peres, I want you to know just one thing. I was in a concentration camp.' In other words, her attitude to Israel was not an abstract matter. They identified with us. We too faced destruction. We too survived a disaster, they felt. Without that, it is very difficult to understand everything that happened."

In the Middle East, Nasser had carried out his first move against Israel. On September 12, 1955, Egypt closed the Straits of Tiran, at the entrance to the Gulf of Aqaba between Sinai and Saudi Arabia, thereby blocking shipping to and from the Israeli port of Eilat. Egypt also barred Israeli aircraft from flying over the straits, thereby preventing El Al, Israel's airline, from flying to South Africa along the route over the Red Sea.

Two weeks later, on September 27, Egypt announced an arms deal with Czechoslovakia. Through the Czechs, Egypt would get $250 million worth of the latest Soviet weaponry.

Israeli military intelligence and the Foreign Ministry predicted that the military balance would now tip dangerously to Egypt's advantage. The media reflected the general sense in the country that, sooner or later, Israel would face another attempt by the Arab states to destroy it. At a meeting in the Defense Ministry in Tel Aviv, Ben-Gurion told Peres and Moshe Dayan: "I suppose they'll attack in the summer."

In October, there were reports from Arab capitals of a plan to set up a united command of the armies of Egypt, Syria, and Jordan, reports that were seen in Israel as foreshadowing an imminent offensive. Almost every night armed bands of *fedayun* infiltrated into Israel from the territory of the Kingdom of Jordan, or from the Gaza Strip, which was under Egyptian control, killing civilians and destroying property. The atmosphere was tense. No one asked *if* there would be a war, only *when*. In the military, there was a sense that the superiority achieved in the War of Independence in 1948 was melting away. Most defense experts, among them chief of staff Dayan, believed that time was working in favor of the enemy, and that therefore a preemptive war was called for. Ben-Gurion opposed this.

Today, few Israelis are aware of the depth of the anxiety that afflicted the founding father of the Jewish state. Ben-Gurion lived constantly with the feeling that at any minute Israel could be conquered and disappear off the face of the globe. He took the threats of the Arab leaders to "throw the Jews into the sea" with utter seriousness. While he generally concealed from the wider public his fears that another Holocaust was about to befall his nation, among his close associates he gave free rein to his emotions. The anxiety caused him actual physical suffering, and he often found it difficult to fall asleep at night. His personal secretary, Yitzhak Navon, reveals: "One morning I asked BG why he was tense, and he said, 'I never closed an eye all night, not even for one second. My heart was full of anxiety over a combined attack of the Arab armies.' This happened to him quite often." Michael Bar-Zohar related: "Ben-Gurion would come to his office in the morning, call in Yitzhak Navon, stand facing the map of the country and say: 'Yitzhak, look at all of those countries around us. How can we stand up to them? How can we survive?'"

His concern did not flow purely from dry analysis of the Middle Eastern power equation, which in the mid-1950s was exceedingly unfavorable to Israel, but mainly from the fact that Israel lacked the support of even one of the great powers. As long as Israel did not have international backing, a preemptive war against Egypt would not fundamentally change the situation, Ben-Gurion told Dayan in December 1955, adding: "The day after our victory, if in fact we do win—and that depends upon the non-intervention of foreign factors, chiefly Britain—we will face precisely the same problems that we face now, but under more difficult conditions, because then we will be presented to the world as an aggressor state." With an offensive ruled out, the Israeli armed forces deployed to defend the country. They constructed fortifications along the borders, and planned and executed civil defense measures. Israel was preparing for a war that would break out at Egypt's initiative.

Once again, Peres was dispatched to Paris to ask for planes and tanks. On October 26, the French minister of defense, General Pierre Billotte, received him and agreed in principle to supply Israel with tanks and artillery. But two days later Billotte retracted, due to pressure from the Quai d'Orsay, the French Foreign Ministry. According to Thomas, the Foreign Ministry was still trying to persuade Nasser to withdraw his support for the FLN rebellion in Algeria. Supplying French arms to Israel, Foreign Ministry officials contended, would sabotage these diplomatic efforts.

As the FLN uprising continued, the French settlers in Algeria grew suspicious that peace would be negotiated at their expense. They staged massive demonstrations. The right in both France and Algeria called on Charles de Gaulle to assume power and to fight until the bitter end. Their protest caused a prolonged political crisis. One government after another collapsed.

A few days after Billotte rescinded his offer, the government of Prime Minister Edgar Faure fell, and France was once again embroiled in an election campaign. Peres remained in France during it. He thought the united front set up by the left and the center, headed by Guy Mollet, leader of the Socialist Party and another former underground fighter, would win. Peres and Mollet, who had been captured three times by the Gestapo and tortured, had become firm friends, based on personal chemistry and shared ideologies.

As the election campaign raged, Mollet met with Peres several times and assured him of his friendly attitude to Israel. Peres recalls that in the course of one conversation, Mollet told him that he felt responsible for Israel's continued existence and promised that if he were elected prime minister, he would not hesitate to arm Israel with the latest French weaponry.

On the eve of the election, Peres was at Orly Airport, preparing to board a plane back to Tel Aviv. He saw banner headlines in the papers reporting the results of a public opinion poll: The right would win, and Mollet would lose.

"But then, the incredible happened," Peres recalls. "Guy Mollet was elected prime minister. The same night he telephoned me in Tel Aviv and said, 'Shimon, I am prime minister. Come and have dinner with me, and I'll keep all of my promises.'"

On February 1, 1956, Mollet's new government was sworn in. Maurice Bourgès-Maunoury was promoted to defense minister (he had been minister for the armed forces briefly a year earlier) and Abel Thomas would run his office. However, the new foreign minister, Christian Pineau, blocked every effort at easing the arms embargo against Israel.

In Paris, a stormy period had begun. The Algerian crisis was becoming an extremely fierce war. Both sides became notorious for their use of terror and torture. The French army was finding it difficult to protect the French colonists against terrorist attacks and scores were massacred. A pitched battle was fought between French commandos and FLN guerrillas near the city of Constantine.

"It was atrocious," says Abel Thomas. "I remember going to Constantine with Jacques Soustelle, the minister in charge of Algeria, to visit the commandos after the terrorist offensive, and the scene was atrocious. We saw an entire family, French *colons*, they were teachers, with their stomachs slashed open." Thomas's right hand draws a line from his chest across his stomach as he recalls the picture. "The grandmother with her stomach cut open, and the heads of two children in her stomach. It was so awful that Soustelle couldn't look at it, and he began vomiting. It was so monstrous."

Mollet was determined to crush the rebellion. To do so, he urgently required intelligence about Egyptian assistance to the FLN. The Israeli defense establishment was following developments in the Algerian war very closely. Until now, Ben-Gurion had been hesitant about intervening in any way in the hostilities. The Mossad had recommended keeping out and military intelligence concurred. But now Peres succeeded in persuading Ben-Gurion that the severe crisis in Algeria had opened a one-time window of opportunity for Israel in France. It is doubtful that at the time Ben-Gurion believed that the window would be as large as it proved to be. He was thinking in terms of modern aircraft and tanks, not in nuclear terms. But circumstances played into his hands, and no one can deny that the "Old Man," as he was known to the younger members of his party, was equal to the challenge. Anyone studying Ben-Gurion's moves in connection with the Israel-France relationship between 1955 and 1960 realizes that he played a brilliant game of political chess. He immediately took two steps: He ordered that the connection between Israeli military intelligence and French intelligence, the SDECE, be stepped up, and sent Peres to Paris to get planes and tanks.[2]

Bourgès-Maunoury approved the sale of French-made Mystère jet fighters to Israel immediately upon his taking up his post as minister of defense. Foreign minister Pineau objected. Without American agreement, he argued, France should not supply arms to Israel, especially because he saw no urgency in it. He quoted Nasser, whom he had visited in Cairo some days before, as saying: "I assure you that I have no intention of attacking Israel." The defense minister's office contended that Pineau was deluding himself and insisted that twelve planes should be dispatched to Israel immediately. The Foreign Ministry reconsidered, but would approve the sale of only nine planes. According to Abel Thomas, "The Defense Ministry then decided to carry out an independent policy. We disobeyed the directive of a senior Foreign Ministry official, who had decided that nine planes were enough for Israel to defend itself. After all, the requests of Dayan and Peres were realistic, and that's a fact." At the Defense Ministry's instructions, twelve planes took off, refueled in Italy, and continued southward to Israel. They never returned to their bases, and the French air force erased them from their inventory. The Quai d'Orsay knew nothing about it. "The moment we decided to help Israel," recalls Thomas, "on that very day, a shipment of armored cars left Marseilles bound for Egypt. The governor of Marseilles was a Jew. We became friendly during the liberation from the Germans. He called me in Paris, and asked me to stop the shipment. I told the defense minister, 'At the same time that we're trying to help Israel, a consignment of armored cars is being sent to Egypt, with the Foreign Ministry's approval.' Bourgès-Maunoury stopped the shipment."

Thomas was not a religious man, but he believed Israel was in danger of destruction and saving it was a mission assigned to him by Providence. His devotion to the fulfillment of Israel's aspirations was not inspired by French interests, nor by a desire to defeat the terrorists in Algeria, but by a grasp of Israel's distress and a humane solidarity with its people. At first the suspicious Israelis did not know how to read him. His naïveté seemed somewhat bizarre. Is it conceivable, they asked themselves, that a gentile would be stricken by the same love for Israel that Jews feel? But after a time they appreciated his honesty and devotion, and the suspicion dissipated. His door was open to Dayan and Peres at all times. Peres recalls that their conversations were world-embracing. Thomas saw a powerful France, free of American patronage, possessing its own nuclear capability. Whether America liked it or not, Thomas said to Peres, France would preserve its status as a power. Peres sensed early on that Bourgès-

Maunoury and Thomas wanted France to get the bomb. In their eyes, this was one of the lessons that France had learned from the shameful surrender to the Germans in World War II. In order to hold on to the status of a world power and in order to redeem itself from American patronage, France had to have the ultimate deterrent. The consideration of scientific cooperation with Israel in the nuclear sphere was on the minds of the Defense Ministry officials right from the start of the negotiations on supplying French arms to the Jewish state, Thomas said.

The twelve Mystere fighter jets landed in Israel in the evening on April 11, 1956. Waiting for them with eager anticipation on the landing strip at the Hazor air base were the leaders of the Israeli defense establishment, headed by the prime minister and the chief of staff. Shimon Peres circulated among them proudly. At last his efforts were bearing fruit. His detractors, who had doubted that the connections he forged in France would ever be of use, came up and shook his hand. The arrival of its first jet fighters heralded a new era for the Israeli Air Force.

In Paris, Israeli Ambassador Tzur had not yet heard about the delivery of the planes. In fact, four days before the Mystères reached Israel, Foreign Minister Pineau had summoned Tzur to the Quai d'Orsay to inform him that the foreign office would refrain from signing the document approving the supply of the jets because it had not been approved by the American-British-French tripartite committee that oversaw the embargo. "France does not intend to be the sole supplier of arms to Israel," Pineau told Tzur. "If the United States and Britain supply 25 percent of the required amount, France will supply the rest." But by then, the Defense Ministry had already issued the orders for the planes to take off for Israel.

Some two weeks later Bourgès-Maunoury dispatched another twelve Mysteres to Israel, despite the Foreign Ministry's opposition. Peres suggested to Ben-Gurion that he propose a defense treaty between Israel and France. Ben-Gurion was not enthusiastic, but said he'd study the proposal. He sent Peres to meet Prime Minister Guy Mollet with another arms list and a personal letter. "The small and young republic of Israel which is facing grave danger," Ben-Gurion wrote, "is appealing to its sister, the great and ancient republic of France, in the hope that its request will not be rejected." Peres says that Mollet responded immediately, declaring: "I believe I will be able to help you." Ambassador Tzur, who was present at the meeting, wrote in his diary: "We met Guy Mollet and handed him the prime minister's letter. His response was positive . . . France will do everything that it is able to do, but, unfortunately, only what it is able to do."

But while Ambassador Tzur was skeptical about the French government's determination to help Israel, in reality things were rolling ahead rapidly. At Ben-Gurion's behest, Peres met Bourgès-Maunoury and proposed a plan for cooperation. France would supply Israel with large quantities of a variety of armaments, and teams of experts from both countries would meet to plan joint operations against Egypt. The French defense minister seized upon the opportunity with enthusiasm, and suggested that the first such meeting be held in Paris in a few days' time. Once again, the Israeli ambassador in Paris was left in the dark.

This exclusion of the Foreign Ministry from key political developments helped cause a government crisis in Israel. There were deep differences between a group of hawks, headed by chief of staff Dayan, and doves led by the foreign minister, Moshe Sharett. Dayan believed war with Egypt was inevitable and preferred initiating hostilities. Sharett thought war could be avoided and advocated exhausting all diplomatic possibilities before even considering such a thing.

Dayan and the army submitted a plan to the government for the conquest of the Tiran Straits by seaborne forces and paratroops. The government, guided by Sharett, refused to approve it. Sharett was also dubious about Peres's initiative for a cooperation pact with France, which Sharett felt was not in Israel's interests. Ben-Gurion made no concessions to appease Sharett, who resigned his post as foreign minister on June 19, 1956. He was replaced by Golda Meir.

On June 23, only four days after the change of guard at the Foreign Ministry in Jerusalem, the joint meeting of Israeli and French military and defense experts was held in Paris. Both sides were represented by impressive arrays of generals, who exchanged ideas in an amicable atmosphere. The foreign ministries of the two countries were excluded. Peres presented Israel's requests: 200 tanks, 72 Mystere fighters, 10,000 antitank rockets, and 40,000 artillery shells—an arms deal worth $70 million. On the plane on the way to Paris, the Israelis joked that when the French saw the list they'd tear it up or burst out laughing, so audacious were the Israeli demands. However, Bourgès-Maunoury's *chef de bureau*, Colonel Louis Mangin, looked at the list and said right away: "Let's sign." Peres took out his fountain pen and signed, even though he had not received his government's permission to do so. It was the biggest arms purchase Israel had undertaken since its inception. "I didn't want to miss the opportunity," Peres explained years later. Thomas remembers Dayan closing the meeting with a speech of thanks and commitment: "My government has asked me to thank you for your readiness to supply us with arms, and I am authorized to say to you that Israel will join with France in any joint operation against Nasser, however far France may go."

Two weeks later Foreign Minister Pineau told Ambassador Tzur about the joint meeting of generals and defense officials. Pineau told Tzur that from now on France would supply Israel with any arms that it required. "The prime minister, and he himself, the foreign minister, had approved this arrangement," Tzur wrote in his diary, adding that Pineau had informed him that "the arms shipments would go through military channels and to prevent mishaps, even the senior officials in Paris would not be informed and the foreign minister would keep the matter a secret and it would be known only to a limited circle of people." Thus, it was the French Foreign Ministry that advised the Israeli Foreign Ministry of the most important military agreement Israel had signed up to that date. Now even the skeptical ambassador was forced to admit, albeit very cautiously, that a turnabout may have been taking place in France's attitude to Israel. "We are standing at the threshold of a new era in our relations with France," Tzur wrote in his diary. "The more I examine it, and the more I force myself to be cautious in my assessments, I can find no other way to describe the turning point that we have reached."

On July 26, three days after the meeting in Paris, Nasser made his move. In a highly emotional speech before hundreds of thousands of his countrymen, he declared that Egypt was nationalizing the Suez Canal. Nassar was furious because of an American and British refusal to finance the construction of the Aswan Dam. That refusal was a direct response to the tightening ties between Egypt and the Soviet Union. President Eisenhower became concerned about Nasser's communist connections following the signing of the arms deal between Czechoslovakia and Egypt in August 1955.

The canal's nationalization was a serious challenge to French and British interests. The waterway was the property of the Suez Canal Company, which was controlled by stockholders in those two countries. Through it passed the tankers that carried most of Europe's oil from the Persian Gulf.

Days after Nasser's dramatic speech, permanent channels of communication opened between France and Israel to deal with arms supplies, intelligence, espionage, and operational planning. In French army camps, work began on packing the large consignments of weaponry to be sent to Israel. Relations between the two armies grew closer by the day.

On July 27, the day after the nationalization and blockade of the canal, Bourgès-Maunoury invited Peres to an operational session of the General Staff of the French army. "How long will it take the Israeli army to overrun the Sinai Peninsula?" the defense minister asked Peres, who replied, "Two weeks, I believe." Recounting the meeting, Peres continued: "All the generals looked at each other as if to say, 'This simpleton, what is he talking about?' Bourgès-Maunoury said, 'Are you interested in conquering Sinai?' I told him that we had other interests: a) Egypt had closed the Tiran Straits and Ben-Gurion had said this was a *casus belli*, and you could rest assured that we have plans to deal with it; b) there is the matter of the *fedayun*, as they were called then, who are embittering our lives; and c) the Egyptians have obtained an abundance of arms, and we are anxious about our security. So Bourgès-Maunoury said to me, 'We have something to talk about.' I said, 'I believe we do.'"

The most important phase of talking began two months later, on Sunday, September 30, when two high-ranking delegations gathered at Mangin's home in Montparnasse in Paris. In the entrance hall hung a portrait of the father of the host, Gen. Charles Mangin, the hero of the battle of Verdun in World War I.[3] The decorations and citations won by the officers of the Mangin clan were displayed in a glass cabinet. One was a certificate signed by Gen. Charles de Gaulle, in which the son, Louis Mangin, is cited. It reads, in part: "In difficult conditions, he took upon himself to carry out an important task in the organization of the military plans for the day of the invasion. Although he was followed by the Gestapo, he was not deterred from doing his duty."

Among those present were the two foreign ministers, Christian Pineau and Golda Meir; IDF Chief of Staff Dayan; the French deputy chief of staff, General Maurice Schall; Shimon Peres; and Abel Thomas. After a round of cognac and an exchange of pleasantries, Pineau opened the discussion: "From one day to the next I become more convinced that we have no choice but to use force against Egypt. To my regret, the British have not yet reached the same conclusion." He said France would have to make a final decision on going to war against Egypt no later than mid-October, before weather conditions could disrupt an attack. If the British did not join, said Pineau, there was still the possibility of a joint French-Israeli operation, or an Israeli campaign with French backing. The next day, Dayan explained Israel's attack plan to a group of French officers, headed by the chief of staff, General Ely. A French military mission under Schall traveled to Israel to examine the readiness of the IDF.

Dayan was satisfied. He saw his plan for a preemptive war coming to fruition. Peres too was satisfied. French weapons shipments were landing in Israel according to plan. Ben-Gurion, however, remained skeptical. His new foreign minister, Meir, was hesitant about putting trust in the weak French government headed by Mollet. "In France, governments rise and fall like dominoes," she told Ben-Gurion. The head of the Mossad, Isser Harel, a close confidant of the prime minister, was firmly opposed to cooperation with France on the intelligence plane. "Algeria isn't in our sphere of activity," he told Ben-Gurion, and he warned against getting embroiled in an international conspiracy. The more Ben-Gurion weighed the advantages and disadvantages of the military operation, the clearer the risks became. There was no guarantee that a war would depose the Egyptian tyrant, he explained, and it was doubtful that anyone could occupy Egypt for any length of time, even for a few months. Also, the reaction of the Soviet Union had to be considered. It might decide to send "volunteers" to help Egypt, "and such help could complicate matters," Ben-Gurion cautioned. "I have no sentiments either for or against the Soviet Union. But we must not forget that it is a nation of 200 million people, a tremendous global force, and let us not forget that they defeated Napoleon . . . The Soviet Union may well extend aid to the Egyptian tyrant, just as it maintained an alliance with Mussolini for a lengthy period, and then with Hitler, because it saw them as the enemies of its enemies. Without the swift elimination of the tyrant, there's no certainty that the conflict will end quickly, even if there are only military successes in the early stages."

The change in French policy thus did nothing to alleviate Ben-Gurion's anxiety. But in fact the die had already been cast. Britain and France would soon propose that Israel join the Big Game, and even the careful Ben-Gurion could not evade such a challenge.

CHAPTER FOUR

An Unprecedented Deal

BETWEEN MID-JULY and the end of October 1956, the deputy head of Israeli military intelligence, Colonel Yuval Neeman, flew to Paris and back eight times. At intelligence headquarters in Tel Aviv, he would collect the information gathered in Israel about cooperation between Egypt and the heads of the Algerian underground. In Paris, he handed the material to the chief of French intelligence, Pierre Georges Boursicot. Thirty-one, of stocky physique, Neeman made a powerful impression on Boursicot. At one of their meetings, Boursicot told him, "You will become the president of a university." And indeed, that is what happened.[1]

Neeman was born in Palestine. His parents established a water pump factory, and for this reason Yuval studied mechanical engineering. At the age of fifteen he had enlisted in the Haganah, and in the War of Independence, at only twenty-three, he commanded a brigade. In his youth, like most of his contemporaries, Neeman was a socialist, and in this he found common ground with the socialist Boursicot, who before World War II had been a union activist. (In years to come, Neeman would traverse the political map. At the end of the 1970s he was head of a right-wing, nationalistic political party.)

"It had been agreed that we would get arms from the French in exchange for intelligence, and I was supplying the intelligence," Neeman recalls. Operational orders for the Algerian underground cells were broadcast in code from Cairo, mainly over Nasser's Saut al-Arab radio station. Israeli intelligence had cracked the codes and deciphered the messages. "Nasser and Saut al-Arab were major pillars of the Algerian revolt and breaking the codes was quite an achievement, and helped the French a great deal," asserts Neeman.

Before his trips to Paris, Neeman had met with the military attaché at the French Embassy in Tel Aviv, Colonel Daniel Divry. Without consulting with Isser Harel, who was the head of both the Mossad and the Shin Bet (Israel's external and internal secret services, respectively), Neeman hinted to the attaché that Israeli intelligence had picked up Egyptian broadcasts that included the encoded names of Algerian underground operatives. But Neeman didn't know that Harel's staffers were aware of the content of the attaché's reports to Paris. When Harel saw the attaché's account of his meeting with Neeman, Harel was furious. A few months before he died in early 2003, Harel said, "This was the first time that a connection with a foreign state on intelligence matters was not carried out through the Mossad. The direct link between the IDF and the French secret services caused damage to the Mossad's activity in France." Harel complained to Ben-Gurion, and Neeman was reprimanded, although he was merely heeding the wishes of his superiors in the defense forces, including Chief of Staff Dayan and Defense Ministry Director General Peres.

A year prior to this, early in 1955, the Mossad had set up three self-defense militias in Algeria to protect the Jewish community there from Muslim terrorists. They bore the name Misgeret (Hebrew for "framework"), operated for five years in the cities of Algiers, Constantine, and Oran, and used arms hidden in secret caches. Some of their commanders were reservists in the French armed forces. Some had been trained in Israel. Senior Mossad officials feared that military cooperation with the French would involve Israel in a superfluous conflict, and endanger the Jews of North Africa.

"It was a very dirty and very dangerous war," Harel said, forty-five years later. "There was no point becoming part of this war. The French expected us to participate in actual operations with them against the Algerians, and I did not like that." For months after the incident with Neeman, Harel repeatedly warned Ben-Gurion against what he called "collusion" with the British and the French. Until his dying day he would accuse Peres of "maneuvering Ben-Gurion, misleading him, and endangering the state in an international intrigue."

As relations with France became institutionalized, Neeman was invited to take a comprehensive tour of North Africa. Traveling on a fake passport, he surveyed the results of the French colonization of the territory since 1830. Just over 120 years later, 1.2 million Frenchmen, known as *colons*—settlers—were living in Algeria and Morocco. On top of all the other connections between France and its vast possessions across the Mediterranean, the French military-industrial complex had built weapons factories and research institutes in the Algerian Sahara, as well as firing ranges to test their products. Close to these facilities they had constructed townships for the scientists and technicians who worked in them. At Colomb-Béchar, in southwest Algeria, the French had set up advanced installations for the development of atomic and chemical munitions, and for the testing of missiles. Near the oasis of Reggane, about 400 miles south of Colomb-Béchar, a nuclear weapons testing site had been planned. The socialist governments that ruled France in the 1950s paid lip service to anticolonialist policies, but Algeria wasn't considered a colony. "Algeria is French" was the slogan that reflected the prevalent assumption.

Neeman's conclusions from his trip were threefold: First, France would hang on to Algeria with all its might, using Israeli intelligence to do so. Second, France was determined to topple Nasser's regime in Egypt. Third, France aspired to become a nuclear power.

In the latter aspiration, France was not alone. "Ben-Gurion told me, 'I want a nuclear option,'" Neeman relates, "and I answered him that I understood, but my connection was in intelligence, and I therefore focused on technical aspects like computers and electronic instruments. I said to him, 'Don't expect me to bring it. But I am working on links with the most important technical services.'"

"I want a nuclear option." That statement, cited publicly for the first time here, is the most explicit ever attributed to Ben-Gurion regarding his vision. Ben-Gurion was willing to reveal his innermost secret to Neeman because he knew of the young officer's broad education and sophistication. Moreover, Neeman's involvement in intelligence was an assurance that the secret would go no further. Unlike the young physicist Amos de Shalit, Neeman did not try to dissuade Ben-Gurion from realizing his nuclear vision.

Neeman therefore nurtured the intelligence connections, and as the Anglo-French-Israeli campaign against Egypt approached, he assisted in coordinating the planning of operations of the Israeli and French armies, reporting to Chief of Staff Dayan. In June, Dayan wrote in his diary: "Relations with the French were honest and warm. There was a spirit of total trust."

This trust, however, was lacking in relations between Israeli diplomats and defense officials. The diplomatic track was handled by Israel's senior representative in Paris, Ambassador Jacob Tzur. He was in constant touch with French Foreign Minister Christian Pineau and the officials of the Quai d'Orsay, but as we have seen, he was excluded from the important transactions. He reported to Foreign Minister Golda Meir, who was also out of the loop of Israeli-French military relations.

In Tel Aviv, the French ambassador, Pierre Gilbert, was in direct contact with Peres. The dynamic Gilbert had learned Hebrew and endeared himself to both the political establishment and to the man in the street. He created a direct connection with the Paris bureau of France's minister for Algerian affairs, Robert Lacoste, and saw to it that the bureau chief would visit Israel and meet the heads of intelligence. As relations between the two countries warmed, Gilbert's enthusiasm increased, but like his Israeli counterpart, he was bypassed by his government when the key decisions about the approaching war and nuclear cooperation were being taken. It was Peres who informed Gilbert of the French government's important decisions.

The third and most important track for negotiations on the Egypt operation was between the defense ministries of the two countries. The Israel military attaché in Paris, Joseph Nahmias, was in daily contact with Abel Thomas, chief aide to French Defense Minister Guy Bourgès-Maunoury, and Nahmias reported not to Tzur but directly to Dayan and Peres, who kept Ben-Gurion informed.

From mid-1956, channels of communication between France and Israel were humming with traffic. Cable offices and telephone exchanges worked overtime. Officers and officials traveled to and fro. The Israeli military elite discovered the delights of Paris. Young generals, many of whom grew up in agricultural settlements, were entertained in magnificent salons, sipping fine cognac and doing their best in broken French.

The French connection provided an unusual element in the life of the young state, where a virtually anorexic austerity reigned, the prime minister wore khakis, and the salary of a ministry director general like Peres was less than two hundred dollars a month.

On each side it was the defense establishment that dominated the alliance; most of the diplomats adopted a skeptical stance. On the French side, Bourgès-Maunoury and his aides stepped on the gas, while Pineau applied the brakes. On the Israeli side, Dayan and Peres whipped the horses forward, while Foreign Minister Meir and Mossad chief Harel tried to hold them back. Meir and Harel were ignorant of the fact that Ben-Gurion's nuclear aspirations had been placed on the agenda right from the beginning of the new relationship with France. "The primary goal," Peres says, "was to obtain a source to supply weapons. The second was a nuclear reactor."

While Peres was steering the effort in the direction of France, Ernst Bergmann was still trying to advance his plan to build a reactor independently. His opponents, Amos de Shalit and some of de Shalit's colleagues in the Weizmann Institute physics department, endeavored to convince Ben-Gurion that adopting Bergmann's plan could cause severe damage to the country.

In April 1956, Bergmann and de Shalit, representing Israel's Atomic Energy Commission, took part in a study tour of nuclear installations in the United States. At a meeting with the heads of the U.S. commission, Bergmann surprised de Shalit when he declared that Israel was planning to build a 10-megawatt swimming-pool reactor (in addition to the small research reactor the U.S. had promised to supply). It would be for research purposes and would be fueled by natural uranium produced in Israel, Bergmann said, adding that the Israeli AEC, which he headed, had already provided several American companies with the specifications and was awaiting bids. He asked the American AEC to allow Israel to acquire enriched uranium and heavy water in the United States. The answer was no to the uranium, but he was told that Israel could purchase heavy water on condition that it be used only for civilian purposes.

This initiative of Bergmann's was something of a shot in the dark, because no decision had as yet been taken in Israel to build a large reactor. After their American tour, de Shalit once more voiced his objections to the Bergmann plan, telling Peres that building a reactor independently would be a "hazardous adventure."

Indeed, Peres had decided to turn to France because he understood that Bergmann's concept of an Israeli-built reactor powerful enough to produce plutonium was a "fantasy." On a visit to Paris, Peres met with Pierre Guillaumat, the administrator general of the French AEC. Peres recalls: "He told me, 'Shimon, let me give you a piece of free advice: In science, one should be lazy, and if something has already been discovered, don't work hard and invent it again. Take whatever already exists, and work at finding what doesn't exist.' It was wise advice, and I understood that we must get hold of everything that could be obtained from abroad." He had consulted Dayan, the only figure in the Israeli defense establishment capable of putting obstacles in his path. Dayan made it clear that his first priority was to get in a preemptive strike at Egypt, and that he was not enthusiastic about the nuclear issue. Peres said, "I told Moshe that I wanted to go ahead with it, and he said, 'OK, I'm with you.' Even though the generals were opposed and he himself had his doubts, he said, 'You'll be responsible? Very well, go ahead.'"

Dayan's doubts were fed by the skepticism of the scientists, according to Peres, and Neeman concurs: "Dayan summoned me, de Shalit, and Dostrovsky, and told us that the military attaché in Paris believed that the French would provide us with the necessary means and assist us. He asked us whether we thought it was serious. I was considered well educated, but I wasn't a physicist yet and my opinion wasn't of much account. De Shalit and Dostrovsky understood the subject, and both were reserved."

In the first stage of the relationship with top French defense officials, discussions of the two countries' nuclear options were general, and noncommittal. At his meetings with Bourgès-Maunoury and Abel Thomas, and with Prime Minister Guy Mollet, Peres remarked a number of times that Ben-Gurion thought a nuclear option would solve Israel's security problems. His interlocutors were interested. Thomas expounded on his own security concept: "If France aspires to free itself of the American embrace, and if it wants to preserve its status as a power, it must build a bomb." It was only at the end of 1954, a year that saw the French defeat at Dien Bien Phu in Vietnam and France's subsequent surrender of control in Indochina, that the government under Pierre Mendès-France decided to build a French atomic bomb. Since the 1940s, the United States, Canada, and Britain had excluded France when it came to sharing nuclear secrets, mainly due to the fear that communists who held senior posts in French nuclear research programs would pass information to the Soviet Union.[2] When Peres discussed nuclear cooperation with his counterparts in Paris, a French bomb was still a distant dream.

One difficulty was a technical one: The French lacked plutonium. By 1956, less than a kilogram of weapons-grade plutonium had been produced in France, and at least four kilograms were needed to make a bomb.[3] Although substantial deposits of uranium had been discovered near the city of Toulouse in 1952 and reactors and a plutonium separation plant had been set up at Marcoule on the bank of the Rhone River in order to process it, industrial-scale production of plutonium began in France only in 1959.

Another obstacle to progress toward a French bomb was the ineptitude of scientific research in the country. The scientists in charge of the mathematical calculations by which the rate was set for compression of fissile material (in order to create nuclear chain reactions that produced the critical mass) could not reach the same results. This made it impossible to complete planning of the nuclear device. The French defense establishment was on tenterhooks as it waited for a breakthrough. Thomas expressed the dismay prevalent in the upper reaches of the French government over the impotence of the scientists when he told Dayan and Peres that French nuclear research "has holes in it, and France is willing to give substantial recompense to whoever could fill them." In a few months' time, however, France's nuclear weapons project would get a big push forward—ironically, due to the deep humiliation France was to suffer in the Suez Campaign.

As the military links between France and Israel tightened, Peres stepped up the discussions on nuclear matters to the practical level. Patiently and resolutely, he wove the fabric of the nuclear pact. Even his harshest political rivals, among them Isser Harel, have admitted that it was Peres, in a magnificent virtuoso performance, who achieved Israel's nuclear breakthrough. "There is one important thing that Peres achieved," Harel told me, "only one thing. And that's Dimona. As critical as I am of Peres, I always credit him with that." For years, Harel had publicly expressed his abhorrence of Peres, and this belated confession of admiration, toward the end of his life, demanded considerable emotional effort.

Isser Harel was, in a way, Israel's J. Edgar Hoover. It would be difficult to exaggerate his political influence. A short man, unassuming, rather inarticulate, but single-minded, he was more aware than anyone else of the weaknesses of politicians. For decades he ruled over the intelligence and espionage services, and was involved in dozens of their exploits. In 1960, he became famous for running the operation that captured Adolf Eichmann, the top Nazi Holocaust bureaucrat in Argentina.

In August 1956, Peres persuaded Ben-Gurion that the time was right to start technical negotiations for the acquisition of a nuclear reactor from the French. Defense Ministry science chief Munya Mardor's deputy, Shalhevet Freier, was sent to Paris to talk with the French AEC. Freier carried the title "scientific attaché," but Peres decided that his office would not be in the embassy, to help ensure maximum secrecy. Isser Harel recalled that this infuriated Ambassador Tzur, who complained to Foreign Minister Meir, who appealed to the prime minister. Peres explained that the heads of the French Defense Ministry dictated the exclusion of both foreign ministries, the French and the Israeli, from the negotiations in order to prevent leaks, and the prime minister accepted his judgment. Harel said the encouragement that Ben-Gurion provided Peres "caused the historical schism" between Golda Meir and Ben-Gurion, compelling many of his most faithful supporters to band together against the prime minister.

In mid-September, the French AEC agreed to sell Israel a nuclear reactor with a maximum 10-megawatt output. In 1952, the French had built a similar reactor, of the EL-2 (or P-2) type, at Saclay, near Paris. Fueled by natural uranium, moderated by heavy water, and cooled by pressurized gas, it was suitable for both civilian and military applications. Peres reported the achievement to Ben-Gurion from Paris, and Ben-Gurion sent him a congratulatory cable: "Well done! I very much appreciate the agreement on that matter."

However, before the deal could go through, the French government had to approve it. It is doubtful that this could have happened without international circumstances playing into Israel's hands. It happened like this: In contacts with France, Britain refused to join a campaign for the conquest of the Suez Canal Zone unless it was given a pretext that would justify warlike action. This was the task that France assigned to Israel, with a tempting reward: Give us the pretext to go to war, and you'll get a nuclear reactor.

The diplomatic drama that preceded the Suez Campaign opened with an episode that could have prevented its taking place at all, because of Israel's bellicose tendencies. Toward the end of September 1955, there was tension on Israel's border, but with Jordan, not Egypt. It threatened to nip in the bud the French plan for setting up a tripartite coalition against Nasser. On September 22, troops of the Jordanian Arab Legion who were stationed north of Bethlehem had opened machine-gun fire on a group of archaeologists at a site on the southern outskirts of Jerusalem, on the Israeli side of the 1949 armistice line. Four of the archaeologists were killed and sixteen wounded. In another sector of Jerusalem, a number of Legion men crossed the lines and stabbed a young Israeli woman to death. They cut off her hand and took it with them. In the northern Jordan Rift, Jordanians shot and killed an Israeli farmer operating a tractor. And in yet another incident, infiltrators from Jordan killed two Israelis working in an orange grove near the border, cutting off their ears and taking them as proof that they had carried out their mission.

It was Israel's policy to retaliate for such actions, usually against police or military posts across the border, into the areas from which the attackers had set out. Despite the precarious international situation, Israel could not resist responding to the grave attacks from Jordanian territory and on October 11, a paratroop detachment was sent to destroy a police station at the northern end of the town of Qalqilya.4 It was the most extensive military operation since the retaliation policy had been in place. The Jordanians put up stiff resistance, and things went wrong for the attacking force; it encountered difficulty in withdrawing, and Israeli casualties were 18 dead and 50 wounded. Over 100 Jordanians were killed.

On the night of the battle, King Hussein of Jordan telephoned General Sir Charles Keightley, commander of the British forces in the Middle East, and demanded that the defense pact between the two countries be activated. (It was Keightley who was to command the Anglo-French force invading the Canal Zone, if and when the plan to conquer it was put into effect.) Hussein asked the British general to order his aircraft out against the Israeli aggressors. The next day, the British government threatened the Israelis that they would send an Iraqi division into Jordan, both Jordan and Iraq being under their protection. Such an action, Israel had made clear, would be seen as *casus belli*. The British chargé d'affaires in Tel Aviv informed Ben-Gurion that if Israel took any action against the Iraqi reinforcements, Britain itself would come to the defense of Jordan. Ben-Gurion replied that Israel reserved the right to freedom of action. "We were apparently not very far from the possibility of British intervention on the Legion's side," Dayan wrote in his memoirs. At one stage it was touch-and-go whether Israel would be fighting against British troops in Jordan, or on the same side in Egypt.

The tension in relations between Britain and Israel was endangering France's efforts to form an alliance against Egypt, so Paris entreated London to drop the plan to dispatch an Iraqi division into Jordan. Britain complied, and the tension eased. In retrospect, it's clear that the tension between Israel and Jordan, and the British threat to act against Israel, had misled the Americans. All eyes in Washington were on the Jordan-Israel border, and the Americans did not notice that at that very time a French-British-Israeli coalition was taking shape and planning an assault on Egypt. When Israel mobilized its reserves, President Eisenhower was convinced that Israel meant to invade Jordan. He would be surprised to discover that right under his nose two of his closest allies had been engaged in a military initiative that was liable to spark a world war.

Two days after the Israel-Jordan border calmed down, on October 14, the Soviet Union vetoed an Anglo-French U.N. Security Council resolution calling for internationalizing the Suez Canal. France was now certain that there was no alternative to military action against Egypt, and it sent a delegation to London to persuade Prime Minister Anthony Eden. The talks were fraught, with Eden insisting that Britain would not move without a pretext. He was caught between conflicting interests. On the one hand, giving in to Nasser's dictates would damage the British economy and be perceived as a humiliation. On the other hand, an attack on Egypt might undermine Britain's special standing in the Arab world. And in the background loomed British public opinion. If Eden went to war without patent justification, the public reaction could have shaken his grip on government.

The French promised Eden that Israel would provide the pretext. French General Maurice Challe said he got the impression from Dayan that Israel was ready to play the aggressor. The British drew up a plan: Israeli forces would attack Egypt, conquer the Sinai peninsula and take up positions on the eastern bank of the Suez Canal. Britain and France would jointly demand that both Israel and Egypt withdraw from the Canal Zone. Israel would comply, as prearranged, but Egypt could be relied upon to refuse. In response, British and French paratroops would be dropped along the entire length of the canal, "to ensure its normal functioning." The French approved of the plan, but in Tel Aviv Ben-Gurion rebelled. He refused to be a "spearhead of aggression against the Arabs," he told his associates. "Israel will not start the war, and will not play the aggressor, while England and France appear as the angels of peace."

Ever since Clement Atlee's Labour Party had reneged on its commitment to a Jewish state in Palestine after it trounced Winston Churchill's Tories in the 1945 elections, Ben-Gurion had developed an obsessive resentment against Britain. His mistrust of Anthony Eden was so profound that he raised the suspicion that even as Britain was cooperating with Israel on the Suez front, it would come to the assistance of its Jordanian allies and launch military operations against Israel on its eastern border. He therefore set two conditions: First, Israel would not go to war alone, and without a clear reason for doing so. Second, Britain must undertake not to intervene against Israel on the Jordanian border. The French were not dismayed. According to Thomas, Bourgès-Maunoury was relying on the indications that Dayan gave to General Challe, and was quite sure that the pairing of Britain and Israel would work.

On October 21, a tripartite summit convened at Sèvres, near Paris. Ben-Gurion, Dayan, and Peres represented Israel. Foreign Minister Golda Meir was not there, although her French and British counterparts, Christian Pineau and Selwyn Lloyd, were. In conversations with Dayan, Ben-Gurion defined his goals: The military operation against Egypt would at least ensure Israel freedom of navigation through the Suez Canal, as well as control of the straits at the southern tip of the Sinai peninsula, and a strip of land running along the eastern shore of Sinai from the Israeli port of Eilat in the north to Sharm el-Sheikh in the south. These were the immediate objectives,5 and they were shared with everyone involved in the preparations. But the main goal, the strategic target, discussed only in the strictest secrecy, was the nuclear option. To achieve it, Israel was ready to pay a huge price—to give the French and the British their pretext for attacking Egypt.

The division of roles among the Israelis at Sèvres emerged only after they published their memoirs. Dayan was to coordinate Israel's military objectives with the Anglo-French invasion plan, specifically, to give them their excuse. Peres was to make sure that by the end of the conference the French government had approved the nuclear deal. Ben-Gurion was there to give a cloak of authority to Israel's agreement to play the handmaiden to the two powers. On October 24, at five o'clock in the afternoon, the three countries signed the Sèvres Protocol, which contained six clauses defining the cooperation among them in their imminent war against Egypt.

It is clear now that it was Ben-Gurion who made the most far-reaching concession and made the signing possible. He gave up on his opening position and agreed to supply the British and French with the pretext for their offensive, albeit with smaller-scale military operations than the British had demanded. Israel would launch an airborne attack in the west of Sinai, not far from the Suez Canal, and only afterward would the British and the French intervene. Britain made a minor concession in agreeing to decrease the time gap between the Israeli operation and the Anglo-French invasion. Britain also undertook not to come to Jordan's assistance if the Hashemite kingdom began hostilities against Israel.

Though Ben-Gurion had compromised on most of the terms he had laid down before the conference, he had recognized the political opportunity in cooperation with the French. "If we do not move now," he declared after Sèvres, "we will have to fight Nasser in the future, without France."

And of course there was another important consideration. Shimon Peres explains: "At Sèvres, when it was all over, I said to Ben-Gurion that there's one more unfinished matter, and that's the nuclear thing. Let me wrap it up before you say no, and he said all right. And then I went into a room with Mollet and Pineau and said: 'Friends, this isn't part of the negotiation, but we are taking a huge risk upon ourselves, and I am asking for this thing and that thing,' and they said all right.

"I asked for more than just the reactor. I asked for other things as well. The uranium too, and that kind of thing. Then I went up to Ben-Gurion, and I said: 'It's fixed.' That's the way it was."

The promise to supply Israel with natural uranium and a small 10-megawatt reactor was made verbally, with the agreement of Pineau and Bourgès-Maunoury. In order to carry it out a formal decision of the French cabinet would be required. No official document had been signed, but this was nevertheless a giant step forward from Israel's point of view.

By agreeing that Israel would take part in the Suez Campaign, Ben-Gurion was taking a grave risk in view of the inevitably angry response of the Soviet Union and the likely displeasure of the United States. His conscience tormented him for his having to deceive President Eisenhower, who had related so humanely to the Jewish refugees when he was commander of the occupying Allied forces in Germany after the war. But this personal remorse was a marginal matter compared to the advantages he had won for Israel: the backing of two powers for a preemptive war that was expected to strike a crushing blow against Egypt's war-making capacity; and the nuclear reactor, whose capacity was more than double that of the research reactor America had promised to supply to Israel, making it possible—according to foreign sources—to produce the small amount of plutonium necessary for weapons purposes.

News of the Sèvres conference was all but buried in an avalanche of international events that week, including new military cooperation between Jordan and Egypt and the capture of five leaders of the Algerian rebellion, including the political leader, Mohammed Khider, and the commander of the underground forces, Ahmed Ben Bella.

But the most dramatic event of that week was a popular revolt that had broken out in Hungary against the communist regime. In the coming days, officials in Washington would be busy weighing their response to the Hungarian uprising, and would entirely miss the plan that had been decided upon in Sèvres. In the Eisenhower administration, foreign policy meant nothing more than planning the next step in the Cold War.

On the evening of October 29, 1956, Israel launched its assault on Egypt. A battalion of paratroops was dropped in western Sinai, near the

Mitla Pass, about 30 miles east of the Suez Canal. Divisions of armor and infantry rolled across the border into Sinai on three axes. Within a week, the entire peninsula would be in Israel's hands, its forces camped on the eastern bank of the canal. In accordance with the plan, the next day Britain and France demanded that Egypt and Israel withdraw from the canal, and Israel agreed. Egypt, as predicted, refused. Now Britain and France were supposed to neutralize the Egyptian air force, and to carry out paratroop drops and landings of forces from the sea, but they put off the launch of their campaign due to stormy weather.

While this was going on, Ben-Gurion was sick in bed, with a high fever and flu, and apprehensive that the Anglo-French operation would be cancelled. He expressed suspicion that Britain's Eden was merely using weather as an excuse to call off the entire campaign. Out of concern for the lives of the soldiers dropped into western Sinai he told Dayan to withdraw them that same night. Dayan, however, argued that even if the Anglo-French invasion were cancelled, Israel could continue alone and win. But Ben-Gurion doubted this. "Only with great difficulty did Ben-Gurion give up on the withdrawal," Dayan wrote.

Mossad chief Harel had the impression that Ben-Gurion's illness was caused by a fear that the cancellation of the invasion would leave him looking like the fool who had given the two powers a pretext for an invasion, playing his part in the deal without getting anything in return. But in three days' time, the French and the British did go into action. On November 5 and 6, their paratroops and marines occupied the canal-side cities of Port Said and Port Fuad. The United States moved to halt the invasion. The Eisenhower administration feared that military action by two Western powers against the leader of the Arab world would give the Soviet Union a free ticket to involvement in the Middle East and throw the Arab states into Moscow's hands. The president's anger focused on Britain, because its involvement surprised him more than that of France.

In London, the Labour opposition organized massive protest against the invasion. The value of the pound sterling sank, and the United States refused to help stabilize it. In France, the operation was seen as part of the war against the Algerian rebellion, and therefore public opinion justified it. Israel was basking in euphoria. The rapid and elegant victory had at one stroke relaxed the tension that had built up in Israel over the years as the country braced for an Egyptian offensive. Israeli public opinion was enthusiastically behind the government.

On November 6, Ben-Gurion formulated a declaration of victory to be read at a parade marking the end of the campaign, at Sharm el-Sheikh. The chief of staff, Dayan, read Ben-Gurion's festive address to the troops. In it, the Israeli prime minister announced the formation of "the Third Kingdom of Israel."[6] The next day, Ben-Gurion delivered an arrogant and bellicose speech in the Knesset with a clear message: Israel intended to annex the Sinai peninsula and the straits at the southern end of the gulfs of Suez and Aqaba.

Hours later, the Soviet Union reacted for the first time, and the euphoria dissipated in one puff. Moscow had held back earlier in the crisis because it was busy crushing the Hungarian uprising, but now it issued an ultimatum: The three attacking countries must cease military operations forthwith. One version of the ultimatum was handed to the French and the British, and another version, couched in much blunter terms, was sent to Israel. "We received the cable from the Marshal [Nikolay] Bulganin," says Abel Thomas, referring to the ultimatum that reached France, "and in it he wrote: 'Don't forget, sirs, that Russia possesses nuclear weapons, and if you do not stop dropping paratroop battalions, we may use it against you.'" On the same day, the United States and the Soviet Union compelled Britain and France to announce that they were withdrawing. United Nations forces were to take their place.

In the separate ultimatum that the Soviet Union presented to Israel, Bulganin, the Soviet premier, wrote to Ben-Gurion that the government of Israel was "playing irresponsibly and criminally with the fate of peace and of its citizens, and placing the very existence of Israel as a state in question." Bulganin warned that the U.S.S.R. could attack it with missiles. In his diary, Ben-Gurion wrote: "The epistle with which Bulganin has honored me, if it were not signed with his name, could have been written by Hitler, and there is no great difference between these two hangmen."

Israel's position was becoming complicated. At the United Nations, sixty-eight countries voted for a complete Israeli withdrawal; Britain and France were among the ten who abstained. Only one was opposed—Israel itself. The Soviet Union once again threatened to take steps if Israel did not comply with the resolution, and Dayan wrote in his diary:

"The French have information on Russian preparations to intervene in the Middle East, and primarily to strike at Israel."

The previous day, Eisenhower had been elected for his second term, and now he was free to step up the pressure. Secretary of State John Foster Dulles sent Israel an unequivocal message: The refusal to pull out of Sinai is endangering world peace. If the Soviets intervene militarily, a third world war is liable to break out. He threatened to cease all American aid to Israel and to support a call in the United Nations for sanctions against Israel.

At dawn on November 8, Golda Meir and Peres flew to Paris. Peres found a despondent French regime. In view of the failure of the invasion, and the U.N.'s orders to France and Britain to withdraw immediately, the Mollet government was incapable of committing itself to come to Israel's aid. According to Thomas, Peres proposed an alternative plan to Mollet and Bourgès-Maunoury: Israel would withdraw from Sinai, in order to preserve its existence in view of the Soviet and Arab threats to destroy it, and France would carry out the verbal promise made at Sèvres to provide it with the means to build a nuclear option. Both men agreed. According to Thomas, the two sides had never before discussed the nuclear deal in such detail as they did that morning in the bureau of the minister of defense.

Ben-Gurion announced that Israel was willing to retreat. Only two days previously, hours before the Soviet ultimatum, he had enthusiastically proclaimed his plan for the annexation of Sinai to Israel, and here he was, prepared to give it all up, even the Red Sea straits. To the military command and the troops the hasty retreat would seem like national self-abasement, and Dayan, in his diary, called it "the disgraceful retreat." But history would judge the dramatic turn of events in a different light. That festive parade at Sharm el-Sheikh, where Dayan read out Ben-Gurion's proclamation of the Third Israeli Kingdom, would disappear entirely from the national memory,7 and the withdrawal would be interpreted as an appropriate solution.

ISRAEL'S REWARD WOULD be revealed only years later, when it became clear that Ben-Gurion and Peres had taken good advantage of the discomfiture of the French leadership at the failure of the Suez Campaign, and collected a handsome price for the shock that the Soviet ultimatum had caused in France. Now the oral promise on the nuclear matter that the French leaders had given Peres at the end of the Sèvres conference was to become a formal undertaking, formulated in written agreements. Moreover, the reactor would be a more powerful one, and various installations and equipment would be appended, by means of which bombs could be built, according to reports from outside Israel.

It would take another eight months of intensive and continuous negotiations and bargaining until a nuclear pact satisfactory to both sides would be formulated, and the signing would be delayed still further. In the wake of the military failure at Suez, the government of Guy Mollet resigned. His successor, Bourgès-Maunoury, had only taken his place at the Hotel Matignon, the prime minister's residence, when yet another serious coalition crisis broke out, leaving the document unsigned.

Early in September 1957, Shalhevet Freier urgently summoned Peres to Paris. The Bourgès-Maunoury government itself was about to fall, and if it did so before the nuclear pact with Israel was signed, the agreement might die. Peres, who fifty years later described the last twenty-four hours of the Bourgès-Maunoury government as "tense and eventful," called at the prime minister's bureau. Bourgès-Maunoury wouldn't sign the pact unless Mollet, a partner in his coalition, and Foreign Minister Pineau gave their consent. Peres promised Pineau that the reactor would be used only for peaceful purposes, and Pineau signed. Peres hurried to Mollet, who made his signature conditional on the agreement of the French AEC chief, Francis Perrin. Peres asked Thomas to persuade Perrin. Thomas clearly remembers that conversation: "Shimon Peres said to me, 'You know Perrin well. Go visit him, and tell him it is impossible to abandon the Israelis.' At one time, Peres or Dayan had told me, 'M. Abel Thomas, if you get us an atomic capability, we can give you information to help you advance in the nuclear sphere.' And then, when I came to Perrin he asked, 'What about the French interest?' And I replied, 'The French interest is that finally we'll get the developments that we do not know yet,' and he was persuaded. Perrin contacted Guy Mollet the day after my visit, and told him that we must give Israel the atomic bomb. That is what happened."

Thomas was the chief catalyst. He persuaded Perrin, who persuaded Mollet, who persuaded Bourgès-Maunoury, who signed the agreement for the delivery to Israel of the nuclear reactor and the necessary appendages. This was the last action of the Bourgès-Maunoury government before it resigned. It took until May 1958 before France united behind Charles de Gaulle. It is doubtful that de Gaulle would have given Israel the equipment that Bourgès-Maunoury agreed to give. Later de Gaulle would give orders to cut the special ties between France and Israel but his officials would ignore those orders so the nuclear deal could go through.

What was it that made the French defense establishment take this extraordinary step in Israel's favor, and sign so unusual an agreement? There were two weighty considerations. One was connected to the Algerian rebellion. The link-up between the Arabs and the Soviet Union had placed French rule in North Africa in jeopardy. As long as France was determined to hang on in North Africa, it needed a powerful ally in the Middle East to neutralize Egypt's Nasser and diminish the threat to French Algeria. (When de Gaulle would decide to pull out of North Africa, he'd no longer need the alliance with Israel, so he'd end it.) The other consideration had to do with French nuclear research. The French believed they would be able to fill holes in their research by using information from Israel. Thomas asserts that Dayan and Peres bolstered this belief and encouraged their French colleagues that it was within their power to direct a flow of nuclear know-how from Israel to France. As we shall see later, the development of the bomb in France advanced in parallel to the construction of the Dimona reactor, and foreign sources state that experts from Israel were invited to witness the first French nuclear test in 1960.

The two sides signed a political pact and a series of technical agreements. France would provide Israel with a large reactor, which Israel said had a 24-megawatt capacity. But according to outside sources the reactor was much larger, reaching as much as 150 megawatts. In addition to the reactor, France would supply Israel with enriched uranium and a plant for the extraction of plutonium, according to U.S. reports. Israel undertook to use the installations only for civilian purposes, but both sides knew this was a fiction.

These agreements had no precedent and are unique even to this day. No country has ever supplied another with a package of equipment and materials for the development of a nuclear option. One of the agreements provided for Israeli scientists and technicians to train at nuclear facilities in France. French authorities on the subject have confirmed that the contract for the construction of the reactor was signed with a straw company behind which stood the Société Alsacienne, the company that built the reactors at Saclay in France. These sources also state that the contract for the installation of the plutonium extraction plant was signed with the Saint-Gobain Nucléaire company that had put up the central French plutonium separation plant near Marcoule. In order to disguise the true purpose of the contract, the company's name was given as SIECC, but no such company existed. Certain technical details, which may have given away the purpose of the reactor and its appendages, were concluded orally with Peres and Freier and were not included in the written contracts. These details remain classified to this day.

Until his death in 2002, Abel Thomas felt that by helping Israel in this way he atoned for the actions of those Frenchmen in the Vichy regime who handed over Jews to the Nazis. Years later, in a letter sent to Thomas when Dayan published his diary, Dayan wrote: "When we met, Israel's existence was in danger. Nasser never concealed his one and only intention—to destroy Israel . . . The help that you gave us was decisive, and enabled us to break the ring that surrounded us and to survive the strangulation that we were threatened with . . . In those days, the existence of Israel was saved."

The Suez Campaign was a dismal failure. France and Britain experienced a military fiasco and profound humiliation. The canal remained out of their hands and the governments of Eden and Mollet fell. Both countries sustained a loss of international standing. Their influence on world affairs shrank. Thus ended the colonial era in the Middle East. Internally, France sank into political chaos. The limpness with which it had been compelled to respond to the Soviet ultimatum spurred movement toward the development of its nuclear option.

Egypt gained the canal. Despite his army's abject defeat in battles with Israel, Nasser's status in the Third World did not suffer. He had brazened it out with the two colonial powers, and thrown them out of his territory.

His disappointment with the Soviet Union for withholding its ultimatum for eight days did not lead him to transfer his loyalties from his communist patron to the Americans. After Suez, Nasser's pan-Arab strategy gained momentum. With his active backing, the Algerian uprising was invigorated. The pro-Western regime in Iraq toppled. In Jordan, the monarchy would be gripped in crisis, and in Lebanon the opponents of the West were strengthened.

The U.S.S.R. had demonstrated to the Arabs that its support could tip the scales in Egypt's favor, and its stock soared in the Third World. Its leaders had successfully managed two crises simultaneously—in Hungary and at the Suez Canal—and had displayed responsible conduct to the West. The decisive Soviet consideration had been to avoid a confrontation with the United States. Moscow had even proposed joint American-Soviet action, which was rejected by Washington, and had presented its ultimatum only after the crisis passed the most dangerous point. The Soviet leaders had emerged as skilled poker players, winning the pot with the worst hand. In retrospect, it is clear that their ultimatum was a bluff. At that time, they lacked the capability of deploying airborne units or sending long-range ballistic missiles, but in the heat of the dramatic, even hysterical, circumstances, France and Israel lacked concrete intelligence about the Red Army and gave the ultimatum a totally incorrect assessment.

The United States played the crisis badly. The CIA and the State Department had failed to put the pieces of the puzzle together to form a complete picture and were caught unprepared. First reports of the Israeli offensive in Sinai were given to Eisenhower nine hours after it started, at the height of the final stages of his election campaign. Secretary of State Dulles was in the hospital after cancer surgery, and the U.S. representative to the United Nations, Henry Cabot Lodge Jr., was advising the president. At the very last moment, the administration tried to halt the Anglo-French intervention, but it was too late to turn the wheel back.

American strategy failed because it saw the world from too narrow an angle. It could see nothing but the threats of the Cold War. Its only aim was to stop communist expansion. It had no plans to help relieve the harsh distress of the countries of the Middle East, and it revealed elementary misunderstanding in its assessment of their interests. Dulles had made no effort to grasp Ben-Gurion's profound anxiety over the very existence of Israel. Ben-Gurion's strategy of placing the nuclear project at the top of his order of priorities, with the intention of forcing the Arabs to come to terms with Israel's existence and realize they could not destroy it, gained no attention in Washington. The Eisenhower administration offered Israel no alternative to the policy of using military force that it had always practiced against its Arab neighbors. If the United States had agreed to guarantee Israel's existence through a defense pact, it is unlikely that Israel would even have considered partnership in the Suez Campaign and Ben-Gurion's determination to acquire the nuclear option might never have been aroused.

The Americans also failed to grasp the sense of humiliation that the loss of Palestine had evoked in the Arabs. Washington courted Nasser out of the idea that he could help the United States block Soviet penetration of the Middle East, but it wouldn't support Egypt by supplying arms. When Egypt recognized Communist China and signed an arms deal with the Soviet Union, the United States reneged on its commitment to build a dam at Aswan, on the Nile River. A week after that, Nasser nationalized the canal. A half-century later, analysis of American strategy in the Middle East lends credence to the theory that the Eisenhower administration's zigzag policy accelerated the development of the crisis over the Suez Canal.

The popularity the United States gained in the Arab world because it opposed the invaders in the Suez Campaign quickly dissipated after Washington came out in early 1957 with the "Eisenhower Doctrine," which called for an alliance of Middle Eastern states against Soviet penetration of the region. The Arabs suspected that America was trying to dominate them the way the colonial powers had, and they put their trust in the Soviet Union. In brief, American strategy accomplished the opposite of the goals it had set out to attain.

Nevertheless, following the defeat of the British and the French and their removal from virtually all their positions of influence in the Middle East, America would now establish itself for the first time as the major Western power in the region. It slowly began drawing conclusions from the failure of its strategy, and in a year's time it would discover Israel's strategic value and become disillusioned with Nasser. But it would take another three years before America would begin to nose around what was going on at Dimona.

It was Israel that reaped major advantages from the Suez crisis. It had accomplished what it wanted. At the very last moment, it had cashed in the French promissory note and set out on the way to nuclear capability. Although Nasser emerged triumphant over the British and French, Israel had humiliated him and demonstrated military superiority over the Arabs.

Judging by the results, there is no doubt that the process begun when Ben-Gurion signed the Sèvres protocol represented a turning point in Israel's history. At the end of 1957, a decade of nuclear development would start in Israel, at the end of which Israel would enter a new era as the possessor of an ultimate deterrent that would remove the existential threat hanging over the country. At the same time, with the help of the nuclear reactor and its appendages, scientific research, both theoretical and applied, would carry Israel forward to the cutting edge of world technology, in both military and civilian industry. Israel's nuclear option and the intensive technological development would reshape strategy in the Middle East. And this is exactly what Ben-Gurion had meant when he said to Ernst Bergmann, on the eve of the establishment of the state, "When the Jewish state arises, the secret of its survival will be in its technological and scientific advantage."

CHAPTER FIVE

First Nuclear Accident

ANYONE WHO EVER had anything to do with Shalhevet Freier couldn't help being impressed by the power of his personality. He was the best possible choice for the position of Israel's special emissary to Paris for nuclear matters. Very little has been published about this unique character. In the pre-state underground he was known for his iron discipline, while his overt interests ranged from nuclear physics to philosophy, music, and classical dance. Duality reigned within him, but in no way did it impinge on the integrity that he radiated. On the one hand he threw himself energetically into the effort to arm Israel with a doomsday weapon, on the other he was elected to the Pugwash Council, the governing body of the organization inspired by two of the most dedicated opponents of nuclear armaments, Albert Einstein and Bertrand Russell. His work was always utterly rational, and remarkable for its analytical approach, yet he would often quote from the Zohar (the "Book of Splendor"), the basic work of the kabbalah, and one of Judaism's most mystical writings. "The open and the hidden functioned within him together and at the same time," Shimon Peres said. His unusual name, Shalhevet, Hebrew for "flame," was taken by his parents from a verse in the biblical Song of Songs: "for love is strong as death; jealousy is cruel as the grave: the coals thereof are coals of the flame of the Lord" (8:6).

Everyone called him Shalhevet, never Mr. Freier (perhaps because "freier" is Yiddish and Hebrew slang for "sucker" or "patsy," and entirely inappropriate in his case). His humility was extreme, to the extent of self-abnegation. He never sought fame, and was photographed only rarely, but his anonymity never bothered him. Men liked him; women, even more. He was shy, and he played the violin. He had delicate features, blue eyes, and a soft voice. He was the antithesis of the aggressive, sharp-tongued, Israel-born sabras, but they admired him.

Shalhevet Freier was born in 1920 in Eschwege, a small, picturesque village in southern Germany. His father, Moritz, was a rabbi at the Alte Schul, the oldest synagogue in Berlin. He was a conscious non-Zionist, while Shalhevet's mother, Recha, was a confirmed Zionist. In January 1933, she set up in Berlin the Youth Aliyah organization, dedicated to taking Jewish children to the Land of Israel. By the time World War II broke out in 1939, Youth Aliyah had been instrumental in the immigration of five thousand European Jewish youngsters to Palestine, saving them from the Nazis. Recha Freier became famous for her courage. On Kristall-nacht,[1] she was in London with her family. When she was told about the tragic events in Germany, she immediately returned to her work in Berlin. She managed to leave Germany surreptitiously just before war broke out, and on her way to Palestine succeeded in rescuing a group of Jewish youngsters in Yugoslavia. Her husband, Moritz, found asylum in England and lived apart from his family for the rest of his life. In the 1950s Albert Einstein nominated Recha for the Nobel Peace Prize, but historians of the Holocaust generally overlooked her.[2] Gradually the injustice was re-dressed and in 1983 she was awarded the Israel Prize, the state's highest award. Shalhevet apparently inherited Recha's courage and her remarkable creative powers as well as her musical talent.

After the Nazis came to power, Shalhevet was expelled from his high school because of what the authorities there termed "harmful influence on the school." His class had been told to write an essay on the subject "Might Is Right," and Shalhevet caused an uproar by writing that strength is not necessarily a guarantee of righteousness. The headmaster gave instructions for his essay to be read out in all the classes as an example of "Jewish degeneracy." Shalhevet's teacher called in his father and suggested that the boy be removed from the school before he was ex-pelled. Rabbi Freier came home, called his son, poured two glasses of wine, and drank a congratulatory toast to him. In the last report he re-ceived from the school, his teacher wrote that "the student Freier is de-veloping in accordance with his race's characteristics."

At the age of sixteen, Shalhevet was sent to England, where he went to a Jewish boarding school. In 1940 he arrived in Palestine in the last passenger boat to cross the Mediterranean before hostilities broke out there. A year later he enlisted in the British army and was posted to the 462 Transport Unit, which saw action in North Africa and then in Italy. In 1943, on the way to Italy, his ship was torpedoed and sank with four hundred of its passengers and crew. Shalhevet hung on to a wooden spar for three hours before he was rescued. After the war he joined the Haganah underground in Italy and worked at preparing cargo boats for the shipping of illegal immigrants from Europe to Palestine. On nine occasions he led convoys of dozens of stolen British army trucks carrying Jewish refugees from the displaced-persons camps to boats waiting for them in ports in Italy and France. Sergeant Shalhevet drove ahead in a jeep, clad in a British officer's uniform. His fluent English opened roadblocks. He also became known as an expert counterfeiter and for some missions was part of Munya Mardor's arms-acquisition teams.

He returned to Palestine in 1947 and began studying physics at the Hebrew University in Jerusalem. Two Haganah officers invited him to the legendary Atarah cafe on Ben-Yehudah Street in downtown Jerusalem, and ordered him to set up a spy network inside the 120,000-strong British army contingent in Palestine, in order to acquire intelligence needed in the struggle for independence. Given the code name "Uri," he recruited his agents from among the underground members he had met in Europe who were now at the university. They worked in their free time, on a volunteer basis, with no financial recompense. In years to come, most of them would hold senior academic or diplomatic positions.

Shalhevet's operation was a veritable production line of valuable information—about army camps, installations and infrastructure, troop movements, intelligence assessments, military plans, and orders. There was an abundance of data not only about the British army, but also about Arab organizations and Jews who collaborated with the mandate authorities. It all went to the Haganah's intelligence service, known by its Hebrew acronym, Shai. Some of the hundreds of maps of districts and localities in Palestine and the neighboring countries were used by the Israel Defense Forces for many years afterward.

As the date of the British departure from Palestine approached, Ben-

Gurion demanded detailed and accurate information about their plans. On March 19, 1948, the Uri network supplied Shai headquarters with the schedule for the evacuation of the British forces. This precise intelligence enabled the Haganah's command to make plans for taking control of British military facilities, including a security zone in central Jerusalem that had been dubbed "Bevingrad" after the British foreign secretary, Ernest Bevin (a man much detested by the Jews of Palestine).3 The fortified perimeter of Bevingrad encompassed the police headquarters in the Russian Compound, the studios of the Palestine broadcasting service, the telephone exchange, the prison, and several government offices. On May 13, two days before the Declaration of Independence, Uri obtained from a source known as "the Romanian" (who remains unidentified to this day) the British plans for the final hours before their official departure from Jerusalem, on May 14 at 6 A.M. Haganah forces were placed on top alert, and they moved in as the British abandoned each facility.

The Arabs were not so well prepared. In fact, by virtue of the high-grade intelligence supplied by the Uri network, the outcome of the battle for the most important of the strategic, dominating positions in Palestine was decided even before a shot was fired. This stunning achievement was organized in its entirety from the modest office that Shalhevet had set up in the basement of a house in the quiet Jerusalem neighborhood of Rehavia, many of whose inhabitants were Jewish immigrants from Germany.

After the War of Independence, Shalhevet headed the Mossad's operations in Europe,4 thwarting arms deals between European merchants and Arab governments. "A steel fist in a velvet glove" is how Arthur Ben-Natan, one of the founders of the Mossad and later Israel's first ambassador to Germany, described Shalhevet Freier—a highly effective operative, but also polished and urbane.

These attributes came into play during his stint in Paris. His job description was vague: to develop close contacts between France and Israel in the scientific and technical sphere. Actually, he was charged with overseeing the implementation of the nuclear pact between the two countries, to manage the shipment of the reactor's components to Israel, to organize the training of Israeli scientists and technicians in the French nuclear facilities, and to obtain scientific and technological information from any and all sources. His primary mission, however, was to conceal the nuclear deal with France and the construction of the Dimona reactor from the eyes and ears of the world.

Shalhevet's office was situated away from the Israeli Embassy in order to ensure that no information about the nuclear deal would leak out, but this caused continual friction with Ambassador Jacob Tzur in Paris and Foreign Minister Golda Meir. In retrospect, it seems clear that separating Shalhevet's duties from the embassy was essential; the strictest secrecy was a precondition for the cooperation with France to succeed. If the true aims of the deal had come out, the administration of President Eisenhower would have done all in its power to foil it. Ben-Gurion needed a heavy smoke screen to keep American intelligence out of the picture for at least five years while he was establishing the reactor and its accompanying installations so deep in the arid soil of Dimona that they could not be uprooted. It was Shalhevet who gave him this international smoke screen.

The method was sophisticated. Ben-Gurion's nuclear vision was never totally denied, but it was kept vague by the few people in on the secret. They admitted that there was a desire to exploit the atom in the service of the nation, for peaceful purposes, but always stressed that a small country poor in means and in population like Israel was not capable of realizing this desire, at least at that time. As Peres put it: "In the air hovered Ben-Gurion's grand vision, a vision that Ben-Gurion was not eager to peg to the ground, because pegging it to the ground would have meant identifying concrete objectives too early."

For the Israeli scientists sent to study nuclear physics in France, Shalhevet was the commander, the boss, the guide, the spiritual father. "He had tremendous charisma and in the eyes of scientists, he was like Moses," recalled Haya Sadeh, widow of the scientist Dror Sadeh. As a young couple, they arrived in Paris in mid-January 1958, and Dror reported to Shalhevet's office, all set to begin his mission of nuclear research. This was his first trip abroad. About three years earlier, while he was still studying for his master's degree in physics at Hebrew University, he had been summoned for an interview at the Defense Ministry in Tel Aviv. Ernst Bergmann and Jenka Ratner sat opposite him and questioned him about his studies. Bergmann was head of the Atomic Energy Commission (AEC) and, non-Israeli sources revealed, Ratner ran Institute 3 at EMET and would head the team that built Israel's first nuclear device.

Engineer Yevgeni Ratner, whom everyone called Jenka, was a close friend of Ben-Gurion, whom he had first met in 1937 at the Haifa Flying Club, the cover for an underground cell where young Jews were trained in various aspects of aviation. Both of them wanted to be pilots. They began with gliding and later learned to fly single-engine aircraft. In the late 1930s, Jenka's role in the underground was to build mines and bombs. Using these devices, the special operations company commanded by Mardor would sabotage strategic installations of His Majesty's government, with the aim of getting the British to leave Palestine so a Jewish state could be established. In the summer of 1939, a unit under Munya Mardor blew up the pipeline of the Iraq Petroleum Company, which carried oil from Iraq to the refineries that the British had built in Haifa. Jenka, who was employed as an engineer by the pipeline company, constructed the bomb.

When World War II broke out, the underground ceased operations against the British, and Jenka proposed to the British command in Palestine a number of ideas for new munitions. He was inducted into the Royal Navy's Mine Design Department and in late 1942 was posted to Britain.

In England Jenka was put to work developing weapons for use against submarines, specializing in chain detonation. After the war, the Royal Navy command offered him British citizenship and a senior position in defense research, but he resisted the temptation, returning to Palestine in mid-1947 and joining the scientific corps of the embryonic Israeli army, where he worked at developing hollow-charge armor-piercing munitions. When the new division for research and development at the Defense Ministry was established, Jenka was appointed to it and worked for two years on a rifle-attached antitank grenade launcher and an improved bazooka, hundreds of thousands of which were produced over the following years. Later, he would develop warheads and fuses for missles.[5]

Armament R&D was not his only task. In 1954 and 1955, Ratner, Bergmann, and other EMET operatives were combing the science faculties of the Weizmann Institute, the Hebrew University in Jerusalem, and the Technion in Haifa. EMET was in dire need of scientific per-

sonnel. Only a few remained of the first wave of researchers who had
been recruited in 1949 and sent to study for doctorates in the United
States and Europe. The most prominent of them, Amos de Shalit, had
left EMET in January 1954, as one of the group of scientists who set up
the nuclear physics department at the Weizmann Institute. "We had to
take various steps to rebuild, as quickly as possible, the scientific potential vital to us in that area," wrote Mardor. Importing scientists from
Europe and the United States was out of the question because of security constraints, and also because Israel could afford to pay only meager
salaries compared to those abroad. Young and talented Israeli scientists
studying for advanced degrees in the United States did not tend to return to Israel. The working conditions and prospects for promotion at
American research institutions were far superior to those that EMET
could offer. The only reserve of manpower available to EMET was in
Israeli universities.

Now, at their first meeting, Bergmann laid on a Zionist speech, in the
spirit of those times, for Sadeh's benefit: "An Israeli scientist's first duty is
to serve the state," he said, and to make the call more tempting, added:
"We have set up an elite unit." Ratner spoke openly about the plans.[6] He
made a depressing impression on Sadeh, who wrote in his diary: "His
eyes were sad." Only years later would Sadeh learn that Jenka's eyes were
always sad, because he was one of the engineers who had made the bomb
for the refugee ship *Patria*.

Bergmann never repeated his error of the first recruitment operation
of 1949. This time, he made the young scientists sign an undertaking of
strict organizational discipline. All of the recruits were told that from
now on their careers were at the disposal of the state. Nevertheless,
Sadeh, for one, was content. The idea that he was one of a very select few,
taking part in such a challenging scientific project for the security of the
state—all of this filled him with satisfaction. "Although we were great
skeptics," says his widow, Haya, "my husband was a patriot."

After a few days, though, Sadeh suffered a blow: The Defense Ministry informed him that his participation in the project had been ruled
out since the Shin Bet was refusing to give him a security clearance. An
agent of security service chief Isser Harel had photographed him and a
fellow student who was also a candidate for a scientific job with the

Atomic Energy Commission, taking part in a political demonstration organized by the United Workers Party (Mapam), whose ideological positions were close to communism.[7]

At first glance, Sadeh's disqualification seems strange. At that time, the prevalent world outlook in Israel was socialist, and Mapam was a partner of long standing in Ben-Gurion's coalition government. But this reflected a contradiction, which has always existed, since the establishment of the state. Because of the electoral system and the consequent multiplicity of parties in the Knesset, the prime minister has to share power with extremist groups. In the cabinet, Ben-Gurion discussed security issues with these parties while at the same time withholding state secrets from them; he called them loyal partners, but instructed his security services to spy on their contacts abroad.

With the help of people who could affirm his loyalty, Sadeh overcame the initial disqualification. In those days, if you belonged to the Israeli equivalent of the "old boys club" you could even get past Isser Harel. Sadeh was first employed by the AEC in a unit setting up the American research reactor at Nahal Soreq, south of Tel Aviv. He did his research work not far from there, at the Weizmann Institute's radioactivity laboratory. His direct supervisor was Yehuda Wolfson, and the head of the department was Amos de Shalit. (The rift between Bergmann and de Shalit regarding the nuclear project did not affect the nuclear physics research of AEC scientists.)

In his research on the energy levels of radioactive materials, Sadeh used polonium-210 (also called radium F),[8] an element that emits alpha-ray radiation, covered by a thin layer of plastic, to concentrate the energy on the target point and prevent it from scattering. But nonetheless, the radiation does find its way out. It later emerged that for a long period radiation levels had not been measured in the radioactivity lab. In mid-1957 the lab was found to be contaminated. Traces of radioactivity were also found on Sadeh's hands, and on objects he had handled at the home he and Haya had rented at Kibbutz Naan, near the Institute.

The AEC, Institute management, and the lab staff handled the mishap with strict secrecy. The Institute was not interested in having its involvement in security projects published abroad, especially not its partnership in a nuclear project being carried out by the AEC. After a brief investigation, whose findings were not published even within the Institute, the lab was locked and hermetically sealed for a number of months.

A month after the lab was closed, a student in the physics department died of blood cancer. A few years later, Sadeh's supervisor, Wolfson, contracted cancer and died. Shalit himself died of cancer twelve years later, in 1969, at the age of forty-three. Sadeh too died prematurely of cancer. No direct link was established between the diseases and deaths of the four researchers and the contamination discovered in the radioactivity lab in 1957.

When the radiation spill was discovered, Dror and Haya Sadeh were terrified, but they were calmed when tests revealed that there was no excess radioactivity in Dror's bodily excretions. His bone marrow was not tested, and it was not known if it had been contaminated. He was instructed to undergo monthly physical examinations and he complied. At the Institute's behest, the couple kept the entire affair a secret from their family and friends. As far as can be ascertained, this was the first nuclear accident in Israel, and it has never before been disclosed.

AFTER THE SADEHS arrived in Paris, the memory of the incident was wiped out by their encounter with the City of Light. Despite the high political tension there due to the escalation in the Algerian conflict, Paris retained its charm. French society had cast off the wartime depression and was blossoming again. The markets were abundantly stocked, places of entertainment were packed, and swarms of tourists, many of them Americans, were back in the streets—an altogether different picture from the austerity and hardship still prevalent in Israel. Few Israelis had their own cars in those days, and at home the Sadehs traveled by bus. In Paris, they bought a small Citroën, taking advantage of an exemption from the sales tax for people with diplomatic status, which the Israeli scientists were granted. In the family album there's a black-and-white photo of the couple with the Eiffel Tower in the background. Dror, handsome and lean, is wearing a suit and a fashionably narrow tie—items which were probably absent from his wardrobe in Israel. Haya is in a white blouse, a wide skirt, and high-heeled shoes. They are leaning over a baby carriage that holds their first child, Shmuel.

Sadeh was a typical scientific researcher: obsessively skeptical, ever suspicious of conventional wisdom. He was a sensitive man, a romantic, who had suffered a difficult childhood in the shadow of a powerful and tyrannical father. From an early age he kept a revealing diary. When his father died, the sixteen-year-old Dror wrote: "A happy orphan am I!"

He recorded how he fell in love for the first time, with his classmate Hava Rofeh, who lived with her family in Haifa's Mount Carmel neighborhood. It was 1946, and he was fourteen. His ability to express himself was impressive: "My love for Hava has driven sleep from my eyes. At night I write in a cramped hand tearful journals of a tormented lover." Hava never even knew of his love. "Part of the magic of love found expression in my suffering and pain and keeping my love a strict secret," he wrote to himself. Using a powerful pair of binoculars that his older brother had brought home from his travels, he would stand for hours opposite her home and gaze at her window. Many years later, he wrote that he used these very binoculars "when I drove on the road near the 'textile factory' trying to discern from the distance the special smokestack of the plant amongst whose founders I was numbered." The "textile factory" was the Dimona reactor, and the "special smokestack" was its dome. In the 1960s, official spokesmen who were asked what was being built near Dimona would say it was a textile factory, and people in the know would use that as a code name for the project. To this day in Israel, many people smile when the words are used.

His beloved Hava died of rheumatic fever a year later. The young Dror was grief-stricken. "I cried without stopping," he wrote of her funeral. "I shall never forget how her parents carried the stretcher bearing Hava's small body wrapped in a black shroud. For a moment, the shroud shifted, and her white foot was uncovered. I burst into inconsolable sobbing." Just as Dror Sadeh's first love was bound up with death, so, we shall see, was the profession that he chose, that of nuclear scientist.

Dror had chosen science as his vocation at the age of ten, thanks to an eccentric teacher. "The nature teacher changed my life forever," he wrote. "For an entire year, he taught us about one single plant." That plant was the *mimosa pudica*, which is Latin for "the shy mimosa," a flower that when touched, closes its petals with "alarming speed." The teacher had ignored the curriculum, and the parents didn't like it. He was dismissed. But his persistence had found favor in the eyes of the curious young lad, who was also something of a rebel, with an independent and sometimes eccentric mind.

At the end of January 1958, following Shalhevet's instructions, Sadeh reported to the holy of holies of the French nuclear project, the Centre de Saclay, some twelve miles southwest of Paris. In Saclay in the 1950s, the French atomic energy commission (CEA) had built three research reactors and dozens of laboratories. To Sadeh's surprise, he was denied entry. A management official came to the gate and explained that there were bureaucratic difficulties; Shalhevet claimed that behind the scenes a struggle was being waged between the CEA and the Saclay management. The management was insisting on getting full details of the goals of the research that the Israelis were going to carry out, and the CEA was naturally refusing to supply them. It took Shalhevet two weeks before he managed to get the head of the CEA, Francis Perrin, to persuade the management of the center to grant the Israelis entry passes.

Sadeh was now in a new world. That year, a new and sophisticated laboratory for the study of irradiated fuels had opened at Saclay. Some of the research projects were conducted in the small and rather old EL2-type reactor (EL stands for *eau lourde* or heavy water), which was built in 1952 and ran on natural uranium. This was a weak reactor, with a maximum capacity of 2.8 megawatts, but it produced 300 grams of plutonium in each operational cycle. In 1957 construction was completed on a second research reactor, EL3, which was fueled by lightly enriched uranium and reached an 18-megawatt capacity. And in 1958, the year Sadeh came to Saclay, a third research reactor was inaugurated, the first to be operated by the CEA using plutonium, which was supplied by the EL2 reactor.

Not far from Saclay, in an ancient fortress in the town of Villeneuve Saint Georges, a few miles southeast of Paris, was France's Los Alamos—the research and development center that housed the central weapons design laboratory where the first French atom bomb, the one that would be tested in the Sahara in 1960, was planned.

The range of reactors, laboratories, materials, and research instruments at Saclay enabled the Israeli researchers to follow scientific processes that in Israel they could study only in theory. For two years at the Weizmann Institute Sadeh had examined energy levels in radioactive substances, some of which were simply not there, and others that were supplied in such tiny quantities that the scope of the research and the chances of reaching results were severely limited. What's more, there wasn't a critical nuclear reactor.9 The American research reactor at Nahal Soreq was still in development and would be operative only in 1960. In contrast, at Saclay, new scientific horizons opened.

Shalhevet urged the scientists to absorb as much knowledge as possible. True to form, he broadened the scope of their missions and instructed each of them to put out feelers in directions other than the narrow confines of their research. Sadeh admired the way Shalhevet worked, and the two became friends. With time, Sadeh came to trust Shalhevet absolutely and although Shalhevet's scientific education was limited, Sadeh did not hesitate to consult him on scientific matters too.

In 1959, Sadeh handed Shalhevet a written request that he be allowed to study for a doctorate at the Sorbonne. The narrow definition of the research project that he had been allotted in the framework of the nuclear project did not satisfy him. He aspired to have a role in pure research, and to develop an independent scientific path. Shalhevet passed the application to Tel Aviv, with his recommendation. Bergmann also recommended approval. He believed that the doctoral studies at the Sorbonne would be excellent cover for Sadeh's secret research at Saclay. Sadeh's request reached Mardor, who wrote in his diary about requests from young scientists like Sadeh to broaden their research boundaries: "These pure research subjects that some of the people are attracted to are fascinating, from their point of view, but they cannot always be applied to practical research. It was therefore not our practice to approve them." Mardor feared that the de Shalit pattern would repeat itself with Sadeh and that he too would leave EMET, make an independent career for himself, and disagree with the establishment's policy on critical matters of principle.

De Shalit, meanwhile, had done very well for himself. In the second week of September 1957, just a few days before the secret nuclear pact with France was signed, he played host at a remarkable event held at the Weizmann Institute. U.S. Air Force planes flew in some 150 scientists from eighteen countries to the International Conference on Nuclear Structure, one of the first scientific meetings in the world—certainly the first in Israel—devoted to exchanges of information in nuclear physics. The young State of Israel was unaccustomed to international events, certainly not on nuclear physics, and the conference was treated by the government as a state occasion. At the festive opening banquet, seated at the head table were the prime minister and defense minister, David Ben-Gurion, and the foreign minister, Golda Meir, together with the head of the Manhattan Project, Robert Oppenheimer, Nobel physics laureate Wolfgang Pauli, and Amos de Shalit, the man behind the conference. Among the other physicists in the hall were six future Nobel laureates.

De Shalit's prestige soared, and Ben-Gurion congratulated him emotionally. The deliberations did not touch on Israel's nuclear aspirations; the deal with France, on which Shalhevet was putting the finishing touches, was not even hinted at. It was a purely academic get-together, and the papers read were devoted to models of the structure of the atomic nucleus and the various processes that take place within it, and to technologies involved in various experiments. On the sidelines, however, more practical matters were raised at meetings between Ben-Gurion, Peres, and Bergmann and some of the top physicists, Oppenheimer among them.

Bergmann was persona non grata at the Weizmann Institute. Moreover, from his point of view de Shalit was the enemy, endeavoring to block the progress of the nuclear project. De Shalit would refer to Peres, Mardor, and Shalhevet contemptuously as "clerks," and Bergmann to him was a chemist, not a specialist in nuclear physics. These men, de Shalit opined, did not correctly grasp the nature of the project and the perils entailed in developing it; their horizons were too narrow.

But the government machine overcame the doubters and the naysayers, and the project was launched. Toward the end of 1957, the first French scientific advisers and technicians arrived, and at Dimona work began on the infrastructure. A vast area of the desert plain was fenced in, roads paved, and electrical lines constructed. The earthworks were on a vast scale, in the terms of the nine-year-old state. Because of the scale of the Dimona project, there was a shortage of cement for housing construction.

On this gigantic platform was to rise a reactor similar to the G-1 installation that the French CEA had first activated at the Marcoule nuclear center on the Rhône River bank in January 1956. (It was closed down in 1968.) The Marcoule reactor could attain 42 megawatts of thermal power, was fueled by natural uranium, and was planned as a dual-purpose facility for the production of both electricity and plutonium for military use. The salient differences between the two reactors: The Marcoule model was moderated by graphite and the Dimona one by heavy water, and the latter reactor would not generate electricity.

According to Israeli statements, the Dimona reactor has a 24-megawatt capacity, but Pierre Péan, the first French journalist to investigate the nuclear connection between France and Israel, reported in his book that the members of the French team planning the plutonium-separation plant were surprised to discover that the pipes of the cooling system permitted a much higher capacity.[10] For years experts have been busy estimating or guessing the actual capacity, and a consensus of a sort has emerged that the reactor was originally built with a 40-megawatt capacity and was upgraded in the 1970s. This meant it could produce 15–20 kilograms of plutonium and four to five bombs a year. Péan's research showed that the Dimona reactor was planned to produce 10–15 kilograms a year. However, working on information publicized by Mordechai Vanunu, the Dimona technician who gave secrets to a London newspaper and was subsequently imprisoned in Israel, American and British experts have concluded that Israel's annual plutonium output is some 40 kilos, and that it manufactures ten bombs a year. One of these experts was Theodore Taylor, who participated in the Manhattan Project and headed the Pentagon's atomic weapons testing program. Israel has never officially admitted that the reactor is used to produce plutonium.

Adjacent to the Dimona reactor itself, which was called Machon 1 (Institute 1), four underground plants were initially built:

- A plutonium separation plant (Machon 2), where plutonium is removed from the spent uranium rods and is reprocessed to be used in new fuel rods.
- A plant where spent uranium fuel rods are coated with aluminum to be sent to the reactor for reuse.

- A laboratory (Machon 8) for testing the purity of uranium samples from Machon 2. In the late 1970s, a gas centrifuge installation for enriching uranium was added, as revealed by Vanunu.
- A waste treatment plant (Machon 4).[11]

What bothered the planners more than anything else was security. How could so gigantic an enterprise be hidden from the world? Not only was Israel's largest building project sure to arouse curiosity in itself, but when dozens of Frenchmen suddenly descended on Beersheba, the nearest city to Dimona, and rented apartments, went shopping, and patronized the restaurants and bars, how could this be explained? And what about the fifteen hundred Israelis working on the project? Could they be fooled into thinking that the giant dome was an observatory? Meanwhile in France dozens of engineers, foremen, technicians, and officials were leaving their families and traveling off to some unknown destination. And some people who saw the huge installations manufactured in France that would have to be conveyed on the roads or rivers to the ports were sure to ask where they were headed.

In both countries, special security apparatuses were set up, not only to ensure that no one in the know would say a word, but also to fabricate and maintain a false front. In France, a special unit was formed within the CEA, while in Israel an entirely new intelligence framework was established under the innocent title of the Bureau for Scientific Relations, or LEKEM (the Anglicized form of the Hebrew acronym). It was tasked with guarding Dimona's secrets, and also with gathering technical intelligence from around the world.[12] The two bodies functioned well, and for several years nothing leaked out.

Péan relates that an engineer friend of his was sent to work on the construction of the reactor and "his wife never knew where he was. His mail was addressed to Morocco or Latin America." The cargo crates containing parts for the reactor were labeled "desalination equipment," and addressed to South America. French security officials imposed strict secrecy regulations, which are in force to this day. Not one of the Frenchmen who worked on the construction of the Dimona reactor agreed to be interviewed for either Péan's book or this one. The fear of the Israeli Mossad still grips them. "Out of all of the Frenchmen who were in Dimona—and I have studied the documents," says Péan, "there was not one worker or engineer who revealed secrets, and that is stunning, when you see how people leak left, right, and center nowadays."

To lead the construction of the nuclear complex at Dimona, Peres chose Colonel Emmanuel Prat, known by his nickname, "Mannes," then serving as Israel's military attaché in Burma (a country with which Israel maintained close military ties at that time). Previously, he had been head of the IDF's logistics corps, and quartermaster general. He remains a shadowy figure, and to this day not many Israelis have heard of the man who headed this costly and complex construction project, but people involved in it respected and admired him as a person who got things done.

Approval for bypassing Bergmann and Mardor and appointing someone from outside the nuclear establishment came from a special subcommittee of three top physicists: de Shalit, Harry J. "Zvi" Lipkin, and Ze'ev "Venya" Hadari. Hadari's role in the building of the reactor remains something of a mystery. At the beginning of World War II and under his original name, Venya Pomerantz, he was sent to represent the Jews of Palestine in Istanbul, where he worked at saving European Jews from the Nazis. In 1943 he returned to Palestine and published an emotional call to the young Jews of Eretz Yisrael to join the British army's Jewish Brigade and get to the front lines in Europe, in order to help the Jews there and show them that there was a Jewish force capable of fighting. Despite the depths to which the Jews had been plunged, Pomerantz declared, "the very belief that there are Jews from the Land of Israel who carry arms" would spur them to try to extricate themselves from their plight. His call reverberated through the small community, and to a certain degree highlighted the equanimity with which the leaders of the Palestine's Jews and public opinion were relating to the victims of the Holocaust.

His encounter with the survivors of the Nazi depredations tormented Hadari's soul, as had happened to Ben-Gurion, Mardor, and Shalhevet. Like them, he was convinced that the Jews needed not only their own state, but also the ultimate deterrent. He studied nuclear physics and received his doctorate from the Sorbonne. He specialized in the properties of radioactive elements in the so-called actinide series.

Hadari and his two partners in the committee of physicists realized that the construction of the reactor was a project of dimensions unprecedented in Israel and that its management had to be entrusted to a professional, a qualified engineer with experience and proven leadership capability. Behind the scenes, the physicists tried to keep Bergmann away from the Dimona project. They were aware of his foibles, his urge to prattle, his tendency to exaggerate. In the end, it was Ben-Gurion who accepted Peres's recommendation and decided that Mannes Prat would direct the project.

Prat had no experience with reactors or with nuclear materials, but Peres asserts that he was looking for "someone with an open mind," capable of learning. "For this position, I wanted someone thoroughgoing, uncompromisingly pedantic, who would strictly maintain the security constraints for this delicate project." And indeed, Prat was a stickler on security matters. "Mannes thought we were all as negligent as could be, and that our negligence would cost the state dearly," says Peres.

The people who recommended Prat did not hide from Peres that he was tough and stubborn. "When I gave him the post, I knew he would make my life difficult, and he did," says Peres. Prat balked at signing documents in the state's name. When he was handed work plans prepared by the French engineers, he would pass them on to Peres. "He didn't want to accept responsibility, and he made me sign all the technical papers," Peres recalls. "Anything with an element of risk, I had to sign. And like a fool, I would sit all night and read documents that I either understood or didn't understand, and I'd ask, and then I'd sign."

Physicist Zvi Lipkin was Prat's personal guide and gave him a quick course in nuclear physics and reactor engineering. Born in the United States, Lipkin was twenty-nine when he came to Israel in 1950 as a Zionist, just after earning his doctorate at Princeton. In 1951, Bergmann recruited him to the army's Science Corps (HEMED), and when the Atomic Energy Commission was set up, he was one of the founders. In the early 1950s, he worked at the first reactor built in Saclay as part of Israel's nuclear project, and later researched and taught at universities in Europe and the United States. He was on the staff of the Weizmann Institute, Tel Aviv University, and the U.S. government's Argonne National Laboratory outside Chicago.

Peres remarked that Mannes assimilated the required material rapidly.

"This gentleman, within three months, became the best expert I ever knew on the nuclear subject," he exclaims, not without hyperbole. In a few years' time, when there was a change of government, Mannes's identification with the project and its founders would be so strong that he would stir up a hornets' nest by refusing to allow his new masters to inspect its operations. But for the time being, he began welcoming the first French engineers at the construction site.

Ben-Gurion then initiated a change in the structure of EMET. On June 5, 1958, he told his inner staff at the Defense Ministry that EMET would become RAFAEL, the Hebrew acronym for the Authority for Weapons Development.[13] To complete the nuclear project, it was necessary to remove the bodies involved from the direct responsibility of the Defense Ministry, for reasons that were primarily organizational. Ben-Gurion wanted to be free of the constraints of the state budget. The operations of the Defense Ministry had to be financed by the Treasury's budgets division, but a public authority would enjoy relative flexibility in both raising and spending funds. But there was also a security-related reason. To maintain secrecy, a public authority could hide its operations from government agencies and the public's eyes more efficiently than a division in a government ministry.

Munya Mardor was made head of RAFAEL, and was appointed to the General Staff of the Defense Forces, the only civilian among the generals. This time he had no hesitation. "I could not pass over such fascinating plans, despite the difficult personal concessions that my family had to endure," he wrote. What he meant was that he once more had to give up his goals of going into business, and sharing with his wife the burden of running the household and educating the children. The challenge proved a more powerful attraction. "I agreed to turn my life upside down," he wrote, because he felt "there were unique prospects of achieving satisfaction and a possibly one-time chance to take part in a creation of the kind that RAFAEL offered."

Without this challenge, Mardor would have left the Defense Ministry. He was frustrated by the bureaucracy such as having to run from one official to another in order to obtain the resources he needed. But the scent of the secret weapon in his nostrils cast its spell over him.

Ben-Gurion ruled that the strategy behind EMET would be transplanted to RAFAEL. Development of arms for operational use would be commissioned by the Israel Defense Forces. Projects requiring long-term research and development, such as missiles and advanced weapons, would be endorsed by the civilian echelon.

The founding of RAFAEL shifted the Israeli weapons industry into a higher class. EMET had been occupied mainly with the development and manufacture of conventional weapons systems; RAFAEL specialized in furthering advanced technological programs. At RAFAEL, research and development were top priority, production was secondary. EMET was organized by field of research—electronics, chemistry, mechanics, physics—but at RAFAEL it was according to projects, which included a surface-to-surface naval missile, an air-to-air missile, a multistage ballistic missile (which was called "the meteorology rocket"), and a computer to control artillery fire. This division by project made it possible to group experts from various scientific fields in one unit.

THE MOST PRESTIGIOUS project was of course the building of the nuclear device, which sources outside Israel have said RAFAEL did at a plant near Haifa, with the production of plutonium carried out at the reactor in Dimona and not as RAFAEL's responsibility. The Negev Nuclear Research Center, known by its Hebrew acronym, KAMAG, was set up in Dimona to organize the erection of the reactor and the production of plutonium.

This was the hierarchy of the nuclear project management: Peres was the director general, Mannes Prat was in charge of KAMAG's construction, and Mardor, according to foreign sources, was responsible for the technical side. Ernst Bergmann continued as head of the Atomic Energy Commission and served as the scientific adviser of RAFAEL, but he would have no say in Dimona. As was the case throughout the history of the project, the names of the directorate were classified as secret.

There was no master plan. In those years, there was no one in Israel with experience in planning so complex a project. Even if an attempt had been made to draw up a comprehensive plan, it is doubtful that it would have succeeded. Many of the key elements were unknown, among them the timetable and the overall cost. Indeed, even control over the pace of construction wasn't in Israel's hands but was set by France, where a period of political instability was setting in. The budgets to be allocated were equally uncertain, especially since no one really knew where the money would come from. Moreover, the professions of management and operations research were still in their infancy. Systems analysis had only just been introduced to Israel, and PERT, or Progress Evaluation Report Technique, which had been devised in the United States for the Polaris missile project, would reach the country only a year later, in 1959.

There was also a positive side. In French politics, circumstances played out in Israel's favor. For the first two years of the cooperation between the two countries, until mid-1960, Jacques Soustelle, a good friend of Israel, was France's minister for atomic energy and in charge of the CEA. He admired the Zionist movement, and the heads of Israel's defense establishment were his friends.[14] He related to the Dimona project as if it were being built for France itself, and when there were delays due to bureaucratic obduracy, or because of a lack of integration between the many French factors involved in the production of the installations and instruments and their transport to Israel, Peres and Shalhevet would bypass the obstacles by turning directly to Soustelle.

By now, Shalhevet was running a large operation in Paris. He was in charge of dozens of local workers and Israelis, including advisers and researchers, an auditor, security officers, interpreters, secretaries, and drivers. During the first two years of his period in Paris, 1956–57, he had spent most of his time in negotiations with the CEA and ministerial bureaus, and then in the phrasing of agreements. "Shalhevet was a man with tremendous diplomatic influence," recalled Haya Sadeh, "and the relationship with France was based on his personality." He worked mostly with a secretary and an assistant, and reported directly to Peres in writing. Each report was headed "Top Secret" and began with a relevant verse from the Book of Proverbs or Psalms or the Talmudic Ethics of the Fathers. His success in France was the result of his personal integrity, according to Peres. His French interlocutors appreciated his honesty.

The next two years of Shalhevet's time in Paris, 1958–59, were hectic, between coordinating with dozens of factors, following up on the consignment of shipments to Israel, overseeing the young Israeli scientists working in French laboratories, briefing security personnel, and gathering information for the researchers. Frequently, the Israeli team asked Shalhevet to come up with a nugget of information to do with either theoretical or applied physics—a formula, a number, the property of a certain material. Shalhevet would usually give the job to one of the young researchers working in the labs at Saclay or Marcoule, who would question French colleagues about the problems.

Shalhevet often talked with the young scientists. The instruction to maintain secrecy even with their families was bothering some of them. What could they tell their wives and what must they keep secret? Was it feasible to leave the wives in ignorance of what their husbands were doing for so long a period? Should cover stories be fabricated, to reduce tensions? "There were probing discussions, and eventually Shalhavet gave Dror permission to speak freely to me," says Haya Sadeh, "and at home he told me about his work." She doesn't know if he told her everything, or what happened in other families.

Some of the scientists were worried about the fact that they were working on such a project. "The moral element," they called it at meetings. This was a period of soul-searching among nuclear scientists who had participated in the Manhattan Project, and some of them were deeply repentant. The Russell-Einstein Manifesto and its dramatic call for nuclear disarmament, which was issued in London in 1955, reverberated loudly. Europe had been terrified by the Soviet threat to launch a nuclear offensive against the aggressors in the Suez Campaign. The Cold War had created a new lexicon of the terminology of war: mass destruction, ultimate weaponry, balance of terror. In schools in the United States bomb shelters were built, and nuclear-attack drills were held.

The moral element profoundly troubled Shalhevet. In years to come, as head of the Israeli Atomic Energy Commission, and in the Pugwash organization, he would tackle issues of nuclear policy and produce a plan for the nuclear disarmament of the Middle East. But he had no doubts about Israel's right to a nuclear capability. The moral justification, he would tell the young scientists, had been provided by his encounter in Europe with the survivors of the Holocaust.

CHAPTER SIX

A Nuclear Complex
Grows in the Desert

SOMETHING PECULIAR HAPPENED in 1960. The head of the security services, Isser Harel, told the prime minister that a Russian satellite had passed over Dimona and photographed the construction site of the nuclear reactor and that the Soviets were planning to share this intelligence with the United States. Ben-Gurion was shocked and summoned Golda Meir, Peres, and Harel to an urgent meeting. Forty years later, Peres provided a detailed account of that meeting.

It began with Harel reporting that the previous day he had learned that the Russian foreign minister, Andrei Gromyko, was flying to Washington to talk to Secretary of State John Foster Dulles, and that Israel had to move quickly or else the two powers would take a stand against her. Harel proposed that Ben-Gurion or Golda fly to Washington to fix things. Peres resisted vigorously. "Let's say a Russian satellite passed over," Peres told Ben-Gurion. "It didn't see a reactor, it didn't see anything. It saw a few bulldozers on the ground. What does that signify? I really do not understand what Gromyko has to tell."

Harel denied emphatically that such an event had ever taken place.[1] "It never happened at all. This is the first time I've ever heard this story," he said with emphasis.

But Peres continued to insist upon the preciseness of his memory. "Golda and Harel kept up the pressure," said Peres, "and the atmosphere at the meeting was terrible." In the end Peres said to Ben-Gurion, "If you want to go to Washington, go. But we have an obligation to the

French to maintain secrecy. First, someone must go to France and tell them that we are going to inform the Americans, and I assure you, that's the end of our relations with France."

Ben-Gurion had accepted Peres's judgment and refrained from any activity. In Washington, the American and Russian foreign ministers had other issues to discuss.

"The story never happened," insisted Harel. "I generally have a good memory. It's impossible that something wouldn't ring a bell for me. I think that it's just another case of Shimon Peres's bluffing."

One fact supports Peres's version. We know now that late in 1960, a Soviet satellite *did* photograph the Dimona construction site, and that the images revealed the structure of a nuclear reactor. A story in the *New York Times* in late December of that year quoted American officials in Washington as saying that Israel was building a reactor in Dimona; their conclusion was based in part on reports from Moscow about these satellite images. However, this item also contradicts Peres's version, for if in late 1960, the structure of a reactor could be discerned in the satellite pictures (as in photographs taken from an American U-2 spy plane, as we shall see), then the description he gave of the site at the meeting was incorrect. Peres also erred in quoting Harel, who clearly could not have spoken about an upcoming meeting in Washington between Gromyko and Dulles, because Dulles died of cancer in late May 1959. However, after more then forty years, being wrong about the identities of the great powers' foreign ministers is not considered a gross error.

There are two reasons for bothering with this story, which may or may not have happened the way that Peres told it. One is connected to the dread amongst the Israeli leadership that the construction of the reactor would be exposed. The pact with France had created a completely novel situation: A peripheral little country was building an ultimate weapon, thereby gate-crashing the exclusive nuclear playground of the big powers. There was no precedent for this. "It would have looked like tremendous audacity, because apart from the powers, no other state had anything like it. We were the first, we were the only ones, we were controversial, we were outrageous," says Peres.

––––––––––––––

ISRAEL'S LEADERS WERE AWARE that they would soon have a very hot potato in their hands. On the one hand, they were sure that the nuclear project was essential to the country's security. On the other hand, they knew that the reaction that it would provoke in the United States could be extreme. The horrors of Hiroshima and Nagasaki were still very vividly engraved on the world's consciousness. Indeed, Ben-Gurion and his allies were determined to go ahead with the development of the ultimate weapon, but they were terrified by the very thought that in the near future they would have to deal with the results of their determination.

But the meeting at Sdeh Boker exposed the deep rift between the Mapai old-timers and Ben-Gurion's young guard. Golda and Harel were engaged in a power struggle with Peres and former chief of staff Moshe Dayan, now a Knesset member and minister of agriculture, over the top positions in the party, in anticipation of taking control after the departure of Ben-Gurion. Ostensibly, Ben-Gurion's regime was stable, and his party was at the height of its power. In the general election of 1959, he achieved his best electoral result since the establishment of the state.[2] But the internal rivalry caused by the ramifications of the Lavon Affair had split the party in a manner that made reconciliation impossible. The old guard, headed by ex-prime minister Moshe Sharett and Golda Meir, had formed an opposition to Ben-Gurion. Harel, who had always been considered loyal to Ben-Gurion, now went with his opponents. Golda and Harel cooperated because they saw the exclusion of the Foreign Ministry and the Mossad from the negotiations with France on the nuclear pact as an endeavor by Ben-Gurion's young allies to deprive them of their influence and squeeze them out. The negative view taken by Golda and Harel was based on three arguments: First, it was impossible to rely on the shaky French regime; second, Peres was not credible and his reports could not be trusted; and third, the decision to try to keep the United States out of the picture was an error.

None of these claims stood the test of time. The government of France, despite its instability, generally fulfilled its obligations under the pact. Peres's reports to Ben-Gurion were reliable (and many years later Harel would praise Peres's initiative and performance in the creation of Dimona, despite his relentless hostility toward him). Ben-Gurion's insistence on keeping the reactor a secret from the Americans caused no damage. The opposite was true. It is doubtful that if Israel had announced to the Americans that it was developing a nuclear option, the project would have been allowed to continue.

After the 1959 elections, Peres, after resigning as director general of the Defense Ministry and being elected to the Knesset, had been promoted by Ben-Gurion to deputy minister of defense. Golda organized a rebellion of the old guard against the move, but Ben-Gurion went ahead with it and eventually the rebels capitulated and joined the government. There can be no doubt that Ben-Gurion was aware of the resentment of the veterans against Dayan and Peres, but they had helped him in his quest for the secret weapon—although Dayan's support had been rather ambiguous—while the old-timers had made things difficult for him, and he had no choice but to prefer the younger men. In retrospect, it is clear that the importance Ben-Gurion attributed to seeing the project through is what spurred him to advance Dayan and Peres to critical decision-making positions at the expense of his longtime partners.

"The reactor was constructed amid extraordinary controversy," said Peres, saying "reactor" to conceal what he really meant. (Indeed, he and the others involved would always avoid being explicit, using words like "it," or occasionally "the secret weapon" or simply "the reactor.") However, there is no available record of any official decision ever taken by any competent governmental body to endorse Ben-Gurion's personal wish to acquire the nuclear option. Ben-Gurion refrained from bringing important parts of the pact with France before the cabinet for discussion or approval. The widest forum was the inner security staff of the defense minister, in which only two elected officials—Ben-Gurion and his deputy, Peres—took part, together with a small group of appointed officials, advisers, and scientists. The Atomic Energy Commission was kept only partly in the picture, and the top officials of the Foreign Ministry and the Treasury not at all. Foreign Minister Meir, Finance Minister Levi Eshkol, and Trade and Industry Minister Pinhas Sapir—the hard core of the ruling Mapai—were personally briefed by Ben-Gurion and Peres.

The Knesset plenum was never told officially by the prime minister of his intention, and there was never any debate on the immense defense-related and economic ramifications of the project. At the first stage, while the reactor was under construction, the Knesset's Foreign Affairs and Defense Committee was not informed at all. For a number of years, most of the members of the parties in the ruling coalition formed by Ben-Gurion in 1959 (comprising 86 of the 120 Knesset members) received no information about the project. The leaders of the coalition parties were told about the pact with France and the construction of the Dimona reactor, but were never officially informed of what foreign sources say was the intention of producing weapons-grade plutonium and manufacturing a bomb. Until early 1962, the parliamentary opposition, on both the left and the right, never took up the subject of the nuclear project. No law obligated the prime minister to report on anything to Menachem Begin, the leader of the largest opposition party, Herut, which won seventeen seats in the Knesset in the 1959 election. Ben-Gurion never took the trouble to brief Begin (whom he despised for historical, ideological, and personal reasons) on any of his activities in general, and defense matters in particular. Even if he had told Begin about the plan to acquire the ultimate deterrent, it is unlikely that Begin would have raised any objections, as it jibed with his extremely hawkish principles. The left-wing opposition consisted only of the Communist Party, with its three seats. Even if they somehow got wind of the project, their ability to organize any substantial opposition to it would have been totally crippled by the close surveillance the security services maintained over their activities. The three Arab parties in the Knesset, with a total of five seats, were affiliated with Ben-Gurion's Mapai and entirely under his thumb.

Any opposition to the Dimona project by the general public, had they been told about it, would have been marginal and insignificant. In the late 1950s, Israeli society was conformist in the extreme and totally docile. Most citizens displayed unquestioning loyalty to the leaders of the tribe, and if there was an occasional dissident voice, it was drowned out in the yea-saying of the compliant majority and the tame media. And if any protestors did raise their heads, the security services intervened and shut them up rapidly. Opposition was confined to an indistinct murmuring on the radical wing of the intellectual community, who had somehow discerned what was going on. But these muted musings aroused no echo whatsoever amongst the broad public.

Apart from the experts engaged in producing uranium and developing the project, the limited number of people who knew what Israel was developing consisted of three circles:

The outer circle comprised a few hundred politicians, diplomats, journalists, and academics who were aware that a nuclear reactor was going up at Dimona. They were not involved in official deliberations about the project, but were connected to members of the two inner circles, who were. They were not given authoritative information, and could only guess the true purpose of the reactor. The discourse in this circle was not related to the practical aspects, but was restricted to the political and moral spheres.

The wider inner circle encompassed some one to two hundred people who knew what the reactor was meant to produce, and it was from among their number that most of the objections to the project were heard. They included some cabinet ministers, some Knesset members from the coalition parties, IDF General Staff members, the upper echelons of the Intelligence Corps (the Mossad and the Shin Bet), and a group of physicists with security clearance. Most of these people took part only in narrow segments of the decision-making process.

The innermost circle comprised a few dozen people who were privy to the details of the whole project, including the materials that Dimona was designated to manufacture and the process of building the bomb device that, according to foreign sources, would be carried out by RAFAEL. They included Ben-Gurion's defense staff group, which consisted of Deputy Minister Peres, the director general of the ministry, and a number of advisers, all Defense Ministry officials. Also in this circle were a few cabinet ministers, the IDF chief of staff and his deputy, the chief of military intelligence, the members of the Atomic Energy Commission (a few, while others only knew parts of the project), the heads of the security services, and scientists with top security clearance. There were many professional arguments, but they were unanimous about the path that Ben-Gurion had chosen. This small group was united around the goal and believed that it could be achieved. The wider circle was skeptical and lacked faith, according to Peres:

> Look, everyone cast doubts. Don't forget, we were doing something out of the ordinary. Some said, "It isn't serious, nothing will come of it." The political types said the whole world would come down on

us, destroy us, ruin us. The money people said Israel would be impoverished, it was such a costly business. The scientists accused us, me too, of promising something that could never be achieved. So that there was a kind of national unity against it. I remember my good friend David Hacohen, the chairman of the [Knesset] Foreign Affairs and Defense Committee, saying, "There won't be rice to eat in Israel, there won't be grain to eat." Abba Eban, then ambassador in Washington, said it was "a crocodile on dry land." Listen, the expressions they used were awful.

Munya Mardor, attempting to explain the obstacles in his path without giving away the nature of the project, wrote in his diary in his economical language:

It was precisely against the main part of the weapons development program that many critics and opponents arose from among the country's academic community, and both civilian and military office-holders. They claimed that our path was unrealistic and not essential to Israel's security deployment, especially the large, long-term projects. More than once we had to calm them down in various ways, to limit the damage they were doing. We explained, among other things, that at the first stage our work was restricted to components only and not the entire system, and "sufficient to the day is the evil thereof"—when we'd go over from the components phase to the subsystems, and then integrating them into the complete weapons system.

Three groups of opponents tried to nip the project in the bud: academic, military, and political. Coping with the academic opposition was the most complex proposition, because its adherents were not subject to the state bureaucracy, and they were accustomed to freedom of thought and expression.

"RAFAEL's intrusion into spheres which the academic institutions regarded as their own private estates was a thorn in their flesh," Mardor wrote. "All of our efforts to bring the key personages in these institutes closer to our work, as advisers or in managerial or guidance roles, and to let them be partners in our research, were unsuccessful." Most of the academic community opposed the nuclear project because they did not believe that Israeli industry was capable of consummating it, and also because in the 1950s the scientific circles that set the tone in the free world denied the legitimacy of military nuclear research. "Sometimes we discerned an 'ideological' resistance to dedication to the military project," Mardor wrote. Thus, in a subtle hint, Mardor depicts the reluctance of Israeli scientists to risk jeopardizing their professional careers. Since a substantial part of Israeli academic research was financed by foundations and institutions abroad, local scientists feared having their names connected with military projects, lest they lose their grants. Mardor described a reality in which "scientific colonialism of the great powers, even the friendly ones, deflected a highly significant scientific potential from taking an interest in and participating in defense research." He warned that the dependence of Israel's academic world on budgets from overseas "embodied the danger that foreign efforts would practically dictate the course of Israeli science." Peres was far more outspoken. In a speech at the Weizmann Institute in 1959, he deplored the fact that scientists "confined themselves to the ivory towers of pure research," at a time when Israel was busy equipping itself with "a secret weapon." The rebuke was aimed at Amos de Shalit, who had refused to cooperate with the project. The military censorship made sure to erase that sentence from press reports of the speech, but details about the event, and the quote from Peres's speech, were leaked to the British Embassy in Tel Aviv.

The dialogue between RAFAEL and the academic community was rather ambiguous. The academics wouldn't admit unequivocally that they were boycotting military research, but they voted with their feet by simply staying away from it. In 1959, RAFAEL set up a special team, headed by the physicist Ephraim Katchalsky (Katzir), to appeal to the institutes of higher learning to encourage scientists occupied in pure research to participate in advanced technological research and development projects. "But all of those repeated appeals, which were accompanied by a variety of tempting perks, bore no fruit, and there was no real positive response, even for a limited period," Mardor complained. In order to circumvent the opposition, he initiated a series of symposiums and closed conferences with academic scientists who had security clearance. But his colleagues at RAFAEL, including Bergmann, negated the idea. Their objections, in Mardor's opinion, sprang from "a psychological tendency to withdrawal" and "the tense relations with the academic institutions." Mardor insisted and ultimately the parleys were held "with the participation of the best scientists in the country" and "gave our people great satisfaction."

The recruitment of Katchalsky to the RAFAEL directorate in January 1960, as the coordinator of research and development on a part-time basis, was "a sign of a thorough turnaround" in the attitude of the scientific community, Mardor wrote. Ephraim's brother, the chemist Aharon Katchalsky-Katzir, also joined RAFAEL as a consultant in the same year. The brothers, both associated with the Weizmann Institute and both highly respected in the academic community, helped Mardor and Bergmann to bring about the attitude change. "During that period," Mardor wrote, "there were many signs that the doubts harbored by top-drawer scientists were dissipating."

Compared to the confrontation with the academics, the clash with the top army brass was a lot easier to handle, since Ben-Gurion was their supreme commander and it was inconceivable that his men would not heed his authority (as happened, incidentally, in France during de Gaulle's presidency). The high command was divided into two groups. A minority—including the commander of the air force, Ezer Weizman, and generals Haim Barlev and Meir Zorea—ardently supported the development of missiles and the ultimate deterrent. The majority demanded that resources be devoted exclusively to projects whose outcome was assured in advance. Generals began using slogans like "Not a cent for missile development." They spoke of the projects using words like "visionary"—in a mocking sense—or even "hallucinatory." "The army found it hard to swallow," says Peres, "because there was a constant shortage of munitions, uniforms, boots, and money for salaries, and the needs were great, and here we were, with our fantasies, taking the bread out of their mouths."

The harshest opponent was Major General Dan Tolkowsky. An esteemed but modest and soft-spoken officer, he insisted on wearing a beret and detested the more dressy visor caps. In 1958, after five years as commander of the Air Force, years of bitter struggle over the form that the force should take and its place in Israel's security doctrine,[3] Tolkowsky retired from the military and Ezer Weizman took over as air force commander. Tolkowsky was given the civilian appointment of adviser to the chief of staff and head of the Defense Ministry's Planning and Development Authority. At his request, he was assigned the task of evaluating the "methods of planning and scientific research" in the defense establishment and determining whether it was worthwhile to try to create a nuclear option. He studied the nuclear issue, visited nuclear installations in Britain and France, and came to a negative conclusion. Building it would be "a stupid move," Tolkowsky wrote, because it would prod the Soviet Union into supplying the Arabs with nuclear weapons. His recommendation was rejected, and of course the U.S.S.R. never gave the Arabs the bomb. When he resigned in April 1959, no reason was given. (As air force commander, when his positions were rejected, he had frequently threatened to resign.) But information about the disagreements in the defense establishment and Tolkowsky's negative stand leaked out to the British and American embassies in Tel Aviv, and we shall discuss this below.

Dayan, as was his wont, kept his feet firmly on both sides of the fence. While he supported Ben-Gurion's vision and never obstructed Peres's efforts to realize it, he also did nothing to restrain the opposition. Dayan was invited to visit RAFAEL, and accepted willingly, Mardor related, "but he had only just entered the door, and was shaking my hand, when he said, 'You know I don't believe in all this, but you invited me so I came.'" Bergmann and Jenka Ratner were standing next to Mardor and were surprised by Dayan's remarks. Mardor summed it up: "We found it difficult to categorize Dayan. Eventually we classified him as one of the skeptics, who although they believed in our development program doubted our ability to implement projects . . . in which even great powers have to invest a supreme effort." With time Dayan's attitude changed and in the mid-1960s, when it became clear to him that a serious option had evolved, he gave it great weight in Israel's deterrent strategy.

Mardor describes a meeting in the defense minister's office in 1958, when Peres asked Ben-Gurion to approve an allocation of a million lira (equal to about a half-million dollars at the time) to RAFAEL for missile development. "Chief of staff Haim Laskov [Dayan's successor] interrupted and pressed Shimon [Peres] to divulge from what source the money would be taken, and at whose expense." Laskov passed a note to Mardor: "I know of no budget where it can come from. Obviously it can't be from the IDF's budget. Perhaps Shimon has got something else."

Indeed, there was "something else" for the nuclear project, as we shall soon see, but the missile project ground to a near standstill. The first decision to start an independent rockets and missiles R&D had been taken at the highest level of the Israeli defense establishment in July 1958, a short time after RAFAEL was established. It followed a substantial analysis of Egyptian armament intentions and an intelligent estimation that before the end of the decade Egypt would acquire medium-range surface-to-surface missiles (SSM). Consequently, RAFAEL was required to imitate a French-designed short-range SSM missile and then assigned to design an original short-range missile, the Luz ("core" in Hebrew). During 1959 and 1960 the Luz project had dragged and testing results were disappointing. Inadequate financing was the major obstacle. Although RAFAEL had spread the missiles development project over ten to fifteen years, the defense establishment refused to grant it budgets for even a relatively short period of three to five years. "The budget that we managed to raise" for the development and testing of missiles, wrote Mardor, "was not sufficient to ensure the required working momentum." This caused a holdup.

Why did Ben-Gurion refrain from finding funding for the missile project, while being avidly concerned with raising money for Dimona? Ben-Gurion's concept was unique. He never considered the nuclear option as an offensive weapon, but rather as an instrument of deterrence. If he had planned to build an offensive weapon, then the means of delivery would have been just as important to him as the weapon itself. But to him it was clear that the bomb would be stored in the basement. It was being built so that it would never have to be used. In the strategic weapons sphere, whose doctrines were only then starting to evolve, this was an original concept. The bomb in the basement was not a decisive weapon, as the strategists of the great powers would have called it, with the aim of destroying the enemy and assuring the hegemony of the strongest, but a political tool in the hands of the weak, dedicated to preventing their destruction. And because the Israeli device would be a defensive rather than an offensive weapon, Ben-Gurion preferred that it remain a virtual entity, with a vague, indistinct nature. That way it wouldn't draw fire, or provoke the enemy into developing his own bomb, or annoy the great powers.

The need to maintain strict secrecy led Ben-Gurion to keep the financial figures away from the Treasury and the army command. If Ben-Gurion, Peres, Prat and Mardor had been obligated to disclose details of the expenditure to the Treasury officials in charge of the national budget, the project would have been exposed to internal and external pressures, and the circle of those sharing in the secret would have grown. If the Dimona budget had been revealed to the army command, its criticism of the project would have been all the sharper.

Concealing the figures from most of the people responsible for the defense budget was not a complicated matter because in its early years the project was mainly financed by a private fund at Ben-Gurion's disposal, and was not included in the annual national budget. In those years, such funds were called "the B budget." They were managed by a special treasurer, someone who could be trusted, and details were known only to the head of the organization and one or two of his aides. Of course they were not under the control of the Treasury's budgets division, nor subject to the audits of the state comptroller. A "B budget" could be used to pay for political party activities or for secret governmental operations. During that period, the identities of the ruling party and the state overlapped almost completely.[4] Ben-Gurion's Mapai party always ensured that the Treasury portfolio would be in its hands and that it would be given to a minister who could be trusted to cooperate fully with the leader. Finance minister Eshkol was informed of the amounts being invested in the project and on the size of the B budget, but he was given reports on a personal basis and did not share them with ministry officials.

Ben-Gurion noted in his diary in 1958 that the cost of the Dimona reactor would be $25 million, but it is doubtful that an accurate estimate was possible at that stage. A later American estimate put the cost of the Israeli project at between $100 million and $200 million, but it is unlikely that this estimate was based on reliable figures. Peres wrote in his memoirs, *Battling for Peace*, that building Dimona cost $80 million, at 1960 prices.[5] There is no certainty that this figure is accurate—because budgetary control over secret projects at that time was decentralized, with some of the money coming from the state budget, and some from unofficial funds, and no centralized accounting was made of all the expenditures. However, comparisons with assessments made by other sources suggests that the figure is realistic. A French source estimated that Israel paid France a total of some $40 million for the installations, expertise, consultation, and training of scientists and technicians. To this we must add the cost of construction of the Dimona complex, for which there are only partial figures. A prominent Israeli economist who was involved in the economic decisions concerning Dimona after 1964 estimates that the construction of the first stage of the project (including the payment to the French) was some 250 million Israeli lira, or $83 million in 1962 terms.[6]

Peres says that there were disputes among the leadership on the volume of the costs as well. In order to set up a separate fund, Ben-Gurion told his staff to "call Abe." Whenever there was a need to raise funds from American Jews for a Zionist cause, or when there was a need for some lobbying in the White House, Ben-Gurion would say, "Call Abe." The same thing happened on the American side. When the Democratic presidents, Truman, Kennedy, or Johnson, needed to convey a message to the Israeli leadership, or when they wanted to persuade Israel to make a sensitive political move, they would also tell their aides, "Call Abe."

Abe was Abraham Feinberg, a New York philanthropist and talented lobbyist whose role in Israel's nuclear project was critical. Some of the missions he performed for both the American and Israeli governments were complex and even dangerous. If Ben-Gurion had not been sure that Feinberg could raise the millions needed for the project from world Jewry, it is doubtful that he would have undertaken the deal with France. Israel of the 1950s and '60s could never have paid for the advanced technology, erected the Dimona reactor, and built a nuclear deterrent out of its own resources.

Born to a poor immigrant family, Feinberg made a fortune out of underwear and stockings. His childhood and adolescence represent the pattern of life of the second generation of the Jewish immigrants from Eastern Europe who landed penniless at Ellis Island around the turn of the century and crowded into the tenements of the Lower East Side of Manhattan. The parents were laborers, peddlers, middlemen, petty merchants; the sons went out to work at a young age to help the family and pay for their own education. They were brainwashed with the words "Education is the key to success," the motto that Jewish mothers everywhere have drummed into children's heads for generations.

Abe's father was a hosiery salesman who could hardly make a living. "I got into business for economic reasons," Abe told an interviewer from the Truman Presidential Library who recorded his life story in 1973. "I came from a family that could not afford to send me to college, so I had to earn some money in order to sustain me during my college years." At age twelve, he was accepted by the elite Townsend Harris High School, which was housed at the City College of New York, and was famous for the classical and humanistic emphasis of its curricula. At fifteen, Feinberg graduated from high school and entered City College night school, where generations of immigrant children were educated and thus saved from poverty. In the daytime he worked for a textile marketing firm. At seventeen, he registered for night classes in law at Fordham University, and on graduating, in 1933, went into business with his father, selling hosiery. But he continued studying for his master's degree at New York University.

Although he later passed the New York state bar exam, Feinberg never practiced law. The war years were good for business. The troops needed socks and underwear, and the manufacturers sold whatever they could produce. But his work in the garment industry never tapped the full skills of this ambitious young man. The rise to power of Hitler in Germany had altered the course of his life, providing challenges and excitement. "I realized very quickly," he told the interviewer, "that Hitler was a great threat, not only to the world, but particularly to my people . . . so, I began to be active organizationally in Jewish affairs."

At the age of twenty-five, Feinberg became active in the United Palestine Appeal, raising funds from textile manufacturers for the Jews who had been forced to leave Europe. Early on, the heads of the appeal recognized his leadership talents and recruited him to the national committee. This level led him to the corridors of power in Washington, and he realized that finding a lasting solution to the problems of the Jews required not only philanthropy, but also political action.

Feinberg was disappointed with the leader of American Zionism, Rabbi

Abba Hillel Silver, believing that he was taking the movement down the wrong path: "Silver was very arrogant, a brilliant speaker, and a despotic type of leader," he said. "He was a very close friend of Senator [Robert] Taft.7 And so his innate feelings toward Roosevelt were inimical."

Silver's support for the Republicans closed the doors of the White House to him. Feinberg believed that in order to mobilize the Democratic administration to support the Zionists and force the British to allow the refugees from the Nazis to settle in Palestine, it was necessary to create a continual and businesslike dialogue with President Roosevelt and with Secretary of State Cordell Hull. The routine way to do this, he related, was to join a local branch of the party—he was a supporter of the Democrats—and to get to know the representatives of the district and the state in the House and the Senate, and to use them to penetrate the power centers. But this was too slow a process for him, and he sought a direct connection, through industrialist acquaintances. A close friend from St. Louis knew Robert Hannegan, a key Democratic political activist.8 "I brashly said to my friend, 'I want to meet Mr. Hannegan, for the purpose of finding a way to talk to Mr. Roosevelt,'" Feinberg related.

Hannegan suggested that Feinberg turn first to Vice President Harry S. Truman, but Feinberg balked. He believed that in order to achieve influence, it was necessary to go straight to the president himself. Nevertheless, Hannegan convinced him to do it step by step. Truman came to New York to address a Jewish conference, after which he attended a meeting of a small group of friends at the Savoy Plaza hotel. Hannegan obtained an invitation for Feinberg. "This was the end of 1944," said Feinberg. "When we gathered, awaiting for the vice president, I noticed four Secret Service men coming into the room. Then came the vice president. In those days the vice president had no Secret Service detail. It immediately struck me that something was going on and that perhaps Hannegan was smarter than I thought when he said to meet the vice president. If they were protecting the vice president this strongly and under these unusual circumstances, there must be something wrong with the president. And, of course, the president was dead within four or five months."

When Roosevelt died, Feinberg was at a business cocktail party. "Of course, when the news came in, the party was over. Everyone wrung their hands. 'Look what we're left with. How is this country going to survive?' And I was regarded as an idiot when I said, 'You don't know the qualities of Truman. I do, and I tell you that we have nothing to worry about.'"

World War II came to an end. The world was horrified by the dimensions of the destruction of the Jews by the Nazis, and Feinberg intensified his public activities on behalf of the survivors of the Holocaust. In the winter of 1946 he traveled to Europe to get a firsthand picture of the displaced-persons camps. In the course of a tour lasting several weeks he visited twenty-two camps, and was shocked by what he saw. "They were the same camps that the Nazis used, with the same barbed wire, the same gallows, the same ovens. I was in those places, so I know the shock is merely seeing the ashes that were not yet scooped out of the oven."

Feinberg talked to thousands of survivors, and realized that most of them were not willing to remain in Europe. Draconian immigration laws had barred the gates of the United States (and other Western countries) to Jewish refugees, and therefore Palestine was the only destination for them, but here too the doors were closed by the British government. Feinberg mobilized to help the Haganah acquire cargo ships and outfit them to carry refugees to the Land of Israel illegally. "In those same weeks, in the winter of 1946, I was involved in an operation in which they secretly transported refugees in trucks," he said. "In one case, 200 kids went by train openly from the city of Ulm [in south Germany] to Marseilles. This was right in front of the American Army, who just closed their eyes. We sent those kids in closed cattle cars. They were surviving children with no parents. It was a pathetic thing to see these little kids. One had a little violin, one had an accordion, a balloon, all the little precious treasures. All they had was one crust of bread and part of a roll of toilet paper, and there were no latrines in cattle cars."

Feinberg found himself at the heart of the Haganah's illegal immigration activity in Europe. He got to know Mardor and Shalhevet, and was thrilled by their exploits. In the summer of 1946, Feinberg accompanied refugees to a cargo ship that sailed from Marseilles to the shores of Palestine. Close to the coast, a British warship blocked its approach to the port. The Haganah command ordered the refugees to leave the ship and reach the beach in the lifeboats. Feinberg was astonished by the solidarity of the Jews of Palestine with the refugees. "They would be received by the people in the Palestine settlements on the beach, who would immediately change clothes or change identity cards with the refugees, so that when the British caught them they didn't know who the hell they had. Did they have a native or did they have an immigrant?"

In his childhood, when Abe's outlook on the world was being shaped, Jewish solidarity was only a theoretical value and not an imperative. He had passed the war years in comparative comfort in New York, having received an exemption from conscription because he was married with two children. Before going to the displaced-persons camps in Europe, his aspirations were fulfilled in his pursuit of the American Dream. The dramatic encounter with the remnants of the Jewish people in the camps and on the shores of Palestine shook the young businessman. As he witnessed the suffering of the Jews, the extent of which can hardly be exaggerated, Feinberg experienced the same process of emotional transformation as Mardor and Shalhevet: a harsh shock first, followed by the development of a deep sense of solidarity, and then the insight that there is no solution to the problems of the Jews other than the establishment of a Jewish state in the Land of Israel, a state that must be made into a defensive fortress. This was the lesson that he learned from the Holocaust.

Feinberg got to know the leaders of the Jews in Palestine and the commanders of the underground army, many of whom would fill key positions in the government of the young state when it arose. The activity in the Haganah got the youthful textile manufacturer involved in a daring operation.

That summer, on his last day in Palestine, Feinberg was imprisoned by the British on suspicion of bringing out military information. He was arrested on Saturday, June 29, when thousands of British soldiers raided Jewish communities, arrested leaders and hundreds of underground members, and found caches of arms and ammunition. It was a severe blow to the Haganah, and in the history of the Zionist struggle it is known as the "Black Sabbath."

That morning, Feinberg was at Lod airport, near Tel Aviv. He boarded a plane bound for Cairo, and took his seat. From Cairo, he intended to fly to Paris and then back home. Sitting near him was a man with an Asian appearance, Moshe Sassoon.[9] Sassoon had lived in Syria and Lebanon on a Haganah mission, gathering information on their military forces, and he had drawn up a report, which he was due to submit to Ben-Gurion in Paris. The report was concealed in Feinberg's baggage.

The pilot was warming up the engines when British police burst in, located Sassoon and Feinberg, ordered them to disembark, and led them away to be interrogated. "Sassoon was stripped naked," related Feinberg. "His shoes were cut, his belt was cut, and his luggage was cut in their looking for what they wanted. He was a Palestinian under their jurisdiction, and therefore they could pretty near do anything they wanted. Then they started on me. I said, 'No, you don't touch me.'" Feinberg was an American citizen and the British knew that he had some influence in the White House.

Feinberg was held for the night in jail but his interrogators allowed his luggage to be taken back to the hotel in Jerusalem and a Haganah messenger replaced it with an identical case. The next day Feinberg was released but the information still had to go to Paris. This time the microfilm was hidden inside a cigarette lighter and Feinberg was asked to carry it to Portugal. Another messenger had waited for him at Lisbon airport and brought the message to Ben-Gurion.

In New York in the fall of 1947, the U.N. General Assembly vote on the proposal to partition Palestine between the Arabs and the Jews was approaching. This was a turning point in Zionist history, and Feinberg was mobilized to exert his influence. Truman was planning to support the proposal, but the top State Department officials were urging him to oppose it. "Truman's position was certainly not a secret," said Feinberg. "The State Department's position was not a secret. Truman was helpful in directing me to the State Department and helping me try to get the point of view across. Almost at the last minute the possibility of the United States voting against it was there."

And then, on November 29, came the dramatic vote with Jews around the world glued to their radio receivers, tensely counting the votes one by one. Feinberg accompanied Chaim Weizmann, who was in New York to lobby the wavering U.N. delegates. "As soon as the vote came in I ran over to Dr. Weizmann, who was at the Plaza Hotel. He was alone . . . and he actually opened the door himself when we came. He was in his shirt sleeves. He used to wear a stiff collar, but the collar was off and he had this neckband and striped shirt; I remember it clearly. And the tears were coming down. He just sat down, and we said nothing but embraced each other. We were very close friends. My wife gave him a kiss. And all he said was, 'At last.'"

Feinberg strengthened his position in the Democratic Party and attended the meetings of the party's top committees. In the late summer of 1948, Truman planned a coast-to-coast campaign journey, and Feinberg devoted himself to fund-raising on the president's behalf, contributing money himself and getting other Jews to do so too. Within two weeks, he and well-connected businessman Ed Kaufman had raised $100,000. "The trip was a triumphant trip from his [Truman's] point of view as a politician," said Feinberg. "He often said, 'If not for my friend Abe, I couldn't have made the trip and I wouldn't have been elected.' This is not true. The trip would have been made one way or another. But I think it was helpful to him to know early that the problem of making the trip was behind him."

Presidents don't forget people who help them get elected, and thanks to his financing of the campaign trip of 1948, Feinberg became a close friend of Truman's, earning the status of an unofficial adviser to the White House on Jewish and Middle Eastern affairs. For the next twenty years, Feinberg was one of the most important lobbyists in the most powerful country in the world, promoting the cause of the Jewish people and the State of Israel.

This should not be taken lightly. National and religious minorities who have no sovereign state to call their own need the mediation of an intercessor with standing in the establishments of powerful countries. This is true of a minority living in a defined territory, and even more so of a minority scattered across many countries, like the Jews. In the political hierarchy of the weak, the intercessor's go-between role is one of the most important, and indeed since the early days of the Jewish Diaspora, for almost two thousand years (from the fall of Jerusalem and the destruction of the Temple in 70 A.D.) intercessors have mediated with rulers on behalf of Jewish communities.

Both the Israeli government and the American administration made use of Abe Feinberg's services and when he reported to Ben-Gurion on October 31, 1958, the discussion centered on the financing of Dimona.

Ben-Gurion called the donors "makdishim," or consecrators, and their contributions "hakdasha," consecration. Both of these Hebrew words derive from the word *kadosh*, sacred, which is also the root of the word *Mikdash*, or Temple—the holiest institution of Judaism. And inside the Temple is the Kodesh Hakodashim, the Holy of Holies. And like the Temple, which was erected with the contributions of the children of Israel (Exodus 25:1), so too Israel's nuclear program would be built with contributions. In Ben-Gurion's eyes, the nuclear project was holy.

Abe Feinberg was the chief consecrator—Ben-Gurion's representative in charge of obtaining donations from the wealthiest Jews in the world.[10] The secret fund-raising campaign began at the end of 1958, and continued for two years. Some twenty-five millionaires contributed a total of about $40 million dollars (in today's terms, some $250 million).

At one of the meetings where the financing of the project was discussed, Ben-Gurion asked for a list of the founders of the Sonneborn Institute—the group formed by the eighteen richest Jews in North America, who had met with Ben-Gurion in June 1945 in the home of one of their number, Rudolf S. Sonneborn in New York. The coordinator of donations on behalf of the Sonneborn Institute was Henry Morgenthau Jr., who had served eleven years as secretary of the Treasury in the Roosevelt administrations, and after resigning from government soon after Truman became president, served as chairman of the United Jewish Appeal and later as chairman of the board of governors of the American Financial and Development Corporation for Israel.[11]

Seventeen of the participants in the institute were Americans—the youngest was Abe Feinberg himself—and one was a Canadian, Samuel Zacks of Toronto, president of the Canadian Zionist Organization, who had made his money from gold mining. Among the donors there were another three Canadians: Louis and Bernard Bloomfield, and Samuel Bronfman, president of the Canadian Jewish Congress and founder of the Seagram whiskey empire. It can be presumed that Morgenthau, Zacks, and other members of the institute, as well as the Bloomfield brothers and Bronfman, gave hefty sums to Feinberg's Dimona campaign. The list of donors is a close-kept secret to this day; they were assured that their names would not be linked to the project so their worldwide business dealings would not be harmed.

From a passage in Ben-Gurion's diary that has been declassified, from some statements by Peres, and utterances of Mardor's, we learn that in Europe, the British and French branches of the Rothschild family were among the donors, as well as Isaac Wolfson (who gave at least $5 million), and the Sieff family, both of Britain. Feinberg kept the names of the American donors a secret, at their request, as well as his own name. No Israeli official has ever confirmed that it was Feinberg who conducted the Dimona appeal.

No less than financial resources, a fundamental requirement for success of the nuclear project was a highly developed scientific infrastructure. The planning and production of a nuclear bomb anywhere relied upon research and development in a variety of spheres: nuclear physics and engineering, radiological chemistry, applied mathematics, electronics, ballistics, metallurgy, fine mechanics—and this is only a partial list. The most difficult scientific task, the one that has foiled most of the developing countries that aspired to possess the bomb, is to master the processes that create the nuclear explosion.

Isotopes of two radioactive elements are capable of producing such explosions. One of these isotopes is uranium 235, which is found in small quantities in natural uranium ores. Only 0.7 percent of natural uranium is fissile, that is, unstable in its nucleus, and it has to be extracted from the ore and separated from the nonfissile material. The Israeli physicist Yuval Neeman has defined the separation process as "disconnecting the fat material from the thin." Nonfissile natural uranium 238 is heavier, as it has 146 neutrons per nucleus, while the fissile uranium 235 has only 143. To make one bomb, about ten kilograms of uranium 235 are needed.

There are several methods for the separation of uranium 235 from natural ore. One method using centrifuges was developed by the Austrian physicist Gernot Zippe while he was in a Soviet prison in the 1950s. The stronger the material with which the centrifuge is built, and the faster it revolves around its axis, the more efficient it is, and the purer the product and the higher the concentration of uranium 235.

A second method of separation was developed in the United States for the Manhattan Project. The uranium ore is vaporized and the gas passes through hundreds of miles of piping fitted with membranes. Since the uranium 235 is the lightest of the materials in the ore, it passes more rapidly through the membranes.

The second of the radioactive elements whose isotopes have unstable, fissile nuclei and can therefore be used to create a nuclear explosion is plutonium, an artificial element formed when natural uranium is used to fuel a reactor, and is irradiated within its core. After the spent fuel rods are removed from the core, the plutonium is extracted in a process that is exceedingly complex. The amount of plutonium in the rods is minute and to build a bomb some four kilograms of plutonium are needed.[12] This amount is known as the critical mass that enables the explosion to take place.

Israel, according to foreign reports, and France used plutonium to build their first bombs. The United States, on the other hand, chose to use both fissile materials in 1945, making one bomb with uranium 235, and two others using plutonium.[13]

This is how the plutonium explosion is set off: A particle accelerator fires a neutron at the unstable isotope nucleus, splitting it into two, releasing energy and two or three other neutrons, which in turn split other nuclei, and so on, creating a chain reaction and the vast release of energy that constitutes the thermonuclear explosion.

In order to construct a bomb, the materials required to create the chain reaction must be prepared in the right proportions and arranged in the right order. The reaction activity must be controlled and regulated so that the fission and release of energy will occur at the planned time and with the planned force. How this is done was the secret the Americans possessed when they succeeded in making the atom bombs dropped on Japan. The first secret was the precise amount of fissile material (the critical mass) needed to create the chain reaction that built up into the blast. The second secret was how to control the pace of the bombardment of the neutrons inside the isotopes' nuclei, so as to regulate the discharge of the energy released when the nuclei break up.

The control of these processes is a complicated matter, and this has caused delays in most of the countries that have built bombs. French scientists had difficulties in working out the exact formula for creating the chain reaction in the fissile material. Russia simply stole the information from the United States.[14] Great Britain obtained assistance from the

Americans. Israel was helped by France, and also by scientists from elsewhere abroad.

The ability to control the reaction is all-important, because both the uranium-235 and the plutonium isotopes are very sensitive to movement. When isotopes are in close conjunction, the neutrons in their nuclei begin to move, and an uncontrolled explosion may result. Because of this danger, the material is stored in two subcritical sections, each of which is incapable of detonation, but which when brought together can produce an explosion within one second.

A simple bomb consists of a container holding two pellets of fissile material that are pressed together by two springs and separated by a wedge. When the wedge is removed, the two balls merge with each other forcefully and rapidly, and the process of nuclear fission begins, resulting in an explosion. The calculation of the critical mass of the fissile material has to be dead accurate, and if the mass created when the two pellets join is even a little less than that called for by the formula, it is unlikely that an explosion will take place. The process for bringing the two pellets together must also be very quick and very precise.

After the exact quantities of the materials have been determined and after the fissile materials have been arranged in the device, the first explosion must be detonated to set off the chain reaction. There are two ways of doing this. The simpler one, the gun method, is appropriate for a uranium-235 bomb. In it, a TNT explosion causes the two subcritical masses of fissile material to merge, creating the critical mass that sets off the chain reaction culminating in the nuclear blast.

The more complex method of detonation is called implosion, and is used for both uranium and plutonium isotopes, or a combination of the two. TNT encircles the fissile material and its detonation sets off two processes that ultimately produce the nuclear explosion: The fissile material is compressed inward and simultaneously an external neutron generator starts to launch a stream of neutrons at the fissile material core. In the first French nuclear test, in 1960, the implosion method was used, and American experts say that the first Israeli bomb was built in the same way.

In the conditions prevalent in Israel, its decision to rely on plutonium rather than highly enriched uranium as the primary fuel for its first nuclear weapons[15] was a wise choice, say foreign experts, mainly because

enriched uranium is very difficult to come by and in the plutonium production process, there is no need for enriched uranium. As early as the
1940s, enriched uranium was being spoken of as a nuclear trigger item,
and its distribution was restricted. Moreover, at that time, the enrichment of uranium was a more complex and expensive process than the extraction of plutonium from natural uranium.[16]

This is why the Dimona reactor was fueled with natural uranium,
from which plutonium was extracted. Small amounts of uranium have
been mined in Israel since the 1950s. We have already related how in
1948, while the War of Independence was raging, an exploration team
headed by the physicist Israel Dostrovsky had located deposits of phosphates containing small quantities of uranium in the Rotem plain, south
of Beersheba in the Negev. Later, Dostrovsky developed a relatively in-
expensive method of extracting the uranium from the phosphate deposits. Since then, Israel has produced some ten tons of uranium a year in
the Negev, a quantity that was sufficient to fuel the reactor in its early
years. Over the years, uranium has also been imported from various
sources. The largest amount, six hundred tons, was purchased from
South Africa in the 1970s, according to non-Israeli reports.

This is how the combustion of natural uranium at the core of the reactor takes place: The uranium is compressed into aluminum rods, which
are inserted into the core, where they are irradiated. (According to the
information leaked by former Dimona technician Mordechai Vanunu to
the London *Sunday Times* in 1986, at the Israeli reactor 140 rods were irradiated simultaneously, in three-month cycles.) After the irradiation,
the burned rods are removed from the core and taken to a chemical laboratory, where the plutonium is extracted in a process known as the "re-
processing of irradiated fuel," similar to the extraction of copper from
iron ore.

The more powerful the reactor, the greater the quantity of plutonium
that it can produce. The American-supplied research reactor at Nahal
Soreq cannot produce plutonium because it is too weak, and its output is
meant mainly for industrial and medical purposes. In contrast, the Dimona reactor was constructed from the start—foreign sources say— in
order to produce plutonium. Foreign experts who follow Israel's nuclear
activities believe that the reactor has been upgraded repeatedly, and that

the plutonium output has increased accordingly. We have already pointed out that there is general agreement among experts that since the late 1970s, the Dimona reactor has had a production capacity of 70 megawatts, enabling it to produce some 40 kilograms of plutonium a year, from which ten bombs can be made.

Another essential component in the operation of a nuclear reactor in which plutonium is extracted from natural uranium is heavy water, the common name for deuterium oxide, whose molecular formula is D_2O. In a nuclear reactor, it is the heavy water that is used to control the release of energy. It does this by moderating the pace of the movement of the neutrons released by the nucleus of the uranium atom, thus enabling a sustained chain reaction, without generating an explosion, for just as in nuclear bombs, in nuclear reactors the chain of reactions of the fissile material liberates an enormous amount of energy.

Ernst Bergmann had tried to find a supplier of heavy water from early in 1956. The natural source was Norway, due to the close nuclear ties it had formed with France. Norsk Hydro,[17] the Norwegian heavy-water manufacturer, had been the one and only supplier of the liquid to Europe in general and France in particular since it was established in 1934. In the 1940s and '50s, Norway had no hesitation about exporting heavy water to friendly countries. Ben-Gurion, however, preferred to acquire it from the United States, which he hoped would treat Israel as it had treated India. (In March 1956, India had purchased twenty-one tons of heavy water in the United States, without being required to place it under supervision.[18]) America was a new factor on the world market in this commodity, and in the mid-1950s was competing with Norway, whose price was more than three times higher $200 per kilogram, compared to the $60 charged by the Americans—a significant difference in Israel's economic situation. Moreover, if the United States agreed to provide Israel with such a key requirement in the production of plutonium, the Israeli nuclear project would derive a high degree of legitimacy.

Israel therefore applied to both Norway and the United States. Bergmann met the heads of the U.S. Atomic Energy Commission (AEC) in Washington and asked for permission to acquire ten tons of heavy water. The AEC agreed, on condition that Israel would agree to the supervision of its use. At the same time, some of the top figures in Mapai put out feelers to the leaders of the Norwegian Labor Party, whose head, Einar Gerhardsen, was prime minister. At that time, the Israeli nuclear project was something of an unlaid egg, because Israel had no reactor, just a vision, and the negotiation dragged along. Only after the nuclear pact with France was signed in late 1957, and when it became clear to Ben-Gurion that it was impossible to budge the Americans from their demand for oversight of the use of the heavy water, did the contacts with the Norwegians gather momentum.

The moving spirit in the Norwegian nuclear industry was the astrophysicist Gunnar Randers, who had spent the war years, when Norway was under Nazi occupation, in exile in London and on his return in 1946 was made head of the Norwegian Institute for Atomic Energy Research. Bergmann met him in Geneva in August 1946, at the first U.N. conference on the use of atomic energy for peaceful purposes. Before the conference, U.N. Secretary General Dag Hammarskjöld appointed Randers his personal adviser, and tasked him with setting the agenda. Randers and Bergmann became friends. They spoke to each other in German, and were on first-name terms. From the start of their acquaintanceship, Randers displayed empathy with Israel. With his elongated face, high forehead, shock of black hair, and thick eyebrows, he was a charismatic and ambitious man. With great pride, he showed Bergmann a photograph of himself with Albert Einstein taken before the war, thus helping to win his admiration. It had been Einstein who recommended to Chaim Weizmann that he appoint Bergmann to head the Sieff Institute (whose name was later changed to the Weizmann Institute).

In his own country Randers had both enthusiastic supporters and sworn enemies. Few remained indifferent toward him. He had developed a wide network of connections in the international nuclear community— in the United Nations and in the European Atomic Energy Community, Euratom. He advised Third World governments and took delight mainly in irritating the American nuclear establishment.

When Bergmann and Randers met, they discussed the issue of small countries and the bomb. Could states like Norway and Israel develop the bomb? Norway was still suffering from the trauma of the Nazi occupation. Its political leadership was agonizing over whether to develop its nuclear industry in a military direction, or to make do with activity in the civilian sphere. The Norwegian military command was not eager to see large resources invested in the building of a bomb, while the civilian defense establishment generally liked the idea. But unlike in Israel, in Norway the discussion of the alternatives and the weighing of the prospects against the risks were systematic. Norway had all the necessary capabilities for building a bomb; not only raw materials, but also an excellent scientific infrastructure. The great Danish physicist Niels Bohr had placed his research institute in Copenhagen and dozens of young researchers that he had recruited in the Nordic states at Norway's disposal.

In mid-1957, the matter of the heavy water had become urgent, and Bergmann wrote a personal letter to Randers. Israel needed to acquire twenty tons. Randers replied immediately in the affirmative, but made the deal conditional on the agreement of the Norwegian Foreign Ministry. The executive board of Noratom, the government corporation responsible for the export of heavy water from Norway, enthusiastically supported the deal, and so did prime minister Gerhardsen. The Norwegians' attitude was not purely commercial. It involved moral considerations connected to the fate of Norway's Jews in the Holocaust, just as a year before France's decision to grant Israel military and nuclear assistance was connected to the abandonment of most of France's Jews to their fate in World War II.

Some 1,800 Jews had been living in Norway in 1940, on the eve of the German invasion and the flight of King Haakon VII and his government to exile in Britain. The German commissioner, Josef Terboven, abolished the monarchy, dispersed Norway's parliament, the Storting, and set up a national council comprised of collaborators, headed by the notorious Vidkun Quisling, whose name became a synonym for collaboration with occupiers. In October and November 1942, the Norwegian police helped the occupation forces round up 769 Jews and deport them to Germany. The Nazis sent them to the Auschwitz death camp and only 25 survived the war. Some 900 Norwegian Jews had escaped to Sweden before that, and were given asylum as refugees there. Another 100-odd Jews joined the Free Norwegian Forces based in London. An anti-Nazi underground was active in Norway, and in touch with the government-in-exile in London.

As in France, after the war the political and military leadership was based on the exiled government and the underground leadership. The collaboration with the Nazi occupation and the abandonment of almost half of the country's Jews to their tragic fate bothered the Norwegian national conscience. That was the moral aspect, to which was added an ideological consideration that sprang from political solidarity. In both Norway and Israel, in the postwar era, the Labor parties were the leading force in politics, and the ties between the leaderships of the parties were close. Like Ben-Gurion, Gerhardsen had headed the government for years, and he too was an adored leader in his country.

Norway's agreement to supply Israel with heavy water may also have been motivated by anger at the United States. The nuclear establishment headed by Randers was very unhappy about the American nuclear monopoly. In the early 1950s, the Norwegian leadership aspired to build an independent, profitable atomic industry but toward the middle of the decade, the American administration, and to a certain extent the British as well, pushed Norway off the nuclear playing field. Norway's joining NATO in 1954 marked the end of Randers's nuclear dream. The country no longer had a need for its own bomb. The American nuclear umbrella provided for its defense (unlike Sweden, which remained outside the alliance and neutral, and therefore was still weighing making a bomb in the mid-1950s). If during that period the United States had invited Israel to join NATO, and had extended its nuclear umbrella over it as well, there is no doubt that Israel would have done what Norway did, and given up its nuclear ambitions.

In the winter of 1958, when the negotiations on the heavy-water deal entered a practical track and the terms of purchase were being discussed, the issue of supervision came up in all its gravity. The Norwegian Foreign Ministry refused to step back from its demand that the agreement be based on inspection regulations, which at that very time were being formulated at the International Atomic Energy Agency in Vienna. Norsk Hydro, the production company, was hesitant about the deal because it had economic interests in Egypt, and even the support of some of the leading figures in Noratom cooled somewhat, due to apprehension over the American reaction. Randers turned to the Americans, and they advised him that the agreement should include an inspection requirement, but Israel resisted obstinately. The Foreign Ministry in Oslo was just as obstinate, and when it seemed that matters were dragging on too slowly, Israel tried a ploy that had proved itself time and again, inviting Randers and his wife to visit Israel as state guests and giving them the royal treatment. But this time it didn't work. The Norwegian Foreign Ministry would not give in, and Randers succeeded in persuading Bergmann to capitulate.

The agreement was signed in Oslo on February 25, 1959, when on the desert plain near Dimona, the skeleton structure of the reactor was already rising. The Israeli ambassador to Norway, Haim Yahil, and the Norwegian foreign minister, Halvard Lange, were the signatories. Israel undertook to use the heavy water for peaceful purposes, and agreed that Norway would have the right to inspect that this indeed was the case. However, Norway agreed that the inspection would be carried out not inside the reactor installation, but outside of it. Norway insisted, and Israel agreed, that when the IAEA regulations for the supervision of heavy water were drawn up, the task of inspection would be transferred to the international body.

Norway provided Israel with twenty tons of heavy water, with which it was possible to make hundreds of bombs. Because of a temporary shortage of stocks, Norway asked Britain, to which it had sold heavy water in the past, to sell back twenty-five tons and to deliver them directly to Israel. The Foreign Office had recommended that the Norwegian request be turned down, but the British Atomic Energy Authority endorsed it, relying on the supervision clause in Norway's contract with Israel, and the British government approved the deal. Eventually, Britain sent Dimona only twenty tons. One shipment of ten tons left Britain in June 1959 and another ten tons were sent in June 1960.

For many years, the inspection clause was dormant, and neither side was interested in activating it. In 1986 Mordechai Vanunu woke things up, creating a fairly complicated crisis between the two countries. But meanwhile, Israel had to contend with a new problem when Dimona was bared to the world.

CHAPTER SEVEN

Dimona Is Uncovered

THE MAN WHO FIRST BARED the secrets of Dimona to the outside world was Henry Jacob Gomberg, a Jewish professor of nuclear engineering in the physics department of the University of Michigan. "Israel, with French assistance is building a powerful nuclear reactor in the Negev, with the intention of producing weapons-grade uranium"—this was the gist of a detailed report that he handed to American intelligence early in December 1960, a few weeks before the end of Eisenhower's presidency and the swearing in of John F. Kennedy.

For the United States, Gomberg turned up two years too late. If they had cracked the secret in 1958, the Americans would have been able to kill the project. For Israel, Gomberg let the cat out of the bag two years too early. In 1962, the construction of the reactor would have been complete. Nevertheless, in retrospect it is clear that the damage he caused to Israel's nuclear program was not substantial, and in fact his revelations may well have been initiated by the heads of that program, the same people who until then had done everything possible to keep it secret.

Gomberg arrived in Israel for the first time in November 1960. He had been invited by the Israeli Atomic Energy Commission for consultations on the training of engineers and technicians to work in the small American research reactor in Nahal Soreq. At forty-two, he was recognized as a successful scientist. Born in Brooklyn, New York, in 1942 he joined the College of Engineering at the University of Michigan in Ann Arbor. After the World War, Gomberg took part in pioneering projects on the possibilities of utilizing fusion power for energy production. Over the years, he participated in initiating business enterprises based on his research in defense-related areas, and at least one of them—Ann Arbor Nuclear Israel Ltd., which he ran in the mid-1980s—was connected to Israeli nuclear research.

On his 1960 trip to Israel, Gomberg visited research institutes and laboratories and met senior officials of the defense establishment who had been coached in advance, and were accompanied by security personnel. Was he working for the CIA? Apparently not as an official agent, but before leaving the United States he had been briefed in the offices of the U.S. Atomic Energy Commission in Washington. He was asked to keep an eye open, and he was given the direct phone number of the American ambassador in Tel Aviv, Ogden Reid.

It was the urge to blabber on the part of some Israelis that ostensibly led to the exposure of the country's nuclear objectives. "Ostensibly" because Gomberg was almost certainly an unwitting part of a sophisticated Israeli ploy to let the Americans know about the reactor without infuriating the French. Gomberg listened attentively to the people that he met, put the facts together and reached the conclusion that in addition to the American research reactor in Nahal Soreq a second reactor was under construction at Dimona. It was not an experimental agricultural facility, as some of the Israelis would have him believe, but a French-made Marcoule-type reactor, which, he understood, Israel intended to use to produce plutonium for the purpose of developing nuclear weapons.

Stunned by his discovery, Gomberg hastened to contact Ambassador Reid and divulge his conclusion: In less than ten years' time, Israel would be in a position to build a bomb. The diplomat understood immediately that what Gomberg was telling him meant the Middle East would never be the same. He advised Gomberg to leave Israel immediately and fly to Paris, and from the U.S. Embassy there to cable his findings to Washington. This advice was well-considered, and Gomberg complied immediately. He had uncovered a state secret of the highest order and because he did not have diplomatic immunity he might be arrested if his conversation with the ambassador was being recorded, or if he cabled Washington from Israel and the security services intercepted the wire.[1]

On November 26, 1960, a coded, classified cable was sent from the U.S. Embassy in Paris to the secretary of state in Washington, reporting that Gomberg had arrived from Israel with urgent and secret information. Formulated in cable-ese, it said that Gomberg "claims personal friend Ben-Gurion told him one week ago that within three weeks Israel would announce five-year plan simultaneously revealing construction nuclear power plant vicinity Beersheba."

Gomberg was instructed to return to the United States immediately and on December 1 he met in Washington with representatives of the AEC, the State Department, and the CIA, and expounded on his findings. His impression was that the construction of the reactor had been under way for about two years, and it would be completed in another year's time, at the end of 1961. The French would supply the uranium for its operation. Israel was interested in extracting plutonium. His information came from various sources, but it was mainly based on a talk with Ernst David Bergmann, the scientific director of the project, who was the "personal friend" of Ben-Gurion's mentioned in the cable. Later, he sat down and wrote up a detailed report:

> I was completely unprepared for the magnitude of the effort in Israel or for the attitude of some of the Israelis in regard to it. What I learned about the large classified project near Beersheba all came indirectly. I spoke with a number of high placed Israelis who were forced to acknowledge the existence of the classified effort in order that any use might be made of my consultative capabilities, but no one spoke to me of it in detail or gave any direct information about it. For this reason I prefer to keep the names of the Israeli officials with whom I spoke, and who were placed in the position of having to acknowledge some of the characterization of the classified project, to myself.

In astonishment, he relates how his interlocutors were surprised when he questioned them about the aims of the nuclear training they were planning.

> As soon as the conversation started it immediately became apparent that the Israelis had not anticipated that to discuss nuclear training with me they would have to reveal the objectives of which the train-

ing was being conducted. As a result I had to ask pertinent questions, the responses to which immediately revealed the existence of a very important project, which the Israeli officials could not discuss with me. This impression was fortified with each of the conversations I had in Israel until it overshadowed everything else about my trip there.

It was the number of students that Israel was preparing for nuclear engineering work that exposed an anomaly, Gomberg wrote. To implement its overt nuclear project, the American research reactor at Nahal Soreq, only a small number of professional workers were needed. But at the Weizmann Institute alone, twenty to thirty people had been trained in an intensive nuclear engineering course, in areas that were not required to operate the Nahal Soreq reactor. Gomberg wrote that one Israeli scientist revealed to him that RAFAEL's Institute 4 was due to receive small quantities of plutonium and polonium,[2] and from the way he spoke, Gomberg realized that France would be providing Israel with enriched uranium.

The next day, Washington cabled Gomberg's report to Ambassador Reid in Tel Aviv and requested confirmation, and the day after, December 3, Reid went to see Bergmann, who told him that within a week Ben-Gurion would make a statement on the nuclear research reactor Israel was building in the Negev. It would be moderated by heavy water, Bergmann told the ambassador, its output would be between 10 and 20 megawatts, and it would begin to function in about a year and a half.

The only difference between Gomberg's report and Bergmann's clarifications to the ambassador was in the definition of the purpose of the reactor. Gomberg described a facility designed to produce plutonium, while Bergmann spoke of a research reactor. The next day, Gomberg was called to another meeting with administration officials in Washington, and repeated his conclusion. The officials believed this conclusion, and not Bergmann's claims, to be the truth. In fact, from that day on the American government related to Israel as a state suspected of aiming to build a bomb. To the American intelligence community, Gomberg's report was in the nature of a watershed. Until he came along, only circumstantial evidence against Israel had been collected. He placed the evidence in context.

So were the Israelis who met and talked with him total idiots? Is it at all possible that they did not foresee that consulting a foreign expert on the training of experts for operating a nuclear reactor would arouse his suspicion that they were in fact building such a reactor? And when scientists and officials were given permission to talk to him, were they expected to discuss archaeology?

It is my opinion that Gomberg had been selected in advance to serve as the conduit to the American administration. Not that the AEC leadership ordered scientists and technicians intentionally to whisper the secret of Dimona into his ear, but exposing them to Gomberg was enough. The background to the affair was this: In mid-1960, the directors of the project had realized that the wall of secrecy surrounding Dimona was weakening. Two years had passed since the launch of the program, and the tracks left in the sand, so to speak, could no longer be concealed. Hundreds of people were employed on the project in Israel and in France—scientists, foremen, drivers, builders. Scores of Frenchmen were living in Beersheba, and no effort was being made to hide their conspicuous presence among the local population. And what's more, to anyone traveling on or near the plain south of Dimona, a remarkable sight revealed itself: a formidable fence, a network of roads, mobile patrols of armed guards, and a gigantic dome that left little to the imagination. The foreign press was sniffing around, foreign military attachés undertook desert reconnaissance trips, and more and more Israelis began asking each other what was really happening at Dimona. The Defense Ministry in Tel Aviv began to understand that the secret was slipping away from its keepers, and it was decided that to keep the hungry lion at bay, it was worth throwing him a chunk of meat.

THE UNITED STATES was interested in uncovering information on countries suspected of concealing clandestine nuclear projects. Known in international jargon as the "nth countries,"[3] they were considered the most likely candidates for nuclear weapons proliferation. But when it came to Dimona, it was British intelligence that excelled. Official documents recently declassified by the British government make it clear that its agents were the first to uncover both Israel's nuclear aspirations and the French-Israeli connection. The information that they gathered was accurate, and had they been interested in baring it to the world, the British could have revealed what Israel was doing as early as 1959 and jeopardized the future of the project.

The first suspicions about Israel's nuclear project were registered in Britain in 1958, when two Israelis visited British nuclear installations separately: the director of the Dimona project, Mannes Prat, and the head of the Defense Ministry's research and development authority, Dan Tolkowsky. The visits were arranged by the military attaché at the Israeli Embassy, Yuval Neeman, who was at the same time completing his doctorate in physics in London. In the Middle Eastern section of the Foreign Office, someone composed a brief memorandum headed, "Why is Israel interested in nuclear power?"

Part of the answer to this question turned up at the British Embassy in Tel Aviv in April 1959. British documents reveal that an unidentified source leaked to the embassy passages from a speech that the director general of the Israeli Ministry of Defense, Shimon Peres, had made at the Weizmann Institute that January. I have already mentioned that in his speech Peres had shown his anger at Amos de Shalit, alleging that his research was marked by "a surfeit of theory," at a time that Israel was "developing secret weaponry." The British ambassador, Patrick Francis Hancock, had trouble interpreting the latter phrase—did it refer to missiles or nuclear arms? So he invited the president of the Institute, Meyer Weisgal, to dinner. His guest did not disappoint him and let his tongue run loose. A dispute had emerged in the Defense Ministry, Weisgal told his host. Peres was keen to get the bomb, but had run into opposition. One of the opponents was Dan Tolkowsky, who had investigated the matter thoroughly and written a report opining that if Israel built a bomb, the Soviet Union would be obliged to supply the Arabs with one too. Ben-Gurion, Weisgal told the ambassador, was positioned between the two. He wanted to build a nuclear reactor, and only after its construction would he decide whether to acquire nuclear capability. The British Embassy conveyed the information to the American naval attaché in Israel, Captain George William Kittredge, who cabled it to Washington in May.[4] The CIA asked the military attaché in Tel Aviv to substantiate the reports from his own sources, but he couldn't do this, so the information was labeled dubious by the Americans.

The British were also the first (apart from the French, of course) to learn that in 1959 and 1960, Norway had sold twenty tons of heavy water to Israel. As mentioned earlier, Norway asked Britain, to which it had sold heavy water in the past, to sell back twenty-five tons and send them direct to Israel. Eventually, Britain shipped to Israel only twenty tons. The shipment of the last five tons was cancelled due to the fact that in December 1960, when the cargo was ready to leave Britain, information had been leaked to the press that Israel was constructing a nuclear reactor in Dimona and intended to build a nuclear bomb. Those were years when international control over the sale of materials that could be used for nuclear armaments was tenuous. Although the United States applied its own supervision measures strictly, they did not obligate its allies. The British therefore sent the twenty tons of heavy water that Norway had requested to Israel, and in the first week of December 1960, they reported the deal to American intelligence. Early in 1961, when a thorough investigation was carried out in Washington over the failure of American intelligence to discover the Israeli project, it transpired that two arms of the U.S. administration—the State Department and the AEC—had received information about the heavy water deal in July 1959. These reports had been filed away and forgotten.

In early 1956, Bergmann had asked the American AEC to approve the sale of ten tons of heavy water. It had been approved, on condition that the U.S. be permitted to maintain control over its use, a condition that led Israel to abandon the idea, as mentioned earlier. But the fact that the request had been made was conveyed to the CIA in July 1956, and then pigeonholed. If a serious analysis of the Israeli request had been made then, it might have aroused the suspicion that Israel was planning to build a reactor more powerful than the one that the Americans had supplied, and to use it for purposes other than civilian ones. In fact, five full years went by between Israel's request to Norway and American intelligence's linking it to the erection of the reactor at Dimona.

The American intelligence community began gathering and analyzing material on Israel's nuclear activities only in January 1956. For over two years, Israel was classified at the third grade of priority, at the bottom of the list of the "nth countries." On September 15, 1958, it was elevated by one grade, to the second level. The change reflected an American decision to keep a closer eye on Israel's activities, but it had already missed the train by then, as the nuclear deal between France and Israel had been signed almost a year earlier, in October 1957. The change in Israel's grading was apparently the result of two meetings between officials of the U.S. Embassy in Tel Aviv and Bergmann, early in 1958. In January, at Washington's request, Bergmann was interviewed and gave a general description of an Israeli interest in producing nuclear energy. He said Israel had produced small quantities of heavy water and uranium from its own resources. After the CIA had studied his remarks, its directorate asked the Tel Aviv embassy three times—in March, June, and July—to obtain more detailed information. The second secretary at the embassy held another meeting with Bergmann and heard from him that Israel had indeed decided to construct a heavy water reactor, but had not yet determined how powerful it would be. In Washington officials reached the conclusion that Bergmann was referring to the American nuclear research facility, and that Israel was not planning an additional reactor. Nevertheless, the suspicion remained, and it was decided that the CIA would step up its surveillance, mainly through aerial photography.

Thus, as of early 1958, once or twice a week a U-2 spy plane would take off from the U.S. Air Force base at Incirlik, Turkey, and after flying over Syria and Lebanon enter Israeli airspace and begin taking photographs from 70,000 feet up of military bases and airfields. Once, totally by coincidence, the construction site at Dimona was also snapped. Israeli radar detected the overflights of a foreign plane, but there was no way of knowing who had dispatched it. The Israeli Air Force could not intercept it, because its most advanced aircraft was the French Super Mystere, which could not fly higher than 60,000 feet.[5] On one of its sorties, the U-2 photographed an artillery firing range in the Negev. When the pictures were studied in Washington, analysts discerned a suspicious site, with a great deal of building activity, a network of roads, and a long perimeter fence. But they failed to conclude what the purpose of the site was. Only with hindsight, in early 1961, immediately after Gomberg's revelations, were the pictures scrutinized once more. Then it became clear that the early stages of the construction of the reactor were to be seen in the aerial photographs.

For an entire year, from mid-1958 to mid-1959, American intelligence failed to obtain substantial information about the Israeli nuclear program. The first report on the building site in the Negev reached American intelligence channels in the middle of 1959, from "special intelligence sources," the nature of which is not known. It was discounted by the analysts in Washington, because other information in the same item was demonstrably untrue.

In December 1959, the Americans were given a golden opportunity to positively identify the Franco-Israeli nuclear connection. Apparently there were suspicions that such a connection existed, and the CIA briefed its agents to find out if Israeli representatives were to be invited to witness the first French nuclear test, to be held in the Algerian Sahara. And indeed, early in 1960, the agency received a report that a certain Israeli representative was due to watch the test. But when it was held, on February 13, the CIA was unable to ascertain if Israelis had been present or not. In fact, at least two were there, and one of them photographed the proceedings and screened the slides later for project personnel. He also showed his family slides taken at a Jewish school in Oran that he had visited. He brought his daughter a doll in traditional Muslim dress, with blue eyes and a tattoo on its forehead. "If your friends ask you, tell them it's from France," he told her.

The most compelling report reached the CIA in August 1960. An American woman, who worked as a secretary at the U.S. Embassy in Tel Aviv, was touring in the Negev with her Israeli boyfriend. When they were near Dimona, he told her that France was building a nuclear reactor there. In Beersheba later, he introduced her to some Frenchmen who were working on the Dimona site. They told her that it was all very hush-hush. Back in Tel Aviv, she told her boss in the political department of the embassy about it, and he cabled her tale to Washington, but at the CIA they ascribed no importance to the account.

That summer, little Israel was humming with rumors about Dimona. They reached the ears of Professor Eugene Wigner of Princeton University, who was teaching in Israel at that time. After he returned to the United States he said at a meeting of the president's scientific advisory committee on December 19 that he had driven past the Dimona installation, and that it was referred to as a power reactor site. Although he spoke about it openly, the CIA failed to verify his information.

That September, Bergmann leaked information like a broken faucet. At a meeting in Vienna with Lawrence B. Hall, assistant general manager of the American AEC for international affairs, he informed the American that Israel was building a reactor and that it was eager to accumulate stocks of uranium, because it had hopes of extracting plutonium from them. The aim was to complete the construction by April or May of 1961, he revealed, and invited Hall to "come and see it some time." Only two months later did Hall report on his conversation with Bergmann to Charles Reichardt, the AEC's head of intelligence. The information was distributed to the American intelligence community more than a month after Gomberg had provided the definitive proof.

While these reports were filtering through, the American and British military attachés in Tel Aviv were vying to put the pieces of the puzzle together. In July 1960, the American attaché, Eugene T. Seaburn, toured the Negev with an Israeli escort officer. They saw the Dimona building site from a distance, and the Israeli officer said it was a metallurgical laboratory. The attaché went back to the site on August 7, this time with a camera. He took high-quality pictures, but couldn't identify a nuclear reactor among the images. On a third Negev trip, in November, he was told once more that it was a metallurgical laboratory. Only in early December, after Gomberg's revelations and when the pieces of information about the reactor had formed a clear picture, did the CIA examine his photographs again; this time they discerned the skeleton of the reactor dome. Meanwhile, the British military attaché had also visited the vicinity of the site a number of times and in early November, shortly before Gomberg collated his findings, he produced some excellent photographs, copies of which were sent to Washington.

According to Israeli sources, an American reconnaissance satellite first photographed Dimona in September 1960. It was one of the Corona military satellites, operated under a CIA program and used from June 1959 for surveillance of the Soviet Union, China, and the Middle East. The objectives of the photographic mission had been set in consultations in which CIA Director Allen Dulles took part. The satellites were fitted with advanced photographic equipment, which produced high-resolution images. In the course of time, images from all over the world have been released for publication, except high-resolution images that were taken over Israel. (It is possible that those images were censored because the reactor is clearly visible in them, and if they were published the Americans would not be able to deny that they were aware of its existence.) The analysis of the pictures taken by the military attachés, and apparently also the satellite's images, supplemented the information provided by Gomberg, and in early December political activity on the Dimona issue gathered momentum. At a meeting of the National Security Council in Washington on December 2, Dulles announced that the CIA and the AEC were convinced that Dimona was "not meant for only peaceful purposes." The language was cautious, phrased in the negative, but within a few days the wording would become sharper.

On December 8, in the light of the Gomberg report, the CIA drew up a special national intelligence assessment on the subject of Dimona, and the director summed it up for outgoing President Eisenhower in a more explicit formulation: Israel is building a nuclear complex in the Negev that will apparently include a reactor capable of producing weapons-grade plutonium. The following day, Secretary of State Christian Herter summoned the Israeli ambassador, Avraham "Abe" Harman, showed him the photographs taken by the military attaché, and spelled out clearly that the United States, on the strength of its intelligence assessments, suspected Israel was planning to manufacture nuclear weaponry. Herter warned him of the repercussions of the action. Herter demanded that the ambassador produce all the relevant facts, and Harman played the innocent, claiming that he had no information on the subject. Afterward, Herter telephoned the chargé d'affaires at the French Embassy in Washington and expressed his surprise at the fact that since 1958 France had been helping Israel build "a reactor which is at least ten times as large as claimed." Herter added that "it appeared from the design [of the reactor] that it was not intended for power but for plutonium which in a comparatively short time would give them considerable weapon potential." The French diplomat, like Harman, also claimed ignorance, saying that he knew "less than nothing" about the matter.

Media reports were not long in cropping up, based on leaks from the British and American governments. On Tuesday, December 13, *Time* magazine scooped the world with a news item reading: "A small power which is neither Communist nor a member of NATO is developing a nuclear option." It was clear that there was only one country that fit the description. On Friday of the same week, Chapman Pincher, the scientific correspondent of the London *Daily Express*, reported that Israel was building an experimental bomb. The Israeli Embassy in London immediately issued a denial: "Israel is not building an atom bomb and has no intention of doing so."

On Sunday, December 18, the chairman of the American AEC, John A. McCone, was interviewed on CBS's *Meet the Press*. Possession of a reactor was not in itself enough for building a bomb, he asserted, but it was possible to use it to extract plutonium, which could be used to make a bomb.

The next day, when Jews were lighting the sixth candle of the Jewish festival of Hanukkah, the *New York Times* weighed in with a detailed news report of its own. On the front page, correspondent John W. Finney reported: "United States officials are studying with mounting concern recent evidence indicating that Israel, with the assistance of France, may be developing the capacity to produce atomic weapons." The item included a denial from Bergmann, who said the report was "flattering but untrue." The *Times* said that Israel had deceived the United States by telling it that the reactor was a textile plant. (In fact, a textile factory had been set up in Dimona, by the Kitan Textiles concern, but identifying it with the reactor had been a bluff.)

The publication in the *New York Times* somewhat disconcerted the fathers of the Israeli nuclear program. They were far from accustomed to media disclosure of security matters, and certainly not to leaks about the nation's most secret project, and they did not know how to handle the situation. A few days later, Ben-Gurion would meet Ambassador Reid and express his surprise that anything and everything could be published in the United States; after all, Ben-Gurion was used to dictating to the Israeli media what news was fit to print, and what would be censored. Ben-Gurion was evidently stressed. The publication would obligate the administration in Washington to issue an official statement. Would the official American reaction place the continued development of the project in jeopardy?

Ben-Gurion would have sighed in relief had details reached him of the discussion that took place that very day, December 19, in the president's office in the White House. It was the most important meeting on the subject of Israel that had taken place since the Suez Campaign, and amazingly, the outcome was highly favorable from Israel's point of view. In some ways, what happened that day in the White House was something of a Hanukkah miracle.

Attending the White House parley were the top figures of the administration. Apart from Eisenhower, there were Secretary of State Christian A. Herter; CIA Director Allen Dulles; Chairman of the Atomic Energy Commission John A. McCone; Defense Secretary Thomas S. Gates; the chairman of the joint chiefs of staff, General Lyman L. Lemnitzer; Treasury Secretary Robert B. Anderson; and various advisers and aides. The facts expounded before the president left no room for doubt: Most of the government agencies were united in the belief that Israel was determined to build an atomic bomb.

According to the records of the meeting, Herter opened the discussion by saying that "the group had come in to talk about the problem raised by information they had received to the effect that the Israelis are operating a plutonium production plant." He said that "he had a statement, which he proposed to make public by the State Department, stressing that the Israelis assert this plant is for peaceful purposes." Gates remarked that "our information is that the plant is not for peaceful purposes." The president's special assistant for science and technology, Dr. George Kistiakowsky,[6] remarked that there was some doubt that Israel was building a bomb, as there was no chemical plant for plutonium extraction at the site. (Another five or six words of his were censored out of the record.) McCone replied that the AEC believed a plutonium extraction plant was in fact under construction there. "The Israelis would not build such a plant just to do part of the job," McCone declared.

It was clear to the participants in the meeting that the gravity of the revelations and the reports in the media obliged the United States to issue an official reaction. And bizarrely, more than the actual political and military repercussions of the Israeli project, they were concerned with the wording of their reaction, and the level at which it should be issued. Since the White House had no interest in revealing its suspicion that Israel was building a bomb, how could the statement be phrased to express the seriousness of the subject, but at the same time keeping it a secret from the rest of the world? And should it be the president who reacts, or the secretary of state?

Eisenhower drew the attention of the meeting to the matter of the source of funding for the project, and various theories were floated: American aid, foreign bank loans, diversion of private and public assistance monies. The president observed that the cost of the project was estimated at between $100 million and $200 million. "We do not know where they obtained the funds, but have a proper interest in this because of the aid we are giving them," he remarked. Herter opined that as far as the funding was concerned, "We could go very far in our demands." Treasury Secretary Anderson added, "They have been sending money out without control over the purposes for which it is extended. There is a real question as to whether these contributions qualify as tax-deductible." The discussion of the finances took up a considerable part of the meeting, and it is worth noting that the sensitivity of this issue is precisely why Israel has to this day preserved the anonymity of the list of "sanctifiers."

The need for supervision of the Israeli project was also discussed at length. McCone thought the United States should insist that Israel be subject to the inspection regulations of the International Atomic Energy Agency. Gates said the official statement should say that the United States expects Israel to open the site to inspection, and Herter observed, "They might reply that they will do so when the U.S. permits inspection of its plants." The president responded sharply: "We do not conceal that our plants are for weapons material production, nor do we make any claim that such production is peaceful." Dulles remarked that "the Israelis seem to be trying to confuse this plant, which is a large production installation, with the very small research reactor on which we are helping them." Dulles, it turns out, was aware of Bergmann's diversionary tactics.

The anticipated reaction of other countries was briefly discussed. Gates said the decisive question was the extent of France's involvement in the project. Dulles warned that "the Soviets and the Arabs are going to cause all the trouble they possibly can" and Herter responded, "This is the reason we are sending this note. We are at least removing ourselves from suspicion." Eisenhower observed that the problem was more complicated, "in that we are now face to face with the question of what to do as farther countries become atomic producers." Herter said that "it may still be possible to head off this production by the Israelis."

The president asked if he himself should issue the statement, noting that then it would become official administration policy, but Herter said it should come from him, the secretary of state. It was important to make it clear that the Americans did not as yet have authoritative information on the Israeli project, the president said, in instructing Herter to make sure that the statement would be cautious and balanced, explaining, "We have simply a report made ten days ago, which was the cause of our concern [referring to Gomberg's revelation]." It was decided that the statement would be the responsibility of the State Department, and that any other department that wanted to react would do so in coordination with Secretary Herter.

In the declassified records of this meeting, the authorities deleted two short passages, but it is unlikely that they would have affected the conclusion that can be drawn: The uppermost echelon of the American government clearly had no intention of making Israel cancel its project, or even freeze it. Although the secretary of state suggested examining this possibility, no one supported him. The president's reaction was very moderate. He expressed no apprehension whatsoever about any possible danger that the United States, NATO, or the world might face if Israel acquired a nuclear deterrent. The possible reactions of the Arabs and the Soviets were mentioned only on the margins of the debate.

The two operative decisions that emerged from the White House meeting were, from Israel's point of view, decidedly unthreatening: The United States would endeavor to institute American or international supervision over the Israeli project, and the Treasury secretary would determine whether money donated by American Jews to the project had illegally enjoyed the tax deductions allowed for charitable gifts. Israel was therefore able to breathe freely. The American government was almost certain that the Jewish state was aiming to produce an ultimate weapon, but was prepared to pretend to the world that the Israeli nuclear project's purposes were peaceful. It is doubtful that three years earlier, after the Suez crisis, any reasonable political observer could have believed that the Eisenhower administration would have allowed Israel to take the first steps on the path to becoming a regional power, and a nuclear one to boot. Was this the start of a strategic turnabout in America's attitude to Israel?

On the same day as the top-level meeting in the White House, the French Foreign Ministry issued a statement that concealed far more than it revealed. It denied that France was helping Israel build a nuclear reactor, claiming that the only assistance Paris was extending was the supply of an experimental installation for the production of heavy water for natural uranium, exactly the same as Canada had given to India.7 The next day, on December 20, Herter met once again with Israeli Ambassador Harman, and received the first official report on the subject from him. Harman confirmed that for the past year and a half, a nuclear reactor for peaceful purposes had been under construction at Dimona. France had helped Israel, as had other countries to a very small degree (he probably meant Norway and Great Britain, which provided heavy water). The reactor had an output of 24 megawatts and its purpose was the development of industrial, agricultural, and medical science. The building would take another three or four years to complete. "Tomorrow," the ambassador told the secretary, "the prime minister will officially unveil the project in the Knesset."

The next day, the eighth and last day of Hanukkah, suspense reigned in the Knesset. For a few days, rumors had been rife in Israel that Ben-Gurion was due to make an important declaration. It took the form not of an official statement initiated by the government, but of a reply by the prime minister to parliamentary questions submitted by two Knesset members regarding the activities at Dimona. The Knesset regulations allowed Ben-Gurion to defer his reply for as long as he desired. But he decided to respond after it became clear to him that a confrontation with the Eisenhower administration was not to be expected. He wore his usual simple khaki clothes, but his voice betrayed his excitement:

> We are presently engaged in building a research reactor with a 24,000 thermal kilowatt (24 megawatt) output, to serve the purposes of industry, agriculture, medicine and science, and to train scientific and technical Israeli manpower . . . The research reactor we are now building in the Negev will not be completed before three or

four years' time. This reactor, like the American reactor, is meant to be used only for peaceful purposes, and is being built under the direction of Israeli experts. On its completion, it will be open to trainees from other countries as well, and it is similar to the reactor that the government of Canada helped to erect in India, although ours will have a smaller output.

Ben-Gurion emphatically denied the reports published abroad that Israel was making a bomb. "This is a false report, either wittingly or unwittingly," he stressed. France was not mentioned in the statement, and neither was Norway. There was no reference to the American reaction. There was not a word about the cost, the energy-producing systems, or the materials that would be used to operate the reactor. There was no reference to any environmental aspects. One sentence related to Israel's neighbors: "Israel proposes general and absolute disarmament in Israel and in the neighboring Arab states, under mutual inspection."

After Ben-Gurion's statement, the Knesset continued with its routine business. Parliamentary procedure did not allow for a debate after a ministerial reply to a question. This was the first time that the citizens of Israel had heard an official confirmation, from the prime minister himself, of the persistent rumors that had been going around the country for years to the effect that a gigantic defense construction project was under way in the Negev. I remember the excitement that I felt as a sixteen-year-old, and that the reaction of the adults around me was restrained. In those days, security matters were discussed behind closed doors, the citizens did not demand to be informed, and the media was not accustomed to inform. In an age of innocence, when the internal strength of society sprang from confidence and faith in itself and its leaders, the citizens of Israel had learned to understand reality mainly from what was left unsaid.

On the same day, Ben-Gurion's statement was read verbatim over Kol Yisrael, the Voice of Israel, the state radio station and the only station in the country that broadcast news. No analysis or commentary was added, no debate on the environmental or moral implications. The print media followed suit the next day. Nevertheless, there can be no doubt that Israeli old-timers understood that the prime minister was planning to create a nuclear option.

Following Ben-Gurion's disclosure, the State Department published the statement whose principles had been hammered out at the White House. The United States welcomed the declaration that the reactor was meant for purely peaceful purposes, and asserted that in this case there was no cause for particular concern. It was a more generous formulation than Israel had hoped for, and the tension that had grown up between the two countries eased.

On December 24, 1960, three days after Ben-Gurion's statement in the Knesset, U.S. Ambassador Reid called on Ben-Gurion at his home in Tel Aviv, conveyed the president's best wishes for the New Year, and had a "serious discussion" about the reactor (to quote a cable from Reid to Washington after the meeting). Reid handed the premier a message from Washington, concerned mainly with the implementation of supervision. The United States was eager to receive a full report on the Israeli project, including its plans for the "removal" of the plutonium created in the reactor, the message said.

The administration really meant that Israel must provide information on what use it meant to make of the plutonium. Nevertheless, the U.S. government does not wish "to exaggerate or prolong this issue," the ambassador told Ben-Gurion. That is the key phrase, precisely reflecting the American position from December 1960 to this day, except perhaps for a brief period of confrontation during the administration of President Kennedy. Reid stressed how important to the president were his "Atoms for Peace" initiative and the principle of the nonproliferation of nuclear weapons. "In response the Prime Minister expressed mild irritation over publication in states of so much data re project. Smiling, he said, why in states is everything being told everybody," Reid wrote in his cable.

For his part, Ben-Gurion called the State Department reaction to his Knesset statement "very decent," and added that "he was very sorry that he has not been able to tell President Eisenhower of this project during his recent visit to Washington [in March 1960]. And said that were it not so close to end of Eisenhower administration, he would wish to give personal account to President, whom he had long known and admired."

The conversation was very friendly, devoid of tensions and anger. Ben-Gurion was relaxed, and even found time to chat about his vision for the development of the Negev. He quoted Homi Jehangir Bhabha, the founder of the Indian atomic energy program, who had told him that the future belonged to cheap energy produced from the atom. He never responded when the ambassador asked "whether there might be any feasibility in having a scientist have a look at this project." (But through other channels Israel informed Washington that when things calmed down, it would enable experts from the United States and other friendly states to visit the site.) It's noteworthy that Reid used the casual phrase "have a look." In a short while, with Kennedy laying down the line on nuclear nonproliferation, Americans would be using the word "inspection" in their discourse with Israel.

When the flurry of activity over the baring of the Dimona reactor died down, the American administration was free to study the lessons of the entire affair. In late January 1961, the CIA placed a seventeen-page report on the desk of new president John F. Kennedy. It contained a detailed analysis of the failure of the American intelligence community to identify the Israeli nuclear project much earlier. The conclusion was unequivocal: From the moment that the first hints of Israel's nuclear activities began coming in, almost three years had been wasted on investigating false leads. Since April 1958, American and foreign—including Israeli—sources had fed American intelligence agencies with dozens of pieces of information on Israel's secret nuclear project, but those in charge of analyzing and assessing the data had failed to focus on the important nuggets, failed to organize them into a clear picture, and failed to appreciate their collective significance. The agencies had not shared much of the information with each other. Differences among them in their style of collection and analysis of intelligence had led to misunderstandings. Information had flowed along the wrong channels or had gathered dust in pigeonholes or had gotten lost in tortuous pipelines. (These conclusions are something of a premonition of the findings of the Joint Congressional Inquiry into the activities of the U.S. intelligence community in connection with the terrorist attacks of September 11, 2001. Anyone studying and comparing them will find common symptoms.)

The CIA report on the failure to identify the Dimona project determined that there was a problem of relying on a preconception: "The general feeling that Israel could not achieve this capability without outside aid from the U.S. or its allies, and the belief that any such aid would be readily known to the U.S., led to the tendency to discount rumors of Israeli reactor construction and French collaboration in the nuclear weapons area."

Also included in the report were bureaucratic excuses: At CIA headquarters there was a shortage of professional personnel, and the U.S. Embassy in Tel Aviv lacked a scientific attaché. Indeed, the report states, since 1956 instructions had occasionally been given to the American embassies in Tel Aviv and Paris to keep an eye on the military cooperation between France and Israel, and American diplomats assigned to Tel Aviv had been briefed to watch for activities in the nuclear sphere, but the surveillance was sporadic. The report pointed out that officials in Israel had disseminated contradictory and confusing information. Bergmann, for instance, changed his version frequently. The compilers of the report did not blame only the errors of American intelligence agencies for the failure; they also considered France, an ally that had acted behind America's back, to be partly responsible. The most egregious instance happened in November 1960 when a representative of the U.S. Atomic Energy Commission attached to the U.S. Embassy met with an official of the French nuclear agency, the CEA, and told him that the United States was aware of "the construction of the nuclear power plant in Beersheba." When he asked for details of the French role, "This individual stated flatly that the French CEA is not collaborating with the Israeli government in the construction of a nuclear power reactor. Furthermore he said that no French company is working with the Israelis on a power reactor since prior permission from the CEA would be required and such permission has neither been requested nor granted."

A week later, on November 27, the CEA had second thoughts and amended its reply to the American request for information. The earlier answer had been incomplete, the French agency explained, and the actual situation was that France was indeed helping Israel build a heavy-water uranium-fueled reactor.

The compilers of the American report admitted that the material gathered in the United States was incomplete: "We lack information on the size, type and numbers of reactors involved and hence their plutonium production potential." This situation prevails to this day. Despite the disclosures of Mordechai Vanunu, the Dimona technician turned whistleblower, on the output of the reactor and its plutonium-production capacity, and despite the massive cooperation between the two countries on security matters, the Americans are still groping in the dark on certain aspects of Israel's nuclear option, testimony to Israel's success in maintaining secrecy over information that it sees as essential to its survival.

As for Henry Gomberg, did the Mossad pursue the scientist for divulging the national secret? No, because in the game of charades Israel was playing with the United States, he had been cast as the messenger. Before meeting him, Bergmann consulted with Ben-Gurion and Peres. Together they formulated the message they wanted him to convey to the Americans, and the timing of its dispatch. Their judgment was correct: It would not be appropriate for the Americans to learn of the secret after everyone else, or for Ben-Gurion to make a statement in the Knesset before the administration in Washington had been apprised of its content. There is no way that the Israeli AEC would have invited Gomberg and shown him Institute 4, where the main nuclear research was made, without the policy makers having taken into account that he would immediately report what he had seen.

At least two elements in the U.S. administration were anxious about Gomberg's fate, and one official of the U.S. AEC inquired whether it was necessary to provide him with bodyguards. But there was no need for such a measure. The Mossad never hunted him down and Israel bore him no grudge. On the contrary. Had he not received affirmation of his suspicions from Bergmann himself?

In the ensuing years, Gomberg went from strength to strength in his scientific work. His links with the U.S. AEC continued, as did his relationship with Israel. But no details of his dealings with Israel have ever been revealed. Together with some American colleagues, Gomberg published pioneering research papers and developed techniques for identifying radioactive elements in metals through autoradiography (creation of an X-ray photograph, which shows the presence of radioactive material). In the mid-1970s he served as chairman of KMS Fusion Inc., a start-up company in Ann Arbor that set up the most advanced laboratory for laser-induced nuclear reactions in the world. The executive scientist of the company was the 1961 Nobel physics laureate Robert Hofstadter, and he and Gomberg devised methods for creating energy through laser-induced fusion in a deuterium-tritium pellet, methods that have both civilian and military applications. The company closed down eventually, because the federal government did not countenance such sensitive defense research being conducted by a private firm.

CHAPTER EIGHT

De Gaulle Throws a Monkey Wrench in the Works

ON A CLEAR SPRING MORNING in April 1960, Dror Sadeh, one of the Israelis engaged in nuclear research in France as part of the Franco-Israeli agreement, drove his small Citroën from his home in Paris to his laboratory in Saclay. The car had a *plaque rouge*—French for the red license plate of a diplomat's vehicle. As he always did, Sadeh parked in the lot close to his lab, walking distance from the nuclear reactor complex. He had no idea that on the same day an important guest was expected at Saclay—no less than Charles de Gaulle, who would be accompanied by a large entourage headed by Francis Perrin, head of the French Atomic Energy Commission (CEA).

Two years earlier, on June 1, 1958, in the midst of a political and economic crisis, de Gaulle had condescended to end his self-declared internal exile at Colombey-les-Deux-Églises, and to return to Paris to lead France. Algeria was in flames, inflation was soaring, and the stock exchange was collapsing. The commanders of paratroop units in the French army, headed by General Jacques Massu, had met on the island of Corsica to plan a military rebellion.[1]

De Gaulle was the last prime minister of the Fourth Republic. In September he had presented a new constitution to the people, who approved it by a large majority in a referendum, paving the way for the declaration of the Fifth Republic. In December, 78 percent of all the French had elected him president with expanded powers. Michel Debré, an ardent supporter of French Algeria, and a good friend of Israel, was named prime minister. Jacques Soustelle, another staunch supporter of Israel, was minister of energy, in charge of the CEA. According to the new constitution, the president had a decisive say on matters of defense and foreign affairs.

In the very same months, between May and December 1958, the CEA, together with the Israeli scientific attaché, Shalhevet Freier, was putting the finishing touches to the preparations for the construction of the nuclear reactor at Dimona, and its related installations. Most of the French professional experts had already been recruited and some had already been sent to Israel; equipment for Dimona had been manufactured in various plants in France.

In the first two years of his presidency, de Gaulle carried out far-reaching strategic moves. He distanced France from the spheres of influence of the two great powers, and was endeavoring to achieve the status of an independent military power for his country by accelerating the pace of development of an atomic bomb.[2] This objective reached fruition at the first French nuclear test in February 1960. (Toward the end of his term of office in 1966, de Gaulle made another strategic move, removing France from the integrated military command of NATO.[3])

In each of the steps he took to strengthen the army and speed up the acquisition of the bomb, de Gaulle received the full cooperation of the defense establishment. This was also true on the Algerian issue, as long as the army's orders were to suppress the FLN rebellion and to keep Algeria French. In July 1958, de Gaulle was brought up to date on the cooperation between the armed forces of France and Israel. He noted in his diary that he had learned of "inappropriate cooperation that had grown between Tel Aviv and Paris after the Suez Campaign, leading to Israeli officers being posted permanently at all levels of the French military." The president ordered that the relations be severed, but his defense establishment did not obey him. Moreover, the details of the nuclear agreement with Israel were never laid before the president. Energy Minister Soustelle held back the information. The cooperation with Israel far exceeded what was customary in international relations in this area, and Soustelle feared that de Gaulle would put an end to it, and that as a result Israel would cease to supply intelligence on the rebellion in Algeria. This would weaken the struggle to maintain the North African territory as part of France, the ideal to which Soustelle was devoted. He eventually resigned from the government in high dudgeon in 1960, when de Gaulle announced that France would separate from Algeria, and in 1962 he joined the rebels of the Organisation de l'Armée Secrète (OAS), a secret army organization.

The French historian Jean Le Coutour, who was the correspondent for *Le Monde* in Cairo in the 1950s and later researched and wrote about the de Gaulle presidency, has said that he cannot believe that in what is so patently an important a strategic area, the president's men failed to comply with his instructions: "Within the core of government in Paris, in the Ministry of Defense, in the circle surrounding the president, how was it possible not to obey the orders of General de Gaulle, in matters such as strategy, defense, and military technology? I fail to grasp how such a diversion, such insubordination, could have been perpetrated, but it happened, and that's a fact," Le Coutour said.

Indeed, how *did* some of the heads of the French defense establishment manage to fool de Gaulle, the very exemplar of the authoritative leader, for over two years? For one thing, it was not as difficult as it sounds: For the first year of his rule, de Gaulle was preoccupied with the acute economic crisis, which he tried to overcome through a series of drastic measures, like issuing the new franc, worth one hundred old ones. Second, although de Gaulle expressed amazement at the special relations with Israel and declared his intention of discontinuing them, he never went beyond the declaration and never followed up to ensure that his orders were being carried out. And third, and according to foreign sources probably most importantly, he was aware that before it could carry out its nuclear tests, France needed Israel's help. As we have recounted, the French scientists responsible for building the bomb had difficulty in reaching agreement on the calculation of the critical mass required to sustain the chain reaction in the fissile material. To perform the calculation, accurate simulation was required, and that could be attained only on the supercomputers of the period. The United States aimed to hold up France's entry into the nuclear club, and refused to supply it with the necessary equipment for building such computers. Israel had the capacity to fulfill this task. Says Le Coutour: "During the first part of his rule, before 1960, although de Gaulle leveled criticism at the degree to which Israeli officers had penetrated the French military, he took no action. There were other matters at the head of his agenda. It was not the Israeli nuclear capability that was the main thing, but the French one."

And indeed, it was to obtain a report on the progress of French nuclear research from Francis Perrin that the president came to Saclay on that spring morning in April 1960. Two months beforehand, the first French nuclear bomb had been tested successfully in the Algerian Sahara, but the building of the second one was stalled, due to a serious lack of weapons-grade plutonium.4 The development of a hydrogen bomb was also under consideration.

De Gaulle's motorcade stopped at the entrance to the main control hall of the reactors. The door of the black presidential Citroën DS limousine opened and de Gaulle stepped out. The first thing he saw was Dror Sadeh's tiny Citroën Deux Chevaux car, with its *plaque rouge*. The bearded, elegantly attired Perrin stood next to the president. He was a short man, and de Gaulle towered over him. What, the president wondered aloud, was a foreign diplomat's car doing in the holy of holies of French national security? Perrin could only stammer. Soustelle, who in 1958 and '59 had protected the Israeli project against the French groups and individuals who wished it ill, was no longer around to smooth things over. That evening, at home, Sadeh told his wife, Haya, that because of his little vehicle, things were in an uproar and an inquiry was under way. The following day, he and the other Israelis were told not to go to their laboratories.

The president was furious over the way senior figures in the defense establishment had deceived him. He asked his foreign minister, Maurice Couve de Murville, to inform his Israeli counterpart, Golda Meir, of the cessation of all cooperation, and he instructed Perrin to terminate all activities connected with the Israeli project.5 Perrin conveyed the instructions to all the units that were under his authority, among them the Saclay center. De Gaulle's decision to impose a nuclear embargo on Israel came at a critical moment. Although, foreign sources have reported, the construction of the skeleton of the Dimona reactor had been completed, the plant for the extraction of plutonium had not, and without plutonium there is no bomb.

Strangely, however, despite Perrin's instructions, when the tumult had died down a week later, Sadeh and his fellow Israelis returned to their labs. In effect, the embargo was felt only in diplomatic channels. On the ground, French cooperation with Israel continued as before. This was the great achievement of Shalhevet Freier, who had set a stable course for the nuclear project's French aspects before he ended his term in Paris and returned to Israel in 1959. French sources have identified two French Jewish CEA officials who assisted Freier: nuclear engineer Jules Horowitz, the chief supervisor of the Israeli trainees, who visited Israel several times, and the director of international relations of the CEA, chemist Bertrand Leopold Goldschmidt, the only Frenchman who had taken part in the Manhattan Project. Goldschmidt was involved in most of the important nuclear events in the 20th century in Europe and North America, and he had a great deal of knowledge about atomic research in the Soviet Union as well. In 1949, he had headed a team of researchers that achieved a breakthrough in French nuclear research, when they succeeded in extracting for the first time a few micrograms of plutonium from spent uranium. Goldschmidt held frequent meetings with the Israelis. He was a friendly man who loved to tell stories, and did not hesitate to put the broad, worldwide network of connections that he had created at Israel's disposal. Another French official who counseled the Israelis was General Jean Thiry, who played a role in the manufacture of France's first bomb, and in the 1960s served as director of the French nuclear test site at Mururoa atoll in the Pacific Ocean. All of this activity carried on even after the declaration of the embargo by de Gaulle, demonstrating that when it came to nuclear cooperation with Israel, the break between the policy makers in Paris and the personnel in the field endured.

In the first two years of his rule, de Gaulle avoided confronting the nationalistic elements that had brought him to power. Only when his presidency stabilized and the economic situation began to improve, as 1960 neared, did he allow himself to begin preparing public opinion for the disengagement from Algeria. When he did so, a broad hawkish opposition front confronted him, at first hesitantly and later vigorously, to the point of declaring a rebellion. In February 1960, de Gaulle had to have recourse to emergency powers, so strong was the opposition to the president's policy on the part of the French settlers in Algeria and some of the military units protecting them. De Gaulle's staff suspected that Israel was using the Mossad to activate Algerian Jews and provide assistance to opponents of the disengagement among the settlers.[6]

The cutting off of the special military relationship with Israel was meant to signal to the Arab world that for the first time since the Suez Campaign, France was extending it a conciliatory hand, and at the same time to weaken the Algerian settlers and the officers who were defying de Gaulle.

In mid-May, foreign ministers Couve de Murville and Meir met during a stopover Meir made in Paris on a flight to the United States. "De Murville told Golda: We have decided to stop all nuclear links with you and we are going to return all your money, and she cabled the 'happy' news to Ben-Gurion," recalled Shimon Peres. Immediately after that Couve de Murville informed Israel that France would not supply it with uranium, unless Israel would publicly declare that the reactor was for peaceful purposes only and would open it to international inspection. The news about the French embargo was imparted to the narrow circle of those in the know about Israel's nuclear secret, and elicited concern. In contrast, the academics who opposed the project rubbed their hands in satisfaction.

In early June 1960, Ben-Gurion dispatched Peres, then deputy minister of defense, to Paris for talks with Couve de Murville, but their meeting failed to produce a solution, so Ben-Gurion himself flew to Paris to meet de Gaulle. They met twice. At the first meeting they discussed world affairs and avoided Dimona. Both of the elderly leaders enjoyed such *tours d'horizon*.

On the day of their first meeting, Sadeh submitted his doctoral thesis to the physics department of the Sorbonne. Entitled "Recognition of Energy Levels in Light Nucleuses by Betatron" (an instrument that speeds up electrons), the dissertation was supervised by professors Christian Magnan and Leon Katz. They were not aware that when Sadeh had asked the Israeli Atomic Energy Commission for permission to enroll for a doctorate, the security department had insisted that the Mossad make sure that the supervisors were not linked to hostile elements. There were certain suspicions, and it took Sadeh considerable efforts to dissipate them.

At the second meeting between the two leaders, three days later, de Gaulle asked Ben-Gurion for what purpose Israel was building a nuclear reactor, and Ben-Gurion pledged that Israel would not build a bomb. De Gaulle promised to reconsider his position, and Ben-Gurion flew back to Tel Aviv. Two weeks later, on August 1, de Gaulle instructed Couve de Murville to tell Israel that he had not changed his mind, and if Israel refused to open Dimona to international inspection, the nuclear pact would be annulled.

Shimon Peres suggested that he go to Paris to try to salvage the French-Israeli cooperation, and Ben-Gurion agreed. A meeting between Couve de Murville and Peres produced a compromise: The French government would cease its direct involvement in the construction of the Dimona reactor, but all the contracts signed with private French companies would remain in force, including the contract with Saint-Gobain Nucléaire, which had undertaken to build the plutonium separation plant, foreign sources have reported. Thus de Gaulle's embargo held up the building at Dimona for only a few months. By the end of 1960, work at the site was proceeding according to plan, under the terms of the compromise. During the next three years, the French companies would complete the construction of the facility. Some of the work that had in the original agreement been assigned to French companies was now allotted to Israeli firms.

But the building of Dimona was only one part of the project, and ironically it was in the other part, whose conduct was entirely in Israeli hands, that delays and difficulties piled up. In mid-1960, the physicist Israel Dostrovsky, who ran Institute 4 of the RAFAEL Weapons Development Authority and carried the main burden of the scientific leadership of Israel's nuclear project on the ground, traveled to the United States for two years of advanced study at the Lawrence Livermore National Laboratory in California, where much of America's defense-related nuclear research was carried out. The facility had been established by the "father of the hydrogen bomb," Edward Teller. Yuval Neeman, who had completed his stint as military attaché at the Israeli Embassy in London and had returned to Israel with a doctorate in physics, was appointed scientific director of Institute 4 in place of Dostrovsky. Neeman was surprised to find that the project was foundering.

"It was like this," Neeman explained forty-four years later. "Mannes Prat controlled KAMAG [the Hebrew acronym for the Nuclear Research Center in Dimona], and Munya Mardor controlled RAFAEL, with Peres and Bergmann coordinating. The three bodies, KAMAG, RAFAEL, and the Atomic Energy Commission, were interconnected and could not be separated." Each week, a coordination meeting would take place at the Defense Ministry in Tel Aviv. Peres presided and the participants were Bergmann, Prat, Mardor, and the chemist Avraham Hermoni, who was the chief scientist at RAFAEL. Clashes of egos occurred among the figures at the head of the project at the coordination meetings, according to Neeman's account, and compartmentalization of information exacerbated the problem.

Bergmann and Mardor were given information by Prat only in very small doses in order to maintain secrecy. For his part, Peres also kept Dimona's secrets totally out of Bergmann's reach, thereby helping Prat keep his Dimona cards very close to his chest. Bergmann also had a professional handicap, not being a nuclear physicist. "Cooperation was dwindling away and the project was in decline," said Neeman.

What was missing therefore was a leader. Bergmann performed three functions: chairman of AEC, chief scientist in the Defense Ministry, and scientific director in RAFAEL, but he could not take charge of the entire project, as he was compartmentalized out of Dimona, as were most of the other members of the AEC. As long as the Dimona facility had not been completed and there was apprehension that the French would cease fulfilling their commitments, or that information would leak out and the Americans would discover the project, the AEC was not given details about decisions regarding Dimona. AEC members knew what the goal was and set the guidelines for basic nuclear research, and Institute 4 was open to their inspection, but the AEC never ran the project nor did it supervise its management. In fact, the AEC, Israel's most secret defense body, was no more than a rubber stamp. Of the seven members of the commission, only two were involved in the detailed planning of Dimona and the everyday activities of Institute 4: the physicists Harry Zvi Lipkin and Igal Talmi (as well as Dostrovsky, of course, but he was in the United States in the early 1960s).

Because of his exclusion, Bergmann now found himself with more time on his hands. He would spend a lot of time sitting in the old-time Prague Café in central Tel Aviv, in the company of *yekkes*—Jewish immigrants from Germany—like himself. The story was told there that after World War II, the chemist Bergmann had volunteered to prepare a poison that a group of youngsters known as Hanokmim (the Avengers) had taken from Palestine to Europe with the intention of taking revenge on the Nazis. Bergmann himself never confirmed this tale.7

Time had taken its toll, and Bergmann had lost much of his vitality and decisiveness, not to mention influence. He had never learned to drive, and in order to get from one RAFAEL institute to another he needed a car and driver, but the management wouldn't always put them at his disposal. Behind his back there were whispers to the effect that he had fallen from grace, and in fact Ben-Gurion tended to consult him less and less.

Nevertheless, despite all the external and internal difficulties, and the personal quarrels, the goal was ultimately reached. On the other hand, the way the operation was run proves the rule that political-military establishments that deal with projects involving gigantic budgets, and because of secrecy are not supervised by a parliament or some watchdog state body, eventually tend to become corrupt or debilitated. Israel's nuclear project was run like a state within a state. In mid-1963, when Ben-Gurion resigned as prime minister, his successor, Levi Eshkol, initiated a cleanup, changed the control structure, and sacked some of the pioneers of the project, including Prat and Bergmann.

By the end of November 1960, de Gaulle's nuclear embargo had evaporated into space, and things had calmed down. The confrontation with France had continued for six months, throughout which both countries observed strict secrecy. No outside body, including the CIA, discerned the storm behind the scenes. In Israel, information about the embargo leaked out to a group of intellectuals and some journalists, but the military censorship and the security services made sure nothing was published.

IN NOVEMBER Dror Sadeh was invited to defend his doctoral thesis at the Sorbonne. A week before the time set for his lecture the new Israeli scientific attaché in Paris, David Peleg, who had replaced Shalhevet Freier, summoned Sadeh to his office and informed him that the Israeli Atomic Energy Commission was demanding his immediate return to Tel Aviv. Sadeh refused, and told Peleg he would go back to Israel right after delivering his dissertation. Peleg insisted. "You have been ordered to return forthwith," he told Sadeh. Voices were raised. Sadeh lost control, picked up an ink pot off Peleg's desk, threw it at the attaché, and stalked out of the room and vanished. In a panic, the office staff began searching the premises for him, and called his home. Some said they feared he would do something desperate. But all that Sadeh did was take a walk in the Bois de Boulogne in order to compose himself.

Sadeh remained in Paris, and a week later successfully defended his thesis. He received a doctorat d'État, the higher of the two doctoral degrees awarded in France. He then traveled back to Israel, and reported for work at the Atomic Energy Commission. Ostensibly, things had calmed down. Sadeh had his degree and the AEC had its scientist. But under the surface, resentment seethed. The rift that had opened up between Sadeh and his colleagues deepened. The envious among them couldn't stomach the fact that one of their number had come back from Paris with a personal achievement under his belt. They were a small, closed group, fanatical about the project they had been entrusted with, whereas Sadeh was an independent type who found it difficult to exhaust his talents within the narrow scientific channel that had been assigned to him. In a few years' time he would abandon the project entirely, and win a name for himself in an academic career.

CHAPTER NINE

The Deception That Worked

ON DECEMBER 31, 1960, a few weeks before the end of the Eisenhower administration, the American ambassador in Tel Aviv, Ogden Reid, received instructions from Washington to present the Israeli government with five questions in writing about its nuclear plans. Reid handed the questions to Foreign Minister Golda Meir on January 3, 1961, giving her twelve hours, until midnight the same night, to come up with the answers. Here, in summary form, are the questions:

1. What did Israel intend to do with the plutonium produced at the Dimona reactor?
2. Would Israel agree to supervision over the plutonium?
3. Would Israel permit officials of the International Atomic Energy Agency (IAEA) to visit the reactor, and when.
4. Did Israel intend to build an additional reactor?
5. Was Israel prepared to declare that it had no plans to produce atomic weapons?

Meir passed the queries on to Prime Minister David Ben-Gurion, who was offended by the "undignified demand" for immediate answers. The next day he summoned Reid to his home at Sdeh Boker in the heart of the Negev desert and rebuked him: "You have to address us as equals, or don't speak to us at all." Nevertheless, Ben-Gurion offered full replies to the questions:[1]

1. "As far as we know," said the prime minister, "those who sell the uranium do so on condition that the plutonium be returned to them," and therefore the plutonium produced at Dimona would be handed to the suppliers of the uranium. Ben-Gurion did not specify who those uranium suppliers were. He might have meant France, or perhaps he was being disingenuous and meant that the uranium would stay in Israel, because the reactor was to be fueled by natural uranium mined in Israel.

2. Representatives of friendly states would be permitted to visit the reactor in 1961.

3. Israel would permit the IAEA to inspect the reactor only if the other countries with such installations also did so, and only as long as there were no Russians among the inspectors, as "we do not wish hostile states to put their spoon into our pot."

4. Israel had no plans to build another reactor.

5. Israel did not plan to make atomic weapons. "What I announced in the Knesset still stands," the prime minister told the ambassador, referring to his statement of December 21 in which he cited "peaceful purposes." "I spoke plainly, and you must accept my words as they were spoken."

John Fitzgerald Kennedy took the presidential oath on January 20, 1961. Only ten days later, the new secretary of state, Dean Rusk, handed the president a memorandum summing up the results of the contacts with Israel on the nuclear issue toward the end of the Eisenhower administration. Rusk wrote that Ben-Gurion's assurances that Israel had no plan to build a bomb "appear to be satisfactory," but "several minor questions still require clarification" and therefore the State Department and intelligence agencies would follow Israel's nuclear activities constantly. "At the moment, we are encouraging the Israelis to permit qualified scientists from the United States or other friendly powers to visit the Dimona installation," read the Rusk memo.

The Kennedy administration's starting line on Israel's nuclear initiative was therefore a moderately worded expression of trust in Ben-Gurion's statements. But Secretary of State Rusk would stick faithfully to the State Department's tendency to prefer the Arab positions, principally because of the dependency of the West on Middle Eastern oil.[2] From Israel's point of view, President Kennedy provided something of a counterbalance to this tendency.

Kennedy's posture toward Israel was more positive than Eisenhower's had been. As a U.S. senator in March 1958, two years before he was elected president, he had laid out the principles that guided his view of Israel's place in the Middle East:

> Quite apart from the values and hopes which the State of Israel enshrines—and the past injuries which it redeems—it twists reality to suggest that it is the democratic tendency of Israel which has interjected discord and dissension into the Near East. Even by the coldest calculations, the removal of Israel would not alter the basic crisis in the area. For, if there is any lesson which the melancholy events of the last two years and more taught us, it is that, though Arab states are generally united in opposition to Israel, their political unities do not rise above this negative position. The basic rivalries within the Arab world, the quarrels over boundaries, the tensions involved in lifting their economies from stagnation, the cross pressures of nationalism—all of these factors would still be there, even if there were no Israel.[3]

The new president shaped the complex network of his relations with Israel on the basis of this somewhat idealistic and even naïve faith, and on the positive values that it represented. Unlike the Eisenhower administration, which had paid only marginal attention to Israel's nuclear aspirations, under Kennedy's presidency this issue dominated the discourse between the two countries. This was because Dimona had been revealed to the world on the eve of the transition between the two administrations, and, more important, Kennedy placed the limitation of the nuclear arms race at the center of American foreign policy. In his judgment the United States, as the leader of the free world, was responsible for restricting the proliferation of nuclear weapons. Kennedy displayed great determination in his fight for disarmament and nuclear nonproliferation. Israel's nuclear enterprise was in direct contradiction with the principles of his policy.

February 1949. Israel's first president, Chaim Weizmann (*left*), at a reception for army officers at the Weizmann Institute. Weizmann was a staunch opponent of Ben-Gurion's nuclear project.

May 1951. President Harry S. Truman (*left*) meets Prime Minister David Ben-Gurion in the White House. Israel's ambassador to the U.S., Abba Eban, stands behind them. Truman had endorsed the partition of Palestine and the creation of the Jewish state.

October 29, 1956. Israel launched its assault on Egypt. Paratroopers dropped in western Sinai, about 30 miles east of the Suez Canal, take their positions in sand trenches.

November 6, 1956. Israel Defense Force Chief of Staff Moshe Dayan (*center*) reads Ben-Gurion's victory address to IDF troops at Sharm el-Sheikh, the southern point of the Sinai peninsula. In his address, the Israeli prime minister announced the formation of "the Third Kingdom of Israel."

Isser Harel, head of Israel's security services, after he retired. Harel dissociated himself from Ben-Gurion's decision to help France with intelligence on the activities of the FLN in Algeria in exchange for military and nuclear aid, and opposed the Anglo-French-Israeli Suez Campaign against Egypt.

June 1958. French Foreign Minister Maurice Bourgès-Maunoury (*left*) and director general of the Defense Ministry Abel Thomas (*right*) meet with Israeli PM Ben-Gurion at his Tel Aviv residence. Thomas and Bourgès-Maunoury had done more than anyone else to help Israel to develop its nuclear option.

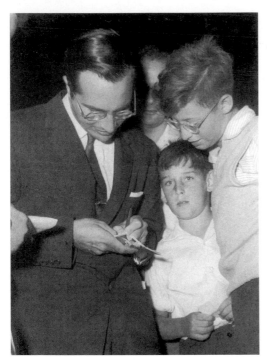

July 4, 1959. U.S. ambassador to Israel Ogden Reid signs autographs at Independence Day reception in Tel Aviv. Reid was involved in exposing the nuclear reactor in Dimona.

February 1960. Final construction of the small American research reactor in Nahal Soreq, south of Tel Aviv. Israeli scientists who were involved in the assembly of the nuclear facilities at Dimona were trained at Nahal Soreq.

June 1960. At the Palais de l'Elysée in Paris, French President Charles de Gaulle meets for the first time with Ben-Gurion. De Gaulle opposed the military and nuclear cooperation between the two governments and ordered that the relations be severed, but his defense establishment did not obey him.

RAFAEL's founder, Munya Mardor, and his wife, Lenka. According to foreign sources, under the leadership of Mardor, RAFAEL developed the first Israeli nuclear weapon.

October 10, 1960. (*Left to right*) Deputy Minister of Defense Shimon Peres, Ben-Gurion, Mardor, and IDF Chief of Staff Zvi Tsur observe the Shavit 2 missile a few minutes before it was launched.

Professor Amos de Shalit, the head of the nuclear physics department of the Weizmann Institute. De Shalit wrote a letter to Mardor warning him against trying to mislead the Americans about Israel's nuclear plans.

Professor Dror Sadeh lectures at Tel Aviv University. Young Sadeh was sent by the Israel Atomic Energy Commission to study at the Saclay Nuclear Research Center near Paris.

An unauthorized photo of the nuclear reactor at Dimona, photographed by Mordechai Vanunu, the Israeli nuclear whistle blower. Inside Dimona, Vanunu took around sixty photos of top-secret buildings, facilities, labs, and production processes.

A laboratory model of a nuclear weapon core that was also secretly photographed by Vanunu inside Dimona and leaked to the London *Sunday Times*. On the basis of Vanunu's testimony and checking by independent experts, the newspaper concluded that Israel had constructed 100 to 200 atomic warheads.

August 1962. President Kennedy agreed to sell Hawk antiaircraft missiles to Israel. A Hawk battery was installed near Dimona to defend the nuclear reactor from air attacks.

November 1962. Prime Minister Ben-Gurion and Foreign Minister Golda Meir talk candidly in the Knesset in Jerusalem during the course of a political rift.

May 1963. German Defense Minister Franz Josef Strauss (*left*) meets Shimon Peres in Tel Aviv. Strauss told Peres that his government was not involved in the activities of the German scientists and technicians who were recruited by Egypt.

November 1963. Prime Minister Levi Eshkol (*left*) expresses condolences to Ambassador Walworth Barbour at the American Embassy in Tel Aviv on the assassination of President Kennedy. The American ambassador is an important player in Israeli politics, and Barbour's long presence hovered constantly over the halls of power.

June 1964. President Lyndon B. Johnson and his wife, Lady Bird (*right*), meet Prime Minister Levi Eshkol and his wife, Miriam, at a reception in Washington given by the Israeli ambassador Avraham Harman (*center*). The chemistry between Johnson and Eshkol led to American acceptance of Israel's nuclear plan.

May 1966. Prime Minister Eshkol presents Professor Ernst D. Bergmann with the annual Defense Prize at a ceremony in the Defense Ministry garden in Tel Aviv. The award was intended to mitigate the sting of Bergmann's removal from his positions at the Defense Ministry and RAFAEL.

June 3, 1967. Two days before Israel would attack, IDF Chief of Staff Yitzhak Rabin (*center*) confers with his deputy Brigadier General Haim Barlev (*left*) and Chief of Operations Brigadier General Ezer Weizman at the general headquarters in Tel Aviv. Israel attained nuclear capability shortly before the 1967 war.

June 9, 1967. Following three days of fighting, Israeli soldiers reached the east bank of the Suez Canal opposite the Egyptian city of Ismailia. Many Israelis saw the victory as a miraculous event, coming only twenty-five years after the Nazis began systematically murdering millions of Jews in Europe.

Paul Warnke, deputy assistant secretary of defense in the administration of Lyndon B. Johnson and director of the Arms Control and Disarmament Agency in the administration of Jimmy Carter. After a series of meetings with Israeli Ambassador to the U.S. Yitzhak Rabin, Warnke was convinced that Israel had attained nuclear capability.

January 1969. A few days before his departure from the White House, President Johnson ordered the sale of fifty F4 Phantom Jets to Israel. High officials at the State and Defense departments expressed reservations about the deal.

September 1969. President Richard M. Nixon welcoming Prime Minister Golda Meir to the White House. Meir went to Washington in order to hold a serious and sincere discussion about Israel's nuclear plan and to tell the truth to the American leaders.

At the beginning of the 1970s, new housing blocks were built at the development town of Dimona, a few miles from the Negev Nuclear Research Center. Approximately 2,700 scientists, technicians, and administrative staff are employed at the research center; many of them reside in the town.

October 26, 1973. On the west bank of the Suez Canal, Israeli soldiers observe destroyed Soviet SAM-2 missiles. A massive effort was required from the Israeli Air Force (IAF) to destroy the SAM missiles that protected the Egyptian and Syrian forces attacking Israel during the first phase of the war.

March 23, 1979. Egyptian President Anwar Sadat (*left*), President Jimmy Carter, and Israeli Prime Minister Menachem Begin at the signing ceremony at the White House of the Israeli-Egyptian Peace Treaty. Sadat initiated the 1973 war to force Israel to enter negotiations on withdrawal from Sinai and to negotiate a peace treaty, and in this he succeeded.

June 9, 1981. In a press conference in Jerusalem, Prime Minister Begin announces the bombing and destruction of Iraq's Osirak nuclear reactor by the IAF. Begin declared: "Israel will not tolerate any nuclear weapons in the region"—a doctrine that is still in force today.

The father of the hydrogen bomb, Edward Teller (*right*), meets Shimon Peres at the prime minister's office in Jerusalem. Teller was the source for the CIA when it drew up the first situation assessment that Israel had begun to produce nuclear weapons.

February 12, 1991. In the first Gulf War, American Patriot missile tracers inter-cept Scud missiles over Tel Aviv. Although Saddam Hussein had chemical war-heads at his disposal, he launched only less damaging conventional TNT warheads in his attacks on Israel.

April 21, 2004. Accompanied by prison officers, Mordechai Vanunu is released after serving eighteen years. The information that Vanunu exposed to the world in words and pictures may have stripped away the veil from Israel's nuclear pro-gram but did not damage it.

Ambassador Paul C. Warnke believed that Kennedy's basic assumption was that it was a mistake for Israel to develop a nuclear weapon. An assistant secretary of defense in the Johnson administration, in the 1970s Warnke would serve as the chief U.S. arms control negotiator, and represent the U.S. government in negotiations with Israel over the American demand for supervision over Dimona. "The more nuclear proliferation there was, the greater chance there was for a nuclear war, and if more and more countries, particularly in sensitive areas like the Middle East, developed nuclear weapons, there was a chance they might be used."

This assumption guided the basic goal of the Americans: to prevent nuclear proliferation among countries considering building a bomb, such as China, France, Yugoslavia, Brazil, Sweden, India, Pakistan, South Africa, and others. Israel, however was a special case. The influence of the Jewish vote and the pro-Israel lobby in the United States was growing, and at least three presidents—Kennedy, Johnson, and Nixon—set their policy toward Israel's nuclear program with one eye on the Jewish electorate. In addition, the Cold War was penetrating into the Middle East, and Israel was emerging as an ally of the West. On top of that, there was the impact of the lessons of the Holocaust, although in the early 1960s, the connection between the Holocaust and Israel's need for a doomsday weapon had only begun to seep into American consciousness, and it would take at least another ten years before it would be fully appreciated.

This complex array of constraints confronted Kennedy with a difficult choice. On the one hand, there was the principle that America was determined to block any initiative aimed at the proliferation of nuclear weaponry. But on the other hand, was the United States really interested in exposing to attack a small nation surrounded by enemies sworn to destroy it? Would it be fair for the United States to handle Israel's nuclear enterprise in the same way as it handled those of powers like China and India, who were liable to use their nuclear weapons offensively against their enemies? It was clear, after all, that Israel's nuclear potential was meant to serve as a deterrent. Said Warnke: "I say the answer is no. I do not think that the U.S. had the feeling that it could physically stop Israel from developing a nuclear weapon. That would be a mistake, Israel was a

friend. There were foreign countries, unfriendly countries, that had nuclear power."

The key sentence—"I do not think that the U.S. had the feeling that it
could physically stop Israel from developing a nuclear weapon"—captures
well the gradual improvement of Israel's status in Washington's eyes since
the total embargo on weapons that the United States had imposed on Israel in the early 1950s, and the deep rift between the two countries that
was caused by Israel's occupation of the Sinai peninsula during the Suez
Campaign. It is difficult to imagine an official of the Eisenhower administration in the mid-1950s being able to talk that way about Israel's aspirations for building an atomic option. It is reasonable to assume that if
Israel's nuclear program had been discovered at that time, the United
States government would have twisted Israel's arm and unceremoniously
forced it to give up the idea of building Dimona, in much the same way
that in early 1957 Washington coerced Israel, by means of the threat of
sanctions, to withdraw from the entire Sinai, which it had conquered in
October 1956.

The shift was set into motion on both sides toward the end of the
1950s, when in American eyes, Israel ceased being a burden and began to
emerge as a strategic asset, and when Israel stopped regarding France as a
reliable ally, and set off on the road to close friendship with the United
States. It would be years before it became clear that these early mutual
steps marked a fateful turning point for Israel.

From the perspective of the early 21st century, it is easy to discern how
most of the Arab Middle East was swallowed into the Soviet sphere of influence, but in the late 1950s the signs of this development were not entirely evident. We have already mentioned that with the Eisenhower
Doctrine in mind, the United States had initiated an attempt to gather
the Arab states of the Middle East under its wing, to counter the penetration of the Soviet Union into the region. Whoever joins us, the Americans promised, will get handsome economic rewards. It is interesting to
speculate what would have happened to the Middle East in general and
Israel in particular, if Egypt's president Nasser had been tempted by the
offer, and had led the revolutionary Arab states into the American sphere
of influence (as his successor, Anwar al-Sadat would do in 1976.4). But
Nasser did precisely the opposite.

In February 1958, Egypt and Syria formed a confederation known as the United Arab Republic, the UAR, based on a pan-Arab ideology with certain pseudo-communist tinges. The establishment of the UAR inflamed revolutionary elements across the Arab world, and they threatened to topple the line of dominoes that formed the pro-Western front line that the United States and Britain had built to avert Soviet penetration. In July, Iraqi Prime Minister Nuri as-Said was assassinated and his government was overthrown, endangering the other pro-Western regimes in the oil states of the Gulf—Kuwait, Bahrain, and the United Arab Emirates—and threatening to break up the American-sponsored Baghdad Pact (1955), whose members were Iraq, Iran, Turkey, and Pakistan. A civil war broke out in Lebanon, and the pro-American government there was close to collapse. In Jordan, the army declared a mutiny, and the Hashemite monarchy was on the brink of elimination. The United States and Britain were forced to put on shows of strength in Lebanon and Jordan, respectively, to stabilize their regimes. U.S. Marines were dispatched to Lebanon, and British troops to Jordan. The reasons for all these troubles could be traced back to Nasser. President Eisenhower later reflected: "This somber turn of events could, without a vigorous response on our part, result in the complete elimination of Western influence in the Middle East."

There's no doubt that the grave crisis that erupted in the Middle East in 1958 opened the eyes of both Eisenhower and of his secretary of state, John Foster Dulles.[5] The president told aides that he believed that in the struggle for influence in the region "to lose would be far worse than the loss of China, because of the strategic position and resources of the Middle East." And Dulles realized that Nasser had become a leader "who whipped up Pan-Arabism much as Hitler whipped up Pan-Germanism as a means of promoting an extension of his power." This equation between Nasser and Hitler, made in a lecture to a conference of the Pan-American Union in late-June 1958, exemplifies the about-face in America's position vis-à-vis the strongest leader in the Arab world.

The crisis sharpened America's appreciation of Israel's strategic dimension in the region. In late July, after it became clear that the pro-Western regimes in Lebanon and Jordan had been rescued, Dulles sent a message to Ben-Gurion to express gratitude to Israel for the assistance it had rendered to Britain and the United States. Dulles thanked Ben-Gurion warmly for the permission Israel had granted to the U.S. and the Royal Air Force to fly through its airspace in order to help King Hussein of Jordan protect his throne. "We believe that Israel should be in a position to deter an attempt at aggression by indigenous forces" who were ready to use force against pro-Western regimes, wrote the secretary of state. "The critical situation in the Middle East today gives Israel manifold opportunities to contribute, from its resources of spiritual strength and determination of purpose, to a stable international order."

Thus for the first time Washington identified Israel as the only stabilizing factor in the region that was ready to mobilize on America's behalf. Saudi Arabia had refused to extend assistance to the Anglo-American military intervention in Lebanon and Jordan, while Israel had helped even as the Soviet Union was threatening to use military force against it. It was this identification of Israel "as the only strong pro-West power in the Middle East" that was capable of counterbalancing the damage wrought by Nasser's revolutionary radicalism—as stated in a report drawn up by the National Security Council in the wake of the crisis—that planted the seed of the U.S.-Israeli alliance, unwritten but strong and stable. Today this partnership seems self-evident, but in the late 1950s it was nothing short of a revolutionary innovation.

Concomitantly, Ben-Gurion, and therefore Israel, changed course. The Israeli prime minister realized that from the moment de Gaulle had decided to disengage from Algeria, the reasons behind France's patronage over Israel had lost their validity; just as in pre-state days, at the end of World War II, he had transferred the Zionist movement from the aegis of Great Britain to that of the United States, so now Ben-Gurion swung Israel onto the course that would lead it to become part of the American camp. Both sides, the superpower and the tiny new state, inched gradually to that point. The United States, although it was as yet not able to define precisely what Israel's place would be in the Cold War confrontation, drew the Jewish state closer, while Israel, despite fairly powerful internal forces trying to drag it toward alliance with the Soviet bloc, or at least neutrality, was drawn toward the United States.

During the brief period that John F. Kennedy was president, the rapprochement between the United States and Israel was uneven. Kennedy's primary concern was Jewish American voters. His attitude toward Israel's nuclear program slid along a scale, with his commitment to the principle of total prevention of nuclear proliferation at one end, and his commitment to the Jewish voters to ensure the existence of Israel on the other. The Kennedy who advocated nonproliferation could never agree to Israel having a nuclear option, while the Kennedy concerned with the Jewish voter couldn't stop Israel from developing it. So Israel would adopt evasive and delaying tactics, everything within the framework of the conventional rules of the diplomatic game, and ultimately bow to reality and compromise.

Two American Jews were instrumental in persuading Ben-Gurion to comply with the demands on the matter of inspection; Abe Feinberg, who was bequeathed to Kennedy by Eisenhower, who had in turn inherited him from Truman, and Myer "Mike" Feldman, who represented the Americans' interests while identifying closely with Israel. Feinberg's great advantage was that the Israeli side trusted him implicitly.

Mike Feldman was a polished attorney from Philadelphia, with close links to the East Coast financial aristocracy. Feldman joined with John Kennedy and his family in the mid-1950s. Early in his second term in the Senate, in 1958, Kennedy made Feldman his legislative assistant. During the preparations for the presidential campaign, Feldman formulated the Middle Eastern plank in Kennedy's foreign policy platform. Kennedy told the voters that he would act to eliminate the economic boycott the Arabs had declared against Israel and companies that traded with her, and to secure the right to free navigation in the Suez Canal for Israeli ships. He also pledged to promote "the resettlement of the Arab refugees in lands where there is room and opportunity for them." At meetings with Jews, Kennedy generously scattered the promises that Feldman had fed him. Appearing before the American Zionist Congress, Kennedy vowed to convene a Middle East peace conference and to act to foster prosperity in the region. "The Middle East needs water, not war; tractors, not tanks; bread, not bombs," intoned the young contender as he laid out his optimistic vision. In May 1960, Feldman organized a visit to Israel for Kennedy to enable the candidate to demonstrate to the Jewish voters in the United States his support for the existence of the Jewish state.

Early in the morning of his election victory, Kennedy informed Feld-man that he would appoint him deputy special counsel at the White House, and asked him to be the president's personal representative on Middle Eastern affairs. Feldman had reservations, telling the president-elect that he feared that his strong emotional ties to Israel might make his advice one-sided. But Kennedy put his fears to rest. "That's exactly why I want you to do it," he said. By appointing Feldman, the first Catholic president was sending a positive message to Jewish Americans, who still remembered the declarations of appeasement toward the Nazis that Kennedy's father, Joseph P. Kennedy Sr., had given while serving as American ambassador in London before World War II.

Feldman's membership in the president's innermost circle of advisers gave him remarkable power in the shaping of Kennedy's policy toward Is-rael, to the extent that sometimes his opinion outweighed those of Na-tional Security Adviser McGeorge Bundy, Assistant Secretary of State Phillips Talbot, and National Security Council member Robert Komer—whose concept of American interests often tended more toward appeasing the Arab side in the Middle East conflict. The president sent Feldman for talks with the Israeli leadership on matters fraught with sig-nificance for the future of the state: finding a solution to the Palestinian refugee problem; requests for arms, including the Hawk antiaircraft mis-sile system; and the dispute over the supervision of the Dimona facility.[6] The last subject was the topic discussed by Feinberg and Feldman with Ben-Gurion in late March 1961.

The Kennedy administration insisted that Israel honor its promise to the Eisenhower administration that American experts would be allowed to visit Dimona. In March it became clear to Ben-Gurion that such visits could not be postponed any longer, and that all he could do now was set the price the Americans would have to pay for them. Feinberg and Feld-man persuaded him that a meeting with the president was the appropri-ate reward. While the prime minister treated Feldman like an official American representative, he regarded Feinberg as "one of us," on the ba-sis of his dedication to assisting the Haganah in the pre-state days. As the man who had been in charge of the special fund-raising campaign to fi-nance the nuclear project, Feinberg knew exactly what its purpose was. Feldman knew only what the American government knew. In the end it was agreed that the visit to Dimona would take place in mid-May, and immediately afterward Ben-Gurion would fly to New York for his meeting with the president.

The precedent of letting foreigners visit Dimona made the directors of the project nervous and led to friction. None of them had any way of knowing if the Kennedy administration was actually determined to discover the truth or merely wanted to go through the motions. Deputy Defense Minister Shimon Peres ordered the director of the Dimona facility, Mannes Prat, to prepare the site for a visit by outsiders. Foreign Minister Golda Meir took issue with this move. She feared that any deception could be discovered and would raise the ire of the president. She believed that it would be appropriate to tell the Americans the truth: that the Arabs were threatening the very existence of the State of Israel and of the survivors of the Holocaust, and this gave Israel the fundamental right to defend itself by any means, including a nuclear option. Ben-Gurion, on the other hand, had no hesitation. He would allow secrets to leak out only in tiny drops. He had no interest in placing the president in an impossible situation. If all the secrets of Dimona were divulged, the principle of nuclear nonproliferation that Kennedy espoused would obligate him to take steps to eliminate the project.

An expression frequently used by those in the know about Dimona during that period reflected the emerging concept of maintaining vagueness about the nuclear project: "What they don't know about doesn't exist, and there's no need to discuss something that doesn't exist." If the president was not fully aware of the purpose of Dimona, he would not have any reason to take any steps against Israel. From a contemporary point of view, there is no doubt that Ben-Gurion was taking the right tack. The American government was not yet ready to digest an official statement that Israel had launched a program aimed at building a nuclear option. Over the years, Washington would gradually get used to the idea, and in ten years' time, when it was Prime Minister Meir's turn to shape Israel's security strategy, she would do what she had urged Ben-Gurion to do, and whisper the truth into the ears of the leaders of the American administration.

The Israeli Atomic Energy Commission set about working assiduously to prepare for the visit at Dimona. The official host, according to the report of the American inspectors, was Ephraim Katchalski, scientific adviser to RAFAEL and head of the Weizmann Institute's biophysics department, whose dignified manner and reputation would create an atmosphere of credibility for the guests. Every detail of the visit was carefully planned. The guests would be allowed to see those parts of the facility that were above ground level. They would not be shown the subterranean levels, where the plutonium extraction plant was then under construction, as non-Israeli publications have revealed. According to atomic whistleblower Mordechai Vanunu, a dummy control room was constructed to show the Americans, and the real control room, which was being built underground, was concealed from the guests.

Two days before the two American experts set out on their mission, a minister at the Israeli Embassy in Washington, Mordechai Gazit, invited Philip J. Farley, deputy assistant secretary of state, out to lunch. Gazit informed Farley that the experts would be official guests of the Israeli government and they would be welcomed at the airport by officials of the Israeli AEC. In order to prevent the media from discovering their presence, it would be better if they avoided contact with the U.S. Embassy in Tel Aviv. But if there were leaks, the Israeli government would issue a statement to the effect that the two had come for routine talks with their counterparts in Israel.

Those were the technical arrangements, but Farley was surprised to learn that Gazit had come to the meeting with additional aims: first, to drop the first hint to the administration of the purpose of Dimona, in order to get a sense of what the Americans already knew, and if they knew something, what they thought about it; and second, to preempt a negative reaction if the experts should, God forbid, uncover the truth about Dimona. The detailed report that Farley composed on his meeting with Gazit is one of the most interesting American documents on the gradual development of communication between the two countries about the Israeli project:

> He [Gazit] pressed me repeatedly on what the U.S. expected to achieve of the visit. Certainly we did not plan to issue an announcement that we have visited Dimona and found it pure? If not, what did we know other than that as yet there was nothing other than

peaceful activities under way? I said that I did not believe we would want to make an announcement.

Gazit also asked repeatedly why the U.S. had been so concerned and had made such an issue of the project. Surely we could understand that the secrecy was in the main a protection for suppliers against the Arab boycott. Even if the reactor would produce some plutonium, it would be many years before it went critical, the plutonium was separated and the first bomb could be made. I said that the thing that most concerned us, other than the fact that the project had come as a surprise to us, was the impact in the area of an apparent Israeli commitment to work toward nuclear weapons. If the Arabs believed that this was Israel's goal, the impact on their planning would be great immediately even if Israel's achievement of the goal would be some years off. While the assurance given by Ben-Gurion and to some extent backed up by the U.S. had done a good deal to take the pressures off the Arabs to achieve a balancing atomic capability, there would be a lingering doubt because of the secrecy of the project; indeed we saw constant evidences of increased determination of the UAR to construct a larger reactor than they had previously done more than talk about.

Gazit also directed the conversation repeatedly to the grim security situation in which Israel found itself surrounded by fanatically hostile Arab neighbors. In this situation Israel naturally looked to whatever means it could find for protecting itself. I said that in the U.S. many of us understand the situation of Israel and many of us could understand how if we were in Israel's situation we would decide that we should develop nuclear weapons in order to capitalize on our technological superiority. However, understanding that looking at the situation of Israel from our own position outside, we felt impelled to say that this would be a terrible mistake for Israel as well as for world stability. I could not see how Israel could long expect to have nuclear weapons without its enemies also getting them in some way. Once there were nuclear weapons on both sides, I thought Israel would be in a desperate state. Its territory is simply too small for it to survive even a small nuclear exchange. I thought from my limited knowledge of the situation that fanatic Arabs might well if it were in their power initiate such an exchange, which would lead to destruction of perhaps 25% of the Arab world but virtually all of Israel. Gazit said that, even if the atomic bomb is not the answer, Israel needs to maintain its deterrence.

It was a sensational bit of news that Gazit had let drop: "Even if the re-actor would produce some plutonium, it would be many years before it went critical, the plutonium was separated and the first bomb could be made." This was tantamount to a declaration that Israel did not rule out the possibility that it would attain a nuclear capability. This phrasing of Gazit's remarks is very similar to the statements that Ben-Gurion would make to Kennedy two weeks later, when they met in New York, evidence that every word Gazit had said to Farley had been weighed in advance and cautiously formulated, as part of the groundwork laid by Israel in ad-vance of the experts' visit to Dimona. Gazit's hint was even more trans-parent when he said, "In this situation Israel naturally looked to whatever means it could find for protecting itself."

And Farley himself was hardly stunned by what he heard. Not only did he refrain from utterly ruling out the very thought that Israel would go all the way with its nuclear program, but he didn't hesitate to show sup-port for the project: "I said that in the U.S. many of us understand the situation of Israel and many of us could understand how if we were in Is-rael's situation we would decide that we should develop nuclear weapons in order to capitalize on our technological superiority."

Gazit's cable on his meeting with Farley was closely studied in Jeru-salem, and did much to dissipate anxiety about the forthcoming visit by the experts.

The two visitors were Ulysses Staebler, an expert on nuclear reactors, and Jesse Croach, whose specialty was heavy water. They were both em-ployed by the Atomic Energy Commission of the United States. In his report, Staebler wrote that they were contacted immediately on deplan-ing and taken to a private room, where they were welcomed by Katchal-ski, who greeted them in the name of the prime minister. Staebler asked if a meeting between them and David Bergmann, then chairman of the Israel AEC, was planned and received a negative answer. "I was advised," Staebler wrote, "that he is a public political figure and as such a meeting therefore seemed undesirable but might be arranged if we really wanted it." The pretext given by the hosts was worded as if it had been phrased by an official in communist Russia. Bergmann was not a political figure, and the two guests were aware of that, for they had been well briefed at the U.S. commission in Washington. Mannes Prat simply didn't want Bergmann interfering in Dimona's affairs, and Peres preferred not to run the risk of exposing the talkative scientist to the guests' questions.

The two Americans spent their first two days in Israel touring the country, visiting the small reactor at Nahal Soreq and the Weizmann Institute. On the third day they were driven to Dimona. "We arrived at the reactor site near Dimona about 11:00 a.m. on Saturday May 20, 1961, after motoring from Tel Aviv. Since this was a holiday, the only people at the site were the security guards and those specifically involved in our discussions," they reported, and listed the names of eight hosts: the director of the site, Mannes Prat, and seven heads of departments. Prat greeted them cordially, explained that they were the first foreign visitors to pass the gates of the site, and forbade them to take photographs. "I am also not allowed to take photographs here," he apologized. The guests felt that this prohibition contradicted the procedure that had been agreed upon, but they did not argue and left their cameras in their cases. Prat gave them technical details on the reactor, all of which they included in their report, appending a sketch of the structures at the site and a legend. The reactor was given the number 1. The external envelope of the reactor had almost been completed, they wrote, as had two-thirds of its concrete shield. There is nothing in the report about any other facilities.

On their return to Washington, Staebler and Croach reported to the AEC, a special State Department team, and to National Security Adviser Bundy. They expressed satisfaction that "nothing was concealed from them" and opined that "the reactor is of the size and the peaceful character previously discussed with U.S. officials by representatives of the government of Israel." Although the reactor was meant to produce small amounts of plutonium, they found no evidence that the Israelis were planning to make nuclear weapons. The estimate that the Israelis had conveyed to them that the construction of the reactor would end in 1964 appeared conservative to them. They believed it would be completed before that.

From the Israelis' point of view, the outcome of the visit was fantastic. The deception had worked. The reactor came out looking harmless, and (forbidden) installations had not been discovered. In Ben-Gurion's office, Katchalski and Prat won high praise, and the Israeli team was triumphant. Although a rather troublesome precedent for visits by foreign experts had been set, a precedent for successful subterfuge had also been established. It would be repeated when the second visit took place, in September 1962, and the third, in January 1964, and on another seven occasions over the next nine years. Whenever delegations of experts from the U.S. AEC visited Dimona, they came back with the same message: The reactor's purpose was not to produce nuclear weapons. Was it Israeli trickery that persuaded the Americans, or did they arrive at Dimona from Washington with conclusions that they had reached in advance? We will tackle this conundrum later.

Meanwhile, Ben-Gurion set out for New York, for his first meeting with John F. Kennedy since he had become president. The dispute over inspection was behind them, but nonetheless Ben-Gurion was tense. When he had met Kennedy for the first time, in 1960, he was still a senator, and Ben-Gurion told his biographer, Michael Bar-Zohar, that "he looked like a boy of 25." Perhaps because of Kennedy's youthfulness, Ben-Gurion had not taken him very seriously. Now the boyish senator was president, and the fate of Dimona was in his hands. There was very little in common between the elderly prime minister, who had acquired his vast political experience over decades of harsh diplomatic struggles, as well as wallowing in the mire of petty party politics, and the young president, scion of an aristocratic American family.

On May 30, 1961, the Stars and Stripes and Israel's blue and white Star of David fluttered over the Waldorf-Astoria Hotel on Park Avenue in New York.[7] The meeting lasted ninety minutes. Straight after the exchange of amenities, "the president and the prime minister plunged into a discussion of Israel's Dimona reactor," according to the American side's record of the meeting, written by Mike Feldman:

> The President said he is glad that the two American scientists had had the opportunity to visit the reactor and had given him a good report of it. Since some nations are disturbed at the prospect of the

construction in Israel of a large reactor, with plutonium producing capability, the President suggested that—"on the theory that a woman could not only be virtuous but also have the appearance of virtue"—our problem is how to disseminate information about the nature of the reactor in such a way as to remove any doubts other nations might have as to Israel's peaceful purposes.

According to the minutes of both sides, the prime minister responded by saying that the main purpose of the reactor, and for the time being the only one, was to produce cheap energy. Israel suffered from a lack of water and in order to desalinate seawater it needed large amounts of electricity. "We are asked if it is for peaceful purposes. As of now, the only purpose is peaceful," the prime minister declared. "Not at present, but in another three or four years' time, we will have an experimental plant for separation (of plutonium), which is in any event necessary for every nuclear power plant reactor. We have no such intention at the moment, and we won't do it during the next four or five years. But we shall see what happens in the Middle East, it doesn't depend on us. Perhaps Russia will give bombs to China or Egypt, or perhaps Egypt will develop them by itself."

It is clear from Ben-Gurion's language that Israel had not ruled out developing a nuclear potential. As he explained, a plutonium separation plant might have to be built in any case, as it was necessary for producing electricity, and when it was completed, within the next three or four or five years, the only question remaining would be the timing of the creation of the nuclear option, if there was to be one at all. And that, Ben-Gurion made clear, depended on the situation in the Middle East. So, Ben-Gurion never actually told a blatant lie, although he did bend the truth. He went as far as it was possible without admitting in explicit terms that Israel was planning to build a bomb. He dropped the broadest of hints to the president, just as Gazit had done with Farley a few days before at their Washington tête-à-tête, that Israel was reserving the option of building a bomb.

After Ben-Gurion's explanation, according to the American record of the meeting, Kennedy repeated his warning: "It is to our common interest that no country believes that Israel is contributing to the proliferation of atomic weapons. It is obvious that the UAR [the United Arab

Republic] would not permit Israel to go ahead in this field without getting into it itself." After the brief part of the conversation that was devoted to Dimona, the president asked the prime minister if the U.S. could convey the conclusions of the American experts who had visited Dimona to Arab governments in order to placate them. Ben-Gurion agreed, and Kennedy expressed his satisfaction. The discussion then passed on to other matters.

Ben-Gurion was pleased. The president had accepted the bluff. He had not made things difficult for the prime minister and never even asked him why Israel needed a plutonium extraction plant. Neither did he demand an explicit promise that Israel would not construct installations that would give it nuclear arms capability in the future. On the contrary, according to Bar-Zohar, Kennedy hinted at his obligations to the Jewish voters who had supported him: "Ben-Gurion told me that at the end of the discussion, when the American delegation had already left the room, Kennedy came back in and told him: 'I'd like to ask you something.' The two of them were alone, and Kennedy said: 'I know that I was elected by the votes of American Jews. What do you think I should do?' And Ben-Gurion played the absolute innocent, or at least that's what he told me. He said that it was as if he had been asked what price the president should pay. He said to Kennedy, 'Do what's good for the United States.' Ben-Gurion was very disappointed by this encounter. 'I thought he was a leader, a statesman,' he said, 'and I saw that he was a politician.'"[8]

Indeed, no great empathy was created between the two men, nothing like the personal friendships that flourished later between Lyndon B. Johnson and Levi Eshkol, Richard M. Nixon and Golda Meir, and especially between Bill Clinton and Yitzhak Rabin. The conversation at the Waldorf was of a technical nature. No human warmth was projected, no friendly gestures were made, no remarks that would go down in history. There was not even a press conference afterward. In that era, too close an American contact with Israel was liable to upset the Arabs. On his return to Israel, Ben-Gurion told Peres that he had learned from his talk with Kennedy that "the Americans do not know exactly what we are doing at Dimona." And Paul Warnke later confirmed that Ben-Gurion's appraisal was correct: "We did not really know anything with that degree of detail. We had inspected Dimona on a couple of occasions, taking into account the tight Israeli restrictions, but we could not really tell, so it was more a question of intuition than anything else."

Forty years later, I asked Peres: "And at that time, did you already know that Israel had a nuclear option?"

His answer: "No question about it."

In other words, the whole struggle that Kennedy waged with Ben-Gurion and then with Eshkol was meaningless?

"From my point of view, yes," Peres said.

CHAPTER TEN

A Mossad Conspiracy

A BLACK AND WHITE PHOTOGRAPH, taken at four o'clock in the morning, shows four men standing on a sand dune on a beach a few miles south of Tel Aviv, looking up at the sky. On the right is Shimon Peres, deputy minister of defense, in a white open-necked shirt and a jacket. He is the only one of the four that has a smile on his face. To his left stands the short and stocky figure of Prime Minister and Defense Minister David Ben-Gurion, wearing a military battle-dress jacket. His shock of white hair stands out in the dim light, and he has a grave and thoughtful expression on his face. Next to him is Munya Mardor, head of the Authority for Weapons Development and host of this event, appropriately togged out in a light-colored safari suit. To his left, in uniform, is the chief of staff of the Israel Defense Forces, Lieutenant General Zvi Tsur. Foreign Minister Golda Meir was also present, in a summery floral dress and a dark jacket, but she's not in this picture.

The distinguished party is facing a gleaming white rocket, ready for launch. This is the Shavit 2 (Comet 2) and the name "RAFAEL" is painted on its side in Hebrew. In a few minutes, the countdown would begin, and the first Israeli rocket would soar 47 miles into space. The date was July 5, 1961, roughly two weeks before Egypt was to celebrate its Revolution Day with a massive show of military power. This unusual event on the beach was meant to take some of the wind out of President Gamal Abdel Nasser's sails.

Shavit 2 was a solid-fueled two-stage meteorological rocket. It was designed to reach a speed of two kilometers (1.2 miles) per second by the

196

end of its flight. Meteorological rockets usually are fitted with a small payload containing electronic instruments for measuring atmospheric pressure and wind currents, but Shavit 2 was an experimental model, and instead of the instruments it carried a load of metallic sodium, which would scatter into the atmosphere at the apogee of its course, creating a shining cloud visible from the ground. The production of such a rocket was an essential stage in the development of a strategic missile capable of carrying an explosive warhead, the most efficient means of delivering a nuclear bomb.

Israel's military attaché in Washington had discovered that the Egyptians were intending to launch a similar rocket to mark their national day on July 23. He had cabled Tel Aviv that the Egyptians had acquired from a California aerospace company civilian rockets capable of reaching an altitude of 125 miles. Ben-Gurion was galvanized into action by this report. He called in Mardor and ordered him to move up the launch date for the Israeli-made rocket "to prevent the Egyptians from scoring a political, psychological and morale-building achievement, particularly in the eyes of the rest of the Arab world," in Mardor's words. The prime minister considered victory over Egypt in the race into space so important that he had ordered that the Shavit program be given top priority and had allocated it unlimited resources.

Israeli military intelligence predicted that Nasser would present the rockets as having been developed in Egypt. "We assumed that Nasser's motive in planning the launch was to make political capital," Mardor wrote. "The efforts the Egyptians invested in urgently acquiring the rockets in the United States were interpreted by us as aimed at building Nasser's prestige in the world, especially in the countries of Africa and Asia." Preparations for the founding conference of the Non-Aligned Movement were being completed in Belgrade, Yugoslavia, at that time. Nasser was one of the initiators of the organization, together with Nehru of India, Tito of Yugoslavia, and Sukarno of Indonesia, and Ben-Gurion didn't like the idea of the launch of an Egyptian space rocket weeks before the conference, to carry Nasser's prestige among his peers to new heights.

On the beach, minutes before the launch of the Shavit 2, the members of the RAFAEL technical team were tense, not only because of their awareness of the great responsibility they bore, but also because Ben-Gurion himself was there to watch the launch, and because of the presence, for the first time at such an event, of a civilian camera crew. If the rocket did not lift off as planned, the ignominy would be comparable to that which their French counterparts had experienced three weeks earlier, at the testing grounds at Hammaguira in the Algerian Sahara, when the launch of three similar rockets, of the Veronique type, had failed. The Paris daily *Le Figaro* described in detail how "Norwegians and Americans were invited to be present at the French fiasco," and fifty French physicists "had waited day after day for nothing." Mardor copied the item from the French daily into his diary, in order to underline the difficulty of the mission, and also of course to boast about RAFAEL's achievement: The Shavit 2 launch was a success.

"We stood on the launch knoll, surrounded by dunes. To the west, the waves were quietly lapping on the shore, and, to the east, there was a dark background of green orange groves and fields. All of this combined to form a remarkably pastoral scene, and a feeling of calm enveloped us all." Mardor allowed himself to wax poetic. In a bunker overlooking the launch site, the assembled VIPs peered through their binoculars as the engine ignited. They heard the countdown through loudspeakers. As the rocket lifted off, the deputy chief of staff, Major General Yitzhak Rabin, blurted out: "Wow! What a sight!" Mardor too felt elated. "The liftoff was impressive, powerful and exciting. Everyone was spellbound," he wrote emotionally. At 7 A.M., a special messenger conveyed the news of the successful launch to the president, Yitzhak Ben-Zvi, in Jerusalem. By 8, the cabinet ministers had been informed. The Foreign Ministry cabled the good news to legations abroad, and Israel's state radio station broadcast a special bulletin.

The following day, the world's press led their front pages with the news of the launch, except for the Eastern European bloc and the Arab world, where it was played down. In the London *Times*, the paper's diplomatic commentator said it was unreasonable to assume that Israel would be able to arm missiles with nuclear warheads, but if the country did manage to develop a nuclear capability, the strategic situation in the Middle East would never be the same.

In Israel, euphoria reigned. Ben-Gurion's office was flooded with cables and letters of congratulation. Mardor quotes with pride in his diary the enthusiastic reaction of Amos de Shalit, the Weizmann Institute physicist who was totally opposed to the Israeli nuclear program, in part because of his skepticism about the country's scientific and technological capabilities. "My blessings and best wishes for a fruitful continuation to Jenka [Ratner, the head of the team that built the rocket] and everyone who was involved, including [RAFAEL Scientific Director, David] Bergmann, and you yourself," de Shalit wrote from the United States, where he was on a sabbatical. He added a brief expression of repentance, which Mardor and Peres would often quote in years to come: "I am happy to admit, without reservations, that a large proportion of my objections and complaints have been shattered by this achievement."

But not everyone applauded. The parliamentary opposition criticized Ben-Gurion for his choice of timing, six weeks before the citizens of Israel were due to go to the polls to elect their representatives in the Knesset. In fact, the launch of the Shavit 2 lifted the morale of the Israeli public, but Ben-Gurion's political spin proved ineffective—his party lost five seats.[1]

In closed defense circles a different kind of objection was raised. It was voiced by a senior scientist, Zeev Bonen, a specialist in weapons technologies and the defense industry who had a doctorate from Cambridge and who would become the director general of RAFAEL after Mardor's retirement. Bonen expressed his surprise at the allocation of unlimited resources to a civilian rocket, at a time when projects for the development of military missiles were being scaled back or cancelled. Why refuse to provide additional manpower "in order to realize the [military] objectives that have been set for this year," he asked, while at the same time dozens of experts were employed on a project whose security value was not clear.

Unlike the nuclear project, very few resources had been invested in the various projects for the development of missiles for the defense forces. Consequently, in the early 1960s, the missiles that RAFAEL was building were bogged down in the early stages of development. They included surface-to-surface, air-to-surface, and sea-to-sea missiles. (The last were called Luz in the experimental stage, and later Gabriel.) The guidance and homing systems of these missiles had not been perfected, and the entire project was on the verge of being shut down. "From my conversations with staffers it is clear to me," Bonen said in summing up his complaints, "that the launch of the meteorological rocket was not received amongst them with elation, as the newspapers reported, but with entirely different emotions."

Although the rockets from California did not reach Egypt—for reasons that have never become known—the Egyptians never gave up on their plans in this area, and the show of power that they had apparently hoped to put on for the occasion of Revolution Day 1961 would take place in more grandiose form on the national day a year later.

The space race between Egypt and Israel shed light for a brief moment on a narrow section of their activity in the strategic sphere. Both were investing vast efforts in acquiring strategic arms, and each was employing significant espionage resources in order to discover the darkest secrets of its rival. Both failed miserably at achieving the latter goal.

In late 1960, the Egyptians suspected that Israel was building an atomic bomb. "There was no tangible intelligence grounding for the suspicion, apart from those items that had appeared in the world press at that time," explained Egyptian journalist Muhammad Hasanin Haikal, in 2002. "We caught the whiff of something in the air, but didn't know exactly what it was," he added. Haikal had been a committed mouthpiece and confidant of Nasser's. He was editor of Egypt's most important newspaper, the daily *Al-Ahram*, and his writings meticulously expressed the president's positions. After Dimona was unveiled, he wrote in an editorial that if Israel acquired nuclear weapons, the Arabs would have to do the same immediately because "it was a matter of life and death" for them.

On December 23, 1960, two days after Ben-Gurion announced in the Knesset plenary that Israel was building a nuclear reactor at Dimona, Nasser made his first public mention of Israel's nuclear program. He vowed that if it became clear to him that Israel was developing nuclear weapons, Egypt would launch a preemptive war, "even if we would have to mobilize four million men," and would invade Israeli territory, "in order to destroy the basis of aggression, before it could be used against us." It was an impressive battle cry, but other parts of the speech revealed that the Egyptian president did not put much store by the reports in the international media to the effect that Israel, with the aid of France, was developing the ability to manufacture nuclear arms.

"Nasser never imagined that Israel was building a bomb," said Haikal in 2002. "Today we know that at least up until the end of 1965, Israel's policy of ambiguity led Egypt up the garden path. Nasser believed that it was Israel that had initiated the publication of the stories in the world press, in order to spread alarm amongst the Arabs." Indeed, the Egyptian president had hinted in his speech that the threat of nuclear weapons would not panic the Egyptians, just as in October 1956 the threat of Britain and France to conquer the Suez Canal had not made them surrender. But nevertheless, Nasser's speech aroused concern in Washington.

U.S. ambassador Ogden Reid cited Nasser's speech when he called on Ben-Gurion at his home in Tel Aviv a day later. But Ben-Gurion showed no sign of dismay. "Nasser will attack when he thinks he can destroy Israel. It is not easy for him to mobilize four million men," he told the ambassador. He added this piece of psychological analysis: Nasser is frustrated by his failure to achieve his ambitions. He has failed in the Arab world, in the Muslim world, and in Africa, and he is learning the hard way that it is impossible to rely on the Russians.

Following the meeting in New York between Kennedy and Ben-Gurion, Secretary of State Dean Rusk reported in writing to Egyptian Foreign Minister Mahmud Fawzi that the American experts who visited Dimona had received the impression on their visit that the reactor was meant for peaceful purposes. In his letter of reply, Fawzi asserted that Egypt was carefully following Israel's nuclear activity and regarded its neighbor's projects in this sphere with "unprecedentedly profound concern." But this was a meaningless statement. In fact Egypt sat up and took notice of Israel's nuclear project for only a very brief period, and straight after Fawzi sent his reply to Rusk's letter, the entire matter was dropped from Egypt's political and propaganda agendas.

It was clearly in Israel's interest to calm the Egyptians and put them to sleep, and in this Israel succeeded far beyond its expectations. Until the middle of 1965, Egypt was completely oblivious to Israel's nuclear plans, and when it woke up it was too late even to raise an international brouhaha about them. The matter of the Dimona reactor was perfunctorily mentioned every now and again in the margins of diplomatic meetings that took place in 1961 through 1965 between American emissaries to Cairo and President Nasser and his foreign minister, and in exchanges of diplomatic memoranda between the two countries. However, the United States seemed to take the Israeli reactor far more seriously than Egypt did. This was not the case with Israel's attitude to Egypt's endeavors to acquire strategic weapons.

The Egyptians had already taken their first practical steps in the sphere of nuclear energy in the early 1950s. In 1955, the Soviet Union began erecting, at Inshas Nuclear Research Center near Cairo, a 2-megawatt reactor for research purposes, not powerful enough to produce weapons-grade plutonium.[2] It was first activated in 1960. Like the small reactor that the United States had supplied to Israel for research purposes, the Egyptian reactor was used to train scientists and to produce radioactive isotopes for medicine and industry. Toward the end of 1960, Egypt asked the Russians for a medium-sized reactor. When the talks ran into snags, Nasser turned in a new, unexpected direction.

On Saturday, July 21, 1962, in a fanfare of publicity, Egypt carried out test launches of four surface-to-surface missiles, just after completing development of their prototype model. Two of the missiles were of a type dubbed al-Zafar (the victor), and they were successfully tested over a range of 233 miles. The others were of the al-Kahar (the conqueror) class, and they flew 372 miles. The al-Zafars carried a warhead weighing 500 kilograms, and the al-Kahars a warhead of 700 kilograms. Both types were powered by liquid fuel. They were fired in a westerly trajectory from a launch site some 43 miles northeast of Cairo, and fell in the desert near the border with Libya.

On that day, Mardor and his family were celebrating the bar mitzvah of his son, Rami, at their home in Haifa. At noon, when the party was at its height, Mardor was called to the phone and informed by a RAFAEL staffer of the Egyptian launch. "The first thought that passed through my mind was: This is Nasser's birthday present to Rami," he wrote in his diary. Rami remembers that the guests crowded round General Meir Amit, head of military intelligence, and asked him for details about the event.

A few days after the successful launch, the Egyptians drove their new missiles, draped in the national flag, through the streets of Cairo, as part of the Revolution Day parade. President Nasser addressed a mass rally and declared that the missiles could hit any target up to "just south of Beirut." In other words, the entire area of Israel was within their range.

Israel was shocked. While the country's defense industry was occupied with the first stage of developing its nuclear option, its enemies had unveiled medium-range ballistic missiles. These were not meteorological rockets purchased in California, but military missiles developed and manufactured by the Egyptians themselves.

Israeli military intelligence had been following Egyptian missile development since 1959, and its estimate as of mid-1961 assumed that at least another five years would go by before the missiles would attain a 400-kilometer range (about 250 miles) and endanger Israel. Suddenly, years before the predicted time, the Egyptians had carried out 600-kilometer (372-mile) test launches, and could threaten targets anywhere in Israel. Moreover, Israeli intelligence had no information whatsoever about the composition of the missiles' warheads. Were they planned to carry conventional explosives? Chemical? Biological? Perhaps even atomic ones? The anxiety that seized the Israeli leadership was tremendous, as was the anger toward the head of the Mossad, Isser Harel, who was accused of falling asleep on sentry duty. The heads of the defense establishment demanded that Harel obtain all the information, and he promised Ben-Gurion that he would do so within a few months.

And indeed, in the middle of August, at a meeting in the prime minister's office, the spy chieftain portrayed a situation that appalled the audience. Since the end of 1959, the Egyptians had recruited hundreds of German scientists and technicians, each an expert in one area of strategic-weaponry development. During World War II, some of them had worked at Peenemunde, on the staff of Wernher von Braun,[3] the rocket scientist who developed for the Nazis the V-2 rocket that had terrorized Londoners late in the war. Harel's agents had located companies in Germany that were acquiring raw materials for the manufacture of missiles and planes in Egypt, and an electronics laboratory in West Germany that was busy planning guidance systems, headed by a scientist named Hans Kleinwachter.

The experts recruited in Germany were employed at secret army bases near Cairo and charged with designing aircraft and missiles. The aircraft-building project was carried out at a site known as Factory 36 at the Helwan military base, and it was run by the renowned engineer Willy E. Messerschmitt, who had developed for the Luftwaffe the fighter plane bearing his name, the Messerschmitt Bf 109, which had ruled the skies of Europe during the early years of World War II. Messerschmitt reported directly to the office of the president.

At another base, known as Factory 333, in the Heliopolis neighborhood of Cairo, another German, Wolfgang Pilz, ran the missile-building operation. Not only were the two types of missiles that were launched before Revolution Day under development there, but also a third type. This was the two-stage al-Raid (pioneer), which had a range of 1,000 kilometers (621 miles). According to Ben-Gurion's diary, Harel read out at the meeting a letter that Pilz had handed in March 1962 to the commander of the Egyptian missile base, in which he undertook to build 500 short-range and 400 medium-range missiles.

Harel reported that the missiles were not ready for operational use, because some key functions had not yet been perfected, including the fueling and guidance systems, and that at the test launch they had missed their targets by some 40 kilometers (24 miles). Nonetheless, the defense chiefs were still very worried. Israel had no reply. "Our scientists have been amateurish, and have not tackled this subject seriously," said chief of staff Zvi Tsur at the meeting.

Following the missile-launch display in Egypt, even before Harel's report Ben-Gurion and Peres had decided to transfer the Israeli missile-development project from RAFAEL to the state-owned Israel Aircraft Industries (IAI). Until that time, all of the research and development for the missile project had been carried out by RAFAEL, while outside bodies, including the IAI, had served as manufacturing contractors for components once their development had been completed. Now, following the failure of RAFAEL, the development of a strategic weapon was for the first time entrusted to another enterprise.

Mardor and his staff objected vigorously. Mardor contended that RAFAEL had bred a generation of experts who only a year earlier had successfully launched the Shavit 2, and that they therefore deserved to be trusted. But Ben-Gurion and Peres stood firm. Mardor wrote in his diary that Bergmann was "hurt and infuriated" and had declared a mutiny, announcing in a memo to Peres that he would not be able to demand from his staff that they supply information on their missiles to the IAI, "without my being able to assure them that they would have a role in this project," and adding: "You decided at the time that development was a matter for RAFAEL and not for the Aircraft Industries. I hope that you will agree with me that our people, who have invested so much energy and a not-negligible number of days of their lives in the project, are entitled to enjoy any further development on this matter." Peres was angry, but Mardor intervened and deftly smoothed things over. There was simply no way to avoid admitting that RAFAEL had failed in the development of strategic missiles, even short-range ones.

Isser Harel—Peres's perennial critic—was gleeful over Peres's embarrassment. Peres was ordered by Ben-Gurion to demand an explanation for the assistance to Egypt from the defense minister of West Germany, Franz Josef Strauss. "I wrote a very sharp letter to Strauss," says Peres. "We were great friends. And he replied, 'Shimon, give me a name, give me a lead. We know nothing about all this.'" The West German government, at least initially, was not willing to interfere in the affairs of its citizens in foreign lands. Foreign Minister Meir tried to enlist the aid of the Americans. She gave Mike Feldman the information that had been collected about the German scientists in Egypt, and asked him to convey it to the president and to tell him that Israel was worried.

Events took a dramatic turn on October 23, 1962, when an Austrian citizen, who identified himself as Dr. Otto Joklik and said he was a nuclear scientist, contacted the Israeli commercial delegation in the West German city of Cologne.[4] He reported at his own initiative that the Egyptians had employed him in a project aimed at the development of radioactive arms. Joklik agreed to travel to Israel, where he was questioned by the Mossad near Tel Aviv. He said that the Egyptians were working on two projects. One was called "Innis" and its aim was to arm missiles with warheads carrying cobalt-60 radioactive waste—something known today as a "dirty bomb." The code name of the second project was "Cleopatra," and its goal was to produce eight nuclear bombs, armed with enriched uranium. Although Egypt had no nuclear reactor, said Joklik, with his help they were planning to acquire centrifuges and to use them to manufacture fissile material.

Harel was stunned. This was a far-reaching initiative aimed at producing nuclear arms. The information given by Joklik and relayed by Harel made Golda Meir's blood boil, and Ben-Gurion too, "was terribly distressed," Harel recalled. At that very time, Israel and West Germany were negotiating mutual diplomatic recognition, a far-reaching move that was in accordance with the strategy of reconciliation with Germany that Ben-Gurion had adopted. The picture drawn by Joklik could halt the negotiations.

Harel suggested that Ben-Gurion appeal directly to West German Chancellor Konrad Adenauer, but Ben-Gurion demurred. Ben-Gurion's reluctance sprang from the strategic—even historic—decision that Ben-Gurion had taken about relations between Israel and the German people. Ben-Gurion recognized that West Germany was not Hitler's Germany, but "the other Germany," an expression he had coined in order to justify his decision to sign an agreement with the Federal Republic in 1952 providing for the payment by Germany of reparations to the Jews for the depredations they had suffered at the hands of the Nazis. Adenauer's Germany accepted responsibility for the crimes of the Nazis and agreed to pay compensation to their victims, and honored its moral commitment to the State of Israel.

Israel's recognition of "the other Germany" was therefore a clear case of realpolitik, and Ben-Gurion anticipated that it would bring Israel substantial political, economic, and military gains, as it in fact did. This was why he did not want the affair of the German scientists in Egypt to escalate and damage relations between Germany and Israel. To Harel, this attitude of Ben-Gurion's and the concept of "the other Germany" were utterly perverse, and he never ceased his opposition, sometimes quite bluntly; Meir strongly supported him. Harel even claimed that the Bonn government was behind the activities of the German scientists in Egypt.

Ben-Gurion ordered Harel to persuade the scientists to leave by using other, covert means. Harel did not hesitate. At that time the Mossad's chief activity was information gathering and it did not have an operations unit, so Harel had to recruit operational personnel from the Shin Bet. This was not a problem, since he ran both organizations. Some of the agents enlisted to plan and carry out the threatening and terrorizing of the German scientists and their families had two years previously taken key parts in the abduction of Adolf Eichmann in Buenos Aires.

In the last months of 1962, and the first quarter of 1963, the Mossad operated intensively in several European countries, but its main focus of activity was in Germany. Here is a list of some of the incidents that were connected to the German scientists but have never been officially solved:

- In September 1962, a private aircraft blew up in the sky over northern Germany. Its owner was a German middleman who supplied weapons and recruited technicians for Egypt. His wife died in the explosion.
- In November 1962, Dr. Heinz Krug, forty-nine, disappeared in Munich. He was the director of an Egyptian front company called Antra that was linked to the development of the Egyptian missiles. His car was found abandoned, but he was never located.
- At the end of November, Pilz's German secretary at Factory 333 opened a letter bomb addressed to him that blew up and left her blinded, deaf, and facially disfigured.
- The following day, a gift-wrapped package blew up at the same plant, killing the Egyptian scientist Michael Khouri and five Egyptian engineers who were in his vicinity. The parcel bomb was addressed to General Kamal Azzar, who was the Egyptian army coordinator for the German scientists' work.
- In February 1963, on a road near the town of Lörrach in southern West Germany, not far from the border with Switzerland, an assailant fired a pistol at Hans Kleinwachter, head of the guidance systems lab in Stuttgart, but missed.
- For several months, German scientists received threatening letters at their Egyptian addresses. Some were sent letter bombs. The scientists' families in Germany received threatening telephone calls.

Otto Joklik also joined the Israeli effort. On March 2, 1963, Joklik and Mossad operative Joseph Ben-Gal were sent to Basel, Switzerland, to warn Hans and Heidi, the children of Paul-Jens Goercke, a German expert in electronic guidance systems employed at Factory 333. The two men met Heidi Goercke at the Drei Könige Hotel and urged her to persuade her father to get out of Egypt.[5] If he refused, they told her, he could expect "serious problems." The Swiss police recorded the conversation and that evening they arrested Joklik and Ben-Gal. Within hours, the German police requested their extradition on suspicion of participation in the abortive assassination attempt against Kleinwachter.

A few days later, the story broke in the media and it soon became an international affair. Ben-Gurion was annoyed that Harel had not informed him in advance that the Mossad intended to carry out an operation in Switzerland. The prime minister urgently summoned the spy chief to a meeting at the hotel in Tiberias, on the shore of the Sea of Galilee, where he was vacationing; Ben-Gurion rebuked Harel and served him with a written instruction: "From now on no action that is not in accordance with the law of the country where the action will be carried out will be taken by the personnel you are responsible for without my knowledge and total agreement, and you will not speak to any person, with no exception, about the above-mentioned matter [the arrest of the two agents in Switzerland] without my knowledge and prior agreement."

Harel himself was in a frenzy, and on that very same evening he broke Ben-Gurion's orders. In coordination with Foreign Minister Meir he called a meeting in Tel Aviv of the editors of Israeli newspapers, and informed them not only about the secret circumstances that led to the arrest of Joklik and Ben-Gal in Basel, but also what the Mossad had uncovered in Egypt and in Germany. The work that the German scientists were doing in Egypt constituted an existential threat to Israel, Harel told the editors, and the German government was aware of it and yet refused to act. At the same time, Mossad staffers briefed three Israeli journalists in Jerusalem, and they were then sent to Germany whence they filed stories to their papers containing the information that had been leaked to them. (Military censorship would have prevented the publication of the material had it been filed in Israel.) The affair and the public storm around it ballooned, and not without good reason. According to the head of the Mossad, this was an existential security matter of the highest degree. In Israel and across the world there were sensational headlines along the lines of "Nazis in Egypt Develop Atomic, Chemical and Biological Weapons to Use Against Israel," or "Egyptian Missiles to Be Armed with Radioactive Material," and "Egypt Arms Bombs with Nuclear Waste."

The media storm forced the government to make a statement in Knesset that reflected the Meir-Harel hysteria more than Ben-Gurion's calmer approach, after which an angry debate ensued. Hearing the reports of the Knesset debate, Israelis wondered how, if German scientists were developing weapons of mass destruction in Egypt with the encouragement of the German government, could the Federal Republic be called the "other Germany"? Meir and Harel, who opposed Ben-Gurion's German initiatives, had put him on the defensive. Ben-Gurion failed to grasp the situation. He didn't bother to interrupt his vacation in the north to attend the Knesset debate, and his confidant, Shimon Peres, who would certainly have warned him in time, was away on a working trip to Bonn and Paris. Golda Meir, who represented the government in the debate, never tried hard to defend the prime minister, and neither did the other cabinet ministers. Ben-Gurion's colleagues had turned their backs on him, and he was frustrated and isolated.

The turnabout began when Peres returned from Paris and found that the affair had assumed unreasonable proportions. All the hysteria was menacing the network of special relations that Ben-Gurion had woven with the West Germans. In exchange for the Jewish state's readiness to recognize "the other Germany," the Federal Republic had secretly supplied Israel with American-made arms—tanks, helicopters, and planes—for a nominal price. In the very days that the affair of the German scientists in Egypt was dominating the media, the two governments were beginning to discuss another, broader arms deal. The Federal Republic had transferred to Jerusalem the initial payments of the half-billion-dollar loan that it had undertaken to give Israel, an enormous sum in Israel in those days. The Israeli economy was due to jump several notches. All this was now in jeopardy. Peres requested that the army conduct a thoroughgoing review of the Mossad's findings. The chief of staff assigned the task to Meir Amit, the head of military intelligence.

On Tuesday, March 25, 1963, Amit delivered his report in the prime minister's office. Peres and chief of staff Tsur were with him, and Ben-Gurion cross-examined him carefully about each of the projects that the Mossad had associated with the German scientists. Amit asserted that they were all either nonexistent or unfeasible.

The assessment that Amit gave Ben-Gurion jibed with that of American intelligence agencies. Amit was unaware of the fact that on July 22, 1962, the day after the test launch of the four Egyptian missiles, the CIA had distributed a document that declared that the launch was "by and large a propaganda stunt of the kind at which Nasir [Nasser] excels." A few days later, in an internal memo to the national security adviser, McGeorge Bundy, the State Department reported that it did not "consider that this development alters significantly the balance of military power in the Middle East." In early January 1963, an evaluation drawn up at the request of the CIA's deputy director of intelligence found that it was possible that Egypt might be able to deploy a few missile batteries in the middle of 1964, as long as the German technicians stayed there and the supply of components from Europe was not disrupted. As far as weapons of mass destruction were concerned, the CIA report repeated that it did not consider that this latest development altered significantly the balance of military power in the Near East.

Joklik, the Austrian who came to the Israeli commercial delegation in Cologne, had made it all up. When Joklik's past was scrutinized, Ben-Gurion recounted later at a meeting of the general staff, it turned out that he was a professional con man, and had forged the academic degrees of which he was so proud. Scientific examinations revealed that the purported Egyptian plans discovered by the Mossad to build cobalt-60 warheads and to produce fissile material by means of centrifuges were impossible to implement.

Amit said that "Isser [Harel] never gave Ben-Gurion accurate information. He claimed that the West German government had egged the scientists on, and that was a lie." Peres too laid most of the blame at Harel's doorstep. "Ben-Gurion was furious at being misled and deluded. Look, today [it is clear that] it was all one big cock-and-bull story. It turned out that there were no German scientists," Peres insisted, virtually calling Harel a liar. Harel insisted that the Mossad had conveyed reliable information and that it was Peres who had deceived Ben-Gurion.

"The Old Man," as Ben-Gurion had been called for years, was going through a severe crisis at that time, a crisis springing from a combination of causes. The fabric of relations with his closest companions had disintegrated. Meir, Eshkol, Harel, and other colleagues who for years had made so much of him, now had ceased to back his policies.

"He was totally isolated," said his secretary, Yitzhak Navon. "Not even a fly came into his office, nothing, and every day the media would be engaged in attacks against him, and anyone with whom Ben-Gurion had ever argued came alive to assail him. This was the chance for everyone to pile onto him, from the left, right, and center."

In fact, Ben-Gurion's "friends" were showing him the way out, and his depression was so great that he said to a close companion, according to Bar-Zohar, "I'd rather skin carcasses in the marketplace than be prime minister." Ben-Gurion's temper quickened, and he reacted fretfully. The criticism of his policy toward Germany by right-wing Knesset members so infuriated him that during a parliamentary debate he fired invective at them, accusing them of having "praised and glorified the name of Hitler, and made him a model." In a letter to the poet and columnist Haim Goury, he called Menachem Begin "a distinctly Hitlerian type." If Begin were to gain control of the country, said the letter, he would replace "the military and police commands with his thugs and rule like Hitler ruled Germany and oppress the labor movement with force and cruelty." Thus, Ben-Gurion's personal crisis found tangible expression in his political behavior. Always fearful of a deterioration in security, and of a surprise attack by the Arabs, he had known how to conceal his anxieties from the outside world. But now he was externalizing his emotions to an embarrassing extent.

In February 1963, the Middle East became embroiled in yet another crisis, similar in some ways to that of 1958. In Iraq, a revolution had led to the seizure of the government by the Baath party.[6] In the Hashemite Kingdom of Jordan, King Hussein's reign was once again tottering. Syria, Egypt, and Iraq set up a federation, a move that threatened a united military front against Israel. Ben-Gurion dispatched letters to world leaders, asking them to urge the Arab states to honor Israel's territorial integrity. He wrote to Khrushchev and Kennedy, requesting a joint Soviet-American guarantee of Israel's security. He warned Kennedy that if Nasser attacked and Israel failed to defeat him, the Jewish people would suffer another Holocaust. He proposed to de Gaulle that the alliance between the two countries be renewed. This was not the vigorous and determined Ben-Gurion of 1956, but an aging, confused leader, showing weakness to the world. His excessive anxiety stood out against a background in which Israel was by no means as menaced as he made it out to be. The Arab federation existed on paper only, and Hussein's monarchy would survive. It may be that Ben-Gurion's exaggerated reaction was a result of his having recognized his own weaknesses, exhaustion, growing anxiety, and forgetfulness. His memory had betrayed him.

When Amit left the prime minister's office that morning in March 1963, Ben-Gurion was enraged. He summoned Harel and told him about military intelligence's latest assessment. A sharp argument ensued between the two, and when Ben-Gurion insisted that the military's evaluation was the right one, Harel resigned. The prime minister, who had apparently not grasped the implications of Harel's disloyal conduct, or feared to become his open enemy, tried to persuade him to stay on. But the veteran Mossad chief, known by the epithet "Hamemuneh," or "The Man in Charge," reflecting both respect and fear, would not retract.

On April 1, Ben-Gurion summoned Amit and handed him his letter of appointment as head of the Mossad, replacing Harel. Amit was surprised. "My throat felt dry. Ostensibly, I should not have been surprised, because after all I was more or less involved in the events, but nevertheless, it came as a sudden blow, like thunder on a clear day," he wrote in his memoirs, adding a few lines on his predecessor: "Isser Harel was not only the head of the Mossad, he embodied the Mossad in himself, somewhat mysterious, with the semi-legendary aura surrounding him. It was only in retrospect, when I was inside and familiar with the secrets of the Mossad that I discovered what a small person he was in spirit, as well as in stature . . . Many days went by before I found out the naked truth, until it became clear to me that this 'legend' was nothing more than a tangle of intrigues, ambitions, and delusions of grandeur, with no real basis underneath it."

Nevertheless, as the head of the Mossad Amit planned to continue clandestine operations against the German scientists in Egypt in order to eliminate their involvement in weapons development, although he was aware that the threat they posed was far smaller than Harel had made it out to be. But Peres dissuaded him. "I thought that I shouldn't take any risks and that we should go on pursuing them," Amit explains, "but Shimon said, 'Let them carry on. They're throwing good money after bad.' And Shimon knew. He was involved in missile development in Israel, and he knew that in Egypt nothing would come of it. I agreed with him."

Continued operations against the German scientists were therefore removed from the agenda. "Now, there were no letter bombs, which had proved ineffective in '62 and hit innocent people and created political and moral problems and aroused strong opposition to the Mossad in Europe," Amit said forty-two years later.

In the next two years, Israel was active in three channels. In the diplomatic channel, it persuaded the West German government to intervene, and to make some of the scientists return to their country. To achieve this, Amit traveled to Munich, where he met the head of the Federal Intelligence Service, Reinhard Gehlen.[7] And indeed, in 1964 the first wave of scientists left Egypt, and a second wave left a year later, after Egypt recognized East Germany.

In a second channel, the Mossad acted by using nonviolent means at the Helge factory in the German city of Freiburg. The plant, which made components for NATO missile-guidance systems using technology supplied by the American electronics giant Litton, was about to be closed because NATO had cut its orders, and several dozens of its workers were recruited by the Egyptians. Mossad agents enlisted a Czech technician at the plant who had a brother living in Israel, and tasked him with persuading fellow workers not to go to Egypt. Most of them were convinced, and others received financial compensation for agreeing to stay in Germany.

The results of these efforts were successful. The colony of German scientists and engineers in Egypt dissolved. All three of the models of missiles that they were developing failed to reach operational capability, and work on them was halted. In 1966, the head of the project at Factory 333, Wolfgang Pilz, the last of the colony, moved to China, where he was employed developing the plans that had not reached fruition in Egypt. This was the final act in the drama of the German scientists in Egypt.

In the third channel, and despite the fact that fears about the Egyptians' winning the space and missiles race had proved unfounded, Peres tried to compensate for RAFAEL's failure to produce the appropriate counter. Dassault directors reported that Peres turned to the French in September 1962. The French government approved Israel's request and Dassault put together a special working team at its aircraft assembly plant near Paris, to build a medium-range ballistic missile for Israel. The first version of the missile was based on the two-stage French MD-600. The archetype was designed to carry a 750-kilogram warhead and to be launched from permanent launching pads to a distance of up to 500 kilo-meters, with an accuracy margin of one kilometer radius from the target. The agreement for the production of the missile was signed in Tel Aviv in April 1963.

Foreign media have reported that a second generation of Jericho missiles was developed in Israel in the early 1980s, on the basis of the Shavit 2. Israel has never admitted to having the Jericho 2 in its arsenal, but U.S. Department of Defense experts have several times reported that Jericho 2 has a range of 1,500 kilometers and carries a 500-kilogram warhead. Other foreign experts assert that Jericho missiles are capable of carrying nuclear warheads.

THE AFFAIR OF the German scientists had highlighted the political reality in Israel in the early 1960s. Despite the fact that Israel had turned the conventional arms balance in its own favor, and although Israel's leaders were already aware that within a few years the Dimona reactor would have nuclear capability, nevertheless their fundamental anxiety over the danger of being devastated by a surprise Arab attack had not dissipated. And this was so, it should be stressed, at a time when Israeli and American intelligence agreed that Egypt, the leading and the strongest Arab state, was not demonstrating the slightest intention or desire to attack Israel, mainly because it did not have any illusions about being able to win. American intelligence believed that Egypt would go to war only if and when it became convinced that Israel was about to acquire a nuclear bomb. This assessment was based on explicit statements by Nasser, on information gathered on the ground, and on a number of articles by Muhammad Hasanin Haikal. In talks with the American ambassador in Cairo, John S. Badeau, and with other American emissaries, Nasser declared several times that he would launch "a defensive war" only if there were no option, if it became evident to him that Israel was about to produce weapons-grade plutonium at Dimona.

In internal Israeli politics, the case of the German scientists was the penultimate act in the series of tragic dramas that had begun in 1955, when the dismal Lavon Affair, *the* Affair, had erupted in Egypt, as related in Chapter 2. That affair had upset the delicate equilibrium at the core of

Israel's leadership and was a prelude to the less significant affair of the scientists.

Strangely, a one-sided and inaccurate version of the affair of the German scientists has remained etched in Israel's collective memory. That is the version that Ben-Gurion's opponents nurtured. Ask any average, well-informed Israeli what happened in Egypt in the early 1960s, and she or he will tell you with the utmost certainty that the Mossad, in its inimitable dedication and ingenuity, succeeded in stopping German scientists, some of whom had served in Hitler's war machine, from developing for Egypt weapons of mass destruction that had been meant to wipe out Israel. This version has seemingly authoritative backing in the history books, articles, and Internet sites. It is taught in the schools. The true version, the one based on the assessment of the situation carried out by military intelligence, and whose accuracy has withstood the test of time, has all but faded into oblivion.

CHAPTER ELEVEN

The Heir

IN MID-1962, the Kennedy administration was still trying to play the unbiased mediator in the Middle East, to the ostensible benefit of both the Arabs and Israel, and thus trying to lure both of them into its bosom. It did this by promoting a peace initiative that was derived from the election platform formulated by adviser Mike Feldman for candidate Kennedy in 1960. One plank said Israel should agree to allow the return of 10–20 percent of the refugees who had fled or been ejected from the territories that it had captured in 1948, and the remainder would be settled in the Arab states. This idea was based on a plan put forward by of Joseph E. Johnson, president of the Carnegie Endowment for Peace, and the special envoy to the Middle East of United Nations secretary General Dag Hammarskjöld.[1] In August 1961, Kennedy adopted the Johnson plan, and immediately dispatched Feldman to test the Israeli reaction.

The Johnson plan was the stick; the carrot was an offer to supply Israel with batteries of Hawk antiaircraft missiles to defend the Dimona reactor and the country's military airfields. The plan was to link the return of some of the refugees to an improvement in Israel's defense capability in order to reduce tension in the Middle East. The missiles would allay Israel's anxiety over a possible Arab attack, and the return of some of the refugees would assuage the Arabs' rage. The refugee problem was then, and still is today, the main bone of contention between the Arabs and Israel.

On his return to Washington, Feldman reported to the White House that he had received the impression that the Israelis would agree to take in Palestinian refugees. Feldman's optimistic impression, however, was colored by his wishes, and not based on the Israeli government's policy. Ben-Gurion and Foreign Minister Meir believed that the return of refugees would endanger the existence of the State of Israel, and they would not accept the plan. The Israeli ambassador in Washington, Avraham Harman, defined Israel's attitude toward the plan as "nonnegotiable."

Nevertheless, Feldman managed to create an impression in Washington that Israel would be ready to soften its stance toward both the Johnson plan and the nuclear project, and thus to persuade the president to sell it Hawk missiles, over the strong objections of the State Department. In late September 1962, Kennedy approved the sale despite the fact that Israel had not changed its positions;[2] it is reasonable to assume that the president preferred Feldman's stand to that of Secretary of State Rusk out of electoral considerations. During the second half of his first term in the White House, Kennedy began wooing the Jewish vote, with an eye on the battle for his second term.

It is possible that the Kennedy administration might have insisted on the implementation of the Johnson plan for the solution of the refugee problem despite the stubborn opposition of the Israelis, if Egypt's president Nasser had not taken an aggressive step that threatened the regimes backed by United States in the Arabian Peninsula and the Persian Gulf. His revolutionary offensive began in Yemen. At the end of September 1962, at his instigation, officers in the Yemeni army mutinied against the local ruler, the imam in San'a. Following a pattern resembling the 1952 revolution of the "Free Officers" headed by General Muhammad Naguib and Colonel Nasser himself, the rebels took over key institutions and declared the establishment of a republic. A civil war broke out. The monarchs of three neighboring countries, whose reigns were propped up by American patronage—Ibn Saud of Saudi Arabia, Hussein of Jordan, and the Shah of Iran, Mohammed Reza Pahlavi—supported the imam with arms and money. Israel too, at the instigation of British intelligence, helped the imam's forces, with shipments of surplus World War II weapons. The Soviet Union, Egypt, and Syria backed the insurgents. Nasser sent army units, and at the height of its involvement, Egypt had

75,000 soldiers in Yemen. The United States feared a domino effect that would endanger the West's control of oil production in the Arabian Peninsula and the Gulf.

Until he evacuated his army from Yemen late in 1967, Nasser would allow his forces to sink into the quagmire of a prolonged and difficult war of attrition, in which he squandered many resources and weapons (years later, he would refer to Yemen as "my Vietnam"). He also lost the last vestige of support that he still retained in the State Department in Washington, both because he jeopardized the Saudi dynasty, and because his army in Yemen used poison gas.

In late December 1962, in Palm Beach, Florida, Golda Meir met with JFK and several of his senior advisers on the Middle East, including Mike Feldman. The seventy-minute meeting included a detailed discussion of the nature of the relationship between Israel and the United States. From Israel's point of view, it was a unique and very important meeting and a landmark in relations between the two countries.

At the outset, Meir congratulated Kennedy on his great victory in the Cuban missile crisis, which had been resolved in October. The revolutionary Arab states had supported the Soviet Union, which had lost face in the resolution of the crisis. President Kennedy thanked Meir for her congratulations.

That was an auspicious start, and what followed was even better. The president said that the United States "has a special relationship with Israel in the Middle East, really comparable only to that which it has with Britain over a wide range of world affairs." Meir was surprised. This was the first time that an American president had, at an official meeting, equated his country's ties with Israel with the special relationship between the United States and the United Kingdom. But she was even more surprised when the president declared: "I think it is quite clear that in the case of an invasion the United States would come to the support of Israel. We have that capacity and it is growing."

Today, such language may sound obvious, but until that meeting no American president had offered to intervene on Israel's behalf if the Arabs invaded its territory. Kennedy was the first president to use the word "special" in defining America's relations with Israel, now an accepted feature of the discourse between the two nations.

It emerged clearly from Kennedy's remarks that he had not given up entirely on the revolutionary Arab states and that he was still interested in removing them from the Soviet camp and linking them with the free world, but not at Israel's expense. In other words, Israel's existence and security was a fundamental element of America's interests in the Middle East. This is what Kennedy said: "To be effective in our own interest and to help Israel, we have to maintain our position in the Middle East generally. Our interest is best served if there is a group of sovereign countries associated with the West. We are in a position then to make clear to the Arabs that we will maintain our friendship with Israel and our security guarantees."

Right at the end of the meeting, according to the records of it, Kennedy said he "would hope that Israel would give consideration to our problems on this atomic reactor. We are opposed to nuclear proliferation. Our interest here is not in prying into Israel's affairs but we have to be concerned because of the overall situation in the Middle East."

The wording was gentle, and Meir replied in the Israeli "everything-is-going-to-be-all-right" style. According to the record, "Mrs. Meir reassured the President that there would not be any difficulty between us on the Israeli nuclear reactor."

The president was therefore offering a very far reaching deal, from Israel's point of view. To these statements of intent, a practical step was added: The president was revoking his support for the Johnson plan for the return of some of the Palestinian refugees.[3] The quid pro quo that Kennedy was demanding from Israel was also clearly defined: Help me strengthen the status of the United States in the Middle East. In order for me to succeed in whittling down Soviet influence in the region, you will have to reduce the use of force against your neighbors, and abstain from drawing attention to Dimona.

This was the second leap forward in the protracted process that saw Israel and the United States growing ever closer. As we have seen, it was the Eisenhower administration that first upped the level of the relationship, immediately after the 1958 crisis in the Middle East. The Cuban missile crisis was the catalyst for the second step up, because the free world had faced a tangible threat and its leader, the president of the United States, had found it necessary to marshal his supporters behind him. Just as it had in the 1958 crisis, Israel had emerged as the strongest pillar of support for the United States policy in the Middle East, while Egypt was exposed as a menace to American assets in the region. Kennedy was at that time losing any illusions that he still had about Nasser. Nasser's massive military involvement in Yemen helped him along, as did the enthusiastic support that the Egyptian media had given the Soviets in the Cuban missile crisis. Indeed, in retrospect it is easy to discern how the meeting in Florida fits in as a defining event in the slow process of the solidification of the special Israeli-American alliance.

Meir returned to Israel and reported to Ben-Gurion on the successful meeting in Florida, and toward the end of January 1963, after Ambassador Walworth Barbour had returned to Israel from his Christmas home leave Ben-Gurion summoned him to a meeting in his office. The purpose was to repeat the president's pledges to the American envoy, and to confirm them as the foundations of the relationship between the two countries (by ensuring that they were acknowledged by the State Department as well as the White House). Barbour's report to Washington (in cable-ese) of the meeting with Ben-Gurion, read: "He opened discussion by expressing appreciation for deep understanding, goodwill, and friendship for Israel shown by President Kennedy in recent talks with Foreign Minister Meir. President's comment that United States special relation with Israel not negotiable appeared touch him particularly. While deeply grateful to hear United States would come quickly to Israel's aid if latter attacked he commented in this respect Israel must nevertheless rely upon itself."

Now Ben-Gurion was expected to make concessions in the matter of visits to Dimona by American experts. He was willing to go a long way toward meeting the president's demands, but he drew the line at opening the reactor facility to inspection, because it was clear to him that the United States was not yet ready to internalize the notion that Israel was preparing to join the small club of countries with nuclear capability. Kennedy stepped up the pressure. He demanded that the supervision of the reactor be continuous, and be carried out twice a year. If the president became convinced that American interests were being harmed because of Dimona, or if he perceived Ben-Gurion's insistent rejection as perverse obstinacy, Israel would have to pay a high price.

Ben-Gurion's reason for resisting the demand for inspection was that the project was progressing faster than expected. Construction of the reactor had been completed in 1962, and the sections had been operationally tested. The reactor at Dimona was due to become critical in December 1963. Indeed, Ben-Gurion and his close advisers were convinced that within a few years, Israel would have nuclear capability.

The United States and Israel exchanged messages concerning the timing of the visits to Dimona by American experts, but no progress was achieved until Kennedy lost his patience and fired off a sharply worded communication to Ben-Gurion that Ambassador Barbour planned to deliver after his Sunday round of golf on June 16, 1963. The language of the president's message was imperious: The United States would send inspectors to visit the Dimona nuclear facility "early this summer." Another visit would take place in June 1964, "and thereafter in intervals of six months." In an accompanying cable, the ambassador was told to inform the prime minister that these were America's minimal demands.

Barbour was a career diplomat. He had replaced Ogden Reid as ambassador to Israel in 1961 and was to hold the position until 1973, still the longest term an American ambassador has served in Israel. The U.S. ambassador is always an important player in Israel's political and diplomatic arena, and Barbour's presence hovered constantly over the halls of power. Barbour was part of the inner core of Israeli society. Sometimes the media referred to him as "the high commissioner."[4]

The period during which Barbour served in Israel was crucial, in both the building of the relationship with the United States and in the building of the nuclear option. It was evident that Barbour had a deep understanding of the existential anxiety that afflicted the Jewish state. He empathized with its perceived need to acquire an ultimate defensive deterrent to the extent that he tended to turn a blind eye to some Israeli moves in the nuclear sphere. Barbour was known as an efficient ambassador, with excellent sources in Israel, and it can therefore be assumed that the true purpose of the Dimona reactor was clear to him early on in his term of office. But some Israelis who met him frequently got the impression that he never tried to show much interest in the nuclear project, and he never insisted that his subordinates make efforts to discover the secrets of Dimona.

During the year that had gone by since the last visit by American sci-entists to Dimona, in September 1962, the American government had demanded several times that Ben-Gurion honor his undertaking to make regular visits possible. On the one hand, the construction of the reactor had been completed, and President Kennedy wanted to know exactly what was going on there, and thereby to show the workd that in the mat-ter of the proliferation of nuclear arms, he was as good as his word. On the other hand, the president and his advisers were understanding, and sometimes even empathetic, toward the Israelis' apprehension at being surrounded by tens of millions of Arabs, and they were therefore ready to consider a quid pro quo in exchange for cancelling the plans to build a nuclear option.

In the same week that Barbour was told to deliver the president's mes-sage to Ben-Gurion, Assistant Secretary of State Phillips Talbot sent a memo to the U.S. ambassador in Cairo, John S. Badeau, to the effect that the United States was worried by the building of the reactor at Dimona, but if Washington wanted to ensure that Israel would not use it to build a bomb, it would have to offer Israel a substitute. He wrote: "The Presi-dent felt it important to give serious consideration to Israel's strong de-sire for more specific security guarantees. He believes it is only through allaying Israel's fears about the long-range threat to its existence that leverage to forestall possible Israeli preventive warfare and to prevent proliferation of nuclear weapons can be maintained." In other words, the president was weighing a substitute for Dimona. Was the United States able to come up with something that would equally satisfy Israel's de-fense requirements? That is one way of asking the question; another way is: Would Israel really be interested in swapping the product of Dimona for security guarantees? But until a quid pro quo bargain would be for-mally put on the table and negotiated, the president wanted to know ex-actly what the Israelis are making in Dimona. This was clear to the prime minister even before Ambassador Barbour was told to deliver to him the president's letter. Ben-Gurion was playing for time, and walking a fine line. He wished to postpone the baring of the secrets of Dimona for as long as possible, without entering a confrontation with the administra-tion in Washington.

While Ambassador Barbour was on the links at Caesarea, an unexpected event disrupted his plans. Ben-Gurion stunned his associates and the nation by announcing that he was resigning as prime minister.

The resignation move had begun the previous night. Every week, on the evening after the Sabbath ended, Ben-Gurion would host a Bible study circle at the prime minister's official residence in Jerusalem. He himself often came up with original interpretations of biblical passages, some of which were so revolutionary as to shock observant Jews and conservative scholars.[5] On Saturday, June 15, the circle convened as usual at his official residence in the leafy Jerusalem neighborhood of Rehavia. Shortly beforehand, his neighbor Golda Meir had walked over to see him. Biographer Bar-Zohar relates that she was agitated. She had come to tell Ben-Gurion that the German News Agency had reported that Israeli soldiers were training in Germany. Meir was aware that Germany was secretly supplying Israel with arms, but she had not been informed that Deputy Defense Minister Peres had reached an agreement with German Defense Minister Franz Josef Strauss that provided for Israeli officers to learn to operate the weapons in Germany before the Israel Defense Forces took delivery. The possibility that the item would be published in Israel appalled the foreign minister. The memory of the Holocaust was still fresh, and less than two years had gone by since Eichmann had been hanged. Meir believed that the Israeli public would not tolerate this news.

That evening at the prime minister's residence, Meir urged that the military censorship be activated to prevent the news being made public in Israel. But Ben-Gurion refused. Meir left the prime minister's residence to call on another neighbor, Finance Minister Levi Eshkol, and asked him to intervene, but he too turned her down. That night, after the Bible study circle had dispersed, Meir came to see Ben-Gurion again. It was not unusual for the *haverim* or "comrades" as they called themselves then, to get together at the prime minister's residence. Sometimes they would sit in his abrasive wife Paula's kitchen, and she would make sure that no one upset him. Meir harshly attacked Ben-Gurion's conciliatory policy toward Germany, and they argued angrily without reaching agreement. Meir went home, and Ben-Gurion went to bed, but he couldn't fall asleep. It seems that his decision to resign took shape that night.

When Ben-Gurion arrived at his office on Sunday morning, he told his secretary, Yitzhak Navon, "I am going to submit my resignation." Navon tried to dissuade him, to no avail. Meir cried when she heard the news. Shimon Peres, his closest associate, was in Paris at an air show, with the chief of staff, Zvi Tsur, and Munya Mardor. "The news came as a shock to Shimon," Mardor wrote in his diary, "and on the same day he flew back to Israel." But there was no way to undo what had been done.

The top leadership of Mapai was summoned to the cabinet meeting room, where Ben-Gurion made a brief announcement of his decision. "Eshkol and Moshe Dayan and some others said that it was not feasible," Ben-Gurion wrote in his diary. "I told them that the responsibility was heavy, and I could not carry it. They argued that the timing was not the best. I told them that the timing would never be right, and I would never find a more convenient time." Later, he went to the president, Zalman Shazar, and handed him his letter of resignation. In the afternoon, generals Meir Amit and Yitzhak Rabin came to see him and urged him to retract. In the army's eyes, he was the outstanding figure of the generation, they told him. Ben-Gurion related that Rabin wept (something that Rabin denied), and about himself he wrote in his diary: "I could hardly stifle my emotions and my tears."

Ambassador Barbour was on his way back from the golf course at Caesarea to his home in Herzliyah when he heard the news of the resignation on his car radio. He phoned the State Department and proposed postponing the delivery of President Kennedy's letter. Israel was busy with other matters right now, he explained, and it would be appropriate to wait and hand the letter to Ben-Gurion's successor. The message therefore was held up until, a short time later, a rephrased version was placed on the desk of Ben-Gurion's successor, Levi Eshkol.

Some of those involved in the development of the nuclear option—among them Yuval Neeman—and some of the historians of the period have suggested that Ben-Gurion chose this particular time to resign because he was sure that the pressure that Kennedy was exerting upon him about Dimona was about to become too great. The theory is based on the assumption that he wanted to gain time. Until his successor settled into the post, and until he learned the subject, and until the dialogue with the Kennedy administration about the visits to Dimona was resumed, a good few months would go by, and then the successor would drag things out, and meanwhile the project would continue to progress, and reach a stage where it could no longer be simply eliminated. Although the reactor was already standing, the extraction plant was still under construction, and plutonium separation was not planned to begin before the end of 1964, foreign media have reported.

There is no evidence for this theory, however. Ben-Gurion never said, and never even hinted that his decision to resign had anything to do with Kennedy's pressure, and the people closest to him, like Peres, Navon, and Bar-Zohar, and others with whom I spoke, rejected the notion. On the contrary, the survival of the Dimona project was the only thing that could have made Ben-Gurion put off his resignation. "If there was anything that could have caused Ben-Gurion not to resign, it was the American pressure on the nuclear issue, which was so important to him that it cost him his life," Bar-Zohar said, and added: "In my opinion, if he foresaw a danger that his resignation would lead to the end of the project, he would not have gone, and the entire claim that it was American pressure that made him resign is pure thumb-sucking."

Yuval Neeman believes the opposite: "I am sure that Ben-Gurion left because of Kennedy's pressure. It was a mortal threat to him. Sapir [Pinhas Sapir, minister of trade and industry in Ben-Gurion's cabinet, and one of the party's strongest men] also believed that Ben-Gurion resigned because he anticipated the Kennedy letter," said Neeman. "Ben-Gurion hoped that the change in prime ministers would gain time." But the explanation of Peres, Navon, and Bar-Zohar is more convincing; they were all much closer to the Old Man than Neeman.

When Ben-Gurion departed, the completion of the Dimona project was already assured, and the nuclear option was within arm's reach. In fact, there is no need to seek explanations for his action, because he explained it himself, writing on that very day in his diary: "Actually, I took this decision two and a half years ago, when the hypocritical vulture [his epithet for Pinhas Lavon, around whom the infamous "Affair" revolved] managed to mobilize the entire party against us . . ."

Ben-Gurion resigned because his colleagues had not backed him up in the fight over the Affair. Clearly, the exact timing of the move was the result of an impulsive decision, prompted perhaps by Meir's importuning over the troops training in Germany. The prime minister was sick and tired of government and, as already mentioned, depressed and isolated. He understood that the symptoms of old age were preventing him from performing his job in the optimal manner. In an obsessive campaign that attested to his deteriorating mental condition, he began to demand that justice be done in the eight-year-old Lavon Affair, even though Lavon had been ousted from the party. It is possible that if, a year or two earlier, the leadership of the party had agreed to set up a judicial committee of inquiry to determine who had given the order to send the cell of innocent and patriotic young Jews to carry out the foolhardy sabotage operations in Cairo and Alexandria, Ben-Gurion would have been satisfied and relations within the party would have returned to normal. But the sad truth is that even without the Lavon Affair, Ben-Gurion was no longer capable of carrying the burden of government, and this is why his resignation came not a moment too soon. On a personal level, the manner in which he resigned and the timing that he chose were mistaken. Ben-Gurion caused himself and the young people who supported him great political damage, but in retrospect, it is clear that in the middle of 1963 the time had come to change the horse that had for so long been pulling the wagon.

Levi Eshkol was the natural heir to Ben-Gurion as prime minister, but perhaps a little less so as minister of defense. The Mapai party central committee picked him unanimously for both posts, and even outside the party no one questioned his appointment. Ten years earlier, in late 1953, when Ben-Gurion had taken a break and moved to Sdeh Boker, he had proposed that Eshkol replace him as prime minister, but Eshkol refused. "Why should I be the guilty party from whose clutches Ben-Gurion will save the country when he returns?" he said, and left that dubious honor to Moshe Sharett. Indeed only a little more than a year later, in February 1955, Sharett was forced to go down to Sdeh Boker, because of the Affair, and ask Ben-Gurion to take the helm again. Sharett returned to the Foreign Ministry, and in June 1956, with the preparations for the Suez War as the backdrop, Ben-Gurion ousted him. Eshkol was angry at this humiliation of Sharett, but stood behind Ben-Gurion. Sharett had been a dove at a time when the country needed hawks. If he had not been a dove, the succession would certainly have been his, but his outlook was outside of the mainstream in both the party and the public, while Eshkol's was within it. He was a confirmed activist on security matters, and there was no substantial difference between him and Ben-Gurion when it came to defense issues. But there was a big difference in their styles of government.

Born Levi Shkolnik in 1895 to a Hasidic family in a small village called Oratovo, near Kiev in the Ukraine, the new prime minister studied at the Hebrew high school in Vilna, and joined a Jewish socialist youth movement. At the age of nineteen, he emigrated to Palestine, and Hebraized his name to Eshkol, which means both "a learned man" and "cluster" in Hebrew, and sounds like Shkolnik. In World War I, he volunteered, like Ben-Gurion, for the Jewish Legion of the British Army, and when he was discharged after the war, he was one of the founders of Kibbutz Degania Bet, on the southwestern shore of the Sea of Galilee. He directed the finance department of the Haganah underground and in 1934 traveled to Berlin to negotiate a deal with the Nazi regime for the sale of property left behind by Jews who emigrated to Palestine and the transfer of the proceeds to the owners when they reached their new country.

Eshkol was first and foremost a doer. "He was much more a man of action and much less a man of words," Golda Meir wrote of him in her memoirs. In the pre-state period, he was responsible for settlements, which eventually determined the borders of the State of Israel. After independence he was one of the architects of economic policy, serving as finance minister from 1952 to 1963, and was given credit for bringing about an economic boom in the early '60s.

Until the Lavon Affair, Eshkol was linked to Ben-Gurion and dependent upon him. As the affair became more complex, it was Eshkol who mediated between Ben-Gurion and his young allies, and the party's old guard. No one in the party leadership but him was capable of doing this, and this is how he freed himself to a certain degree from Ben-Gurion's domination, and from his dependency on him. Unlike Ben-Gurion, Eshkol was a prime minister devoid of charisma, and he shunned the regal behavior of his predecessor. Yitzhak Rabin described the difference between the two nicely: "Eshkol was cut from different cloth. He was easy to talk to, abundantly endowed with humor and folksiness, a man of the people, without the aloofness of status, or any aura of glamour. He never soared like Ben-Gurion into the stratosphere, but had his feet firmly planted in the ground of reality."

With the end of Ben-Gurion's authoritarian and oppressive reign, the Israeli public could heave a sigh of relief. Eshkol's moderation and tolerance helped reduce stress and tension in the country. He looked a little like a bumpkin, with a black beret perched on his head and baggy khaki trousers held up by a belt that sat closer to his chest than to his waist. He related to his surroundings and to himself with big doses of irony, spoke a rich Yiddish, told jokes, and made up adages and epigrams, some of them memorable, such as "Put three Zionists in a room and they'll form four political parties." He was no great orator, and quite often his words would get stuck in his throat, but everyone loved him, especially women, and he loved them. He married three times and had four daughters. (His biographer, Yossi Goldstein, has said that he found that Eshkol had "special intimate relationships" with another twelve women.)

At the end of June 1963, when Eshkol was ensconced in the prime minister's office, Dimona was no longer an issue of internal contention. The leading figures in Israeli politics, even those who from the start were not happy about the reactor and were deeply suspicious of Peres's promises, had accepted the necessity for a nuclear option. Ben-Gurion had been aware of this, and if he had believed that his successors would jeopardize the project, or hold up its completion, it is doubtful that he would have retired. Eshkol himself, who in the 1950s had not made any effort to help the project along, now regarded the nuclear option as essential. Meir also supported it; although she objected to the way that Ben-Gurion had conducted the dialogue with the Kennedy administration about the inspections, she had no reservations at all about the need for the doomsday weapon. In an internal Foreign Ministry discussion, three days before Ben-Gurion's resignation, she said:

> There is no need to stop the activities at Dimona, but we have put ourselves into a position in which we are unable to make a profit from the thing. The argument with them [the Americans] now is about whether we are telling them the truth or not. On this I had doubts from the beginning of the American intervention. I was always of the opinion that we should tell them the truth and explain why, and it does not interest us whether the Americans think, as we do, that Nasser does represent a danger for us. But if we deny that

Dimona exists, then we can't use it as a bargaining point, because it is impossible to bargain about something that doesn't exist.

By mid-1963, there was no one of influence who knew what was behind the high fence at Dimona who entertained the possibility that the project should be stopped. The broad opposition of the late '50s had become broad support. It was the facts on the ground that had created this situation: France had honored its commitments, the reactor actually worked, and the launch of the Shavit 2 missile had succeeded. Although the launch had been an exercise in public relations, and its pre-election spin had flopped, its encouragement of national pride and admiration for Israel abroad had made a difference.

Not only were there no objections among the influential to the construction of Dimona, there were also no objections to the claim that a nuclear option was a necessity as an instrument of deterrence. Some analysts have come up with a theory to the effect that there were two contending schools of thought among defense experts: the nuclear option school and the conventional weapons school. But this too is a groundless hypothesis. When the nuclear reactor was up and working, not one of Israel's leading figures cast any doubt on the strategic considerations that were behind Ben-Gurion's plan to achieve ultimate deterrence. As the nuclear option began appearing more and more realistic, the opposition to it by politicians, scientists, and generals had abated. The resentment heard from the general staff in the 1950s over the valuable resources being squandered on long-term projects whose completion was in doubt, were no longer voiced in the 1960s.

Ben-Gurion had always been careful not to put all his eggs in one basket. In his defense concept, a nuclear option never took the place of tanks and planes. When he felt that there was a lack of conventional arms, he took every step possible to acquire them, and he generally succeeded. The fundamental element in his strategic thinking was that the nuclear option was never part of the basic security balance between Israel and its neighbors. It remained hidden, deep in the basement, the last defensive resort in the event of a threat of destruction.

Nevertheless, a small group did stand up against the project—"the Committee for Nuclear Demilitarization of the Middle East," which was founded on humanitarian principles, and made sincere efforts to make it-self heard, but with little success, partly because the security services ef-fectively gagged it, but mainly because the general public wasn't interested and lined up squarely behind the leadership on the nuclear is-sue. The taboo against raising the matter for public debate was not im-posed from above, but adopted by the public of its own free will.

In 1962, the committee had published a petition calling on the gov-ernment of Israel to initiate measures to make the Middle East a nuclear-free zone. The petition was framed by Eliezer Livneh, a prominent socialist intellectual (who eventually became a conservative, joining the Greater Israel movement after the Six-Day War of 1967[6]). The most prominent of the signatories to the petition was the venerable philoso-pher Martin Buber, whose ideas carried more weight in Europe than they did in Israel, probably because he refused to stay on the conven-tional Zionist path. He advocated a binational Arab-Jewish state in Palestine, as one of the leaders of Brit Shalom, the movement that Ben-Gurion had dismissed with contempt in the 1930s. Two other important scholars, both orthodox Jews, also joined the group: Talmud professor Ephraim Urbach, who in 1973 would run unsuccessfully for president against Ephraim Katchalsky, and Yeshayahu Leibowitz, a scientist and philosopher known as the *enfant terrible* of Israel's academe.[7] Two other signatories—Gabriel Stein and Franz Ollendorf—had been members of the Israeli Atomic Energy Commission until 1958. Only one Knesset member signed the petition—Zalman Abramov of the Liberal Party.

Leibowitz was the group's spokesman. He was brilliant and sharp-witted, but also somewhat quarrelsome and clamorous. In 1962, at a meeting of the Hebrew University debating club at Hillel House in Jerusalem, he asserted that the authorities were "secretly perpetrating a disaster at Dimona" and railed against the media's silence about the nu-clear issue, but his warnings had a negligible effect. The committee planned to hold a press conference, and approached the chairman of the military correspondents section of the Journalists Association, Ze'ev Schiff, of the *Ha'aretz* daily. "I invited the heads of the committee to give a background briefing to the military correspondents, and arranged for it to take place at Beit Sokolov (the Journalists Association headquarters)," Schiff recalled nearly forty years later. 'But then, when I arrived, the secretary of the association, the late Moshe Ronn, came out to me and said, 'We've decided to call the briefing off.' I said, 'What on earth made you do that?' He said, 'We got a call from the Ministry of Defense.' I said, 'But this isn't the Ministry of Defense, it's the Journalists Association.' And he wouldn't give up, and we stood on the stairs outside arguing, but in the end the briefing was cancelled. And then some very important people came to me and explained to me why it was not a good idea to meet with the committee members."

The media refrained from reporting on the committee. There was no television yet in Israel, and the only two radio stations were government-controlled. The influential daily newspaper *Davar* was owned by Ben-Gurion's party. In the three important independent papers, there was also no significant coverage of the committee's initiative, because their editors identified with what in those days was called "security needs." The correspondent for *Ha'aretz* in Washington during the Kennedy and Johnson presidencies, Amos Elon, filed a report saying that in a background talk with James Reston of the *New York Times*, Kennedy had said that in nuclear matters Ben-Gurion was "a wild man." Israel's military censorship blue-penciled the item, and Elon has written that "my publisher [Gershom Schocken], no doubt influenced by the powerful, almost tribal sense of national solidarity that dominated Israel at the time, asked me to concentrate on other subjects."

The nuclear issue was not on the agenda of any of the political parties, except for the minuscule Communist Party, whose ideological platform was laid down in Moscow. One of Ben-Gurion's senior coalition partners, Meir Yaari, the charismatic leader of the left-wing Hashomer Hatza'ir youth movement and its affiliated party, Mapam (the United Workers Party), was opposed to the nuclear program, both out of humanitarian reasons—based on the fear that it would increase the danger of a nuclear conflagration—and the pragmatic fear that Israel's acquisition of a nuclear potential would prod the Soviet Union into giving nuclear weapons to the Arabs as well. Ernst Bergmann, head of the Atomic Energy Commission, was surprised by Yaari's objections, and in a 1966 letter urged him to be more realistic. It would not be possible to prevent the spread of nuclear weapons in the world, and the Arabs too would acquire nuclear capability, Bergmann wrote to Yaari, and added: "I can not forget that the Holocaust came as a surprise to the Jewish people. The Jewish people can not afford to be similarly deluded once again." Yaari spoke to Ben-Gurion about the project several times, and demanded that the repercussions of Israel's nuclear capability be discussed, but Ben-Gurion would not hear of the subject being raised for debate in the cabinet. He did, however, agree to the setting up of a secret parliamentary subcommittee of the Knesset's Foreign Affairs and Defense Committee. The panel met a few times in early 1963, but after it became clear that the relevant authorities would not supply it with any information, it broke up without making any decisions.

On July 5, 1963, a week after Levi Eshkol acceded to the premiership, Ambassador Barbour came to his office and delivered the letter that had originally been addressed to Ben-Gurion. His advisers had warned Eshkol that the letter would be framed in harsh language, but the new prime minister was nonetheless surprised. Forty years later, his close aide Zvi Dinstein was still rattled when he remembered: "Kennedy was presenting him [Eshkol] with an ultimatum; it certainly was an ultimatum. It caused us a great deal of anxiety, a great deal." Indeed, no American president had ever threatened an Israeli prime minister so bluntly during political negotiations in time of peace. True, there had already been an American threat to implement sanctions against Israel, when in November 1956 at the height of the Suez Campaign, President Eisenhower had demanded that Ben-Gurion order Israeli forces to retreat immediately from all of its conquests in the Sinai peninsula, and warned that the United States would take measures if he did not, but that was a warning at a time of crisis, when in the background the Soviets were threatening to intervene in the fighting.

Kennedy's letter was a test for the nerves and the leadership qualities of the new prime minister. The president was demanding "reliable information" on Israel's nuclear program, and warning that if Israel did not open Dimona fully to American inspection, American support for Israel "could be seriously jeopardized." Kennedy added: "I regret having to add to your burden so soon after your assumption of office, but I feel the crucial importance of this problem." He also mentioned the commitment given to him by the previous prime minister to permit periodic visits to Dimona, and straight afterward issued his warning:

I am sure you would agree that these visits should be as nearly as possible in accord with international standards, thereby resolving all doubts as to the peaceful intent of the Dimona project. As I wrote Mr. Ben-Gurion, this government's commitment to and support of Israel could be seriously jeopardized if it should be thought that we were unable to obtain reliable information on a subject as vital to peace as the question of Israel's effort in the nuclear field.

The president dictated the times for the visits. Because the first would take place "early this summer," it would be due almost immediately. "It would be essential that our scientists have access to all areas of the Dimona site and to any related part of the complex, such as fuel fabrication facilities or plutonium separation plant, and that sufficient time be allotted for a thorough examination," wrote the president. At the end of the message came yet another warning, to stress that this time the demands were serious. "Knowing that you fully appreciate the vital significance of this matter to the future well-being of Israel, to the United States and internationally, I am sure our carefully considered request will have your most sympathetic attention."

The letter caused consternation in the prime minister's office, and for some six weeks, Eshkol and his advisers devoted most of their energy to it. At the first stage, they met Ambassador Barbour and asked for clarifications. Then there were consultations in various forums, and dozens of different formulations of draft replies were drawn up. Eshkol wondered why Kennedy had used threatening language after two years during which he had refrained from exerting pressure on Israel about Dimona. What had happened, he asked his advisers. After all, there was no crisis in relations between the two countries and only a few months before, in Florida, Kennedy had done his best to put on a show of friendship for Golda Meir, pledging to come to Israel's aid if it were attacked. The advisers had no answers.

Ambassador Barbour explained to the prime minister that the Cuban missile crisis had highlighted the need for nuclear disarmament and prevention of proliferation. This was the main lesson that Kennedy had learned from the confrontation with the Soviet Union that had almost spilled over into nuclear war, and this is what had moved him to write the letter. There was a link, the ambassador explained to the prime minister, between the American goal of resuming inspection of Dimona and the negotiations between the United States and the Soviet Union on a partial nuclear-test-ban treaty. A special presidential envoy, Averell Harriman, was set to travel to Moscow to resume the talks, and Kennedy wanted him to come with clean hands.

A month after the president's letter was handed to the prime minister, on August 5, Harriman and a Soviet representative signed the treaty barring testing of nuclear weapons in the atmosphere and in space. Israel welcomed the treaty, and a few days later became the twenty-third country to sign it. It had nothing to lose. Israel never planned to conduct nuclear tests in the atmosphere or in space, or even underground for that matter.

In preparing his reply to the president, Eshkol agonized over whether presenting a false depiction of Dimona to the American administration would do any good. How many of the secrets of Dimona was the prime minister of Israel entitled to hide from the president of the United States without being exposed as a liar? This is precisely the way in which he framed his hesitation in discussions with his advisers. Ben-Gurion would not have put it that way. Ethics in international relations were of no import to him when Israel's security was at stake.

Eshkol's great advantage over Ben-Gurion was that he knew how to defuse political mines. If Ben-Gurion's personality and style of government were autocratic, Eshkol's were just the opposite. He was a liberal and a democrat, a confirmed man of compromise, who always sought the consensus. These qualities made it possible for him, a year later, to find a path to President Lyndon Johnson's heart, and create a special chemistry with him, personal ties that would turn out to have a far-reaching effect on the nuclear dispute between the two countries.

But at the outset of his term, the new prime minister was a greenhorn in nuclear matters, and he needed guidance before framing a reply to Kennedy's letter. At one extraordinary consultation that Eshkol called, there were six participants: Foreign Minister Meir, Agriculture Minister Moshe Dayan, Deputy Defense Minister Peres, ambassador to the United States Abba Eban and Chief of Staff Tsur. Bergmann was not invited; although as head of the Atomic Energy Commission he was ostensibly in charge of the entire project, he in fact had very little to do with what was happening at Dimona.

The question to be decided was a fairly simple one: Should Israel agree to the proposal put forward by the president that Israel give up the nuclear option and accept American security guarantees as a substitute? Ostensibly, Israel's reply should have been affirmative, because since the early days of the state Ben-Gurion had decided to go for the nuclear option only when it became clear to him that the United States was not prepared to extend an umbrella of protection over Israel. If the U.S. was now prepared to do so, why was there a need for a nuclear option, which was so expensive to develop and so complicated to possess?

In the early part of 1963 the Kennedy administration shaped a broad initiative that Israel and Egypt give up their plans to acquire strategic weapons in exchange for rewards from the United States. Israel would relinquish its efforts to reach nuclear capability and would receive a security guarantee, and Egypt would abandon its ballistic missile program and would get economic and technological assistance. The initiative never took off, mainly because Nasser didn't like it, and so Kennedy restricted the initiative to the attainment of an American-Israeli deal: Dimona for the security guarantee that had been Israel's wish since its birth.

But it was not that simple. What exactly was the nature of the security guarantee or defensive alliance that the Kennedy administration was offering? Could it replace the deterrence that the nuclear option was supposed to provide? Was the United States willing to offer Israel the same nuclear umbrella that it had granted the members of NATO and Japan? Would the United States arm Israel with all the weapons it needed to defend itself? Would American troops be stationed in Israel, and American bases be set up on Israeli territory, like those in Europe? Would there be an unconditional defense treaty, to be activated every time Israel was attacked, and would the United States send its military to defend Israel whatever the circumstances? And if Israel decided to initiate a preemptive war, and it ran into trouble on the battlefield, would the American guarantee be valid?

This was, therefore, a political-military decision of the highest order: The nuclear deterrent, or a defense pact with the United States?

At the meeting in Eshkol's office, various elements of a possible defense pact were discussed. For example, who in the United States would be authorized to activate the pact when that became necessary: the president alone, or the Senate? If the president would require congressional approval, Israel might well be defeated before the U.S. military was authorized to intervene. Would the United States be prepared to hold regular strategic consultations with Israel? Without them, it was doubtful that a joint defensive deployment could be worked out. Would the U.S. Sixth Fleet be integrated into the defense of Israel?[8] Amid a long and detailed debate about definitions of alliances, Moshe Dayan cut right to the chase, as he usually did.

Dayan put forth reasons against having a defense pact. He had no interest in seeing Israel waive its exclusive power to decide on how the struggle against the Arabs should be conducted, and he doubted whether the United States would come to Israel's help when it was attacked: "Even if all the guaranteed conditions would be written down and signed Israel would not rely on it." Dayan's conclusion was clear:

> The most important thing from the security point of view, the thing that can change the balance of our security, will be the finished product of Dimona. There's no point in discussing any substitute.

Chief of Staff Tzur expressed caution about the distant future. He was doubtful the country would be able to stand up to the competition of the arms race. "In the seventies, there will be a need for something nonconventional," Tzur declared. He called it "the big thing that will have to ensure the future for us" and urged that it not be given up. The IDF's chief also preferred nuclear deterrence over a defense alliance.

Eshkol took the floor. For the time being, the prime minister wasn't proposing that the project be suspended, nor that a treaty be signed. Eshkol had never been a partner to detailed discussions on the nuclear project while Ben-Gurion was prime minister of defense. Ben-Gurion and his associates, in particular Peres and Bergmann, had delved into the issue for over ten years. They had examined it from all angles, consulted with the greatest experts in the world, and studied the scientific, technical, economic, and ethical aspects. Eshkol had not been occupied with all this, and he even had little to do with the finances of the project. Ben-Gurion and others had updated him on the contacts with the Kennedy administration, and had even briefed him on what they thought he should do, but the decision had to be his alone, and in order to reach it, he had to clarify the issues with the help of his advisers. He would have preferred to put off the confrontation with Kennedy until he had mastered the issues more thoroughly, and mainly he was frustrated by the idea that he would have to lie to the president. Eshkol's frankness surprised his colleagues:

> What am I frightened of? His man [Kennedy's messenger] will come, and he will actually be told that he can visit [the Dimona site] and go anywhere he wishes, but when he wants a door opened at some place or another, then Pratt will tell him: "Not that." So he'll tell Barbour and Kennedy about it. I too would feel better perhaps if the visit were put off for two or three months. The whole matter is new to me, and even though I'm not activating it, it is there. The question is how important it is to us that [the president] will hear that the prime minister, or the foreign minister, and the entire government, are not lying to him.

Dayan agreed with Eshkol. "This is not the way," he said, meaning that misleading the American government would be wrong. Eshkol was still worried: "It is a little hard to suppose that there will be a first visit and a second, and a third [at Dimona] and [the visitors] will not ask questions to which we will have to reply. We can not assume that we are the only clever ones and that the others don't understand, and we cannot assume that they don't have some sort of Prat of their own, who knows all the tricks, and who has also done this sort of thing, and who can lift the blanket and see what's going on underneath it. We mustn't assume that the whole world are idiots."

The alternative to the nuclear project, Eshkol said, was a request to the president that he supply defensive conventional weapons—hundreds of missiles, planes, and tanks—that would protect Israel and deter its neighbors. Those armaments, said the prime minister, required the construction of army bases and launch bases, "and hundreds of millions of dollars to build them, and they too can be bombed." If I knew that it was a deterrent force, that would be that," said the prime minister. "I could live with it. But we know that straightaway other weapons turn up and this [area of advanced conventional weapons] is making giant strides forward."

Eshkol's grasp of the subject was tenuous, and his attitude to the project was not at all clear-cut, but he was a man who usually made excellent decisions after consultations, and this time was no exception. He would go with Dayan's advice: "The product of Dimona" was better than a defense pact that no one knew whether or how it would be implemented.

It is interesting to note that in the course of the discussion the word "bomb" was not used in the context of Israel's efforts and neither were the words "nuclear" or "nuclear project," or "atomic." Instead the speakers used substitutes like "Dimona," "it," "something nonconventional," "the big thing," "that sort of thing," "the finished product of Dimona," "the activity at Dimona," and other circumlocutory euphemisms. At that time, no one dared to use the taboo words, even in a forum where everybody knew the secret.

Some writers have tended to blame the U.S. State Department for the fact that the contacts between the two countries on the matter of security guarantees in exchange for abandoning Dimona never reached fruition. And it is true that the State Department did express the fear that a publicly declared security guarantee for Israel would harm America's relations with the Arab states, and would give Israel a free hand to conduct aggressive policies in the Middle East [9].

However, it was not the objections of the State Department that removed the matter from the agenda, but the reservations of the Israeli defense authorities, who were not interested in exchanging Dimona for a security arrangement that would tie their hands. If the Eisenhower administration had proposed that Israel swap Dimona for a security alliance, there can be no doubt that Israel would have happily accepted. But by the early '60s Israel was a much stronger country, militarily and economically, and this is why Dayan, Peres, and Tsur saw things from a totally different perspective than in the mid-'50s. Thus Israel waived the guarantees, because it wasn't interested in giving up Dimona. Israel wanted both the "product" of Dimona, as well as offensive weaponry from the United States. And this, ultimately, is what it got.

The series of consultations on the formulation of the reply to Kennedy's threatening letter continued for several days, and then came another prolonged period during which several draft responses were drawn up. "Eshkol was not able to give them [the Americans] what they wanted," says his aide Zvi Dinstein, "and he was trying to gain time while behind the scenes, in an unofficial channel, they succeeded in getting the message through to Kennedy that Israel was able [to attain nuclear capability], and that it therefore wasn't interested in inspection, because it was an existential matter." Dinstein did not know who conveyed the message "behind the scenes" but it is reasonable to assume it was Abe Feinberg. On July 17, Eshkol wrote to the White House asking for patience while Israel put the finishing touches to its response, and a month later, on August 19, Eshkol sent his reply to Kennedy: Israel agreed to permit American experts to visit Dimona, out of consideration for the "special intimacy of relations between the United States and Israel." Eshkol suggested that the first visit take place at the end of 1963, because "by then the French group would have handed the reactor over to us" to check whether all the parameters were in order. The scheduling of the later visits would remain open. "I am quite sure that we will manage to come to an agreement on the timetable for future visits," he wrote to the president, indicating that Israel did not rule out Kennedy's demand that additional visits be set, but for the time being was not prepared to schedule them on the calendar. There would be one visit, and after that the next one would be discussed.

If the president accepted the Israeli reply, each side would emerge with half of its desires satisfied. Israel would have to accept another visit of experts to Dimona, and to prepare it properly so as to conceal the secret installations, while the president would have to apply pressure once more to get Israel to allow further visits.

There was tense anticipation in the prime minister's office until the reply arrived in Jerusalem ten days later. Then Eshkol and his aides heaved a sigh of relief. "Your letter of August 19 was received here with satisfaction," Kennedy wrote. In the complicated dialogue with the president about Dimona, Eshkol had said the right words.

"Eshkol stood up to all the pressures," Dinstein said. "He would always say, 'I spoke to Ben-Gurion,' 'I decided with Ben-Gurion.' He consulted with Ben-Gurion and carried out his policy, but still Ben-Gurion came with complaints." Indeed, from the circles of Ben-Gurion's young guard, there were whispers of doubts and complaints against Eshkol for having allegedly given in to American dictates. At first, it was only a rustle, but the dissenting voices would steadily gain in volume.

The timetable for the American inspection at Dimona would be altered by the assassination of President Kennedy. On January 18, 1964, an inspection team from the United States spent eleven hours at the Dimona complex, reporting to Washington that "the reactor was activated on December 26, 1963, and has no weapons making capability." The inspectors found no evidence that plutonium could be produced at Dimona, nor any signs of any other kind of treatment of irradiated uranium.

Ostensibly, Israel had once again been given a passing grade by Washington, but Eshkol was reluctant to base relations with the United States on fraud, and from then on he would try as hard as he could to limit the false elements in the way the project was presented to the Americans. He did this in the simple form of gradually divulging the secrets of Dimona. In conjunction with the United States, a formula would be found that would enable the cake to be eaten and remain intact at the same time.

ONE DAY AFTER his heir had taken over, on June 27, 1963, Ben-Gurion went to bid farewell to RAFAEL. The senior personnel of all the departments and plants from all over the country gathered in honor of "the Old Man," who was wearing a civilian suit with a white open-necked shirt. Smiling and cheerful, he circulated among the crowd, joking and shaking hands. His hosts felt that a heavy burden had been lifted from his shoulders. "We demonstrated for him the advances in sophisticated weapons systems, and we explained our plans for the future. This was a kind of last salute to him," Mardor wrote.

After a festive luncheon, everyone assembled outside on the lawn in front of the library for "the farewell ceremony," as Mardor called it. Hundreds of RAFAEL staffers sat on the grass and heard the address by the most senior of the scientific personnel, Ernst Bergmann, the chemist who fifteen years before had, at Ben-Gurion's behest, forsaken his spiritual mentor, Chaim Weizmann, and the Institute that he had founded, in order to set up the Science Corps of the army, from which RAFAEL had sprung. "Since I am the son of a rabbi," Bergmann said, turning to Ben-Gurion, "permit me to express my feelings at this moment, and I hope the feelings of all the friends whom you see before you, with the same words that were said of the kings of Israel: 'suffer no stranger to sit upon his throne, no other to inherit his glory.'" A sorrowful murmur emanated from the audience. Some wiped away tears.

"I won't tell you what I learned today, although I learned many important things, and I am a little frightened to speak," Ben-Gurion said in his long, impromptu, but well-phrased speech, hinting twice about the project. Referring to the shortage of arms, he said: "We need all possible means of self-defense, and I do not want to say here what the most effective means of defense is, and what its significance is." Later, he reviewed scientific developments and said that science was capable of "giving us the weapon that will ensure peace and deter our enemies." These were two of the code phrases through which at that time the nuclear option was characterized: "the weapon that will deter" and "the weapon that will ensure peace." As usual, Ben-Gurion devoted a sentence to Jewish brainpower: "There is one thing in which we are not inferior to any nation on earth, and that is the Jewish brain. And the source of science, if an ignoramus like me may say so, is in the brain . . . and the Jewish brain has not caused disappointment."

Those at the gathering knew that an era had come to its end, and Mardor observed in his diary: "His departure has left many question marks." He had no idea how many questions he would have to answer, and how exhausting and difficult the road ahead would be for him in the new era.

CHAPTER TWELVE

Cleaning the Stables

"YOU HAVE LOST A GOOD FRIEND," President Johnson told a delegation of Jews who came to the White House shortly after President Kennedy's assassination in November 1963, "but you have found a better one in me." He was right. The Jews of the United States found an extraordinary friend in Johnson, as did the State of Israel. During his presidency, the third and highest hurdle in relations between the two countries was cleared. For the first time, the United States directly sold offensive weapons to Israel. Together with Johnson's favorable attitude, it was the American Jewish community that deserved the credit. For the first time since the great migration of Jews from Eastern Europe at the end of the 19th century the Jewish community had accumulated the political and economic power that enabled it to exercise self-confidence and resolve, and through those qualities to advance its agenda. Against the backdrop of the painful failure of the Jewish leaders of the 1930s and '40s to persuade America to grant a haven to refugees from the Nazis, it was a revolutionary change.[1]

In the 1960s, the American mood underwent an extreme shift. The xenophobic age ended in an outburst of openness and tolerance. Anti-Semitism receded and the human rights of minorities became enshrined in law. The Jews experienced the birth of a golden age, the likes of which had not been seen since the 10th and 11th centuries in Spain. The political and cultural influence of American Jews and their integration into all spheres of life was achieved for the first time, and shaped America's commitment to Israel's security. The contours of this commitment had been sketched by the Kennedy administration, but it was the Johnson administration that gave it actual substance. Among the elements that benefitted from the dramatic change was "the product" of Dimona.

Far more than the considerations of utilitarian politics, Johnson's fundamental ties to Judaism and Israel sprang from a profound emotional impulse, something that few identified as such during his term of office. Johnson's entire world outlook had idealistic roots: a profound social conscience that he had absorbed from the Bible as a child. And the deep understanding that he had for Israel's existential anxiety, arising from the Holocaust experience, also had religious roots.

In the pious Christian family tradition of the Texan president, the Jews in the Land of Israel were of special importance. His paternal grandfather, Sam Ealy Johnson Sr., and other members of the family had adopted the principles of faith of the Christadelphians, who call themselves "Bible Believing People," and conducted their lives according to a literal interpretation of both the Old and the New Testaments.[2] As well as Jesus and the Apostles, their faith focused on leaders of the Israelites, such as Moses, and the Prophets, especially Isaiah and Jeremiah,[3] whose visions of the End of Days elementary school children in Israel learn by heart. Of special importance to the sect is the covenant struck between God and the people of Israel at Mount Sinai—"You shall be to me a kingdom of priests and a holy nation." (Exodus, 19:6) The Christadelphians call the Jews "the People of the Book," and they are certain that at the End of Days when the Jews are gathered in the Land of Israel, the Second Coming of the messiah will occur.

In the family album, Lyndon Johnson's grandfather inscribed on a picture of himself "Take care of the Jews, God's chosen people. Consider them your friends and help them any way you can." After Sam Ealy Johnson's death in 1915, his daughter, Jessie Johnson Hatcher, Lyndon's aunt, took over his position and kept the family's faith alive.

She would often preach to Lyndon about the importance of helping the Jews. Even while he was president, his relations with his aunt were close. Almost every summer, he and his wife would invite Jessie and the members of her congregation to a reception in their honor at their ranch. Jessie would recite sayings she had composed, such as "If Israel is destroyed, that day the world will end."

To Israeli ears, this sort of utterance sounded strange. Only in recent years have the ways of the American Bible Belt become more familiar to Israelis,4 as the number of fundamentalist Christians in the United States has grown, and some sects set themselves an aim of helping the Jews take over the entire Land, the principles of their faith reverberating through Israel as well. In the 1960s, Israelis' knowledge of such American mores and phenomena was much more limited than it is today, and perhaps this is why only a small number were aware of these special religious roots that tied President Johnson to them and their state.

At encounters with Jewish groups, Johnson liked to mention the sources of his faith and he would frequently cite biblical verses. At a meeting with members of the Jewish organization B'nai B'rith in September 1968 he described his close connection with Israel thus:

> Most if not all of you have very deep ties with the land and with the people of Israel, as I do, for my Christian faith sprang from yours. . . . The Bible stories are woven into my childhood memories as the gallant struggle of modern Jews to be free of persecution is also woven into our souls.

Then he quoted passages from Isaiah and made a connection between the heritage of the biblical prophets and the codes of values common to the United States and Israel: "Our society is illuminated by the spiritual insights of the Hebrew prophets. America and Israel have a common love of human freedom and they have a common faith in a democratic way of life."

In that same year, when he hosted Prime Minister Levi Eshkol and his entourage at his ranch in Texas, Johnson toasted the prime minister and once more made use of a biblical citation, citing a verse from Ezekiel (37:26) accurately from memory:

> That is our intention in the Middle East and throughout our world. To pursue peace. To find peace. To keep peace forever among men. If we are wise, if we are fortunate, if we work together—perhaps our Nation and all nations may know the joys of that promise God once

made about the children of Israel: "I will make a covenant of peace with them . . . it shall be an everlasting covenant."

Immediately after Hitler annexed Austria to Germany in March 1938, Johnson was a freshman member of the House of Representatives. He received an urgent request from his friend and financial backer, the publisher Charles Edward Marsh, and his companion Alice Glass, who were active in rescuing Jewish refugees from Germany and Austria.[5] During a visit to the Salzburg Festival, the two had befriended a twenty-five-year-old Austrian Jewish conductor, Erich Leinsdorf. They had set up a connection between him and the New York City Metropolitan Opera orchestra and helped him come to the United States. Leinsdorf worked with the orchestra, and remained in New York after his temporary visa ran out. If he were forced to return to Austria, the couple told Johnson, he was doomed. Johnson met Leinsdorf at the Mayflower Hotel in Washington, listened to his story, and the next day intervened on his behalf with the immigration authorities. Following Johnson's guidance, the conductor flew to Havana, Cuba, went to the American Embassy there, and returned with a permanent resident's visa.

Leinsdorf's experience led Johnson to try to get to the bottom of the difficulty in rescuing Jews from Germany and Austria. In 1938, a leader of the Jewish community in Austin, James Novy, a businessman who supported Johnson and contributed to his election campaigns, told him that he was planning a trip to Palestine to celebrate his son's bar mitzvah there, and that on the way they would visit with family in Germany and Poland. That was the time that Hitler was demanding the annexation of the Czechoslovakian region of Sudetenland, and Novy many years later recalled that Johnson said: "They're all going to be killed, get as many Jewish people as possible out of both countries." Johnson gave Novy a letter of recommendation and immigration forms, and phoned the U.S. consul in Warsaw and asked him to cooperate and to sign the forms. In this way, forty-two Jews from Poland and Germany, including four of Novy's relatives, gained entry visas to the United States. That's a small number, but it's worth remembering that in mid-1938, a Jew's chances of finding asylum were exceedingly slim. Passenger ships carrying Jewish refugees would ply the coast of North and Central America in search of a port where they would be allowed to land. Some of them had to return to Europe.

Jewish leaders in Texas pressed Johnson to do something, and he did. With a group of friends, Jews and non-Jews, he helped organize a network that smuggled Jews into the United States, through the port on the island of Galveston, in the Gulf of Mexico off southeastern Texas. He gave the network the stamp of authority and enlisted the assistance of Texan institutions on its behalf. Novy financed most of the costs. Jewish refugees, using false passports of countries in Central or South America, arrived in Cuba or Mexico, where they received American visas. From there they sailed to Galveston, where they were housed by the Texas National Youth Administration, a federal organization Johnson had headed in the mid-'30s. Altogether, some five hundred Jewish refugees entered the United States through "Operation Texas," the name given to the initiative by its organizers, who continued to deny its existence for many years because of its illegal aspects.

In December 1963, a short time after Johnson was sworn in as president, Jim Novy divulged part of the operation in a speech he delivered at the dedication of a new synagogue in Austin. Lyndon and Lady Bird Johnson were the guests of honor. The four hundred members of the congregation, among them some of the "Johnson refugees," listened to Novy as he emotionally expressed his gratitude to the president: "We can't ever thank him enough for all those Jews he got out of Germany during the days of Hitler." After Johnson addressed the gathering, the audience gathered around him and the first lady. "Person after person plucked at my sleeve and said, 'I wouldn't be here today if it weren't for him. He helped get me out,'" Lady Bird said later in her *White House Diary*. In 1942, Jim Novy went to Europe on a secret mission. When he returned to the United States, he was awarded the Purple Heart, usually given to military personnel who are wounded in action. Neither he nor Johnson ever divulged the nature of the mission, and both took the secret with them to their graves.[6]

In March 1942, Johnson took part in a fund-raising effort on behalf of the Haganah militia. Novy had gathered thirty wealthy Jews in an Austin hotel for a U.S. War Bond drive party. When the target sum had been reached, Johnson took the floor to speak of the distress of the Jews in Eastern Europe and the difficult situation in Palestine. He asked his audience to donate money to the underground in the Land of Israel, using those very words.

In June 1945, Johnson joined a delegation of members of Congress who traveled to Europe to study the effects of the war. The itinerary included a visit to the Dachau concentration camp. Lady Bird related that her husband returned in a state of shock. He was "bursting with an overpowering revulsion and incredulous horror at what he had seen," she said.

For Johnson therefore, the fate of the Jews of Europe was not merely of theoretical or academic interest. When, in diplomatic talks at the White House, the Israelis played on the Holocaust theme, they found an empathetic listener in the president. Johnson had a deep understanding of Ben-Gurion's concept of an ultimate defensive weapon, the idea that had motivated him to launch Israel's nuclear project. What's more, he was unlikely to impose obstacles to the attainment of Israel's goal.

Paul Warnke, who served as chief U.S. disarmament negotiator in the Johnson administration, noted that Johnson's loyalty to the Jewish community was a key component in his policy toward Dimona: "President Johnson was very responsive to the American Jewish community. He realized that he would not want anything that would jeopardize that relationship. That would be bad for him. That would be bad for his party. They were strong supporters of president Johnson and he liked his supporters."

Toward the end of October 1963, before the death of Kennedy, Prime Minister Eshkol had already asked the United States for offensive weaponry: modern tanks and attack aircraft. Israel argued that the massive shipments of arms from the Soviet Union to Egypt and Syria were upsetting the military balance in the Middle East in favor of the Arabs. We have already mentioned that in 1962 the Kennedy administration had supplied Israel with Hawk surface-to-air missiles, but had adamantly refused to sell it offensive weapons. The Johnson administration too rejected Israel's requests for such arms, but it related to them in a gentle and friendly manner, as can be learned from the language of a message Johnson sent Eshkol in February 1964:

As you know, we have been giving careful thought to your expressed concerns about Israel's security needs. In particular we can
understand your worries over the growing imbalance between Israeli and Arab armor, and can see the justification for your feeling
that you must take steps to modernize Israel's tank forces and antitank defenses. We are fully prepared to discuss this problem further with you.

At the same time we are disturbed lest other steps which Israel
may contemplate taking may unnecessarily contribute to a height-
ened arms race in the region without in fact contributing to your security. Among other things, we seem to have quite different
estimates with respect to the likely UAR [Egyptian] [ballistic] missile threat, and the potential costs and risks of various ways of meeting it.

Such language was entirely different from that which the Kennedy administration had used in its messages to Israel only a year before. The
desire for cooperation is clear, and there are no threats. The link between
the discussion about the supply of conventional offensive weapons and
Israel's nuclear project is blurred, and Israel's strategic capability is only
hinted at (the phrase "various ways" in the last line is code for Israel's deterrence weapon). There's no mention of the principle of nuclear non-
proliferation, which cropped up in every communication from Kennedy
to Israel. For unlike Kennedy, Johnson did not make nuclear weapons
the focus of his policy, and this is why as soon as he entered the White
House the pressure on Israel on the Dimona issue eased. What's more,
Kennedy's initiative to find a substitute for Dimona through security
guarantees was dropped. In fact, under Johnson's administrations, the
United States was reconciled to the existence of Dimona, and at the same
time consented to arm Israel with conventional offensive weaponry.

The pattern of Washington's behavior toward Israel during the Johnson era would as a rule go like this: Officials of the State Department, the
Defense Department, and the National Security Council would demand
that the supply of offensive weapons be made conditional on Israel's divulging its strategic projects—the nuclear and missile programs—but at
the presidential level the conditions would fall away. In other cases, the

gap between the positions would be expressed in a kind of arm-wrestling—polite and civilized, but also serious and tough—between the officials at State, Defense, and the NSC on the one hand, and the president's advisers on the other. Mostly, it was Mike Feldman, who held a key position in the White House, who would squelch the objections of the officials, with the help of the president's two Abes—big-time donor Feinberg and close adviser Abe Fortas. At least once, in a dispute over the sale of tanks to Israel, Feldman on his own managed to bend the collective arm of Secretary of State Dean Rusk, Secretary of Defense Robert McNamara, and Robert Komer, the NSC's Middle East expert. Then too, the bone of contention was Israel's activity in the strategic sphere.

Israel never hid from the United States that it was developing medium-range missiles as a counter to the Egyptian missiles, but it denied that they were part of any nuclear plans. The American defense experts never accepted this claim, and believed that the missiles were meant to be equipped with nuclear warheads. They saw no economic logic in manufacture of medium- or long-range missiles with conventional warheads. The development of the missiles therefore supplied Washington with the best proof that Israel was engaged in creating a nuclear option, and it was on this assumption that Washington officialdom demanded a clear conditioning of the supply of tanks on Israel's baring of its strategic weapons potential, but Feldman managed to persuade the president to drop the condition. The only compromise that Johnson agreed to reach with the officials was that the tanks would be supplied to Israel not directly from the United States, but from the stockpiles of its allies in Europe. The British government was supposed to provide Centurion tanks, but Israel preferred the more advanced American-made Patton M48, which was considered the best in the world at that time. West Germany was persuaded to supply the Pattons from NATO bases on its territory over the objections of Chancellor Ludwig Erhard, Konrad Adenauer's successor, who was not happy at being designated as arms supplier to Israel by the United States. In the mid-'60s, West Germany's foreign and defense policies were determined in close coordination with the Americans, and Erhard accepted the role on one condition: that Israel keep it a secret.

At a meeting in the White House situation room on April 30, 1964, senior American officials finalized the arrangement and resolved that "it would be highly desirable to communicate the decision on this matter to the Israelis before the visit to Washington of Prime Minister Eshkol on June 1." Mike Feldman was therefore immediately sent off to Jerusalem to inform Eshkol of the matter. As far as secrecy was concerned, the Israeli media was trained to obey the dictates of the government. And neither was the "moral" issue a real obstacle, as Israel had in the past already received American arms from Germany.

In consultations prior to his trip to Washington, Eshkol and his advisers pondered how to define the nuclear project when it came up in discussions with Johnson, bearing in mind Eshkol's musings over how many of Dimona's secrets he could withhold from the president without being considered an inveterate liar. Ben-Gurion had declared in his first statement in the Knesset and in contacts with Kennedy and his officials that the reactor was meant for "peaceful purposes." He had voiced this assurance with total certitude. However, Eshkol refrained from repeating it. He also was incapable of baldly stating that the reactor's purpose was scientific and industrial. How then would the aim of the Dimona project be defined truthfully? This was the conundrum Eshkol asked his advisers to solve, and they came up with this: "Israel will not be the first to introduce nuclear weapons to the Middle East." This simple and brief formulation was in fact a work of genius in its very ambiguity, in that it reveals nothing but says everything. There was no admission that Israel was making a bomb, but neither was there a denial of its capability of doing so. It was not an outright lie, but it was not all the truth. It was a statement that induced calmness in those to whom it was addressed, because it indicates a passive and defensive tendency, and contains no hint of aggression or active intent.

Eshkol's close aide Zvi Dinstein believed that the masterly vagueness of the sentence was the work of Jacob Herzog, director general of the prime minister's office and an expert in international relations. At first, Dinstein recalls, Eshkol wasn't very impressed by the formula, "but then he got used to it and then he fell in love with it."

But a short while later, Eshkol learned that a very similar formula had already been used in a meeting with an American president. That was in Washington on April 2, 1963, when deputy Defense Minister Shimon

Peres, accompanied by Ambassador Avraham Harman and minister Mordechai Gazit came to the White House for a meeting with Mike Feldman about Israel's request for Hawk antiaircraft missiles. "We are sitting in Feldman's cellar," Peres recalled, "and then there's a call from Kennedy's office: 'The president wants to see Peres.' We go up, Kennedy's sitting in his rocking chair, and he begins bombarding me with questions. Suddenly, he says, 'Are you making an atom bomb?' I said to him, 'Mr. President, Israel will not be the first to introduce nuclear weapons to the Middle East.'"

According to the protocol written down by the Israeli side, Kennedy said to Peres, "You know that we are following with great interest every sign of the development of nuclear capability in the region? That would create a most dangerous situation. We have therefore taken pains to keep in touch with your efforts in the nuclear sphere. What can you tell me about this matter?" And Peres replied, "I can say to you clearly that we shall not introduce atomic weapons into the region. We will certainly not be the first to do so. We have no interest in it, indeed the contrary is true. Our interest is in the lessening of the tension of the arms race, even in total disarmament."

"When that cable was sent to Israel," Peres said forty years later, "it was received by some very sour faces," and there is no doubt that in mid-1963, two months before Ben-Gurion resigned, it was a daring formula. Peres was taken by surprise by the president's question, and had to ad-lib. "I was under pressure. I didn't know what to say," he later recalled. Peres's improvisation was adopted by Eshkol, first as an oral declaration, and later as a written Israeli undertaking. In May 1966, the vague language was included in a declaration in the Knesset plenum in Jerusalem.

The ambiguity of the formula was of supreme importance in the relaxation of tension between the United States and Israel over the nuclear issue. It allayed American suspicions that Israel was not telling the truth.

Eshkol went to Washington in order to achieve two goals: to institutionalize America's role as Israel's permanent weapons supplier, and to neutralize the threat that Washington would hamper the progress of the nuclear program. Johnson's goal was to preserve the tenuous equilibrium in the Middle East or, in other words, to both halt the arms race and help Israel as far as possible, without upsetting Egypt's Nasser too much.

This was the first-ever state visit of an Israeli prime minister at the White House, and Eshkol was given red-carpet treatment. For Israelis, an official reception for their leader in the U.S. capital, with all due ceremony, an honor guard, and a twenty-one-gun salute, was an exciting innovation. There was as yet no television in Israel, and only rarely did the state radio stations broadcast live descriptions of news events. Only a week later the newsreel accounts screened in movie theaters, with the announcer proclaiming: "Washington. A magnificent reception was prepared for the prime minister . . ."

Unlike Kennedy, Johnson was not eager for a confrontation. He preferred compromise. Unlike Ben-Gurion, Eshkol never emanated an aura of aloofness. He behaved like a simple man and couldn't resist telling a joke or two. No one appreciated a good joke like Johnson. The chemistry was good and the two men hit it off from the start.

According to the protocol of the meeting, Johnson opened by saying that "he was foursquare behind Israel on all matters that affected their vital security interests. Just as the U.S. was in Southeast Asia, they would be wherever they were needed." Johnson repeated the good news that Feldman had brought to Jerusalem, that the United States would help Israel in any way to obtain tanks in Europe. He did not make the supply of tanks conditional upon revealing Dimona's secrets, and Eshkol said only that Israel was "not engaged in nuclear weapons production."

According to the protocol, the president asked: "If Israel is not going to get into nuclear production, why not accept IAEA [International Atomic Energy Agency] controls and let the U.S. reassure Nasser about Dimona?"

Eshkol's answer was negative; he would not allow inspectors who were not Americans to set foot inside Dimona, and he refused to permit the United States to pass information about Dimona to the Egyptians, although after the first visit of American experts there in 1961, Ben-Gurion had replied in the affirmative when Kennedy had made a similar request. Instead, according to the American account, Eshkol replied to Johnson as follows:

I cannot agree that Nasser should be told the real situation in Dimona because Nasser is an enemy. It would be a great thing if you could induce our neighbors to change the armistice into peace instead of pursuing escalation in tanks and missiles. In the meantime, while the UAR remains an enemy and is committed to the destruction of Israel, it would seem inadvisable to communicate such matters to them. Besides, Nasser has worked for years to become a nuclear power. He will continue to do so. A message that Dimona is not manufacturing nuclear weapons would have no effect.

The president responded that it was firm U.S. policy to keep the UAR from getting into nuclear production and it would do everything it could to restrain them. "I want to assure you," the president said, "that we are not being naive about Nasser. What we want to do is to try and prevent him from leaning over too far towards the Russians."

Once again a disagreement emerged about the gravity of the Egyptian military threat. Eshkol said that Egypt had two hundred missiles and Israel would have to produce its own, although it would be ready to wait a year or two to see how the threat would evolve.[7] "I think that Nasser is planning to build these missiles in the hundreds," said Eshkol, but Johnson defined Egypt's prospects for success in developing effective missiles as "feeble"—and he was right, as it emerged in the Six-Day War of June 1967. "We are more confident of the Israeli deterrent edge than the Israelis seem to be," the president added. "We don't blame them for running scared, but we hope they will listen to well meant advice." In other words, it behooved the Israelis to take America's advice and refrain from developing strategic weaponry.

And once again, Nasser made the Israeli prime minister's job an easier one. Egypt's military involvement in Yemen, the massive flow of Soviet arms to Egypt, and Nasser's constant stream of statements against the American military activity in Vietnam all combined to make Congress and the president heartily sick and tired of the Egyptian leader, and accelerated the process of disaffection between the two countries. Moreover, Egypt simply refused to discuss the termination of its strategic projects—ballistic missiles and chemical weapons—with the United States, and for its part, the Soviet Union would do nothing to halt the arms race. In February 1966, the State Department approached the Soviet ambassador in Washington, Anatoly Dobrynin, and proposed that an understanding be reached on the restriction of the supply of airplanes and missiles to the Middle East. Several weeks later, Dobrynin replied in the negative, suggesting instead that the Middle East be declared a nuclear-free zone. Rusk agreed, and suggested that each of the two powers request assurances from its client state and then convey them to the other side. Rusk told Dobrynin that the United States was convinced that the Israelis were not planning to make nuclear weapons, but Dobrynin was not persuaded and nothing came of this initiative.

When he met Eshkol, therefore, the president was aware of the scope of Egypt's arms acquisition, but nevertheless suggested that "Israel should not hasten to counter it and accelerate an arms race. It can always count on the United States in an emergency." Eshkol retorted that a verbal American undertaking was not sufficient, and that he needed offensive weapons: "We are told that there is a United States commitment to Israel. But I cannot ask my people to rely on this alone. When I discuss this matter with my people, the question they ask me is 'do you have enough tanks?'"

Eshkol devoted most of his exposition before the president to the dangers menacing Israel. He depicted the next armed confrontation with the Arabs in terms of a war of Gog and Magog:

> We cannot afford to lose. This may be our last stand in history. The Jewish people have something to give to the world. I believe that if you look at our history and at all the difficulties we have survived, it means that history wants us to continue. We cannot survive if we experience again what happened to us under Hitler. You may view the situation otherwise and it may be difficult to grasp how we feel. I believe you should understand us. It is important that you should understand us.

But Eshkol was breaking down an open door. Johnson saw things no differently. His upbringing in Texas had brought him to a close identification with the Jews' destiny.

The following day, the two men had a fifteen-minute private meeting. They spoke about Dimona. The president once again requested Eshkol's permission to convey to Nasser information about the American inspectors' visit, and Eshkol once again turned him down. Later, Robert Komer met with Peres and scolded him for the way that Israel had humiliated the president. This is how Komer reported to the president on his conversation with Peres:

> I told Peres that the secretive and evasive way in which Israel responded to our frequent inquiries on this [strategic missiles] and Dimona inevitably raised suspicions on our part. For the President of the US to have to intervene personally and repeatedly to get the necessary reassurances was frankly counter-productive; it only made us feel that Israel really did have something to hide. As for Israel's missile program, why was it that they wouldn't even answer our queries? Peres said that when one made an arrangement with a third country [France] and that country laid down certain conditions, it tied Israel's hands. [I] replied that this was the first cogent explanation we'd had, but wasn't the US/Israel relationship such that we were entitled to greater candor? He said we'd want to talk with Israel further about missiles.

By the next morning, Eshkol had second thoughts, and informed the Americans that he now agreed that the information they had about Dimona could be transferred to the Egyptians. And so, both sides came out of the summit meeting satisfied, and Komer wrote a memo to the president in a positive vein:

> While all returns aren't in, this visit seems to have netted out a distinct plus. So far Arab reaction, especially from Cairo, is most restrained . . . while Israelis are highly pleased. We also managed to steer press successfully (so far) away from sensitive arms issue.

This was an election year, and Johnson needed the support of his Jewish constituency. But Johnson won a gigantic victory. It was the high point for him: For the next four years, the further the American military sank into the Vietnam quagmire, the more the public's support for Johnson waned.

The tank deal with Germany and Britain did not remain a secret. In

October 1964, it was leaked to the German media, and in February 1965, Chancellor Erhard ordered a halt to the supply of tanks. By then, only 40 of the 200 Pattons had been shipped to Israel, which asked the United States to make good the shortfall. It also added to its shopping list Skyhawk attack planes, and the United States once more responded that it had no desire to become Israel's arms supplier. But if it emerged that there was no alternative supplier, the U.S. would weigh the request again.

As the negotiations between Israel and the United States dragged on, King Hussein of Jordan sent a distress signal to the U.S. Embassy in Amman: Egypt and Syria, his partners in the Unified Arab Command, were pressing him to enlarge and upgrade his armed forces with Soviet weapons.[8] Hussein preferred American arms, and he asked for Patton tanks and Phantom fighter aircraft. Israel strongly opposed such a deal, despite Washington's attempts to explain that if the king didn't get American arms, he would turn to the Soviets. Israel didn't give in, and negotiations were stalled.

Early in 1965, Johnson sent Komer of the NSC and ambassador at large Averell W. Harriman to Israel. The two emissaries once again made it clear that the supply of arms to Israel was dependent on Israel's disclosure of its plans for developing nuclear weapons and missiles. Yitzhak Rabin, who was now the IDF chief of staff, wrote in his diary: "Komer—and Harriman to a lesser extent—were severe and tough on the matter of nuclear arms. Our contention that prime minister Eshkol had said on his last visit to the United States that Israel would not be the first country to introduce nuclear weapons into the Middle East did not work." Komer was known for his toughness. In Washington they called him "Blowtorch Bob."[9] This is how Rabin described their meeting: "He came to the chief of staff's bureau, and spoke harshly, and even menacingly: 'If Israel goes that way it is liable to create the worst crisis ever in its relations with the United States.' I tried to assuage his concern. 'Your representatives visit the reactor at Dimona. You know exactly what is happening there.'" Harriman and Komer had similar views on the toughness of the Israelis. "Even the Soviets are less tough bargainers than the Israelis," Harriman said.

And of course the Israelis had the advantage of their powerful proxies in Washington, the Jewish lobby, who could be brought into the game when nothing else had worked. The harshness of the positions taken by officialdom was generally softened in the White House, where two additional elements were at play: the Jewish vote, and Johnson's special emotional relationship with the Jews and the State of Israel. This was why Komer blinked first, and cabled Washington:

> WE [ARE] SEVEN MONTHS PREGNANT ON ARMS SALES TO ISRAEL AS WELL AS JORDAN. IF WE SELL TO JORDAN WE MUST SELL TO ISRAEL TOO. IF WE DON'T SELL TO JORDAN, SOVIETS WILL. THEN WE'LL HAVE TO SELL TO ISRAEL ANYWAY.

And that's what happened. The United States sold Israel, directly, offensive weapons in the form of forty-eight Skyhawk planes and two hundred Patton tanks. Israel agreed to America's selling of Pattons to Jordan too, on condition that they would not be based on the East Bank of the Jordan River and did not threaten Israel. To solve the issue of linkage that the American side made between the tank deal and Israel's development of a strategic-weapons potential, the formula that Eshkol had used with Johnson, and Peres had used with Kennedy, was brought in: Israel will not be the first to introduce nuclear weapons into the Middle East. This formula, which so far had been used only orally, became a written principle for the first time in the agreement between the United States and Israel that was signed in March 1965. Its two most important provisions were:

> Article II. The Government of Israel has reaffirmed that Israel will not be the first to introduce nuclear weapons into the Arab-Israel area . . .

> Article V. [The] United States will sell Israel on favorable credit terms, or otherwise help Israel procure, certain arms and military equipment as follows:

> A. The United States will ensure the sale directly to Israel at her request of at least the same number and quality of tanks that it sells to Jordan.

> B. In the event of the Federal Government of Germany not sup-

plying to Israel the remainder of the 150 M48 tanks outstanding under the German-Israeli tank deal of 1964, the United States will ensure the completion of this program.

This was the third time that United States–Israeli relations took a leap to a higher level. The first was taken under the Eisenhower administration, in the wake of the tension in the Middle East in the summer of 1958. The second was taken by President Kennedy at the end of 1962, when at his meeting in Florida with Golda Meir he spoke of the "special relationship" between the two countries and compared the ties to those between the United States and Britain. The third leap, carried out by Johnson, was the most effective. Yitzhak Rabin, in his memoirs, wrote, "The United States has openly and publicly undertaken a far-reaching commitment to balance the forces of Israel and its neighbors in the Middle East."

ESHKOL COULD NOW begin to tackle the internal Israeli front, which was close to boiling point. Ben-Gurion's departure from the prime minister's office had failed to bring the Old Man tranquility. In fact it had only stoked his passion to see absolute justice done in the aftermath of the Lavon Affair. Late in 1964, he presented the minister of justice with a comprehensive report on the issue that leading jurists had volunteered to draw up for him, and he once again demanded a judicial inquiry. Now, for the first time, Eshkol opposed him publicly. When it transpired that some of the leaders of the party had held talks with supporters of Pinhas Lavon with an eye to securing the annulment of his expulsion, Ben-Gurion was mortally offended, and he wrote to Eshkol, "This is my last personal appeal to you . . . before an abyss opens up [between us]." In response, Eshkol took a step that Ben-Gurion himself had taken many times as prime minister: He went to President Shazar and submitted his resignation, thereby coercing everyone who feared a governmental crisis to line up behind him. And indeed, his colleagues in the party leadership hastened to persuade him to retract his resignation, a move for which he laid down an explicit condition: The Lavon Affair would have to be removed from the agenda once and for all.

And the party backed him. In mid-February 1965, at a dramatic party convention, Moshe Sharett delivered a speech that caused a stir. This was the same Sharett who had acted as prime minister when Ben-Gurion took a year's leave at Sdeh Boker late in 1953, and had been ousted from his post as foreign minister by Ben-Gurion when the latter returned to office. Now, in the autumn of his days, bound to a wheelchair, wan and withered by cancer, Sharett settled accounts with his partner of forty years, a man whom he both admired and despised. "Ben-Gurion earned a unique position," Sharett declared. "He earned the glories of the hero of the great historical epic . . . this elevated him to dizzying heights and, in my opinion, burdened him with a tremendously heavy load, perhaps too heavy to bear . . . and when such a contradiction appears, tragedy is the result."[10] After the speech Golda Meir hurried over to him and planted a kiss on his forehead. When it was her turn to speak, she attacked Ben-Gurion still more harshly, and he wrote in his diary: "The ugliest thing about the convention was Golda's venomous speech." Ben-Gurion lost the vote, with 60 percent of the delegates casting their ballots against him.

But Eshkol's hope that the Affair would now go away was short-lived. The tension that had arisen between Ben-Gurion's followers who were still in key positions and the members of the new regime was already beyond repair. Eshkol was determined "to clean out the stables," as he put it, meaning to clear Ben-Gurion's crowd out of the defense establishment. But they would not go quietly and instead put up a bitter struggle for survival. The first to go were the directors of the nuclear project. Eshkol's adviser economist Zvi Dinstein was the executor of the cleanup. Previously he had been controller of foreign currency and head of fuel matters in the Ministry of Finance under Eshkol. His wife, Aya, belonged to the Zionist aristocracy. Her father was Arthur Ruppin, the "father of Zionist settlement," who starting in 1908 had run the Jaffa-based Zionist Organization's Eretz Yisrael Office, which was responsible for acquiring land and establishing Jewish settlements.[11]

Forty years later international oil trade consultant Dinstein explained the policy that he executed on Eshkol's behalf: "We wanted to introduce economic sense into the defense establishment, and that is what we did. It was a network that had evolved on its own. In some of its operations, there was no economic logic, and there was no control. I came there in order to question the conventions that Peres had dictated." Eshkol's people called the hierarchy that Peres had created in the defense establishment "a Byzantine court." They accused him of advancing his associates and adopting divide-and-rule tactics, which Peres denied.

The tension between the two camps remained beneath the surface, because Ben-Gurion's spirit still hovered over the defense establishment and Eshkol hesitated to take extreme measures against Ben-Gurion's associates. Then, in June 1965, Ben-Gurion launched his open political struggle against Eshkol, hinting that he would be ready to return to the prime minister's office in order to "purify the murky atmosphere." But the party central committee convened to choose its candidate for the upcoming November general election, and once again Eshkol won hands-down. Only 36.5 percent supported Ben-Gurion.

After this victory, Eshkol felt for the first time that he was free to implement an independent policy. He demanded that Ben-Gurion's young supporters express confidence in him, and he forced Peres to resign as deputy defense minister. The intellectual elite backed Eshkol and held Peres in contempt. They had been shaped by the era in which loyalty to the Zionist cause was measured by action in combat, and Peres could claim no heroic aura, having served only in staff positions during the War of Independence, and then acquiring the stigma of being a bureaucrat. In the political salons, he had the reputation of having acquired his power through intrigue. At that time, a song called "How the Bug Got to the Top" was part of a satirical cabaret show in Tel Aviv, and though its writer denied that it had anything to do with Peres, the catchy phrase stuck to his name and he had to contend with it for several years.

Eshkol had pushed Ben-Gurion into a corner, and the Old Man had the choice of two alternatives—to withdraw entirely from political life, or to form a breakaway party. He chose the latter, and set up a party called Rafi, a Hebrew acronym for Israeli Workers List (though the party by no means represented the proletariat; at that time it was still considered an asset to be associated with the working class). A large group of younger politicians followed him, headed by Peres. Moshe Dayan hesitated for a few days, and then he too joined Ben-Gurion.

In the election campaign Ben-Gurion's new party ran as a technocratic and progressive grouping, without any ideological predisposition, and promised to refresh the stagnant establishment. Ben-Gurion leveled personal attacks and insults at Eshkol. "This man is going from bad to worse," he said about his successor as prime minister. "He is dishonest," and "not worthy of standing at the helm of the state." Some party spokesmen dropped hints that while Ben-Gurion had nurtured the nuclear project, Eshkol was endangering it, but these claims did not seep into the public's consciousness. In the Israeli citizen's web of political considerations, the nuclear project played no part at all.

In retrospect it is clear that the attacks on Eshkol were unfair, even malicious. Eshkol was conducting security policy in general and nuclear policy in particular, both proficiently and confidently. Proof of this was his achievement in negotiations with the United States on the supply of arms, and Johnson's acceptance of the vague formulation on the nuclear option.

In the November elections, Eshkol was victorious. His party won 45 seats, only five fewer than in 1961. Ben-Gurion tasted failure for the first time, and admitted that Rafi had "suffered a great defeat." The party won only 10 seats, less than half of what it had aimed for. Israeli public opinion punished Ben-Gurion for his petty vindictiveness against his rival, and for his obsessive stubbornness in the matter of the inquiry into the Affair. Eshkol was seen as a popular and humane prime minister, suitable for that period of relative peace and prosperity.

The most conspicuous outcome of the election was the relegation to the opposition of the prominent figures who were identified with the country's security. For the first time in their political careers, Ben-Gurion, Dayan, and Peres found themselves no longer part of the decision-making process. Dinstein was elected to the Knesset and Eshkol appointed him his deputy at the Defense Ministry, replacing Peres. Before that, Yitzhak Rabin had succeeded Zvi Tsur as chief of staff, and he too would have a role in the weakening of the old defense establishment, and in particular in the changes in the order of priorities of RAFAEL. Now, with Ben-Gurion and his "young guard" away from the hub of influence, the new regime could dare to unsheathe their daggers.

Of all those slated to be dismissed, Munya Mardor was the only one to fight back. He stood at a key crossroads, and it was impossible to dismantle RAFAEL without shifting him out of the way first. He was not considered an unmitigated Ben-Gurionist. Unlike Ernst Bergmann, he had stayed away from any political involvement. He also enjoyed wide support because of the close friendships he had forged during the underground era with everyone who was anyone in the security and political elite of the state. He had friends in both camps, and therefore, although Dinstein had sharpened his arrows for use against Mardor, Eshkol was compelled to blunt their points, due to the heavy pressures exerted by members of his own camp, among them the two strong leaders of the party, Golda Meir and Pinhas Sapir, who had succeeded Eshkol as finance minister.

Mardor had sensed that a black cat had passed between him and Eshkol at the outset of the new prime minister's term back in 1963. In April of that year, two months before he resigned, Ben-Gurion had agreed to allow Mardor to be interviewed by the defense correspondent of the *Ha'aretz* daily, Ze'ev Schiff. Both the chief military censor and the security officer of RAFAEL sat in on the interview, and the nuclear project was not mentioned at all. The interview was supposed to be published on July 5, a few days after Eshkol became prime minister. "On that same day, hints of the prime minister's displeasure began to reach my ears," Mardor wrote. Eshkol held up publication of the interview, and Mardor anticipated disaster. Colleagues told him he was imagining a conspiracy, because of his habits formed in the underground, but Mardor was right. Not only was the interview never published, but the prime minister decided to remove the Gabriel sea-to-sea missile project from RAFAEL and to transfer it to Israel Aircraft Industries.[12] Later, according to foreign sources, he also cancelled the Jericho missile project. These were two debilitating blows at an esteemed organization, whose heads were considered the crème de la crème of the defense establishment.

Eshkol's decision to kill the missile development project had two reasons. First, he wanted to reduce the state budget. Second, Eshkol was trying to cut friction with the Johnson administration. Dinstein recalled the bitter criticism Ben-Gurion hurled at Eshkol: "Ben-Gurion said it would be a 'cause of weeping for generations to come.' Those were his words. And we thought that to take on another huge project [in addition to the nuclear project] was beyond our power, and could lead to economic devastation, or devastation for all of our other development projects. To take this thing on, in addition to everything else, was impossible."

Eshkol explained that if Israel needed missiles, it would acquire them abroad, as it had done with other weapons in the past. But Mardor warned him: "If we need missiles urgently we cannot rely on the French or anyone else." "In my opinion, canceling the [missiles] project damaged not only the infrastructure of our security," Mardor wrote, "but it also meant contempt for the [RAFAEL] team, whose members for 16 years spared no effort and no talent in the defense research work and the initiatives in this area. This outstanding team stood there bewildered, humiliated and shamed."

Bergmann was not informed about Eshkol's decision on the missiles, although he still held the titles of scientific adviser to the defense minister and head of research and development. Since Eshkol became prime minister and minister of defense, Bergmann's advisory was devoid of content. The AEC, which he still headed, was neutralized. At RAFAEL too his scientific authority was on the wane. Mardor thought that relations between Eshkol and Bergmann became more tense because Bergmann was a confirmed Ben-Gurionist. Peres also believed that Bergmann's political affiliation tipped the scales against him.

Eventually, Bergmann took the hint and resigned on April 1, 1966. The only scientist with an international reputation, who had joined the top echelon of Israel's military research and had remained there continuously since the establishment of the state, was sent home humiliated. On the altar of his worship of Ben-Gurion and his dedication to the nuclear project, Bergmann had sacrificed a promising scientific career at the Weizmann Institute as well as his relationship with his mentor, Chaim Weizmann. The scientific community of Israel had recoiled from him because of his total identification with the military establishment. Now, Eshkol awarded him the Israel Security Prize, the country's top award for contributions to security, and Mardor convened the senior staff of RAFAEL for a farewell reception.

The next in line for dismissal was the director of the Dimona "research complex," Mannes Prat. Eshkol summoned him to Jerusalem, to get a briefing on the status of the reactor, and Prat's response was, "Why should I go to him? Let him come here." Prat was so closely identified with Dimona that it had become part of his very being. "Mannes was crazy, because he was a genius. Every genius is half crazy," said Peres.

Two leading physicists, Amos de Shalit and Igal Talmi, who were involved in all the stages of construction at Dimona and whose opinions were valued in the security establishment, wrote to Eshkol to say that if Prat was replaced, a catastrophe would occur at Dimona, that it would collapse. But the prime minister was determined and Dinstein handed Prat his dismissal notice. "When I heard that Mannes wouldn't give Eshkol a briefing—that he thought that he was the ruler of his realm, and would brook no interference . . . I'll never forget it," Dinstein said. "I called him to the Ministry and told him, 'The time has come. You have performed a wondrous feat, perhaps the Jewish people owes you its gratitude, and perhaps in a few score years no one will know what you achieved and what you did, and what gratitude they owe you, but we have to part company.' He looked around [to see if there was anyone else in the room] and said: 'Isn't this a private conversation between us? Who are you talking to?' He could not imagine that I was saying these things to him. He said, 'I don't understand. You told me this was a private conversation, who are you saying these things to?'"

However, these struggles were secondary. The hardest battles were fought over the demand by Eshkol and Dinstein to transfer professional units that, according to foreign sources, were engaged in nuclear research and production, from RAFAEL to the direct control of the Defense Ministry. Mardor wrote that the ultimate intention of Eshkol's plan "was to deprive RAFAEL of one of its principal projects." In foreign media reports this "principal project" has been identified as the nuclear project. This disclosure sent shock waves through RAFAEL's staff. "It was interpreted as an expression of a lack of confidence in the ability of our technical teams to master the production processes," Mardor wrote. He notes that there were mutinous murmurs amongst his staff, but he himself persuaded them "not to go too far."

Mardor ran his campaign to save RAFAEL for almost six months. He used all his influence in the academic and political worlds, and his family joined in. Cabinet ministers, scientists, and IDF officers lobbied Eshkol on Mardor's behalf, and he was invited to "a chat over a cup of tea" at the prime minister's official residence in Jerusalem. "Eshkol made things easy for me in the way he conducted the conversation, in a relaxed Saturday afternoon atmosphere," Mardor said. A day earlier, Dinstein had suggested to Mardor that instead of heading RAFAEL, he should become head of the Defense Ministry mission to the United States. Mardor refused, with the backing of his wife, Lenka. Their son Rami was due to enlist in the IDF the following year, and they didn't want to be abroad during his service. "Dinstein tried to talk him into giving up the post," daughter Gonnie recalled, "and we told him to keep up the fight."

On that Saturday afternoon at the prime minister's residence in Jerusalem, Eshkol, Dinstein, and Mardor spoke openly, mostly about the "principal project." On the table lay one of the country's most significant matters: who would control the "project." Would the project be completely supervised by the new prime minister, or would it continue to be commanded by the messengers of the "old man," the young Ben-Gurionists whom Eshkol decided to dismiss from the defense administration?

The conversation went on for about two hours. Mardor had grasped the meaning of Eshkol's ambition, but he wanted to save RAFAEL. He felt responsible for many of RAFAEL's senior personnel, who had linked their careers to him, and poured out his bitterness at being ordered by the new regime to preside over the dismantling of the organization: "Every defense minister is entitled to change the policies of his successor, but I wondered how it was possible to conceive of giving none other than me the 'mission' of wiping out a creation in which I believed and to which I had devoted 14 years of my life."

Immediately after the meeting in Jerusalem, Mardor dispatched a letter to the prime minister. "There is no way to understand a change in the organization of a project—that has reached the stage of assembly into a weapons system—but as an announcement of its failure," he wrote. "Is this the intention? I believe that you, Mr. Defense Minister, do not see things in that way after your visit to the Institute and the reports that you have received recently." Mardor proposed that an independent committee be set up to determine who would run the project, and Eshkol agreed.

Scientists, politicians, and many underground veterans took part in the lobbying campaign. And when the gamut of consultations in a series of committees and in the upper echelons of government was over and the reorganization of the project became a fact, Mardor saw that things were far less terrible than they had seemed to be at first. RAFAEL was not broken up, and he was not fired. Not only was the "principal project" not taken away from RAFAEL, but—according to foreign sources—even the development of the missiles was returned to it after a short while. RAFAEL's budget was enlarged by some 50 percent and it was permitted to hire hundreds of new workers.

In the framework of the reorganization, the Atomic Energy Commission was reinstated with the prime minister as its chairman, and it was given the responsibility for the nuclear program. The director of the AEC would be the physicist Israel Dostrovsky, who had been involved in almost all stages of the project. The AEC would advise the government on all matters connected to nuclear research and development, carry out government policy, and represent Israel vis-à-vis international organizations and foreign governments' atomic agencies. It would be responsible for two facilities: the Negev Nuclear Research Center at Dimona, including the reactor, where nuclear materials were produced, and the Nahal Soreq Nuclear Research Center, containing the small American reactor. The RAFAEL Institute located near Haifa, where the actual nuclear device was assembled, was also placed under the AEC's responsibility, foreign sources have reported.

Simultaneously, control over the scientific projects of the defense establishment, including those at RAFAEL, were transferred to a new Scientific Administration that was set up at the Defense Ministry under Ephraim Katchalsky, who now Hebraized his name to Katzir. Katzir's appointment was approved by the prime minister in late June 1966. At Mardor's request, the new Scientific Administration was defined as a staff unit and did not contain executive units, all of which remained at RAFAEL.

The struggle over the reorganization had taken several months. During this time, Ben-Gurion and some of his supporters sharply criticized Eshkol behind the scenes, claiming that he was jeopardizing the future of the nuclear project. Dinstein says that Eshkol was racked by the criticism. "He was in anguish," said Dinstein. "Only those who were closest to him knew what anguish he was in, and Ben-Gurion would repeat the allegations over and over, emphatically, and all of his many admirers would do the same, and there was no truth in any of it. But it tormented him, I think it even may have caused his death."

CHAPTER THIRTEEN

"We Have the Option"

ISRAEL ATTAINED NUCLEAR CAPABILITY during the second half of 1966. Foreign experts have concluded that fissile materials in adequate quantities were made at Dimona, and that in the laboratories and workshops of RAFAEL a nuclear device was completed and tested by a procedure known in the professional jargon as "cold testing," in which each one of the processes that together create the explosion is checked by simulation.

The cold test of the "critical mass proceeding" within the device was carried out by RAFAEL in November 1966, foreign experts have said. They deduced this from a passage in Munya Mardor's diary. They believed that in the following passage Mardor is describing how a RAFAEL team, headed by Yevgeni "Jenka" Ratner, test-simulated the implosion in the nuclear device. Though there has never been any official Israeli confirmation of this interpretation, it has become a fixture of the international discourse among professionals in the nuclear sphere. Here is the way Mardor described the test in his diary, in his characteristically vague language: "On November 2 1966, a test of special import was carried out. It represented the culmination of a period in the development of one of the principal weapons systems and the step which brought it to the final stages of its development and manufacture at RAFAEL. The success of the test was complete, for we achieved through it unambiguous experimental proof of the efficacy of the system . . . We had waited many years for this result."

Israel has never published an official announcement that fissile materials were being produced at the Dimona reactor, but French journalist Pierre Péan has written—based on French sources that over the years have proved to be utterly reliable—that by the end of 1966 Israel had accumulated enough weapons-grade plutonium to build a bomb. This means that at the plutonium separation plant that went into operation at Dimona in 1965 (according to evidence collected by Péan, and the disclosures made by Mordechai Vanunu) four kilograms of plutonium had been produced. By the end of 1966, American documents indicate, the CIA had also reached the conclusion that Israel was capable of assembling a bomb within a few weeks.

That remarkable event at RAFAEL on November 2, the day Israel is said by foreign experts to have achieved nuclear capability, passed without being marked publicly. This was, after all, a titanic achievement: Israel had become the sixth country in the world to attain nuclear capability, although it was far from being in the league of the powers that had preceded it. Nuclear capability was produced in the basement, and there it has remained, until this day.

Only eight years had passed since the signing of the unprecedented nuclear deal with France and the laying of the cornerstone of the Dimona reactor. In that year, 1958, Israel had celebrated the tenth anniversary of its independence, and Ben-Gurion set ten goals for the second ten years. In his good years that was what he always did—pose long-term challenges to Israeli society. The fifth goal in his list was formulated thus: "To develop atomic power for the needs of the economy, to utilize solar energy, and desalination of sea water for irrigation." But Ben-Gurion was not going to use atomic power to serve the economy; it is clear today that he meant to use it for defense.[1]

The governments headed by Ben-Gurion initiated four large development projects in the state's second ten years, and from the Old Man's point of view, "to develop atomic power" was the most vital and important of all. The other projects were the National Water Carrier, leading from the Sea of Galilee to the Negev; the port at Ashdod, 25 miles south of Tel Aviv; and the Dead Sea Industries, where potash, bromine, and phosphates are produced. The breakthrough in the nuclear project occurred toward the end of Israel's second decade of independence. After the severe security and economic difficulty that typified the state's first ten years, the second decade was a good one. The borders were relatively quiet, military power grew, and the economy flourished—with industry expanding, the Gross National Product increasing by an average of 5 percent a year, and per capita productivity doubling.[2] The massive investment in defense, in industrial infrastructure, and in the educational and welfare systems were made possible by the reparations agreement with Germany, the donations of Diaspora Jews, and the sale of Israeli government bonds.

It was a mobilized society, in more ways than one, disciplined and rigid, but for the first time since it began to struggle with the Arabs over the narrow strip of land between the Jordan River and the Mediterranean Sea,[3] this determined and Spartan community (which now numbered 2.8 million, compared to only 2 million at the end of the first ten-year period) allowed itself to indulge in a small degree of tranquility and to enjoy a better quality of life. Which bloc Israel would join, an issue that had bothered the Eisenhower and Kennedy administrations, was no longer a pertinent question: Israel had chosen the route that would lead it into the democratic-capitalist camp.

Higher education had expanded substantially, and the media had undergone a process of liberalization: The privately owned, independent newspapers had flourished, at the expense of the hitherto dominant party press, and the Kol Yisrael radio network was freed of the control of the prime minister's office and given the status of a quasi-independent governmental authority.[4] However, the relative openness of the media never had any effect at all on the observance of the nuclear taboo—in this area, the collusion continued between the government, which chose to keep the dosage of published information down to almost zero; the media, which chose not to even try to cover the issue; and the public, which chose not to want to know.

There is no doubt that the years of intensive activity in the various fields of nuclear research and development sent Israeli scientific and technological prowess soaring, and at the same time injected entrepreneurial energy and initiative from the military into the civilian economy. At that time, the shift was not discernible to the man in the street, both because of the secrecy in which the strategic projects were cloaked and because the research and development were spread over several fields, but in retrospect and especially in view of the results, this process is now crystal clear.

Nuclear capability, in theory at least, should have granted Israel's leadership a large degree of mental peace and confidence that the threat of destruction had been removed once and for all, but the existential angst never receded. In reality, Israel already possessed the potential of a regional power, but mentally it remained a country besieged. The tenacity of the anxiety may well have been the result of a strengthening of consciousness of the Holocaust. After the Eichmann trial in 1961, public debates about the Nazis' war on the Jews and its consequences had erupted for the first time. These discussions arose first and foremost from what amounted to a need for mass group therapy, but there certainly were also some aspects manifestly in the nature of propaganda.

The main conclusion that Israelis drew from the destruction of European Jewry was that only political sovereignty and a strong military could serve as a guarantee of Jewish security. But the growing awareness of, and preoccupation with, the Holocaust also had a rather disconcerting effect, in that it aroused fear that another similar catastrophe could occur and that the enemies surrounding the Jewish state would rise up to destroy it. This pattern of Israeli apprehension would emerge in full strength in the period preceding the 1967 Six-Day War; this period became known to Israelis as "the Waiting" and dragged out for three anxiety-ridden weeks. Fear of the possibility of another Holocaust played a critical role in causing the panic and the confusion that characterized Israeli society during this period.

Nineteen sixty-seven was the most significant year in the short history of the state. Everything that happened was totally unanticipated, but the events of that year determined the fate of the country for the coming decades. In February, in the presence of Prime Minister and Defense Minister Levi Eshkol, the senior officers of the Israel Defense Forces and the top echelons of the Defense Ministry convened in the war room of the supreme command to hear the chief of staff, Lieutenant General Yitzhak Rabin, present his annual situation assessment. The conclusion was unequivocal: War with the Arabs was not expected before 1973, based on three main reasons supplied by military intelligence. First, about a quarter of the Egyptian army was pinned down by the war in Yemen; second, Nasser was not convinced that his army was capable of defeating Israel; and third, the Soviet Union was trying to keep the Cold War in check, as demonstrated by Moscow's behavior in the Cuban missile crisis. These forecasts jibed with American evaluations.

But then, exactly three months later, in yet another conspicuous example of the fallibility of intelligence agencies, Egypt suddenly deployed sizeable military formations in the Sinai peninsula, thereby lighting the fuse of war.

What led Nasser to take this fateful step? Was it the warnings that the Soviet Union had conveyed to Egypt that Israel was concentrating forces on its northern border with the intention of attacking Syria, Egypt's ally and partner in the United Arab Republic? Israel had emphatically denied that it had massed troops on the border or that it had any aggressive intentions, but in the preceding months it had adopted a clear policy of escalation in the perennial border war with Syria, in order to protect its water sources and to put a stop to Syrian plans to divert them, so there were grounds for Egyptian suspicion. And if Cairo had in fact been misled by Moscow's warnings, was it a case of innocent error, or was it intentional manipulation on the part of the Soviets? If so, what was the purpose? Then again, perhaps Egypt's warlike measures against Israel sprang from its ruler's need to divert attention from his army's involvement in the war in Yemen, in order to help him find a way out of the quagmire into which he was sinking. Or could it have been a sudden whim of Nasser's, springing from a surfeit of self-confidence and disregard for Israel's military power? Or a need to seek revenge for his army's ignominious defeat in 1956? One should also not rule out the possibility that Nasser initially acted because of the Soviet Union's warning, and when he realized that it had been based on a distortion, and in fact there was no untoward Israeli concentration on its border with Syria, he had already lost control because of the wave of enthusiasm that his belligerent steps had aroused throughout the Arab world, and in particular in Egypt.

Historical research has not yet come up with precise answers to these questions but could there have been a possible link between Nasser's belligerence and the reactor at Dimona? Is it feasible that the destruction of the nuclear installations at Dimona was the primary aim of the Soviet Union or of Egypt, or both, when they initiated the escalation? Some researchers have ascribed importance to Dimona when discussing Nasser's motives. Others, including Michael Oren, who has written a comprehensive history, *The Six-Day War,* attribute only marginal significance to Israel's nuclear reactor. In order to answer this question, one must examine how Egypt perceived its northern neighbor's nuclear capability.

The fact that Israel was clearly occupied in nuclear research and development never drew the Arabs into a significant nuclear arms race, notwithstanding the Kennedy administration's apprehensions that it would. Nor did the Soviet Union ever give the Arabs the technology or the materials for building a bomb.[5] All of Nasser's efforts to achieve nuclear capability from other sources came to naught. Clearly, Egypt had no genuine powerful motivation to make it a supreme national goal to get a bomb, as long as the United States and Israel did not provoke it; we have seen how in the early 1960s, Israel lulled Egypt to sleep with the help of the soothing reports of the American experts who had visited Dimona. This was why the Arab world had no reason to be preoccupied with Israel's nuclear program to any substantial extent, until the end of 1965.

At the beginning of 1966, reports were published in Europe saying that Dassault Industries in France had supplied Israel with thirty medium-range strategic missiles. These reports spurred security analysts in the Arab world to look at Israeli strategy in a new light. After all, no country would purchase exceedingly expensive missiles in order to deliver a warhead containing a half-ton or even a ton of TNT to enemy territory. The damage it would do would be too small to decide the outcome of the war and justify the expense. A country acquires ballistic missiles in order to arm them with warheads containing means of mass destruction, in order to achieve decisive results. Not only the Arabs reached that conclusion—so did the United States, initially. In May, Ambassador Walworth Barbour was told to meet Prime Minister Eshkol and demand explanations for the purchase of the ballistic missiles in France. According to the cable he sent to Washington afterward, Barbour came out satisfied: "PM assured me (a) there are no strategic missiles in Israel now; (b) there will be no such missiles in Israel for at least two more years from now, perhaps three." And in a postscript, Barbour added a personal note:

COMMENT: NOTEWORTHY THAT ESHKOL DID NOT TAKE ISSUE WITH MY POINT THAT IN PRESENT CIRCUMSTANCES, PRESENCE OF SSM'S IN

ISRAEL WOULD CONSTITUTE ISRAELI INTRODUCTION OF NEW
WEAPONS INTO AREA. PM IMPRESSED US AS FERVENTLY DESIROUS
AVOIDING FURTHER QUALITATIVE ESCALATION IN AREA ARMS.

In the wake of the reports of the French missile deal, the Arab media began discussing Israel's nuclear capability for the first time. Two issues were raised: Was Israel really building nuclear weapons, and what effect would such weapons have in the Middle East? Muhammad Hasanin Haikal led the debate in the Cairo paper *Al-Ahram*. Several times he predicted that Israel would have a bomb within three years. Forty years later, Haikal admitted that he had been wrong, but only in the timing. "I made no error on the substance. After all, every child knows Israel made a bomb," he said. "The timing makes no difference, the principle is important. I wrote that the Arab world must mobilize all its resources in order to close the gap. That's all I could do. I couldn't be expected to build a bomb myself." Haikal spoke to Nasser about the Israeli nuclear option several times. Nasser reassured him that the Soviet Union would supply Egypt with a nuclear umbrella if Israel or the United States threatened to use strategic weapons against it. That proved inaccurate. "Israel wants to scare us," Nasser told Haikal, but the latter thought that his president was belittling Israel's scientific development. "The Jewish connection frightened me," he said.

In response to the reports in the world media about Israeli nuclear activity, on May 8, 1966, Nasser gave Haikal an interview in which he declared that this activity was a breach of Israel's international commitments, and therefore Egypt too was planning to develop nuclear arms. If Israel manufactured atomic weapons, Nasser asserted, the Arab states would be obliged "to destroy immediately everything that enables Israel to build an atomic bomb," or in other words to initiate a preventive war in order to destroy Israel's nuclear installations. But such declarations from Nasser had often been heard in the past, and this time too no action was taken.[6]

Ten days later, on May 18, in a speech in the Knesset devoted to Israel's achievements in the second decade of its existence, Prime Minister Eshkol responded to Nasser:

It is odd to hear him [Nasser] speak of international pledges and obligations. Egypt does not abstain from threats and acts of aggression . . . The President of Egypt attempts to deceive the world and divert attention from the peril of existing aggressive arms in the area by drawing attention to nuclear weapons which do not exist in our region, and in whose existence in the region we are not interested. I have said before, and I repeat, that Israel has no atomic arms and will not be the first to introduce them into our region. Anybody who really has the interests of the area's nations at heart, who truly wants to free the nations of the Middle East from the nightmare of an arms race with all the constant dangers it involves, including the diversion of vital resources for unconstructive ends, ought to work for general disarmament in the Middle East or, at least, for the limitation of armaments of all kinds establishing a reasonable balance— including the non-introduction of nuclear arms into our region.

Nasser kept his feet on both sides of the fence: He did not relate to Eshkol's challenge on disarmament but neither did he allow himself to be carried away by Haikal's militant articles, and he never initiated any special action on the nuclear issue (except his unsuccessful attempt to build strategic weapons with the help of the German scientists at the beginning of the sixties).

Over the course of 1966, Israel's security situation deteriorated. In Damascus, on May 8, Syrian Air Force Commander Hafez al-Assad launched a coup d'état and installed a radical Baathist regime that actively supported Palestinian guerrilla operations against Israeli frontier settlements. Egypt and Syria signed a military alliance to coordinate their activities. Incidents multiplied along Israel's borders with Syria, Egypt, and Jordan. A minor border incident on April 7, 1967, escalated into a full-scale aerial dogfight involving 130 planes, in which Syria lost 6 MiG-21s to Israeli Air Force Mirages. Two of the MiGs were downed above Damascus.

Tension mounted on May 15, 1967, Israel's 19th Day of Independence. The first intelligence report of the entrance into Sinai of Egyptian forces was conveyed to Chief of Staff Rabin on the saluting stand during a military parade in Jerusalem. The next day, Egypt demanded that the United Nations secretary general, U Thant, order the evacuation of the U.N. Emergency Force, which had been stationed in Sinai with the task of ensuring the freedom of navigation through the Straits of Tiran since 1957. Israel had withdrawn from its conquests of the Sinai Campaign the previous year. U Thant complied with unnecessary haste; if he had not, the course of history might have been different.

On May 17, the Egyptian Air Force carried out an aerial reconnaissance and photography flight over Israel. That afternoon, two MiG-21 jets entered Israeli airspace from Jordan in the east, and flew west at a height of 55,000 feet, traversing the Negev and photographing the Dimona reactor site. By the time the Israeli Air Force managed to scramble its Mirage aircraft,7 the MiGs had crossed the border with Egypt and vanished into thin air over the Sinai peninsula. At any rate, the Mirage could not attain the altitude reached by the MiGs. This was the first Egyptian aerial penetration into Israeli airspace since 1956.

Red lights went on at Israeli military intelligence and the officers at the Egyptian desk pulled out the files containing the warnings Nasser had been sounding about Israeli nuclear weapons development since 1960. The first time Nasser spoke publicly about it was after Ben-Gurion's Knesset speech in December 1960, when he made the original disclosure about Dimona. If it emerges that Israel is developing nuclear weapons, Nasser said, Egypt would launch a preventive war, "even if it has to mobilize four million men to do so" and would invade Israeli territory "in order to destroy the basis of aggression, before it is activated against us." On another occasion, Nasser declared that in order to stop Israel from arming with nuclear weapons, he was prepared to initiate "a suicide war," and in yet another statement, he said "the Arabs would take preemptive action." Nevertheless it was only after the Egyptian aerial photography sortie over Dimona that Rabin ordered a high state of alert in the IDF, and the prime minister approved a massive mobilization of reserves. "There's going to be a war, I'm telling you, there will be a war," Eshkol told his deputy at the Defense Ministry, Zvi Dinstein.

From the early days of the alert, the fear of an attack on Dimona was the main motive behind the IDF General Staff's demand that Israel take preemptive action and take the war into enemy territory to prevent the

Egyptian army from invading the Negev and trying to destroy or conquer Dimona. It was not the ejection of the U.N. forces, nor the closure of the Straits of Tiran to Israeli shipping—which Nasser declared on May 22, and his forces implemented the following day—that led Israel to mobilize its reserves, thereby causing almost total paralysis of the economy; rather, it was the fear the Dimona would be bombed or overrun. On May 21, Eshkol said at a Cabinet meeting: "In my opinion, the Egyptians will want to stop Israeli shipping in the straits, and to bomb the atomic reactor at Dimona. After that, a general offensive may ensue." The reactor had been critical since December 1963. The plutonium extraction plant—foreign experts have stated—had begun operating in 1965. A strike on the reactor could cause a disaster of horrendous proportions, with radioactive fallout reaching Israel's most populous regions, inciting chaos throughout the region. The defenses of the reactor were thoroughly beefed up, but the idea that the defensive line would not withstand an onslaught, that Egyptian armor would break into the Negev and reach Dimona, and that the reactor would be the target of volleys of missiles, artillery barrages, or aerial bombardment, could not be evaded. Despite the fact that the concrete envelope surrounding it had been built to withstand tremendous pressures, earthquakes, and vast amounts of TNT, the specter of these scenarios and the reactor's destruction haunted those responsible for the country's defense. In the history of warfare, there was no precedent for an active atomic reactor being at the center of the battlefield and facing the danger of destruction.

Israeli intelligence assumed that Egypt would launch a combined air-land offensive, with the aim of snatching a strip of the northern Negev, with Dimona inside it, cut off from Israel.[8] The head of military intelligence, Major General Aharon Yariv, informed the prime minister that the offensive could be expected at any moment. On the same day, Egyptian MiGs once again overflew Dimona and took photographs. Eshkol received the reports of this sortie while he was chairing a meeting of the Cabinet Defense Committee, where the degree of urgency for launching an Israeli offensive was being discussed. The meeting was tense, and some ministers voiced gloomy forecasts of what would happen to Israel if war broke out. According to the minutes, the National Religious Party's minister of the interior, Haim Moshe Shapira, proposed that Ben-

Gurion be asked to return to the government and be appointed defense minister. Eshkol was astounded. Turning to Shapira, he asked, "Egyptian fighter planes are flying over Dimona and we have to argue about Ben-Gurion?"

Ben-Gurion's giant shadow followed Eshkol constantly. The Old Man was so bitter that he made no bones about exploiting the crisis to accuse his successor of imaginary lapses and to fling abusive epithets at him. "The cowardly and lying prime minister" he called him, and claimed that Eshkol was responsible for the escalation on the Egyptian and Jordanian borders, and that he had mobilized the reserves unnecessarily. At a meeting of the leaders of his new party, Rafi, Ben-Gurion proposed a demand that the Knesset oust Eshkol, "just as was done in 1940 to [British Prime Minister Neville] Chamberlain."[9] It may have been horror at the possibility that the reactor would be attacked or conquered that affected Ben-Gurion's judgment; as prime minister he had demonstrated daring and determination, whereas now, despite the provocations of the Egyptian president, he was preaching moderation and restraint, the demobilization of the reserves, and avoidance of war. "If we go on the offensive, there will be a disaster," he warned Dayan. Senior army officers, Rabin among them, as well as several political figures, including Menachem Begin, the leader of the opposition right-wing Herut Party, came out of meetings with Ben-Gurion astonished at his attitude.

On the one hand, the opposition was demanding vociferously that Eshkol surrender the defense portfolio to either Ben-Gurion or Dayan; on the other hand most of the General Staff was urging him to order an offensive before it was too late. The IDF chief of operations, Major General Ezer Weizman, stormed into his office and declared: "If you give the order to attack, Jewish history will remember you as a great leader and if you do not, you will never be excused." The minister of justice, Yaacov Shimson Shapira, wept when he heard Weizman's words. The cabinet was radiating hesitancy and self-doubt, and the home front was overcome by a sense of despair and despondency. The economy had slowed down and there were shortages of basic foodstuffs. Huge numbers of casualties were expected. Tens of thousands of additional beds were prepared in hospitals, and rows of graves were dug in a Tel Aviv park. The alert declared in all the Arab countries in the region, the movement of the armies of Iraq and Saudi Arabia in the direction of Israel, and the reports of the use of poison gas by the Egyptian army in Yemen all combined to erode the morale of the Israeli population. Arab propaganda somehow blocked out the weak points in the Arab armies: Nasser was quarreling with the commander in chief of Egypt's armed forces, Field Marshal Abd al-Hakim Amer, and some orders issued by the military command never reached units in the field; 20 percent of Egypt's armor and artillery was out of commission; Egyptian troops transferred from the Yemen front were suffering from malnutrition and were incapable of combat. But none of this reached the Israeli public's ears.

Moreover, the Johnson administration estimated that the Arabs had no chance of defeating Israel.[10] European intelligence agencies came to the same conclusion. Many years later Johnson's secretary of defense, Robert S. McNamara, related that a few days before war broke out, the president hosted British Prime Minister Harold Wilson in the White House and in their discussion of the Middle East crisis the only disagreement between the two was whether it would take Israel seven or ten days to win the war.[11]

Israeli leaders had another good reason for not succumbing to the confusion and despondency that were threatening to overcome them. On the eve of the war that was about to break out, they had been given the option of confronting the enemy with the ultimate weapon, according to foreign sources. After the fighting, sources within the American government divulged that very close to commencement of hostilities, Israel was in possession of two nuclear devices. This is borne out in a passage from Mardor's diary, written on Sunday, May 28, eight days before Israel launched its offensive. At RAFAEL they were working around the clock and Mardor was visiting the various "institutions." Late at night, he entered a workshop in the north of the country, where he met Jenka Ratner, together with the heads of four of RAFAEL's units, overseeing teams who were completing the assembly of a device that Mardor describes as "a weapons system." Foreign experts have stated that this device was the prototype of a nuclear bomb. This is the way Mardor described the scene:

> It was after midnight. Engineers and technicians, most of them young, were focused on their tasks, with serious, introspective ex-

pressions on their faces, like people who were aware of the great—perhaps fateful—value of the weapons system they had succeeded in bringing to operational readiness. They were working under obvious strain, making supreme efforts, both mental and physical. I stepped outside to talk to Jenka. Only outside, in the clear air, I managed with great difficulty to persuade him to take a short nap.

Twenty-seven years had passed since the high command of the Haganah underground had them carry out the sabotage of the *Patria*, the ship in which the British were about to deport 1,800 illegal Jewish immigrants, in November 1940. As described in Chapter 2, the bomb they placed on the ship as it lay berthed in Haifa port sank it instead of merely disabling it, with the loss of 250 lives. Both men were plagued by their consciences for the rest of their lives. It is unlikely that the *Patria* was mentioned as they talked that night, and if it was, Mardor never wrote of it in his diary. But nevertheless, the situation was a dramatic one: The suspenseful anticipation on that cold night in early May, on the eve of the war that everyone knew was about to break out; the finishing touches being applied to the fateful device inside; and the two men who had carried out the act of sabotage that ended in disaster, now on the brink of realizing their lives' ambition of giving the Jews the ultimate defensive weapon. Would this device, whose completion they were overseeing, provide them with expiation for the bomb on the *Patria*?

Mardor's son, Rami, recalled that on one night toward the end of May, his father came home a little earlier than usual. "He came with [the chemist] Aharon Katzir [who had also Hebraized his name from Katchalsky]," said Rami, who was then a high school senior and preparing to enlist in the military in a few months' time. The Mardors were now living in Tel Aviv, in Hashoftim Street, opposite the home of Aharon's brother, the physicist Ephraim Katzir. "It was still light," said Rami, "and I saw something in their faces that I cannot describe in words. There was a kind of glow on their faces, radiating happiness. That was what happened on that day." And Rami's sister, Gonnie, chipped in immediately, "They were radiating happiness, in more senses than one."

Strangely, however, this all-important event did not ease the sense of impending destruction and the acute political tension among Israel's leaders. Eshkol continued to struggle obstinately to assert his prime ministerial authority, but the popular movement for the return of Ben-Gurion to the government swelled, and with it came a call for the appointment of Dayan as minister of defense. Confidence in Eshkol and the national morale waned to unprecedented depths after he stuttered while making a statement to the nation on the radio, and he was forced to concede. Dayan took over the defense portfolio.

Toward the end of May, at the height of the political brouhaha that preceded the government's eventual decision to attack Egypt, Shimon Peres came up with a surprising idea, foreign researchers have written. Since Ben-Gurion's new party, Rafi, had been established, Peres had not belonged to the decision-making echelon, but because of the state of emergency, from time to time the prime minister had asked him and Dayan to sit in on meetings of the Cabinet Defense Committee, and both of them had complied. Peres's proposal to Eshkol was that Israel state publicly that it had acquired the nuclear option, and thus prevent war from breaking out. Behind the idea was the assumption that the announcement itself would reshuffle the deck, and give Nasser an excuse to descend from the high tree he had climbed. In effect, Peres was suggesting that Eshkol forsake the principle of nuclear ambiguity that he himself had invented, as described in the previous chapter, and officially join the five states that had already announced that they had the bomb.[12] Eshkol and Dayan, whom Peres consulted, rejected the proposal. No official document on this matter has been released for publication as yet, so there is no authoritative information on the reasons for their opposition.

It is difficult to calculate today whether an Israeli declaration that it had the nuclear option would have defused the Egyptian president's belligerent disposition, or whether it would have made him still more eager to go to war. One must take into account that the Soviet Union could have been compelled to take action, something that would have caused the two superpowers to reenact the dangerous brinkmanship of the Cuban missile crisis. Israeli military analyst Ze'ev Schiff, an expert on Israeli nuclear policy, said: "I do not think that it would have been justified to break the ambiguity at that stage; with all the panic on the eve of the

Six-Day War, there was no reason to do so. I also do not believe that it would have prevented the war."

With Peres's notion unrealized, matters took their own course. The main offensive planned by Egypt's Field Marshal Amer was set to begin at sunrise on May 27. In the early hours of that morning feverish activity was registered on the lines of communication between Washington, Moscow, Cairo, and Tel Aviv. The day before, Israel had informed the Americans that Egypt was about to attack. Washington alerted Soviet Premier Aleksey Kosygin, who took the warning seriously, and hastily ordered the Soviet embassies in Cairo and Tel Aviv to contact the parties. At 2:15 A.M., the Soviet ambassador in Tel Aviv, Sergei Chuvakhin, wakened Prime Minister Eshkol and read him Kosygin's message. A little later, Chuvakhin's counterpart in Cairo, Dimitri Pojidaev, woke Nasser, and read him the following text: "One hour ago, President Johnson informed me that Egyptian forces are preparing an attack on Israeli positions and that this attack is about to be launched. If such a thing happens, then the US will consider itself freed from the commitments it gave to the USSR to exercise restraint."

Nasser understood the implications and immediately ordered Amer to call off the attack. Amer disputed the decision with Nasser, thought it over, and in the end informed unit commanders that the offensive was being postponed. After the war, it turned out that the operation, codenamed "Dawn," aimed to cut off the Negev from the rest of Israel (something that the Egyptian forces had succeeded in doing in 1948; before the IDF pushed them back into Sinai, Mardor had been responsible for organizing the airlift that carried troops, equipment, and supplies to and from the Negev). The reactor at Dimona was one of the targets to be bombed from the air as part of Operation Dawn. It was not a top-priority objective, and the operation had not been planned in order to conquer or destroy the site. There was thus a gap between Israeli expectations of the Egyptian objectives, and the plan itself, springing from Egypt's evaluation of Israel's nuclear option. The Israelis, aware that they possessed the option, predicted Nasser's moves according to what for them were rational criteria. (In 1981, when Israel saw the Iraqi nuclear reactor as a strategic threat, its planes were dispatched to destroy the reactor, then nearing completion near Baghdad.) Nasser, however, had other considerations.

He assumed that the reports in the international media about Israel hav-ing developed nuclear capability were not correct, and he therefore at-tributed less importance to Dimona. This assumption was accepted by the United States as well, despite their awareness of some aspects of the activity there. At a meeting of the National Security Council in the White House on May 24, attended by the president, the secretary of state, and the secretary of defense, CIA Director Richard Helms stated clearly that there were no nuclear weapons in the Middle East. If the United States, whose experts had visited Dimona, believed that Israel did not have the bomb *and was not about to get it*, then Nasser had no reason to presume otherwise. It is therefore reasonable to assume that the con-clusions drawn by historian Michael Oren are correct: "Several re-spectable authors have posited that Nasser sought to precipitate a conventional showdown with Israel before it could develop non-conventional weapons. My own research, based on dozens of Arabic sources, has shown no evidence whatsoever to support the theory."

Amid the general anxiety over the possibility of an attack on Dimona, the Israeli Air Force conducted an interesting experiment. Through a brilliant feat of the Mossad, Israel had acquired a Soviet-made MiG-21 fighter plane, the most advanced aircraft in Arab hands at the time. A dis-affected pilot, Captain Munir Rodfa, had been located in Iraq, promised money, and persuaded to steal the jet and fly it to Israel in August 1966. It was the first such plane to fall into Western hands. The air force got RAFAEL to fit the stolen MiG with Shafrir 1 air-to-air missiles,[13] and sent it to attempt to intercept Egyptian MiGs entering Israeli airspace. Flown by veteran test pilot Danni Shapira, the MiG was painted in IAF colors, and escorted by two Israeli Mirage aircraft, so that Israeli planes that happened to be in the vicinity would not attack it. "We used espe-cially conspicuous colors, so that our guys would see them and not shoot us down," Shapira said thirty-seven years later. The Israeli MiG was ready to ambush the Egyptians, but they never appeared again.

But as the "Waiting" continued, the tension over Dimona abated. Is-raeli intelligence concluded that since the Egyptians had not moved rapidly to destroy the reactor, they would not try to do so anymore, and this turned out to be correct. The only aircraft shot down over Dimona was an Israeli French-made Ouragan bomber. It had been crippled while on attack over Sinai on the first day of the fighting, and was limping back to base when hit by a Hawk missile as it approached the site of the reactor. The pilot was killed.

On June 5, at 7:15 A.M., the IAF dealt the Egyptian air force a death blow and determined the outcome of the war. On that first day, 70 percent of all the aircraft belonging to the air forces of the Arab states were destroyed. Within six days, the IDF had conquered the Sinai peninsula from Egypt; the West Bank and East Jerusalem from Jordan; and the Golan Heights from Syria. The area now under Israeli control was about three times the size of the state itself.

Many saw the victory as a miraculous event. Only a little more than twenty years had gone by since in Europe millions of defenseless Jews had been penned up in ghettos, sent in cattle trucks to concentration camps, and systematically murdered by the Nazis. Now it had taken only six days for the army of the Jewish state to defeat an enemy whose forces had the advantage in both numbers and weaponry. It is no wonder that a wave of spiritual intoxication swept over the Jews of Israel and the Diaspora. Mardor reflected the mood of many Israelis when, with all the innocence of an enlightened, reluctant conqueror, he wrote in his diary: "The elation of great days in the nation's annals engulfed us. For the first time since the establishment of the state, there was a chance of peace with our neighbors."

Mardor claimed some of the credit for the victory as belonging to RAFAEL. "The beginning of June 1967 found RAFAEL in a situation where the main objectives for the development of weapons systems and their production, set 15 years before, had in fact been attained, and its most important products had reached fruition," he wrote in his diary. He invited defense minister Dayan to pay another visit to RAFAEL's "institutes." "This time," he wrote, "Dayan ended his visit expressing full admiration and acknowledgement of the results of our work. Whereas 10 years before he had been skeptical of RAFAEL's ability to realize its long-range goals." Indeed Dayan appreciated the achievement. Addressing the Knesset's Foreign Affairs and Defense Committee right after the victory, he said: "It is a good thing that we have it." "It" was the nuclear option. Like his colleagues, Dayan never used the ineffable name in public.

But the primitive nuclear devices that, according to American sources,

Israel possessed in June 1967 did not influence the course or the outcome of the war. In their book *Critical Mass* William Burrows and Robert
Windrem claimed that on the eve of the war, Eshkol issued orders for the
arming of the two devices that had been assembled. No evidence has ever
been produced to bear out this contention, but senior officials of the
Johnson administration repeated it, and one of them reiterated it to me.
The nuclear option was absent from the considerations of the planners
of the war. They thought in the purely conventional terms current in the
armies of the West in the 1960s and were restricted to two chief aims: to
destroy the enemy's air power rapidly and to conquer the Soviet-style defensive strongholds by storming them with armor and infantry. In those
days, the nuclear option had not been factored into the balance of power.
In the 1973 Yom Kippur war, however, things would be different.

"MY MISSION AT RAFAEL is complete," Mardor wrote after the Six-Day
War. "The time has come to take my leave." He described the time he
spent in the organization as "my life's work." The new army chief of staff,
Haim Barlev, held a farewell reception for him in the garden of his home.
They were old friends, and the Mardor family turned out in full force.
More than ten years had passed since the members of the General Staff
had bandied about the slogan "not a cent for missile development," but
Barlev had always swum against the current and unlike many of his fellow
generals had supported the investment of resources in long-term research and development of what at that time were considered overly futuristic projects, and he had assisted Mardor in overcoming the military
resistance to RAFAEL's work. During the "Waiting" before the war, Barlev was one of the generals who had kept his cool. He had famously predicted the outcome in a brief, oft-quoted sentence: "We will screw them
hard, fast, and in an elegant manner." At the party, Barlev presented Mardor with a farewell letter he had written on behalf of the IDF. "You
placed in our hands the weapons which are capable of providing the answer . . ." he wrote, intentionally leaving the sentence incomplete. Defense Minister Dayan also spoke at the reception. He said that Mardor
had known how to see into the future, and how "to advance the development of sophisticated and vital weapons."

Mardor went home and sat down to write a history of RAFAEL. In 1980, he was awarded the Israel Security Prize, and a year later, when his book came out, few people noticed that the cover illustration was a blurred photograph of an atomic explosion. Later on, a cancerous tumor was discovered in his chest. "It happened from one day to the next," said his daughter, Gonnie. "The doctors gave him a year, and that is exactly what happened. The day after being given the news, he put a drum in the yard, in Kfar Shmaryahu, and for days he stood there burning documents in it." Many years before that, when they lived in Haifa, he would burn papers in the sink, or flush them down the toilet. Now, he burned the evidence systematically. But he preserved his secret diary. He deposited it with a friend who, like him, had spent many years in a very senior position in the defense establishment. "Dad stood there, sad, and burned the secret papers," said Gonnie, "and I showed him my solidarity with him by standing next to him and I burned all the letters I had kept over the years, every one. I was thirty-three, and I burned it all."

CHAPTER FOURTEEN

A Secret Compromise

IT WAS EDWARD TELLER, the father of the hydrogen bomb, who was the source for the CIA when, early in 1968, it drew up a situation assessment in which the agency concluded for the first time that Israel had begun to produce nuclear weapons. The information was imparted exclusively to President Johnson.

There were three things that tied this towering genius to Israel and its nuclear program: his being a Jew, his Israeli relatives, and the conclusions that he had drawn from the Holocaust. "No one could have had a greater influence on me than Hitler," he would say to anyone who wondered about his pessimistic way of looking at the world. He argued that Hitler's crimes had taught him an important lesson: Withdrawing into the ivory tower of science was tantamount to denial of one's basic humanity. "One cannot ignore the worst evils in politics," he declared. The Bolsheviks too had few opponents more vehement than he. "I hardly dare to ask this question: what would have happened if Stalin got the hydrogen bomb, and we did not," was his reply to journalists trying to get to the bottom of his abhorrence of communism.

He was born in 1908 to an assimilated Jewish family in Budapest, Hungary. His father, Max, was a lawyer. His mother, Ilona, née Deutsch, was a pianist who taught him to play. He loved Bach and Beethoven in particular. The family's residential neighborhood was the birthplace of a group of remarkably creative Jewish scientists in the early 20th century, each of whom played an important role in the advancement of science: the physicists Eugene Paul Wigner, winner of a Nobel Prize for physics in 1963; Leo Szilard, renowned for discovering the nuclear chain reaction; John von Neumann, who developed the fundamentals of the high-speed electronic computer; and the prolific mathematician Paul Erdos.

Wigner, Szilard, and Teller worked together on the Manhattan Project. Szilard was Teller's close friend. In 1945, after the bombs were dropped on Hiroshima and Nagasaki, Szilard moved far to the political left, condemned the bombings, and earned the epithet "scientist of conscience." Teller became famous for moving just as far in the other direction.

Teller studied theoretical physics with the best teachers of his day: Niels Bohr at Munich and Copenhagen, and Werner Heisenberg at the University of Leipzig, where Teller was awarded his doctorate in 1930. On completion of his studies, he almost found himself at the Hebrew University, just established on Mount Scopus in Jerusalem. The first president of that institution, Yehuda Leib Magnes (who was active in the Peace League, Brit Shalom, as mentioned in Chapter 1), was searching for a scientist of repute to head its physics department. No less a physicist than the young Albert Einstein wanted the post, but Magnes turned him down. Chaim Weizmann advised Magnes to approach Max Born, a specialist in quantum mechanics, but his wife wouldn't move to Palestine, and he took a job at Cambridge University. Magnes corresponded with Felix Bloch, who was teaching at Leipzig, but he wasn't tempted and preferred Stanford University.[1] George Placzek, another member of the Leipzig faculty, agreed to go to Jerusalem to see what it was like. He requested that a laboratory be built for him, but Magnes said that for the time being he would have to make do with teaching theory. Placzek said he wanted to bring an assistant with him by the name of Teller. Magnes explained that he had no money for assistants, and a disappointed Placzek departed. Only in the 1950s did Teller hear that Placzek had fought to get him an appointment at the Hebrew University but failed.

Teller became one of the hundreds of Jewish scientists who found refuge in the United States in the mid-1930s, while Hitler was preparing to conquer Europe. His first involvement in politics in the land of endless opportunity occurred when he agreed to drive his friend Szilard from Manhattan to Albert Einstein's home at the eastern end of Long Island, on August 2, 1939. Szilard did not drive, and Teller had a new Plymouth.

This journey has gone down in history. The two young physicists took the trip in order to secure Einstein's signature on a letter to President Roosevelt drafted by a number of scientists, warning that Germany intended to build an atomic bomb. This was a few months after the Germans succeeded in splitting an atom of matter for the first time.[2] The letter convinced Roosevelt to invest vast resources in making an American bomb. It is doubtful that the United States would have undertaken such a great expenditure if these European scientists in exile had not infected the top levels of the American political establishment with a terrible fear of the danger that Germany would come to dominate the world by means of the atom.

In the spring of 1940, when he was teaching physics at George Washington University in Washington, Teller was invited to a conference of scientists addressed by Roosevelt. A few days before, Hitler's forces had invaded the Netherlands and Belgium, and Teller thought it essential to encourage the president to take the United States into the war. This was the first and only time that he came close to Roosevelt.

"I am a pacifist, and you, my friends, are pacifists," Roosevelt told the assembled scientists. "But I am telling you, if you are not going to work on the instruments of war, freedom will be lost everywhere." Teller was charged with emotion. "I had the impression that Roosevelt was talking to me," he related years later.

From 1942 until 1946, Teller was involved in the making of the first atom bomb at Los Alamos, New Mexico. He took part in the construction of the first nuclear reactor there, and made the theoretical mathematical calculations of the fission chain-reaction process. After the two bombs were dropped on Japan, Teller spent the seven years from 1946 to 1953 developing the hydrogen bomb, which took the atomic bomb a stage farther. In the H bomb, in addition to the fission of a nucleus of matter, a process of fusion also takes place, in which the nuclei of heavy isotopes of hydrogen, known as deuterium and tritium, unite and become helium. The integration of these two processes—fission and fusion—in a thermonuclear bomb produces nuclear energy several times more powerful than that created in a regular atom bomb.

Foreign experts believe that for some twenty years, Teller advised Israel on nuclear matters in general, and on the building of a hydrogen bomb in particular. The first connection between Teller and Israel was made by the physicist Yuval Neeman. In 1964, the two men had been invited to a dinner hosted by Shulamith and Gershon Goldhaber, scientists who lived in Berkeley, California. Shulamith, who did research in radiochemistry, was born in Vienna and grew up in Palestine. Gershon, a professor of physics at the University of California in Berkeley who worked at developing particle accelerators, was born in Jerusalem.[3] Neeman was then a visiting professor in theoretical physics at Berkeley, and Teller was head of the Livermore Laboratory. "After that dinner with the Goldhabers, a close connection between Teller and me grew up," said Neeman.

They suited each other like hand and glove. Both were geniuses at physics, and both took an exceedingly gloomy view of the world. During the Cold War, they were among those who saw the Soviets as being focused exclusively on one goal, the destruction of the West. They both were given the nickname "Dr. Strangelove," after the scientist in Stanley Kubrick's satirical movie.

As mentioned previously Teller and Robert Oppenheimer had a long meeting with Ben-Gurion in Tel Aviv in 1952. In all likelihood, it was then that Ben-Gurion became convinced that if Israel managed to build a nuclear reactor, it would have an excellent chance of acquiring a nuclear weapons option. Teller and Oppenheimer told Ben-Gurion that the best way to accumulate plutonium was to burn natural uranium in a nuclear reactor.

Between 1964 and 1967, Teller visited Israel six times. At Neeman's initiative, he gave a series of ten lectures at Tel Aviv University. "There was a tremendous demand for places at his lectures," Neeman, then vice president of the university, recalled. "It was a real event." However, Teller's contribution to Israel was not limited to the academic sphere. During that period, he was a familiar figure in Israel's scientific-security circle and he advised its chiefs as well as the prime ministers and cabinet members. Rami Mardor, Munya's son, remembered meeting Teller at the Cameri Theater in Tel Aviv, where they saw a production of Arthur Miller's *The Crucible*, an allegory on the witch hunts of the McCarthy era. Rami was sitting with Shimon Peres, and Munya and Lenka Mardor, and when the lights went out Teller joined them. The security services did not want that visit to Israel exposed. "They didn't introduce him to me,"

Rami said, "only as a friend of father's from America. Later, at home, they told me that he was the father of the hydrogen bomb."

In those years, the Democrats were in power in the United States, and Teller's views were hardly heard at all. His evidence against Oppenheimer at the U.S. Atomic Energy Commission hearings on the latter's security clearance was still fresh in the public's memory, and most of his colleagues on the Manhattan Project despised him.[4] But in Israel he found support, and people listened eagerly to his tirades against the Soviet Union. The victory in the Six-Day War filled him with admiration and pride. To him, Israel was a prime example of a country that had succeeded in defeating the enemies who were determined to destroy it. At each of his talks with members of the Israeli security establishment's highest levels he would make them swear that they would never be tempted into signing the Nuclear Non-Proliferation Treaty. "Teller enjoyed his stays in Israel very much. He felt good here," said Neeman.

How does one reconcile the support that the Israeli establishment bestowed upon Teller and his undeclared ostracism from most of the scientific community in the United States and Europe? The resolution of the contradiction lies in the fact that Israeli public opinion had always drawn a clear distinction between morality and ethics on the one hand and the country's security on the other. When it came to its security, Israel was prepared to make compromises on moral issues. We have seen how the Jewish state never flinched at importing weapons from Germany, and it also cooperated with the apartheid regime in South Africa.

Teller visited the home of the physicist Dror Sadeh in a Tel Aviv suburb three times. The first was supposed to be a brief courtesy call, and Teller left his driver waiting outside, expecting to be inside for only a few minutes' chat. But, Sadeh's widow, Haya, recalls that Teller looked at his watch and was amazed that two hours had gone by. For a number of years, the two scientists maintained an unbroken relationship and dialogue. Sadeh disagreed with Teller's political positions, but admired his indefatigable creativity. Teller never stopped coming up with new ideas, and some of them were astonishing.[5] The two men found a common interest in the study of outer space. Sadeh had specialized in astrophysics. He ran the operations of the Israeli space agency (and believed in the Strategic Defense Initiative, commonly known as Star Wars, which

Ronald Reagan adopted at Teller's suggestion early in 1983). The principle of transferring the arms race from Earth's surface to space was a notion that gripped both Sadeh and Teller. The futuristic vision of the placement of huge mirrors in space from which tremendously powerful laser beams or particle beams could be transmitted appeared to them as quite feasible. Sadeh wrote of a laser beam fired from a spacecraft at the speed of light at a missile carrying an atomic warhead, destroying it long before a missile fired from the ground could come anywhere near it. "Rather than killing human beings," he asserted, "missiles would be destroyed. Rather than war on earth, war in space." Sadeh's wife, Haya, had different feelings about Teller. "A repulsive type, who was mainly focused on himself," she said years later.

Teller had a somewhat theatrical appearance. For one thing, he had a wooden leg and a pronounced limp, having lost his own limb after slipping under a tram car in Munich in 1928. He was ponderous, with thick eyebrows, a cold countenance, and a booming voice, making gloomy prophesies in a heavy Hungarian accent. There was a Dr. Jekyll and Mr. Hyde aspect to his personality. He could be warm and friendly, and he loved children while at the same time he was obsessive, frightening, and actually dangerous. Conservatives adored Teller, liberals abhorred him. He was ready to slay any sacred cow, but not Israel, said one of his colleagues at the Livermore Laboratory. Teller never hesitated to dismiss technicians or scientists who expressed doubts about the justice of Israel's case, and on the other hand, he opened the door of his institute to Israeli scientists.

In 1967, shortly after the Six-Day War, Neeman met Teller at an international physics conference in Rochester, New York. "Teller said to me, 'I want to see you,'" Neeman recalled, "and that evening, we met outside." It was a peculiar meeting, with a remarkable outcome. Here is the detailed description given by Neeman, thirty-five years later: "There was a tree there, with stones around its thick trunk. We sat down, back to back, on either side of the tree. He sat on a stone on the one side, and I sat on a stone on the other side. Teller said, and I am quoting, 'I think that you are not idiots, and I am impressed by your high level, and I think that you have already finished, and the thing is now behind you. I do not think that the cat and mouse game with the Americans is healthy, and it will cause problems in the future, so I am going to tell the CIA of my impressions, and I'll explain that it is justified, on the background of the Six-Day War.' I was surprised that he chose this way to raise the matter. He did everything to ensure that I wouldn't be shocked, and that's why he sat us down back to back."

On his return to Israel, Neeman described this meeting to Prime Minister Eshkol, who was in favor of Teller's initiative. It was in line with his own wish to get away from a policy based on half-truths and instead to coordinate Israel's nuclear activities with the Americans. Teller went ahead with his plan. He went to the head of the CIA's Office of Science and Technology, Carl Duckett, and told him that in the wake of talks with scientists and senior figures in the Israeli defense establishment, he had reached the conclusion that Israel had attained a nuclear capability. Duckett asked him if Israel was not going to test its nuclear device, and Teller told him not to expect this, because it would not happen. Duckett was not immediately persuaded. He insisted on evidence, and Teller told him everything he knew. "It took him a year to persuade them," said Neeman. "The CIA claimed that Israel had not yet achieved the nuclear option, but in the end Teller did convince them, and the question was what next, and he delicately coaxed them to stop the visits [of American inspectors at Dimona]. He truly and sincerely cared for the Jewish people, and he did it."

Duckett presented the information to his boss, CIA Director Richard Helms, who brought it to the attention of the president. In testimony before the U.S. Nuclear Regulatory Commission in February 1976, Duckett revealed what Teller had told him. In 1996, part of Duckett's testimony was quoted by *The Risk Report* of the Wisconsin Project on Nuclear Arms Control: "Duckett reported that Israel was already making bombs with plutonium produced in its Dimona reactor." Duckett told the commission that Helms had ordered him not to divulge this to anyone, even the secretaries of state and defense. Eshkol never managed to make any political capital from Teller's disclosure before he died in 1969.

EARLY IN 1968, Israel was still elated about its triumph in the Six-Day War, but a certain degree of the old anxiety over the military power that was being rebuilt in Egypt and Syria sneaked into Israeli hearts. From the middle of June 1967, airlifts and cargo ships had been bringing massive consignments of arms from the U.S.S.R. to the two countries, and thousands of Soviet instructors were training their forces. Within eighteen months, the Soviets had replenished the arsenals of the two Arab countries, bringing them to their prewar levels. The United States was prepared to supply Israel with more Skyhawk fighters, and Ambassador Barbour was sent to persuade Eshkol that these aircraft would provide an adequate security umbrella. But Eshkol argued that his air force was at a distinct disadvantage in the face of the advanced MiGs the Arabs had been provided with. He insisted that what Israel needed was the superior American F-4 Phantom, and asked Johnson to approve the request.

The president responded by inviting Eshkol to be his guest on his ranch in Texas to discuss the subject. On the eve of the visit, in January 1968, the president's three top advisers, Defense Secretary Robert McNamara, Secretary of State Dean Rusk, and Special Counsel Walt Rostow, were all opposed to the supply of Phantoms to Israel, out of the fear that it would spur the Soviets to step up the pace of arming the Arabs.

On January 7, Johnson welcomed Eshkol at the San Antonio airport with warm words: "Mr. Prime Minister, we will be together for only two short days. But they will be long days full of friendship and happiness because you have come here to be with us." They flew to the ranch together, and the chemistry worked. Both were farmers, and although they had spent most of their lives in politics, the Texas rancher and the former member of a communal settlement on the shore of the Sea of Galilee both knew how to handle a tractor, and when to pray for rain. Johnson knew the stories of the Bible, and where Jesus walked on the water, and there was no need for Eshkol to tell him where he came from.

Both of the men enjoyed telling stories, and both had a history of heart illness (and their weak hearts would ultimately be the death of both of them, at relatively young ages). The two had so much in common that their advisers described the meeting as resembling a reunion between two old friends. Eshkol's aide, Zvi Dinstein, attested that the relationship was unique and that it was the chemistry that developed between them that paved the way for the eventual supply of America's most advanced plane to the Israeli Air Force, for the first time in the history of the relations between the two countries.

After the tour of the ranch, as the two men sat facing each other in the living room, Johnson did his best to persuade Eshkol that since the war, "Israel was operating from a position of strength in dealing with the Arabs and could afford to be flexible and magnanimous," according to the American account. In response, Eshkol painted a picture of Israel in the role of what he used to enjoy describing (usually in Yiddish) as "Samson the Weakling." Despite the stunning victory of June 1967, the danger of destruction was still present, he said, and he therefore "felt he could only rely upon superior military strength." Not only did the president refrain from applying pressure, but several times during the conversation he reiterated America's commitment to Israel's security, without laying down any conditions at all.

Both leaders identified Nasser as the root of evil in the Middle East. After the war, the Egyptian president had accused the United States of direct involvement in the combat, and had broken off diplomatic relations with Washington. There were no grounds for the allegation, but Nasser needed an excuse to explain his military's ignominious defeat to the Egyptian people and to the Arab world. The United States never demanded that he apologize for the false accusation, because it understood that he was in a delicate situation, but its confidence in him and his regime reached rock bottom. The Indian Embassy represented the interests of Egypt in Washington. At the very time that Eshkol was in Texas, the Egyptian chargé d'affaires, Ashraf Ghorbal, approached the State Department on behalf of the foreign ministers of Egypt and Syria with a request that ties be resumed. Johnson was in no hurry to comply. Unlike President Kennedy, who had endeavored to please Nasser, and deluded himself into thinking that Egypt could be lured into joining the Western bloc, Johnson had no illusions. He thought of Nasser as an irresponsible and ungrateful leader, and halted American aid to Egypt almost entirely.

Exactly ten years after the Eisenhower administration had first discerned that Nasser's Egypt was a threat to American interests in the Middle East, the confrontation between the two countries reached a peak. From the American point of view, Nasser himself constituted an obstacle to any kind of compromise, and as long as he ruled Egypt, a rapprochement between the two countries was unfeasible. (Indeed, it was only after Nasser passed away in 1970 and Anwar al-Sadat replaced him, that Egypt abandoned the Soviet Union and attached itself to the American sphere of influence, making it possible for President Jimmy Carter to hold the September 1978 Camp David summit, where the principles for peace between Egypt and Israel were hammered out.) As we have indicated, an iron law of Middle Eastern diplomacy was that the wider the gap between the United States and Egypt, the warmer were American-Israeli relations. And this time too, as in the past, before the second meeting between Eshkol and Johnson, the president of Egypt spared the prime minister of Israel a great deal of persuasion and pressure.

On the second day of Eshkol's Texas sojourn, the nuclear issue was discussed. Before the meeting, the president was given a comprehensive survey prepared by the State Department on Israel's strategic weapons projects. The bottom line on the nuclear project was: "We are reasonably, though not entirely, confident that Israel has not embarked on a program to produce a nuclear weapon. However, our visits to Dimona research facility do not guarantee that production facilities are not being built elsewhere in Israel."

How is this conclusion to be reconciled with the assessment being drawn up at that very time by the CIA in the wake of Teller's revelations? The blatant contradiction between the two assessments springs from the fact that the State Department had not been informed of what Teller had told Duckett, and only the president had been put in the picture. The State Department survey submitted to Johnson stated that a French company (the Dassault concern) was close to completing the development of a medium-range land missile for Israel. It would be possible to attach a nuclear warhead to the missile, the survey said, and there were signs that because of the French embargo on arms to Israel (declared by President de Gaulle when the Six-Day War broke out), Israel was developing such a missile on its own.

Acting on the advice of his aides, Johnson—although he was aware of Teller's and the CIA's view that Israel already achieved nuclear capability—reiterated at the meeting with Eshkol that the United States was opposed to the presence of nuclear weapons and strategic missiles in the Middle East, and that introducing them to the region would cause escalation. Eshkol reiterated that Israel would not be the first to do so. Part of the conversation was between the two leaders only, and the protocol of this section is still classified.

Eshkol's visit to Texas resulted in the supply of another forty Skyhawks to the IAF, but Israel was still not satisfied. The request for Phantoms took on new urgency when fighting broke out again in the fall of 1968, after Egypt unleashed artillery barrages against Israel's positions on the Suez Canal, and launched commando raids against them. Since the end of the war, over a year before, Israel's forces had dug in and constructed fortified positions on the east bank of the canal. Nasser dubbed this round of fighting "the phase of standing firm" and in Israel it came to be called "the War of Attrition." Nasser calculated that the bombardments and raids would force Israel to retreat from the canal bank.

When Eshkol returned from Texas, Yitzhak Rabin, Israel's new ambassador to the United States, left for Washington. The first year of his term was one of the saddest and most agonizing in American history; while the U.S. forces were bleeding in Vietnam, and the number of casualties topped thirty thousand, the home front was racked by violent struggles between opponents of the war and its supporters and police. During this time Martin Luther King was shot dead in Memphis, and Robert Kennedy was assassinated in Los Angeles.

The new Israeli ambassador, who had spent most of his life in the military and whose exposure to the world at large had been minimal, was staggered by the dynamics of American society (in much the same way that Ben-Gurion had been in the 1920s, as discussed in Chapter 1). In Israel, that year saw the first experimental television broadcasts, while in the United States the networks were bringing the war in Vietnam into every home. In Israel, a bank clerk would list transactions in handwriting in savings booklets; in Philadelphia, the first cash-dispensing machine had gone into operation. In Israel, a citizen would wait months for the installation of a telephone; in New York the line would be up and working the day after the application was made.

Rabin grasped that with America embroiled in mighty internal struggles, this was no time for widespread diplomatic activity on Middle Eastern issues. The collapse of President Johnson's moral authority and the shrinking power of the Democratic Party led him to invest his efforts in building a relationship with the Republican candidate in the November presidential election. In the fight between Democratic candidate, Hubert Humphrey, and Richard Nixon, Rabin quietly threw his weight behind Nixon, in coordination with the dominant circles in the Jewish lobby. At that time, after Nixon won, it seemed that he had made the right move, but as time went by it became clear to him that the strength of the unwritten alliance between the United States and Israel was no longer dependent on which party's representative was occupying the White House. From the time that Johnson took over from Kennedy, the engine of the relations between the two states moved on a separate track from partisan politics and was fueled by the fact that both sides in the Middle East had clearly defined their choices. A clear majority of the Arab states was relying totally on the Soviet Union, while Israel gave itself up entirely to the United States, diminishing its own sovereignty in no small degree, but also creating an identity of interests.

In view of the escalation in the War of Attrition, Rabin's top priority was to secure the Phantoms. Israel claimed that the Americans were dragging their feet on the matter. Usually, election years are good years for Israeli diplomacy in the United States, because the candidates for the presidency, with their eyes on the Jewish voters, generally comply with Israel's requests. But in 1968, the incumbent president wasn't running for reelection, severely restricting Israel's election-year advantage. But Rabin never gave up. He played the candidates against each other, and efficiently exploited the Jewish lobby and the many friends of Israel in Congress, who for their part lined up behind the Phantom deal, even passing a special law (within the Foreign Assistance Act of October 1968). Rabin met Secretary of State Rusk and told him: "You have closed off the sources of weapons essential for our existence." Rusk replied that Johnson had promised Eshkol that the United States government would make a decision in December, and this is what happened.

In September and October, Rusk also met Foreign Minister Abba Eban, who had replaced Golda Meir in 1966, and according to American accounts the ritual was repeated: If you come clean about the strategic weaponry, we'll sell you conventional arms. Rusk demanded that Israel sign the Non-Proliferation Treaty, and Eban was evasive. The Israeli government had not yet completed its discussions on the subject, he said. At both meetings, Eban repeated the standard response formulated by the Eshkol administration: Israel will not be the first to introduce nuclear weapons in the area. The secretary of state said the United States had reason to believe that Israel was involved in programs to build nuclear weapons and strategic missiles and that "these were matters of utmost seriousness affecting our fundamental relationship and we must have clarifications with respect to them." But it was dialogue of the deaf, with each side pressing the issues closest to its heart, and ignoring the other side's arguments.

For his part, Johnson refused to decide on the Phantoms, which had become a matter of urgency, with the war across the canal intensifying. Egypt inflicted large number of casualties on Israel with its shelling, and Israel responded with air raids on targets deep inside Egypt. But Rusk would not comply with Israel's requests, saying that he remained concerned about the arms spiral, and asking Eban if the Soviets would not "respond by providing additional aircraft to the Arabs." Rusk expressed concern about the uses to which Israel would put the American planes, and asked how "we could assure that the Phantoms would not carry nuclear weapons." Ambassador Rabin, who was present at the meeting, replied that Israel was ready to pledge not to arm the Phantoms with nuclear bombs, just as it had done in the deal for the purchase of the Skyhawks, which was signed in 1966.

However, all of these lengthy meetings and discussions were fruitless. The adamant objections of the senior bureaucrats of the State Department to the sale of the Phantoms made the president hesitate. As America sank deeper and deeper into the morass in Vietnam, Israel was not at the center of his attention.

Israel complained that the State Department was tainted with pro-Arabism, and insisted that the authority for negotiating on Israel's request for Phantoms be transferred to the Department of Defense. The president agreed, and Defense Secretary Clark Clifford, who had recently replaced McNamara, took over the reins from Rusk. He appointed Paul Warnke, deputy assistant secretary of defense for international security affairs, to discuss the matter with Rabin. Warnke, as we have seen, was an arms control specialist, and from the mid-'60s he had negotiated strategic disarmament issues with Yuli Vorontsov, the minister counselor of the Soviet Embassy in Washington.

Once more, he confronted the Israeli ambassador with America's perennial dilemma: To what extent will you be prepared to bare your strategic projects to the United States in order to get the Phantoms? On October 18, a document drawn up by the State Department under the headline: "Structuring negotiations with the Israelis" stated: "Secretary Clifford apparently wishes to obtain very firm assurances from the Israelis in respect to the missile/nuclear issue." Straight after that, in consultation with Rusk, Clifford instructed Warnke that the aim of the negotiation was "to make the sale of the planes conditional upon Israel's willingness to shelve its nuclear program." Clear and to the point.

Ambassador Rabin wondered how to describe Clifford's attitude to Israel. "The man was a mystery to me," he wrote in his memoirs. In 1948, Clifford had been an adviser to President Truman, and had become known as a confirmed friend of Israel, because when the subject of the American position on Israel's impending declaration of independence was being discussed, he urged the president to support it. But a rumor had reached Rabin that he had changed his mind over the years. Rabin tried to set up a meeting with the secretary, but Clifford avoided him. "His refusal to meet a representative of Israel was constant and obstinate," Rabin wrote, and added: "Clifford aroused and provoked my curiosity more and more, the longer his obstinacy lasted."

An opportunity to converse with Clifford occurred when Warnke invited Rabin to a cocktail party at the Defense Department. "Warnke made an effort to push Clifford and me into each other's arms and to leave us alone," Rabin recounted. "We exchanged some pleasantries. He was cold and indifferent, and I almost regretted that I had played along with Warnke." After a few minutes, however, Clifford seemed to have second thoughts, and he turned to Rabin and told him how in May 1948, the president had summoned him, along with Secretary of State George C. Marshall and his deputy Robert Lovett to the White House. "'The president asked us to present our opinions for and against recognition of Israel,'" Rabin quoted Clifford as telling him, "'and he said that after hearing us he would make a final decision. "I'll be the judge," is the way Truman put it.'"

According to Rabin's account, Clifford made it clear that in that discussion in the president's office, there were differences of opinion among the advisers. Marshall advised the president not to recognize Israel. "It's a lost cause," he said to Truman, "and doesn't have a chance of standing up to the Arabs." But Clifford took the opposite position. "It would be better for you to recognize Israel," he told the president. To Rabin's surprise, when he asked the secretary what his reasoning was, "Clifford once again wrapped himself in silence." And that was the end of the brief conversation. "I could see that he was sorry that he'd said the little that he did say. His decisive reasons for supporting Israel, he kept to himself," Rabin wrote.

Rabin never gave up. "My curiosity nagged at me," he recalled, and he therefore took the matter up with people in the know. It became clear to him that when Truman was wavering on whether to recognize Israel, his 1948 presidential campaign was at its height. He was running against New York Governor Thomas E. Dewey, the Republican candidate, in a closely contested race, and he needed the Jewish vote, especially in the state of New York, where Dewey was strong because of his fight against organized crime there. Rabin concluded that what Clifford had said to the president was that if he recognized Israel, the New York Jewish vote would go his way, and Jewish money would be placed at his disposal.[6] So why had Clifford changed his position? Rabin had no answer. "At any rate," he wrote, "Israel can be grateful to Clifford on his part in assuring American support in 1948, and derive satisfaction from the fact that in 1968, president Johnson did not take his advice." Indeed, Clifford vehemently urged Johnson not to supply the Phantoms to Israel, unless it complied with the demand that it take the wraps off its strategic weaponry, and it was Paul Warnke who was given the task of persuading Israel to do so.

Rabin came to the negotiations with bitter memories of his meetings with Robert Komer, the NSC official whom Johnson had sent to Israel together with the special envoy Averell W. Harriman in early 1965, when Rabin was still chief of staff. As we saw in Chapter 12, the two had bluntly conditioned the supply of tanks to Israel on its readiness to divulge its plans for the development of missiles and nuclear weapons. "The nuclear issue," Rabin wrote in his memoirs, "for many years lay like a disturbing shadow over the relations between Israel and the United States." Like Prime Minister Eshkol, Rabin too wanted to get rid of the shadow, but the conditions for doing so had not yet matured. Rabin was therefore compelled to overcome the hostility of the undecipherable Clifford as well as Warnke's conviction that all strategic weapons should be destroyed. This was also Warnke's basic position on Israel's nuclear option, and he expressed it unambiguously: By ignoring the development of the bomb in Israel, American presidents had not contributed to world peace. "Both Kennedy and Johnson waxed eloquent about the dangers of an increase in the nuclear club, but key officials appear to have been either indifferent or ready to accept an Israeli bomb," he wrote years later.

Warnke maintained this critical position until the 1990s, but in the last years of his life he displayed comprehension of Israel's special position: "The United States, France, Britain, China and Russia—if not other former Soviet republics—all plan to retain nuclear weapons although faced with no external threats. Who will fault a beleaguered Israel for going nuclear?" He said this thirty-three years after the series of meetings with Rabin, and only months before his death. He had been weakened by illness, but his memory was completely clear.

Although Warnke expressed his understanding of Israel's wish to develop an absolute deterrent, he also maintained that the efforts Israel had invested in building its nuclear capability were superfluous, because if it had ever found itself facing a threat of destruction, the United States would have come to its defense. He believed this with all his heart, but he also attached a reservation: "They [Israel] could rely entirely on the U.S. Would I have done it if I had been an Israeli policy maker? The answer is, probably not. I think I would have been developing a nuclear capability." If Rabin had heard this sort of thing from Warnke in late 1968, he would of course have been able to enter the negotiations with a far greater degree of equanimity.

During his meeting with Mordechai Gazit, the minister at the Israeli Embassy in Washington, a few days before President Kennedy met with Prime Minister Ben-Gurion at the Waldorf-Astoria Hotel in New York, Philip J. Farley, deputy assistant secretary of state in the Kennedy administration, according to his own report, had said that "in the U.S. many of us understand the situation of Israel and many of us could understand how if we were in Israel's situation we would decide that we should develop nuclear weapons in order to capitalize on our technological superiority." This statement and Warnke's much-later remark show that there were high officials in the American administration who identified with Israel's compelling need to develop the absolute deterrent.

When his talks with Rabin began, Warnke was not aware of the CIA situation assessment drawn up in January 1968 on the basis of the information Teller gave Duckett. Years later Warnke recalled: "I think my own feeling was that Israel has the capacity to be a nuclear power, and that it would perhaps be a risky development, particularly if they acknowledged the fact that they are a nuclear power."

Warnke didn't receive hard factual intelligence about Israel's nuclear research and development and his private assumptions were based on conversations with Israeli representatives. Because of Israel's policy of ambiguity, Warnke could not know for sure that Dimona was part of an overall nuclear program.

The aims of Warnke's team in the negotiations were clearly defined, as he said much later: "We hoped that we would persuade Israel not to develop nuclear weapons or at least not to admit that they have nuclear weapons. So my own sense was, if it became a declared nuclear power then there was a greater risk of proliferation. If you got one keep it undercover, don't publicly advertise the fact that you are a nuclear power."

For its part, the Israeli team's goal was to get the Phantoms without paying the price of coming clean about any aspect of the development of strategic weaponry in Israel. These were the overt opening positions. But behind the scenes there lay an old unsettled account between the Department of Defense and the man who had been chief of staff of the Israel Defense Forces in the Six-Day War of 1967. The account was opened on June 7, at the height of the fighting, when Israel's air force and navy attacked the American spy ship *Liberty* off the coast of Sinai. The results were horrific: 34 Americans on board the ship were killed and 171 wounded. Israel claimed that the attack was an error and apologized several times. But because Rabin was the supreme commander of the IDF, many of the Pentagon's top officials held him responsible, although no one alleged that he had given the order to attack the ship, or had even known about it.[7] Warnke had been serving as undersecretary of the navy at that time, and he later declared on several occasions that he did not believe Israel's claim that the attack on the ship had been the result of an error.[8] "I suspect that in the heat of the battle they figured that the presence of this American ship was inimical to their interests, and that somebody without authorization attacked it," he said. No one mentioned the *Liberty* during the negotiations with Rabin over the supply of the Phantoms, but the crippled ship and its decimated crew were there in the background constantly.

The first session of the talks was held in Warnke's Pentagon office on November 4. It was of a technical nature, and lasted forty-five minutes.

Warnke opened by saying that President Johnson had approved the supply of the Phantoms in principle. "It is a difficult decision, not because we are not interested in Israel's security, but precisely because we are interested," he said. Johnson's agreement in principle, Warnke continued, would make the United States Israel's biggest supplier of arms, creating a new reality in the Middle East by expanding America's involvement in Israel's security affairs. It was not only a matter of the 50 Phantoms, but also of 100 Skyhawks (most of which had already been delivered) and other military materiel. "Nevertheless," he declared, "the U.S. is interested in doing what is necessary to assist Israel. Our goal is the same. It is for this reason that we are so concerned with Israel's missiles and nuclear plans and intentions, and this is why we need to update your assurances to us on this matter."

Warnke ended by saying that for the next day's meeting, he would prepare a draft agreement and deliver it to the ambassador for his response.

As the president had already given approval in principle to the Phantom sale, Rabin thought only the technical details still had to be finalized. He therefore listed in detail Israel's preferences as to the delivery and payment dates, as if the deal had already been wrapped up. The novice diplomat thought that Warnke had mentioned the nuclear and missiles issues merely because the American side would make do with hearing once again the routine pledge that Israel would not be the first to introduce nuclear weapons to the Middle East. The Israeli delegation went away confident that the deal would be signed soon.

The next day, November 5, the two teams met again. Warnke handed Rabin a memorandum. Rabin asked for time to study it. When the Israelis read the draft agreement in Rabin's office at the embassy, they were stunned. To the day of his assassination in November 1995, Rabin would not talk about the memorandum with journalists or historians, and in his memoirs he related his reaction only briefly. He was usually careful about his language and the purple expressions he used were rare:

After all that, Warnke, undersecretary of defense, took off his silken gloves and the claws that he bared transfixed me to my chair, and made my blood boil. As a condition for the supply of the Phantoms, the United States was demanding that Israel sign a shocking document, the likes of which no sovereign nation had ever been asked to sign. In the five years of my service in Washington, I never came across anything like it.

Rabin's angry reaction was sparked by paragraph three of the memorandum, in which in return for the Phantoms the United States demanded that Israel would allow it access to every place in Israel connected to the development of strategic weapons: air and sea ports, in order to examine imports; research institutions and universities, to vet research projects; corporations and industrial plants, to check planning and production. In his memoirs Rabin wrote that Israel was being asked to agree "to American supervision and an American presence in every installation of Israel's military and aerospace industries, and in every Israeli military facility connected to research and development or production, as well as every civilian research institute, such as the Weizmann Institute and the universities in Israel." In addition, Israel was required to sign the Non-Proliferation Treaty and to undertake to refrain from testing strategic missiles.

In the three days between the second and the third sessions of the negotiation, the text of the memorandum was transmitted to Jerusalem, and an unequivocal order was issued by the prime minister's office: The demands in paragraph three were to be rejected out of hand, and no discussion about them should be held. Before the third meeting, Rabin's Deputy, Shlomo Argov, called Warnke's assistant, Harry Schwartz, and told him that paragraph three was not acceptable to Israel. Argov proposed that the Americans reconsider including it in the draft agreement. Schwartz listened but did not respond. Warnke was on a visit to Europe.

Although Warnke later insisted that he never had the formal authority to decide whether to hold up the sale of arms, from Rabin's statements it is evident that the Israeli delegation believed that Warnke was expressing precisely the positions of secretaries Rusk and Clifford.

The third session took place in the evening of November 8 and paragraph three was of course the subject of discussion. At the outset, Rabin asked if Warnke had changed his mind about the phrasing of the draft agreement, and received a negative reply. The United States was insisting on the inclusion of paragraph three, as it stood. Rabin was fuming. The American protocol attests as much: "Saying his words might not be diplomatic," it reads, the record indicates that Rabin stated that he had prepared a written response, which he proceeded to read aloud:

> I am now in a position to confirm that my original personal reaction upon first reading this paragraph—namely that it is completely unacceptable—is indeed my government's official position. We have come here for the purpose of purchasing 50 Phantoms. We have not come here in order to mortgage the sovereignty of the State of Israel, not even for 50 Phantoms. Furthermore, I wish to state that we consider paragraph three to be in the nature of a very major condition precedent to the sale of aircrafts and it is therefore not acceptable to us also as a matter of principle. My government's position is that matters raised in paragraph three are extraneous to the question before us, namely terms of the sale of 50 F-4 aircrafts. These matters have been the subject of separate discussions between our two governments . . . Accordingly, I should like to propose that Israel's assurances in connection with the theoretical question of the use of the planes for the delivery of nuclear weapons remains as submitted to you in our original proposal, namely, that the government of Israel agrees not to use any aircraft supplied by the US as a nuclear weapons carrier. I am also authorized to reaffirm that it is Israel's long-standing policy not to be the first to introduce nuclear weapons to the Middle East. Assurances to that effect can be incorporated into the agreement . . . This is my government's position and the only basis on which we consider it possible to conduct negotiations for the purchase of military equipment—in this case 50 Phantoms.

Israel was in effect saying: Either you cancel this paragraph, or we leave the negotiations. Rabin wrote in his memoirs: "I rejected the document, which was an expression of American apprehensions, out of hand." And he added later: "Although I had promised Warnke to transmit it for governmental perusal in Jerusalem, I told him that if Israel agreed to sign the document, it would be waiving its sovereignty. It was a shameful document."

In view of the Israeli response, it was impossible to carry on with the discussion. Warnke had to consult his superiors and get new instructions. Rabin said resignedly, "So there we are," and Warnke responded, "Yes, Mr. Ambassador. We have managed to isolate a major difference."

Before the meeting broke up, Warnke reacted to two points made by Rabin. On the ambassador's claim that the demands made by the Americans in paragraph three were not relevant to the sale of the planes, Warnke made it clear that any use of strategic missiles or nuclear weapons by Israel would affect America's national security:

> It is the national security of the U.S. that I am charged with protecting. By law I am required to consider the impact of the sale on the U.S. You, from your vantage point, do not have to accept my judgments, but I am required to make them.

On Rabin's remarks concerning Israeli sovereignty, Warnke claimed that the undertakings requested by the United States in paragraph three were not intended to limit Israel's sovereignty, and that all international agreements "impinge on national sovereignty." Then, apparently in response to the angry expression on Rabin's face, Warnke observed that however the negotiations ended, there was value to the dialogue. "I have felt that it was important to get across to you how we feel about Israel's acquisition of strategic missiles and nuclear weapons," he stated, and in order that his words should not be construed as an apology, he added immediately that in all of its arms sales agreements, the United States always included a provision making it possible to cancel them if "unusual and compelling circumstances" arose. "To me, if Israel goes ahead with its missile and nuclear programs, this would involve the paragraph . . . and while I cannot speak for the next administration, I feel sure they would feel the same way too."

A stunned Rabin was incapable of confining himself to diplomatic language: "You are only selling arms. How do you feel you have the right to ask all these things?" he asked. "I think I do, otherwise I would not bring it up," Warnke replied. On this acerbic note, the meeting ended. "We will think about what you have said and talk with Secretary Clifford and [Deputy Defense] Secretary [Paul H.] Nitze," Warnke promised. "I will talk with you again tomorrow."

After that third meeting, Rabin concluded that if he wanted to move the Phantoms deal ahead he would have to influence the president through indirect means. He acted rapidly, in two parallel channels: In the one, he got Abe Feinberg and Arthur Goldberg, U.S. ambassador to the United Nations, to go and talk to Johnson, and in the other he peppered the heads of the Democratic Party with messages to the effect that it was worth their while before the elections to present the Jewish voter with a show of support for Israel, not the spectacle of a delay in the supply of essential arms. Rabin wrote in his memoirs: "I dropped hints as heavy as elephants to Democratic friends of Israel: A new president [Nixon], if he is elected, will order that we be supplied the Phantoms as soon as he takes power, and he will get all the credit . . . I think it can be assumed that those who heard me hurried to the White House."

Rabin had the advantage over Warnke. He had met Nixon in a Washington hotel in August, and he had understood that if Johnson delayed the supply of Phantoms, the Republican candidate, if elected, would give the deal the green light without any hesitation. This evaluation had been strengthened a few days before the talks with Warnke began, on October 21, when Nixon declared in a speech at a session of the Conference of Presidents of Major American Jewish Organizations that the United States must pledge in an unequivocal manner to ensure the maintenance of Israel's superiority over its Arab neighbors.

In his memoirs, Rabin describes how in those days he agonized over the propriety of a foreign ambassador making use of a lobby within the American governmental system.

It isn't nice, the fastidious [in Israel] will say with turned-up noses, to set a president against a president, Democrats against Republicans, to incite them against each other, but at the same time they will admit that they are not familiar with the political system in the United States and have no experience in its workings. It is not enough to say that the Israeli ambassador in the United States is entitled to exploit the political competition prevalent in the United States in accordance with its constitution. He *must* do so in order that his efforts will bear fruit. There is not a soul who resents American Jews because of their support for Israel, their loyalty to it, and on their weighing whom to vote for according to the candidates' attitudes to Israel. An ambassador who represents a state over which there hovers a danger of extinction and who does not get involved in the fabric of American political life in order to use it to Israel's benefit—it would be better for him to go home.

At that stage, Warnke was not aware of the Jewish lobby activities and had no daily contact with the White House. He could not know that Rabin sent Feinberg and Goldberg to persuade President Johnson.

On November 9, secretaries Clifford and Rusk raised the dispute between the two sides over paragraph three with the president. In view of the Israeli government's rejection of the paragraph, both secretaries proposed postponing the delivery of the Phantom aircraft, but Johnson did not accept their recommendation. He decided that the planes should be supplied without any conditions. The assault of the Jewish lobby on the White House and the heads of the Democratic Party had apparently worked.

Neither Rabin nor Warnke was told about the meeting with the president and its results. The fourth negotiating session began on November 12. Warnke summed up the two sides' respective positions. Rabin did not respond, as he had received instructions not to discuss paragraph three. But Warnke tried to get Rabin to speak, and remarked incidentally that he had not found any written explanation for Israel's declaration that it would not be the first to introduce nuclear weapons into the Middle East. He asked the ambassador to clarify this. Rabin was caught unprepared. He reluctantly came up with, "It means what we have said, namely that we would not be the first to introduce nuclear weapons." Warnke asked what the specific meaning of "to introduce" was in this context. Rabin replied impatiently, "You are more familiar with these things than we are. What is your definition of nuclear weapons?" Warnke said there were two aspects to the question: the definition of what is and what is not nuclear, and what is and what is not introducing them into the area. "Regarding the first," Warnke said, "if there are components available that could be assembled to make a nuclear weapon, although part A may be in one room and part B in another room, then that is a nuclear weapon. As for 'introduction,' that is your term and you will have to define it." He asked: "Does it mean no physical presence?"

Rabin replied, "I suppose so.

Warnke continued: "What if you have access to nuclear weapons that are in another country? Is that 'introduction'?"

Rabin wasn't interested in developing the theme, and responded with a question that indicated he was uncomfortable with the cross-examination: "Do you believe that this is the situation?"

Warnke eased off and replied that he was just trying to find out the Israeli definitions, and immediately added it was also possible that a country in the region had access to nuclear weapons but did not keep them in its territory.

Rabin now saw an opportunity to shift the discussion to the dangers facing Israel and to break the deadlock. He said that a situation was possible in which China would claim that it was holding nuclear weapons for Egypt, but he did not know how Israel would react to such a situation. Rabin said he believed that "introduction" would require their physical presence in the area.

Rabin's adviser air force Major General Motti Hod asked if there was not an accepted international definition of the term "introduction." Warnke replied in the negative. Hod said that throughout the world, experience indicated that the introduction of a weapon could only occur after testing. You could not introduce a weapon until after it actually became a weapon.

Rabin asked Warnke, "Do you consider a nuclear weapon one that has not been tested, and has been done by a country without previous experience?"

"Certainly," replied Warnke. "China with a strategic missile capability would be assumed to have nuclear weapons even if it had not tested these weapons."

Rabin: "All nuclear powers—the U.S., Russia, the United Kingdom, France, China—have tested nuclear weapons. Do you believe that introduction comes before testing?"

Rabin added that he had experience with conventional weapons, and "would not consider a weapon that had not been tested to be a weapon."

Warnke asked, "If Egypt had missiles with nuclear warheads that had not been tested, would Israel consider that Egypt had not introduced nuclear weapons?"

Rabin: "Weapons serve policy, not vice versa. Since Egypt's goal is to destroy us, I would take it with very great concern. Our policy is not to destroy Egypt. You must combine the weapons with the policy."

Hod mentioned that when Egypt had unveiled its strategic missiles in 1963, it announced that they were capable of hitting anything south of Beirut. Rabin said that he worried more about Egyptian missiles with chemical warheads than he worried about missiles with nuclear warheads. But Warnke was determined not to let the Israelis divert the discussion to the danger that Egypt represented toward the Jewish state, and quickly returned to the topic of a definition for the term "to introduce." Warnke said that Rabin had given two meanings, "notoriety" and "testing," and he insisted on a detailed explanation, and the ambassador complied: "There must be public acknowledgement. The purpose of nuclear weapons is not to use the weapon itself, but to use its deterrent power. I don't believe any power that has nuclear weapons plans to use them, although you can not ever be sure. Ninety-nine percent of their values is deterrence."

Warnke pointed out that the ambassador had mentioned the factor of intent. If Egypt has missiles, Israel should be worried. If Israel has missiles, there is no cause for concern because from the Israeli point of view, the aim of the missiles is to deter. Warnke accurately interpreted Rabin's words, and in so doing stressed their one-sidedness. Turning to Rabin, he said: "Then in your view, an unadvertised, untested nuclear device is not a nuclear weapon. What about an advertised but untested nuclear device or weapon, would that be introduction?"

Rabin replied in the affirmative, "Yes. That would be introduction."

Warnke summed up the disagreement: "At this time, with respect to 'introduction' there is not much clarity and no agreement." Nonetheless, after the meeting, Hod received permission to meet with U.S. Air Force personnel and discuss technical matters about the Phantom deal with them.

In the meantime, between the fourth and the fifth meetings, Clifford's office ordered Warnke to erase paragraph three from the draft agreement. Because Warnke still did not know that the president had approved the unconditional supply of the planes, at this point Ambassador Rabin had a clear advantage over him, as the president's decision had been leaked to the ambassador from the White House. Rabin kept up the discussion with Warnke only because he did not wish to divulge that the final outcome was already known to him.

The fifth and final meeting took place at Warnke's office, as had all the meetings, on November 22, at 5.40 P.M. Paragraph three had been eliminated, and it therefore remained only to iron out the differences over paragraph two. That paragraph stated that the United States would be entitled to cancel the contract and to demand the return of the planes if Israel failed to honor its undertakings about their use—that is to say, used them to carry nuclear weapons. The wording in the American draft read: "It is understood by the government of Israel that action contrary to any of the understandings specified in paragraph two of this memorandum shall constitute 'unusual and compelling circumstances' and shall permit the U.S. to recover any aircraft already delivered under this agreement."

Warnke read the paragraph aloud, and Rabin once again was filled with indignation. This language related to Israel as if it were "the bad guy," he protested, and declared that there was "no precedent. It creates something that I do not believe exists anywhere." Warnke said that his superiors were responsible and that secretaries Clifford and Rusk insisted on the paragraph. Rabin remarked: "The U.S. could ask in ten years time for the aircraft to be returned," and Warnke immediately responded: "Suppose you deliver nuclear weapons in these aircraft in 10 years time?" The matter was left open, and left out of the eventual agreement.

Ten years later, this is what Rabin wrote in his memoirs about the talks:

Three or four days before he departed from the White House, Johnson put an end to the issue. He firmly ordered the signing of the agreement for the supply of 50 Phantoms to Israel, in spite of the officials of the State and Defense Departments, who did not wish to yield their intention of using the planes to force Israel to agree to full American supervision over its research institutes and defense production plants.

And in his home in Washington, thirty-four years later, Warnke claimed that he had predicted in advance that the Phantoms would be sold to Israel without any conditions. He knew Johnson well, and was aware of his attitude to Israel and the Jews.

> I could suspect very strongly that when the ultimate decision had to be made, it would be made in favor of Israel. I think that there was a sense in the part of the Israeli negotiators that there was more of a debate about the American decision than it was in fact. They could not know what I knew. They could not know that Johnson was so dedicated to the security of Israel that he would have done a great deal more than he in fact ever had to do.

After the series of meetings, Warnke was convinced that Israel had a bomb. "When I pressed for Israel's objections to the Nuclear Non-Proliferation Treaty, Ambassador Rabin asked, 'What is it to have a nuclear weapon? Do you have one if you do not say that you have one?' When I said that I believed Israel did indeed have one, Rabin did not deny it."

Warnke admitted that he drew his conclusion on the basis of intuition, rather than intelligence.

> Did I have factual information that would convince a jury that Israel had a nuclear weapon? The answer is no. I based it on various indications that I had received and on the fact that Israel has a scientific capability of becoming a nuclear power, and then of course I talked with Yitzhak Rabin at considerable length.

As for Rabin, the negotiation with Warnke left him with a lingering sense of humiliation. In his memoirs, he directed his hostility not only at Rusk, Clifford, and Warnke, but also at the president himself. This, despite the fact that during Johnson's term, aid to Israel had grown substantially over previous administrations, and the share received by the military multiplied tremendously.[9] (Rabin even translated his anger at Warnke into concrete action. In 1977, when Warnke's candidacy for the post of director of the Arms Control and Disarmament Agency came before the Senate, Rabin assisted the conservative politicians who tried to block the appointment. That was during Rabin's first term as prime minister (1974–77). He conveyed his objections regarding Warnke to the senators via CIA official James J. Angleton, who was known for his good relations with the Mossad. The efforts failed, however, and Warnke got the job.)

In January 1969, soon after Johnson's final decision to supply the Phantoms to Israel, and at the outset of the presidency of Richard M. Nixon, first reports that Israel was building a bomb appeared in the American media. *New York Times* correspondent John W. Finney reported that sources in the Johnson administration had confirmed to him that Israel was close to nuclear capability, though it had not yet built a bomb. NBC broadcast a similar item. Israel issued a blanket denial and repeated the formula that it would not be the first to introduce nuclear weapons to the Middle East. "Were you the source of the leak?" I asked Warnke in 2001. He smiled and kept silent.

Late in December 1968, Rabin flew to Israel for consultations on the Phantoms deal with Prime Minister Eshkol. "It was my last meeting with Eshkol, whom I liked so much," he wrote in his memoirs. When he returned to Washington, he told his wife, Leah, "I saw the signs of death engraved on Eshkol's face."

Eshkol died of a heart attack on February 26, 1969. The party gave Golda Meir the mandate to form a government. It was a very tense period. On the banks of the Suez Canal the War of Attrition was raging. The Israeli Air Force's attacks deep inside Egyptian territory had forced the Soviet Union to carry out an unprecedented act of escalation. A few days after the change of government in Israel, the Soviets deployed surface-to-air (SAM) missiles and took upon themselves responsibility for providing the entire area of Egypt with protection against air raids. The operators of the SAM batteries were Russian officers and men. On April 1, the Soviet Union sent three fighter squadrons and their crews to Egypt.

The clash was not late in coming. On July 30, in dogfights over the northern canal sector, five MiGs flown by Soviet pilots were shot down by Israeli planes. Two of the pilots were killed, another was wounded, and the other two escaped unhurt. All of the Israeli planes and pilots safely returned to base. The Israelis had set an ambush for the enemy aircraft, but they did not know that there would be Soviet pilots in their cockpits. Neither side published the outcome of the battle; Israel did not wish to vex the Soviets and the Soviets and the Egyptians were too ashamed.

The aerial clash had far-reaching implications. In Washington apprehension grew that the Soviet involvement would lead to a confrontation between the two powers, and the United States therefore stepped up efforts to keep the sides apart. The wing of the American administration that wanted to neutralize Israel's efforts to obtain strategic weaponry depicted the fight between Israeli and Soviet pilots as a classic case of how a minor player in the international arena with nuclear potential was liable to bring relations between the two great powers to a crisis point, and to damage the interests of the United States.

In late September, Prime Minister Golda Meir traveled to Washington to meet President Nixon, National Security Adviser Henry Kissinger, and Secretary of State William P. Rogers. This hard-bitten woman, who was born in Russia and grew up in the United States, had a distinct advantage over her predecessors as prime minister: She could speak to the leaders of America in their own language, in her distinctive Milwaukee accent. Nixon related with respect to the assertive stateswoman, who formulated her statements with precise simplicity; he too expressed his ideas in the form of brief and understandable sound bites.

Meir went to Washington in order to hold a serious and sincere discussion on Israel's strategic weapons and to tell the truth to the American leaders. Indeed, this is what she believed should have been done since the early 1960s. But in order to achieve the full effect of the unveiling of the truth, the cooperation of the Nixon administration was required, and to Meir's delight it transpired that the ground had been well prepared for the seed of truth. The new administration was about to create a new world order—disengagement from Vietnam, détente with the Soviet Union, and a thaw in the frozen relations with China. And, for the sake of balance, it was aiming to strengthen the bonds of the Western alliance.

The clearest expression of the new outlook now prevalent in Washing-

ton was its attitude to the proliferation of strategic weaponry. It was a di-
ametrical change, executed by Kissinger. There were many who took issue with the permissive positions Kissinger adopted on nuclear
proliferation, but no one contested his status as an expert. His first book,
Nuclear Weapons and Foreign Policy, was considered a classic discussion of
the subject and from 1961 to 1968 he had served as a consultant to the
U.S. Arms Control and Disarmament Agency. Kissinger argued that instead of fighting a rear-guard action against friendly states that were developing nuclear weapons—among them Israel and India—it would be
better to assist them, or at least not to hinder their efforts, and thereby to
strengthen the Western camp. He stated explicitly that friendly states,
including West Germany and Israel, should not be pressured into signing the Nuclear Non-Proliferation Treaty.

Prior to Meir's visit to Washington, a senior State Department official,
Theodore L. Eliot, prepared a background memo for Kissinger entitled
"Israel's Nuclear Weapon and Missile Program." In contrast to all the
dozens of similar papers in which American government agencies had
analyzed Israel's nuclear program in the ten preceding years, this memorandum was remarkable in that the author made no effort to embellish or
blur reality and to depict Israel as not having what it did have. Until now,
the bureaucrats had tended to cooperate with the politicians over the fic-
tions associated with Dimona. Although it was Israel that had initiated
the fabrications, American politicians never dared to expose them for
what they were, presumably for these two reasons: First, because in terms
of realpolitik, an Israel that possessed the nuclear option was a more
valuable asset to the defense of the West than an Israel without such an
option. And second, from the point of view of any presidential candidate,
the advantages of Jewish votes and money were more powerful than the
liability of a nuclear Israel.

The first of two important conclusions to which Eliot drew Kissinger's
attention in his memorandum was that Israel might already have nuclear
weapons. He wrote:

All the facilities required for production of plutonium have been
identified with the exception of a separation plant. Israel may also
have acquired highly enriched u-235, possibly through develop-

ment of a small gas centrifuge separation capability. Some [of our experts] have reservations about whether or not Israel has produced and assembled a complete nuclear weapon, but do not dispute the likelihood that she could and soon might; others feel confident that Israel already has one or more complete nuclear weapons now. The first of such weapons would probably be in an air drop configuration, so that Israel might very well now have a nuclear bomb.

In making this assessment, Eliot was diverging radically from, if not entirely contradicting, the briefing that the State Department had given Johnson almost two years earlier, prior to Eshkol's visit to his Texas ranch. Then, the president had been told: "We are reasonably, though not entirely, confident that Israel has not embarked on a program to produce a nuclear weapon." What had happened to overturn the intelligence assessment between January 1968 and September 1969? The information supplied by Edward Teller had seeped down from the White House to the State Department and, as Warnke later said, an analysis of the minutes of his talks with Rabin had convinced the Americans that Israel had built a bomb.

The second conclusion that Eliot stressed for Kissinger's benefit was that the "visits" that American experts paid at Dimona were in fact stage-managed by Israel, and that they should be called off, because as seen from a distance, they might cause the United States harm. This is how he put it:

> Since the visits are arranged far in advance, Israel has every opportunity for concealment. If eventually Israel were in some way to confirm its possession of a nuclear capability, a substantial part of world opinion would assume that we had played a supporting role. The Soviets, and perhaps others, might see great benefit in attempting to confirm that assumption. We can have no assurance that our "visits" to Dimona would remain unnoticed in this context.

The notion that the visits were an exercise in concealment by Israel was expressed here for the first time in an official American document that has been declassified, and this straight talk was emblematic of the change in course. The leadership and officialdom in Washington no longer had any cause to play along with the Dimona theatricals and to pretend to the outside world that the reports of the visiting experts represented the actual truth. From the moment that the Nixon administration recognized Israel's atomic capability, and in effect granted it retroactive legitimacy, the inspection visits had become redundant, and could even cause the United States harm if and when Israel openly declared that it had a bomb at its disposal.

The Eliot document bolstered the pragmatic element in the policy that Kissinger adopted toward Israel, because if Israel's nuclear capability was a fait accompli, and if it could not be eliminated, it would be better for Israel to keep it under conditions favorable to the interests of the United States. It was this pragmatic consideration that led Kissinger to the conclusion that Israel should not be coerced into joining the Nuclear Non-Proliferation Treaty, nor should it be pressured to reveal its plans and its strategic weapons inventory. From Israel's point of view, this was the beginning of a new era. This is how Rabin described the new situation in his memoirs: "The various arms of the Nixon administration left Israel alone on the subject of signing the NPT, and the matter dropped off the agenda."

The precise understandings reached between Meir and Nixon and Kissinger have still not been declassified, but various utterances by politicians and officials over the last thirty years make it possible to sketch a picture that is in all likelihood close to reality. For its part, the United States accepted the fact that Israel possessed nuclear capability, ceased to demand that Israel sign the Non-Proliferation Treaty, and stopped sending its experts to inspect Dimona. Israel committed itself to three nos: no publication, no testing, and no provoking of the Arabs with its nuclear option. The Nixon administration had been assured that Israel would not take its bomb out of the basement, and if they were ever forced to use it, that would happen only in the most extreme emergency. In exchange for these Israeli pledges, Nixon promised Meir that as long as he was president, Israel would never reach a situation of conventional military weakness. And as far as she was concerned, that was sufficient. In her memoirs, Meir said this about the nuclear aspects of her talks with Nixon: "I could not quote him then [after the meeting], and I shall not quote him now." And in his book, Rabin observed only that the discussion was about "sensitive" subjects.

This was the fourth and most important leap forward in the development of the informal defense pact between the United States and Israel, after the Eisenhower administration's 1958 decision to relate to Israel as an asset, Kennedy's definition of relations with Israel as "special," and Johnson's silent consent to Israel's nuclear capability. Now, at the end of 1969, Nixon and Kissinger had closed the circle.

The granting of legitimate status to Israel's nuclear capability by the United States was an historic achievement on the part of Golda Meir. Only rarely is it attributed to her. If someone had prophesized in the later 1950s that it would take only about ten years from the beginning of the development of the Israeli nuclear option to the time that the United States would recognize it as an acceptable means of deterrent, cease to press Israel to join the NPT, and drop the surveillance of Dimona, Ben-Gurion would have looked at that person as if he or she had just dropped in from Mars.

When Golda Meir returned from her visit to Washington, the War of Attrition along the Suez Canal was at its height. Egyptian artillery pounded Israeli positions and Israeli aircraft bombed strategic targets deep inside Egypt. For the first time the IAF deployed the F-4 Phantom fighters that President Johnson had agreed to sell to Israel in the midst of the tough Warnke-Rabin negotiations.

A moment of opportunity to start silencing the guns on the canal occurred in the spring and summer of 1970. In a speech on May Day, Nasser appealed to the American president to help settle the conflict with Israel. Nixon complied and hastened to send his secretary of state, William Rogers, to the Middle East with a cease-fire proposal that both sides accepted and signed in August. But as soon as it went into effect, Egypt moved batteries of SAMs close to the canal. Israel demanded that they be removed, but the Egyptians refused. A special U.N. envoy, Gunnar Jarring of Sweden, was sent to the region, with America's blessing, to seek a permanent settlement, but as long as Egypt refused to move the SAMs back, Israel refused to cooperate with him, and the result was diplomatic deadlock.

THROUGH HIS TOP POSITIONS at the Lawrence Livermore National Laboratory and then at Stanford University's Hoover Institute, as well as key consultative positions in most United States administrations from the 1950s into the '90s, Edward Teller was one of the important guiding lights, possibly the most important, in the evolution of America's strategic arsenal. There was no other scientist of his standing who defended the development and use of nuclear arms with his determination. Thinkers and scientists argued against him that in his desire to defend liberty, he masterminded the production of weapons of mass destruction whose potential for harming the innocent was no different than the means employed by the enemies of liberty. Teller was never reticent in the face of criticism. His belief in his own righteousness was rock solid. To an interviewer who asked him if he had any regrets about his role in the development of nuclear weaponry, he replied dismissively: "Can you tell me why I should have regrets?"

The lesson that Teller learned from the events of the 20th century was very Jewish in the pessimism that it radiated: "The future is uncertain. That indeed, what we say, what we do in each individual case, may move the whole world. And that puts an exceptional responsibility on our shoulders." This skeptical attitude was also evident in his statements about the relations between Jews and Arabs. Teller advocated perhaps under the influence of Yuval Neeman, who was a pillar of the Greater Israel movement, that Israel should hold on to all the territories that it had occupied in 1967.

Teller never mentioned Israel by name, but among foreign experts who keep a close eye on Israel's strategic capability, it is an accepted presumption that Israel has in fact built hydrogen warheads and has put them in cruise missiles deployed on submarines. In June 2000, the Sunday *Times* of London, quoting "Israeli defence sources," reported that Israel "has secretly carried out its first test launches from submarines of cruise missiles capable of carrying nuclear warheads." The launches took place from a submarine sailing in the Indian Ocean, the paper said, and "were designed to simulate swift retaliation against a preemptive nuclear attack from Iran." According to the *Times*, whose Israeli sources are considered reliable, one missile hit a target nine hundred miles away. Israel has acquired three Dolphin-class submarines from Germany, and according to foreign publications, has armed them with missiles fitted with nuclear warheads. Some newspapers in the United States, Germany, and Britain cited Israeli sources as saying that this maritime deployment gave Israel the capability of responding to a preemptive attack and complemented its ability to launch nuclear weapons from the land and from the air. These foreign media reports that Israel was beginning to plan a second strike deterrent capability in 1999 came shortly after the Mossad warned the government that Iran would be capable of carrying out a nuclear attack on Israel as early as the year 2000. Although Iran never did fulfill that forecast and five years later was still not considered to have a nuclear option at its disposal, Israel very quickly acquired the response, according to those reports.

In order to operate its fleet of Dolphins, Israel set up a special unit of submarine crews, known in military jargon as "Unit 700"—the number of points that a student is required to obtain in order to gain admission to the prestigious faculties at Israeli universities, considered the equivalent of an IQ of 130. Each one of the three submarines has a crew of thirty-five officers and men. According to publications abroad, one of these submarines regularly cruises the Indian Ocean.

CHAPTER FIFTEEN

The Sadat-Kissinger Axis

ON OCTOBER 9, 1973, Prime Minister Golda Meir thought of killing herself. She told her friends before she died in 1978 that it was the hardest day of her life until then. Three days before that, at 2 P.M. on Saturday, October 6, Yom Kippur (the Day of Atonement), the holiest day in the Jewish calendar, the armed forces of Egypt and Syria had launched a coordinated surprise attack against Israel. In the south, wave after wave of Egyptian infantry crossed the Suez Canal in rubber boats, and overran the Barlev Line, a series of sixteen fortresses that Israel had built along the eastern bank of the waterway at about five-mile increments. Although they were heavily fortified, fifteen of the strong points were conquered, with only the northernmost one, code-named Budapest, not falling to the Egyptian onslaught. Those Israeli soldiers who were not killed and did not manage to escape were taken prisoner. The spectacle of the surrender of Israeli troops, filmed by Egyptian television, came as a rude shock to Israelis, still intoxicated by their army's triumphant victory of 1967.

The Egyptian army that crossed the canal was no longer controlled by Gamal Abdel Nasser, who died in 1970, but by his trusted deputy and partner in the 1952 Free Officers coup, Anwar Sadat. The Egypt that Sadat inherited from Nasser suffered from a chronic economic crisis. Sadat's requests to the Soviets for military support, to replace the devastation of the 1967 war, were ignored, and in July 1972 he expelled from Egypt most Soviet military advisers, including thousands of air combat personnel.

Exploiting his triumph in the first phase of his surprise attack along the Suez Canal, Sadat could theoretically order his army to keep moving eastward, traversing the 125-mile width of the Sinai peninsula, which Israel had conquered from Egypt in 1967, and taking the war into sovereign Israeli territory. But the Egyptian forces had no intention of advancing eastward. The Egyptians' aim was entirely different.

On the northern front, five hundred Syrian tanks rolled westward, and conquered large tracts of the Golan Heights, the Syrian territory that Israel had occupied in the 1967 war. The Syrians threatened to invade the Galilee. Helicopter-borne Syrian commando units conquered the Israeli-fortified position on Mount Hermon, the highest peak on the Syria-Lebanon border, at 9,232 feet high. Since it was taken by Israel in June 1967, the fortified listening post constructed there had served as the eyes and ears of the country's intelligence on the northern front.

The Egyptians and Syrians enjoyed a clear advantage, mainly because Israel had been caught napping. On the Saturday that they launched their attack, the Israeli forces in their defensive positions in both the north and the south were far from ready to handle a large-scale offensive. This was the first act in the nightmare scenario that had terrified Ben-Gurion during his many sleepless nights, and led him to conceive the idea of building a nuclear option in order to prevent it from ever coming true.

The Israel Defense Forces immediately declared an emergency mobilization of all the reserves. Throughout the night and the next day, October 7, the reserve divisions armed themselves and began moving toward the front. At three o'clock in the afternoon of October 7, Defense Minister Moshe Dayan came to the prime minister's office in Tel Aviv. He described the grave situation on both fronts to Meir, and proposed that in the south the government order a retreat to a new line of defense. After Dayan had finished talking, Meir summoned the chief of staff, Lieutenant General David Elazar, known to everyone by his nickname, "Dado." Elazar admitted that the situation was grave, but recommended waiting before carrying out a retreat, and Meir took his advice. She wrote in her memoirs, "In the arguments between Dayan and Dado, to my good fortune I always backed Dado." After the war, she said, "Dado saved the State of Israel." (This did not help Elazar when, after the war, a state commission of inquiry, headed by Chief Justice Shimon Agranat, blamed him for most of the shortcomings of the war and ordered that he be replaced. Political figures like Meir and Dayan were not censured.)

That evening, Dayan decided to take a far-reaching step. Non-Israeli sources have reported that for the first time since Israel had attained nuclear capability, the minister of defense ordered that nuclear bombs be loaded on fighter planes and nuclear warheads fitted to Jericho missiles, and that they be readied to attack the targets that had been assigned to them if it transpired that the Arab offensive was endangering the existence of the state. This information has never been confirmed by any official Israeli source. Two contradicting versions have been published about Meir's reaction to Dayan's orders. One version says that she instructed him to cancel the order, out of fear that the Soviets would detect and identify the activity, and react by threatening to use force against Israel. The other version says the opposite—that the prime minister informed U.S. Secretary of State Henry Kissinger that Israel was instituting a state of nuclear readiness, and that she cancelled it only after President Nixon immediately ordered an airlift of weapons and ammunition to Israel to replace what had been lost in combat. Those who adhere to the latter version accuse Meir of extorting large amounts of military equipment from the United States by threatening to declare a nuclear alert. Both versions rely heavily on fragments of evidence and hearsay, and before the truth is known we will have to wait for the publication of the relevant official documents in Washington and Jerusalem.

After she had heard both Dayan and Elazar, Meir called a cabinet meeting, where Dayan repeated his gloomy description of the situation. "The prime minister and the other ministers were shocked by what I had to say," he wrote in his diary. "I could see from the expressions on their faces that I had not persuaded them. It seems to me that they believe that the weakness is not in our military power, but in my character; that I had lost my confidence and therefore my evaluation is incorrect, that it is too pessimistic." Once again Dayan proposed retreating from the Suez Canal deep into Sinai, but the cabinet accepted the chief of staff's position and gave the army the task of pushing the Egyptians back across the canal.

The next day, October 8, was even worse. At dawn, an armored Israeli division under the command of Major General Avraham "Bren" Adan launched a counteroffensive on the southern front, in an attempt to dislodge the Egyptian forces that had established bridgeheads in the northern sector of the Israeli side of the canal.[1] At noon, the attack was blocked and the division was forced to retreat, after suffering serious casualties. Scores of soldiers had been killed, and dozens of tanks destroyed. In the afternoon, the division regrouped and launched another attack, but that also failed. In the lead battalion, thirty-two tank crewmen were killed and four were taken prisoner, including the battalion commander. Another armored division, commanded by Major General Ariel Sharon, which according to the chief of staff's plan was supposed to attack the Egyptian bridgeheads in the central sector of the canal, never even engaged the enemy. The Southern Command, which should have been directing the counterattack, never read the battle correctly and lost control over the movement of the forces. "It seems to me that the current commander of the Southern front is not capable of directing this war," wrote Dayan. The commander, Major General Shmuel Gorodish, was not removed, but a former chief of staff, Lieutenant General Haim Barlev (after whom the line of canal fortresses had been named) was sent to the Southern Command to oversee its operation.

The setbacks on the ground might have been redeemable had the Israeli Air Force not been almost totally neutralized by the Egyptians' dense and effective deployment of some fifty batteries of surface-to-air missiles, some of them mobile, in the vicinity of the Suez Canal. Most of the batteries had been moved forward close to the canal under the guidance of the Soviets directly after the signing of the Israel-Egyptian ceasefire in the summer of 1970. Israel was now paying a terrible price for not insisting then that the missiles be moved back.

The next day, on October 9, at 7:20 A.M., Dayan once again met Meir in the prime minister's Tel Aviv office, and told her that the counterattack in the south had failed. The minister of defense was tense and weary. The situation was so grave, he said, that he feared "the destruction of the Third Commonwealth" (a reference to the two previous sovereign Jewish governments, or kingdoms, and their symbol—the Temple in Jerusalem—the first destroyed by the Babylonians in the fourth century BCE and the second by the Romans in the 1st century CE). The stain of having voiced this dreadful prediction, foreseeing a possible end to the Jewish state, was to stick to Dayan until his dying day, tarnishing the heroic aura he had basked in for most of his life. "I reported to her the instructions I had given to the Northern Command—not to retreat at any cost—the meaning of which was that there were liable to be heavy casualties among our forces," Dayan wrote in his diary. "Golda nodded her head in agreement," he continued. "I have known Golda for many years, and I have seen her shed tears more than once. But never in time of war. War is not a crying matter." Meir may not have wept, but whoever met her that day could clearly see the shock on her face.

Dayan asked for the prime minister's permission to bomb civilian targets in Damascus, and said that if the Syrian army advanced into Israeli territory, it was possible that Iraq and Jordan would join the Arab offensive. Later, Dayan admitted that he had been mistaken in all of his assessments on the eve of the war and in its early days, and he offered his resignation, but Meir refused to accept it.[2] Dayan also asked to be allowed to appear on television and to tell the public the truth about the situation on the battlefronts, but the prime minister refused. She saw how dejected he was, and feared that if he appeared on television he would depress the nation's morale.

After the war, the deputy chief of staff, Major General Yisrael Tal, described the atmosphere at the General Staff headquarters that morning: "The ninth of October was the blackest day of the war, because on it we learned of the extent of the failure of October 8 [the defeat on the southern front] and we had no more reserves. There was nothing more. The war was perceived at that moment not only as at a critical juncture and almost beyond despair, but as a war for our very national and physical existence." Tal's description of the state of shock was accurate. In the General Staff, senior officers were stunned. Some even broke down and wept.

At the very height of the crisis, Meir Amit drove from Tel Aviv airport to Dayan's office. A general in the reserves, Amit had taken over from Isser Harel as head of the Mossad during the German scientists affair (see Chapter 10), but was now a civilian and head of Koor, Israel's largest industrial concern. On the day that the war had broken out, he was just ending a business visit to Bangkok, the capital of Thailand. Thirty years later, he recalled:

I was already on the plane to Teheran at Bangkok airport, when the Israeli ambassador to Thailand came running up and yelled, "War has broken out! War!" Then I got stuck in Teheran, because El Al airlines had stopped its flights. Two days later, when I finally arrived, I reported to Dayan, and told him, "I'm back. At your service." "Good thing you came," he said. "I'm not on good terms with Dado [General Elazar], and I suggest that you liaise between us. I'm giving you the authority, including on the delicate matters. If they have to decide, and I am not around, I'm giving you the authority to decide." He didn't put it in writing, it was only oral. He wanted me to be in the supreme command bunker. "I come only at night," he said. [Dayan preferred to tour the front lines and most of the time was away from his Tel Aviv office.] It was all based on personal relations. We had grown up together, I at Alonim and he at Nahalal [two adjacent agricultural communities in the Jezreel Valley]. I was in charge of the command group. I was not in the army anymore, but I had sufficient authority.

Although Amit no longer had an official role in the defense establishment, he had kept abreast of the developments in the nuclear program by virtue of his closeness to Dayan, and this is why he agreed to accept responsibility for "the delicate matters," or in other words, the implementation of the nuclear option. "To the best of my knowledge," Amit later said, "the use of the nuclear option [in this war] had never been discussed in any civilian or military forum, despite the fact that Dayan was hysterical, and spoke of 'the destruction of the Third Commonwealth.' I do not know if anyone did discuss using this option, and if [president] Katzir said anything about arming a plane, I do not know about it, but it is doubtful that the president would receive a report about it, and if I do not know about a plane being armed, then it apparently never happened."

Amit was referring to an unusual remark by the president of Israel in 1973, the physicist Ephraim (Katchalsky) Katzir, who had been involved in the nuclear program earlier. A few years after the war, he said in a television broadcast that in 1973 "Israel armed an aircraft with a nuclear bomb."[3] The statement slipped through military censorship and brought the subject out into the open. Later, on several occasions, official Israeli spokesmen denied Katzir's utterance. Amit was not denying that Defense Minister Dayan had weighed the possibility of preparing the nuclear option for use, but was expressing doubt as to whether practical steps were actually taken. According to a detailed account published in *Time* magazine in October 1973, Israel assembled about a dozen bombs and prepared them for delivery by aircraft or missiles.

In retrospect, it emerged that most of Dayan's judgments had indeed been wrong, both before the war broke out and during its early course. In the months leading up to the war, Dayan never realized that the diplomatic deadlock would force Sadat into war, and after the hostilities began he failed to identify the strategic objectives of the Egyptian war plan. Moreover, the panic and despondency that seized him in the first days of the fighting because of the magnitude of the surprise, the large numbers of Israeli casualties and prisoners,[4] and the failure of the counteroffensive of October 8, all blurred the excellent soldierly senses that Dayan had in his youth, and led him to give extremely erroneous interpretations to the events on the battlefield. The situation was in fact very grave on both fronts, but not critical. Israel was never in danger of annihilation. On both fronts the enemy armored forces enjoyed superiority as long as they were protected by the umbrella of SAM missiles that prevented Israeli aircraft from attacking them. On the first days of fighting, on both fronts, the Israeli Air Force failed in its efforts to overcome the SAMs, and was therefore unable to operate against the ground forces, but from the moment that it learned the lessons of its errors and developed effective tactics against the missile batteries, the Egyptian and the Syrian armored units were exposed to the accurate fire from the air, and were forced to retreat.[5]

Moreover, today we know with certainty that Sadat's war plan was a limited one. The Egyptian president's aim was to conquer a narrow strip of land along the eastern bank of the Suez Canal and to stop his forces there, without advancing toward the Israeli border. His entire object was to break the deadlock and force Israel into negotiations on withdrawal from Sinai, and in this he succeeded.

This strategy of Sadat's was described in a surprising revelation published by Henry Kissinger in a recent book, *Crisis*, and in official documents declassified in Washington in October 2003. The day after Egypt and Syria went to war, on October 7, 1973, Sadat's national security adviser, Muhammad Hafez Ismail, conveyed a message to the American administration in which the Egyptian president laid out his strategic plans for the war and for the negotiations that would come in its wake. Ismail delivered the letter to the Cairo CIA station, which he was in touch with. At that time, diplomatic relations between Washington and Cairo, which Nasser had broken off after the 1967 war, had not yet been renewed.[6]

Under the heading "Conditions for stopping the war," Sadat stated explicitly in the letter that he was not interested in intensifying the combat or to "widen the confrontation." On the contrary, he wanted to negotiate with Israel on peace in exchange for a return to the 1967 border. Kissinger understood from the missive that Sadat was asking the United States to handle the negotiations for a cease-fire and then for a permanent settlement. Imparting his war plans to the United States was a bold move, calculated but not without risk. In fact, the president of Egypt was depositing the fate of his country's war effort in the hands of the foreign minister of a country that had extended its patronage over the very enemy it was fighting. The publication of parts of Sadat's letter (the full text has not yet been declassified) cast an entirely new light on the interpretation of the 1973 crisis and war.

The opening of a secret channel of communication between Egypt and the United States enabled Sadat to display flexibility in the diplomatic contacts and to take the necessary steps toward achieving a cease-fire at the time that suited him: as soon as his forces had established control of the strip ten to fifteen miles wide on the east bank of the Suez Canal. Aside from the United States, no one else was aware of Sadat's true war aims. He had deceived his Syrian ally by concealing not only the war plan, but also the fact that he had turned to the United States. Syria was expecting a comprehensive and determined Egyptian offensive, starting with the crossing of the canal and continuing with an eastward thrust across Sinai and an invasion of Israeli territory. If Syria had been aware that Sadat's goals were limited to conquering a strip along the canal, it is doubtful that it would have agreed to join his initiative and gone to war. Neither did the Soviet Union know of the direct contact between Sadat and Kissinger, and in the early days of the war Moscow was still trying to persuade other Arab countries, among them Jordan and Algeria, to join the offensive.

Clearly Israel was unaware of the Sadat-Kissinger contacts and the Egyptian plans. If the Israeli leaders had known that Sadat's intentions were so restricted in scope, they would certainly have reacted more temperately to the surprise attack, and avoided the hysteria that engulfed many of them in the first days of the war. However, Kissinger kept the Egyptian overtures a secret, giving himself a giant advantage over both the Soviet Union and Israel in managing the crisis. This way, the deck was stacked in his favor, and he could conduct the moves toward a solution independently. He was also lucky. Not only had both the main adversaries—Israel and Egypt—requested his mediation, but it was exactly at that time that the Watergate affair was becoming messy, and President Nixon and his closest advisers were busy trying to deflect the steady onslaught of the media. This meant that Kissinger was free to direct the Middle East show virtually unhindered, and he did so with great skill.

Why did Sadat limit his war goals? Why did he not exploit the tremendous success of his forces' canal-crossing operation and thrust eastward with his armor before the Israelis could mobilize their reserves and organize a defense? The answer is that he had accurately read the strategic situation as dictated by Israel's nuclear capability. Meir Amit, who, it will be recalled, had received authority over "the nuclear matter" from the defense minister, confirms that in talks with Israeli, Egyptian, and American officers and military experts it emerged that Sadat, in contrast to his predecessor, Nasser, had assumed that Israel possessed the nuclear option and would threaten Egypt with it if he dared to endanger the existence of Israel. The way he saw it, this was the line in the sand that said "this far and no further."

Looking back after thirty years, and since the disclosure of Sadat's overture to Kissinger at the start of the war, it is clear that the Egyptian leader was illustrating Carl von Clausewitz's famous dictum, "War is not an independent phenomenon, but the continuation of politics by different means." Sadat's strategy was carefully calculated and very clever. He was aware of the limits that Israel's nuclear capability placed upon his power, and with great skill he exploited the impact of his surprise, and the panic and instability that it sowed in the enemy's camp, in order to achieve a diplomatic objective without going so far as to provoke Israel into using its ultimate defense. In this way he was keeping the promise he had made to his nation when he inherited Nasser's mantle: to return to Egyptian control every grain of sand that had been lost in 1967. Step by step, with stubborn determination, Sadat brought the Middle East into a new era, from the surprise attack and the seizure of the bridgeheads on the east bank of the canal, through his secret appeal to the United States, and his efforts to secure a cease-fire once his forces were established in what had been Israeli-occupied territory, despite the fact that the Israelis had also crossed the canal during the war and were holding territory on the western bank. He persisted throughout, with the disengagement talks at Kilometer 101 on the Cairo-Suez road and the implementation of the interim agreements for Israeli withdrawal reached there in January 1974. All this was followed by his dramatic peace initiative in 1977, and the signing of a peace agreement with Israel the following year (because of which he was assassinated by a Muslim Brotherhood activist, while taking the salute at a military parade held in Cairo in 1981, to mark the eighth anniversary of the successful offensive).

In addition to securing the full withdrawal from the Sinai, Sadat prepared the ground for Israel's agreeing to the establishment of the Palestinian Authority in the West Bank and Gaza as part of the 1993 Oslo accords, and the eventual adoption of the two-state solution to the Israel-Palestinian problem by the Clinton and George W. Bush administrations. Before the October 1973 war, the consensus in Israel was that the territories conquered in 1967 would remain in Israeli hands for many years. Israelis viewed arguments in favor of a Palestinian state as totally unrealistic. The surprise offensive launched by Sadat was also the beginning of the process of Israel's return to its pre-1967 borders, despite its possession of the tremendous strategic advantage accorded by the nuclear option.

In contrast to Sadat, the Israeli leadership's performance during the October 1973 crisis was manifestly unskillful. On the military level, preparation for a coordinated offensive on two fronts was negligent; intelligence failed to uncover the Arab plan to attack[7] and the command botched the conduct of the early battles, all of which was a result of excessive self-satisfaction at the results of the 1967 war, contempt for the enemy, and a surfeit of arrogance. More important, the hysteria evinced by the political leadership in the first days of the war exposed a grave and fundamental malfunction: the lack of basic tools for the analysis and conduct of policy, and amateurishness to the point of charlatanism of those at the top of the political and military hierarchy in everything connected with the management of crisis situations. (Similar dysfunction on the part of both the government and the military had also marked the three weeks of the "Waiting" period prior to the Six-Day War, as we have seen in Chapter 13.) Possession of nuclear potential, it transpires, is no guarantee of superiority in the conduct of tactical and even strategic warfare.

Historical research since 1973 has shown that an intelligent analysis of Egypt's strategy, grounded in overt moves by Sadat and his public declarations, would have led to the conclusion that there was no need for Israel to arm its Jericho missiles or aircraft with nuclear warheads and bombs, as non-Israeli sources have said was done. The nuclear option could safely have been left deep in the basement, because its aim—precisely as Ben-Gurion had conceived it, deterrence against destruction of the state—had been fully achieved without preparing to exercise it. Keeping it in the cellar had been sufficient to persuade the main enemy of that time that it should not even think of threatening Israel's existence, because the response would be a threat to the existence of Egypt.

The issue of Israel's nuclear potential came into play once more toward the end of the war. On the night of October 15–16, a unit of paratroops from Ariel Sharon's division had crossed the canal at the seam between the Egyptian Third and Second Armies, and established a bridgehead on the western bank. The next day, a floating bridge was constructed across the canal and for the next few days, armored and infantry brigades streamed to the Egyptian side. From the bridgehead, the Israelis moved north, up to the outskirts of Ismailiya, and south, to Suez City, threatening to encircle the Egyptian Third Army. On October 22, Israeli units pushing westward reached the Cairo-Suez road, and stopped exactly 100 kilometers (62 miles) from the Egyptian capital.

On that evening, a cease-fire, set the previous day by Kissinger and Soviet President Leonid I. Brezhnev at a meeting in Moscow, was due to take effect. The Israeli forces were rushing forward, and needed another day or two to complete the encirclement of the Third Army, an achievement that would give Israel a trump card when it came to demanding that the Egyptians return their forces that had crossed the canal in the early days of the war and were stubbornly clinging to their positions there. Israel therefore wanted the fighting to go on, and Kissinger decided to let them proceed, although he had agreed with the Russians that it would stop. In a cable he sent to the State Department from Moscow, he gave instructions that Israel be informed that "we would understand if Israelis felt they required some additional time for military dispositions." Then he flew to Tel Aviv, where he met Meir and once again advised Israel to ignore the cease-fire in order to improve its positions. Here is an extract from the American record of the conversation:

> Meir: The Egyptians and the Syrians haven't said anything [about the cease-fire]. They have said that the fighting continues.

> Kissinger: You won't get violent protests from Washington if something happens during the night, while I'm flying [back to Washington]. Nothing can happen in Washington until noon tomorrow.

> Meir: If they don't stop, we won't.

> Kissinger: Even if they do . . .

Thus, egged on by the secretary of state,[8] Israel violated the terms of the cease-fire and surrounded the Third Army, while in Moscow, Brezhnev boiled over with rage. In a message he fired off directly to Kissinger, he deplored "the flagrant deceit on the part of the Israelis to violate the cease-fire."

The cease-fire violations rekindled the crisis, and the Soviets demanded that Israel retreat to the lines of October 22. To back up his demand, Brezhnev ordered two Warsaw Pact divisions stationed in Bulgaria to go on alert. He then called President Nixon twice on the red phone and reiterated the demand that Israel withdraw. When Israel nevertheless continued its advance, he took an extreme step. On October 24, at ten o'clock at night, the Soviet ambassador in Washington, Anatoly Dobrynin, contacted Kissinger and dictated a furious message from Brezhnev to Nixon, including a protest against Israel's continuing "to seize new and new territory from Egypt" and also a threat: "I will say it to you straight that if you find it impossible to act jointly with us . . . we should be faced with the necessity urgently to consider the question of taking appropriate steps unilaterally."

Now it was the United States' turn to respond firmly. According to Kissinger, on the night of October 25–26, Washington ordered America's nuclear forces around the world to raise the level of their alert from DEFCON (Defense Condition) 4 to DEFCON 3.[9] "The basic purpose," Kissinger related after the crisis, "was to generate a lot of [communications] traffic that the Soviet Union would pick up before they received our reply—to know that this was getting serious." So the orders transmitted on American military networks to step up the nuclear alert were not motivated by a genuine concern that the Soviets would carry out Brezhnev's threat and use force against Israel, but in order to fabricate tension so that at its height it would be possible to relax it and once more reach an agreement. In reality, it had not been necessary for the United States to raise the level of the nuclear alert, because it was already high due to the continuing war in Vietnam, despite the peace agreement that had been signed early in 1973.

The American nuclear alert, which was in fact a ploy engineered by Kissinger, has led some pundits to be carried away by their imaginations. In Israel, for example, one version was published claiming that at the height of the crisis, American intelligence had discovered in satellite photographs that a Soviet ship in Egypt had unloaded Scud surface missile batteries manned by Soviet crews and armed with nuclear warheads that had not been camouflaged, and that this was in fact the reason for America's declaration of a nuclear alert.[10] However, an in-depth examination of American and Israeli intelligence sources revealed that no such event had taken place. The Soviet Union had deployed Scud missiles in Egypt some months before the war, and there had been apprehension in Israel that they were armed with nuclear warheads, but further inquiries had dispelled the fears. The warheads were conventional. Just as it had in earlier crises in the Middle East, in 1973 the Soviet Union behaved responsibly and left its strategic forces out of the game, as did the United States.

Nevertheless, from the point of view of the administration in Washington, the danger that the crisis would degenerate into a nuclear confrontation was not merely hypothetical, because now, for the first time, there were three parties with nuclear capability involved, and the Americans feared that the Israelis would interpret the Soviet warning as a threat to its existence and take drastic countermeasures. Washington therefore advised Israel to halt its advance immediately, to stop shooting, and to supply the besieged Third Army with food and water. Israel was compelled to heed the advice. Prime Minister Meir was very angry with Kissinger for insisting on rescuing the Third Army from surrendering to Israel.[11]

On October 24, the cease-fire took effect. After eighteen days of fighting, Egyptian units were lodged firmly on the east bank of the canal, and Israeli units were in a similar position on the Egyptian side. At Kissinger's initiative, talks between the two countries began negotiating a separation of forces in a tent pitched on the western side of the canal, 101 kilometers (63 miles) east of Cairo, on the road to Suez. The outcome of the talks was an Israeli withdrawal from the territory it had conquered on the western bank and, eventually, Sadat's peace initiative, in the wake of which the Camp David accords were signed, under the auspices of President Jimmy Carter.

Years later, Kissinger regretted that he had encouraged Israel not to observe the cease-fire and to continue advancing. In *Crisis*, he wrote that he "had a sinking feeling" that he "might have emboldened them" to keep on fighting.

GOLDA MEIR'S NUCLEAR dilemma in the 1973 war was a key element in the plot of the one-woman play *Golda's Balcony* that was staged at the Helen Hayes Theater on Broadway in 2004.[12] Playwright William Gibson had interviewed Meir at length and she told him how she stood on the "balcony"—the observation deck at Dimona, from which important guests were invited to view the operation of the nuclear reactor. He sketched her character with a great deal of sympathy, and New York audiences seemed to have identified easily with her. But anyone who actually experienced the shock of the first days of the war found it much more difficult to admire her.

The most dramatic scene in the play occurs during the first days of the war. In Meir's office, the phones are ringing ceaselessly with news of fresh disasters at the battlefronts. The prime minister has to make the most difficult decision of her life: Should the bomb be used? According to the play, the bombs had already been loaded onto the warplanes, and the pilots were buckled up in their cockpits, waiting for the order to take off. In Washington, Nixon and Kissinger agree that if Golda is persuaded that the Jewish state is facing destruction, she will not hesitate to give the orders, and they therefore decide to provide Israel with conventional weaponry in order to stave off the danger. (On the stage, actress Tovah Feldshuh, who played Golda, imitated Kissinger's voice with great accuracy, and the audience laughed out loud.)

At least four peopple heard Meir say that on October 9 she had contemplated suicide. Late in 2003, the elderly Ephraim Katzir, president of Israel in 1973, told a journalist: "It is a picture that I can not forget. She felt that the responsibility was on her shoulders. She said to me: 'Ephraim, I am to blame for the deaths of 2,500 soldiers. It is my fault.'" He said that she told him, "Ephraim, I have had enough of my life." She told two officers, Brigadier General Avner Shalev, who was the chief aide to Chief of Staff Elazar, and Major General Rehavam Ze'evi, "On the second day of the war I decided to commit suicide."[13]

At a conference in Tel Aviv three years after the war, the novelist Amos Oz asked Meir, "What do you dream about," and she replied: "I have no time to dream. I don't sleep, because the phone rings at night to inform me about the casualties." When she wrote her memoirs, she put it this way: "And how I dream, but only one nightmare. Suddenly all the phones in the house start ringing, and there are a lot of them, in every corner of the house, and there's no end to the ringing. I know what the ringing means, and I'm scared to pick up all the many phones. I wake up covered in cold sweat. In a silent house. I breathe a sigh of relief, but I don't fall asleep again. I know that if I fall asleep, the same dream will come back. I keep on thinking when that dream will let me go. Then I'll begin dreaming all the dreams about our beautiful lives."

CHAPTER SIXTEEN

Two Scenarios:
War (with Iran) or Peace

FAST-FORWARD THIRTY years from where we left a shaken Israel after the Yom Kippur war to Israel today. It took fifty years for the Jews to establish and stabilize the sovereign state that had been the goal of the Zionist movement since its inception at the end of the 19th century. Almost certainly, when historians look back with the added perspective of another two decades, they will conclude that Israel's nuclear capability was the decisive element in persuading the Arab world that the Jewish presence in the narrow strip of land at the eastern end of the Mediterranean Sea was a permanent reality.

The warlike confrontation between the Arabs and the Jews settled into an equilibrium after the 1973 war. The results of the war enabled both sides to shift from continuous struggle to negotiations toward a peace settlement. Egypt's victories on the battlefield—the conquest of the Barlev Line and taking 250 Israeli soldiers prisoner—spurred Egypt to shift from a state of utter rejection of the Jewish state to one of reconcilement with its existence. For Israel too the 1973 war was a defining moment. Despite the many casualties and the gigantic economic damage that it sustained, Israel emerged from the war stronger than it was at its outbreak. Thirty-two years after the bloodcurdling sirens that wailed throughout Israel on its holiest day, it can be said that the final outcome of the military confrontation was good for both sides: Egypt had forced Israel to recognize the limitations of its power, nuclear capability notwithstanding, and for its part, Egypt, and in its wake most of the Arab states, were compelled to come to terms with the existence of Israel.

Since the war, three processes have shaped Israel's image:

The first one is what is known in Israel as "the diplomatic process," which is in essence the gradual withdrawal of Israel's forces and settlements from the vast areas it captured in 1967, and attempts to solve the disputes with the Palestinians, all in exchange for a peaceful settlement with the Arab world. This diplomatic process was set in motion by the letter that Anwar Sadat wrote to Henry Kissinger on the second day of the 1973 war, as related in the previous chapter. The Sadat initiative gave birth to the negotiations between Egypt and Israel at the 1978 Camp David summit, under the aegis of President Jimmy Carter. At the end of the talks, Prime Minister Menachem Begin and President Sadat signed a peace treaty at the historic ceremony on the lawn of the White House.

The peace between Israel and Egypt has survived for over twenty-five years, although there have been prolonged troughs and profound crises between Israel and the Arabs during that period. The most serious were in 1982, when Israel invaded Lebanon (it occupied the southern part of that country for two decades), and during the two Palestinian uprisings against the Israeli occupation of Gaza and the West Bank, which together lasted some ten years.

By 2005, Israel had reached peace agreements with two of its neighbors, Egypt in 1978 and Jordan in 1994. Talks began with Syria in 1992, but were broken off; they were renewed in 1996, and once again broken off. As for the dispute with the Palestinians, here too the sides made progress in the peace process, troughs and crises notwithstanding. In 1993, after the first Palestinian uprising, Israel recognized the Palestine Liberation Organization, carried out its first withdrawal from occupied Palestinian lands in the Gaza Strip and in the West Bank, and handed them over to an autonomous entity that had been set up for this purpose, known as the Palestinian Authority.

The giving up of land caused severe internal rifts within Israeli society, and even led to the 1995 assassination of Prime Minister Yitzhak Rabin. During the protracted period while peace negotiations were stymied, violence flourished, and a second uprising, or *intifada*, broke out in late 2000, with the Palestinians resorting to suicide terrorism of unprecedented proportions and the Israelis taking extreme measures against the civilian population, including the destruction of homes, roadblocks, curfews, closures, and mass arrests. After four and a half years of vicious combat, both sides reached a state of exhaustion.

In February 2005, after the death of Palestinian Authority chairman Yasser Arafat, the longtime uncontested leader of his nation, the second uprising came to an end with an official statement to this effect by Arafat's successor, Mahmoud Abbas, made at a regional summit at Sharm el-Sheikh in Sinai. The peace process resumed according to a plan conceived by the George W. Bush administration and known as the "road map," whose final aim was the establishment of an independent Palestinian state coexisting peacefully with Israel. Shortly after the summit, Israel began withdrawing from some of the territories of the Palestinian Authority that it had reoccupied during the second *intifada* uprising, and promised to evacuate the settlements in the Gaza Strip and the northern West Bank. Three key disputes remain to be resolved: the ultimate extent of the Israeli withdrawal from the West Bank, the fate of the Palestinian refugees who had left the country in 1948, and the question of sovereignty in Jerusalem.

At the same time, Syria expressed an interest in renewing negotiations with Israel, and it appeared reasonable to assume that negotiations could get under way once Israel had completed its withdrawal from the Gaza Strip and northern Samaria (on the West Bank), and that any arrangement reached would apply to Lebanon as well.

The political process has been going on for thirty-five years and it seems that before a comprehensive settlement is reached, at least another decade will have to elapse. Traffic on the road to conciliation between Jews and Arabs moves slowly, stops frequently, and even goes backward sometimes. But if there is no major setback, by the year 2015 a map of the State of Israel may be drawn showing permanent borders, recognized by the countries of the region, for the first time. It will have taken over 120 years since the first Zionist Jews hailing from Eastern Europe came to settle in the Land of Israel.

The second major development that has occurred in the last generation has been the wave of migration of Jews from the former Soviet Union to Israel since the late 1980s, as a result of the success of an international propaganda campaign led by Jewish organizations in the United States. The flow of immigration swelled in the 1990s after the collapse of the Soviet empire. Within five years, the Israeli population increased by one million people, or 20 percent;[1] it was as if the United States were to absorb some 60 million immigrants. The Russian immigrants were remarkably well educated, so much so that all at once Israel became the country with the highest average educational level in the world, something that strengthened its technological infrastructure considerably. One may assume that the dramatic increase in the population bolstered the confidence of the Israelis and lightened their burden of existential anxiety, thereby leading to a reduction in their resistance to giving up the occupied territories and to a willingness to make compromises with the Arabs.

The third process affecting contemporary Israeli reality is an outcome of the terrorist attacks carried out by al-Qaida in the United States on September 11, 2001. The shock waves of those attacks reverberated for years in many other states, especially in the Muslim world: Afghanistan, where the Taliban regime sheltered al-Qaida; Iraq, where Saddam Hussein's terrorist regime was toppled; Pakistan, Saudi Arabia, and Syria, which were urged to take new political and ethical directions; and Libya, where the sight of the invasion of Iraq gave ruler Mu'ammar Gadhafi the final shove to dismantle his nuclear project. In Israel, the impact of 9/11 had the opposite effect; its strategic position improved greatly, because the Arab threat to its existence shrank substantially. The 2003 conquest of Iraq by a coalition led by the United States and the demise of the Saddam regime—the only one in the Arab world that had not hesitated, in 1991, to attack civilian targets in Israel with volleys of ballistic missiles— liberated Israel from a menace to the east. This new reality, in which large forces of Israel's most important ally were positioned a stone's throw away, gave the country strategic reinforcement, and also played a part in the shaping of a general consensus that made it possible to resume withdrawing from Palestinian territory.

Simultaneously, Syria's military power was declining appreciably, due to a protracted economic crisis and the fact that the United States had put Syria on the list of states that provide havens for terrorist organizations, threatening to impose sanctions on Syria unless it removed the terrorists. In the winter of 2005, another threat to Israel, the Syrian domination of Lebanon, appeared close to termination, as a popular uprising in Lebanon, combined with American pressure, led to the withdrawal of the Syrian army from that country.

From Israel's point of view, the war that the United States declared on international terrorism, the end of the Saddam dictatorship, and occupation of Iraq by the U.S. coalition, had caused some favorable changes. They wiped away the eastern front that had threatened Israel for years, expedited the waning of the Palestinian armed uprising, and accelerated the pace of the peace process.

Nevertheless, it is doubtful that all these dramatic events would have persuaded the Arabs to accept the sovereign Jewish presence in the heart of the Middle East were it not for the bomb in the basement. Israel's nuclear deterrent actually served exactly that function—it deterred the country's enemies. This is amazing because no foreign government has ever proved that Israel in fact possesses the bomb, although that fact is generally accepted. How is it that Israel actually managed to persuade everyone that it had at its disposal that amorphous entity known as "nuclear capability" and to use it to achieve effective deterrence without making the rest of the world nervous and compelling it to force Israel to allow inspectors to visit its nuclear installations or face sanctions, while countries like Iraq and Iran failed to do the same?

There are many reasons for this, but first one should emphasize that if the United States had not wanted Israel to have the nuclear option, it is doubtful that Israel would have been able to do so. Every president from John Kennedy on made it possible for Israel's nuclear program to progress, as did most of the senior legislators in Congress. On the other hand, the top bureaucrats usually objected to the program, or opposed it outright. But in view of the powerful support of the upper political echelons, U.S. officialdom had no chance of eliminating the program, or delaying it. Israel for its part tried hard to help the American politicians who supported the program. For Israel it was a matter of life and death. In the history of the young state, there have been very few issues around which both the political leadership, in all its incarnations, and public opinion have formed so united and harmonious an approach as the nuclear program.

Israel succeeded where many other states have failed, first because until the end of 1960, Ben-Gurion managed to hide from the world, and most importantly from the United States, the decisive stages in the development of Israel's nuclear capability. When the United States finally grasped what was under way at Dimona, Israel's nuclear option was already a fait accompli. Second, Ben-Gurion had succeeded in initiating and fulfilling the program in an era before strict international oversight had been instituted. Third, at an advanced stage in the nuclear program, Israel preferred to coordinate its development with the United States. And fourth, Israel benefited from the fact that under Nixon and Kissinger, the United States changed its criteria regarding nuclear initiatives of friendly states, ceased demanding that they open their nuclear facilities to international inspection, and allowed them to refrain from joining the Nuclear Non-Proliferation Treaty. Fifth, and perhaps most essentially, Israel always was careful to meet the conditions set by the United States: It made the purpose of its nuclear capability purely defensive, presenting the world with a display of nuclear ambiguity, and never, even in days of dire emergency, when its leaders feared the country was in existential danger, resorted to warning its enemies that it possessed nuclear weapons; and principally, Israel abstained from carrying out nuclear tests.

Intermittent reports have appeared in the world media of events that have been interpreted as indicating that Israel has indeed carried out such tests, but there has never been clear evidence of testing. One such report is still cited: On September 22, 1979, a few minutes before 1 A.M. GMT, an American Vela-type spy satellite, designed to detect signs of nuclear activity, photographed a double flash over the Indian Ocean that was similar to the flashes that had been photographed from space when China and France had carried out nuclear tests. The photographs sparked a wave of rumors that Israel had carried out a nuclear test with the logistical support of South Africa.

Experts in the American national laboratories at Los Alamos examined the photographs, and raised the possibility that the flashes were indeed a nuclear explosion, but an external examining committee of experts appointed by President Carter concluded that it was possible the flashes were a climatic phenomenon resulting from unusual weather conditions.² The committee was headed by Jack Ruina, professor of electrical engineering at MIT, and its members included Nobel physics laureate Luis Alvarez.

In his book *The Samson Option*, American journalist Seymour M. Hersh quotes unidentified official Israeli sources who told him that Israel and South Africa had together carried out three nuclear test explosions, one of which had been caught by the Vela satellite's camera, but to this day no official Israeli or South African source has confirmed this information.³ Shimon Peres declared that Israel has never carried out a nuclear test. "If Israel was to perform a nuclear test, it would be inviting horrendous pressure," he told me.

The late ambassador Paul C. Warnke confirmed that the United States had conditioned the supply of offensive weapons to Israel on its refraining from conducting nuclear tests. If Israel carried out a test, the United States had the legal instruments not only to cease the supply of attack weapons, but also to demand that Israel return some of the armaments already supplied. Warnke added that Israel had adopted the nuclear ambiguity policy at America's insistence. He put it like this: "I think we preferred the fact that Israel was not declaring that it had targeted some potential enemy with nuclear weapons."

The Israeli who developed and elaborated the concept of nuclear ambiguity into a political doctrine was Shalhevet Freier. He explained to members of the nuclear inner circle that the concept was meant to achieve three goals: against the enemy, deterrence; to friendly nations, maintenance of a responsible image that makes normal relations possible; and for the Israeli people, a boost of self-confidence in the face of their security challenges.

Maintaining ambiguity requires extreme discipline and modesty, and the small closed group that conducted Israeli defense policy generally managed to conquer any impulse to boast or gain publicity, of course with the help of strict censorship and a sympathetic public, which never demanded of its leaders that they tell it the truth. When there's a sword across your throat, apparently, prudence and reason are the best policy.

In retrospect, no one disagrees that ambiguity was a success. Ze'ev Schiff, Israel's leading military analyst, said that if there was an Israel Prize (the country's top award) for an idea or concept, he would give it to the person who thought up nuclear ambiguity. "It worked well. It is still working. It is very likely that we will live with it for a long time into the future," said Schiff, and continued: "Toward our enemies, toward our allies, and even within the internal Israeli system, it made maintaining security and foreign relations easier; this is a theory that functioned well in practice, and it makes no difference if it was conceived as such in advance, or if it was built up brick by brick, until the wall was standing."

Warnke held a similar opinion. "Ambiguity gives the Arab states a good excuse for not doing more to eliminate Israel," he said. "I think there is a feeling in part of the Arab states that they cannot do anything about it and I think that they are happy that way. They are happy not being in a position in which somebody is going to say, 'Why don't you attack Israel, why don't you bomb Jerusalem?' So I think that everybody is more comfortable with the situation that exists than they would be with any other situation."

There was no erosion in Israel's ambiguous position even after the revelations of Mordechai Vanunu, the Dimona technician who in 1986 leaked the secrets of the reactor to the *Sunday Times* of London. Abroad he was praised as a "whistleblower," but in Israel he was convicted of treason. Vanunu supplied the paper with a detailed description of the production processes at Dimona, as well as photographs he had taken secretly. He exposed Institute 2, where he worked for nine years and which, according to him, housed the plutonium extraction installation. After checking the information and consulting experts, the *Sunday Times* concluded that the Dimona reactor had a 150-megawatt output and could produce forty kilograms of plutonium a year. On the basis of Vanunu's information, Theodore Taylor, a nuclear physicist who studied with Robert Oppenheimer, told the paper that Israel has the "capacity to produce 10 nuclear weapons a year that are significantly smaller, lighter and more efficient than the first types of weapons developed by Russia, America, Britain, France, or China."

Before Vanunu's revelations, most of the world's experts on nuclear weaponry believed that Israel had a program to build atomic bombs, but was still at an early stage. (However, as we have pointed out, American intelligence had estimated early in the 1970s that Israel had already made at least one bomb.)

Vanunu completed his full eighteen-year jail term, nine years in solitary confinement, in April 2004. After his release, his freedom of movement and speech were restricted. He was barred from going abroad or meeting foreign journalists. The security services kept him under close surveillance. The information that Vanunu exposed to the world in words and pictures may have stripped the veil away from Israel's nuclear program, but it never damaged it. On the contrary, the revelations increased the weight of the nuclear deterrent, according to the evaluations of many Israeli security experts, including a former head of the General Security Services (the Shin Bet), who preferred to remain anonymous, and a former chief of staff of the Israel Defense Forces, reserves Lieutenant General Amnon Lipkin-Shahak.

In recent years, American and European liberals friendly to Israel have been advising the Israeli defense establishment to relax the strict adherence to the policy of ambiguity. But the Israeli defense establishment is firmly opposed to any change. This position represents an apparent Israeli consensus. Public opinion in Israel has never been in favor of opening the nuclear question to public scrutiny and debate, not even nonmilitary nuclear issues such as the safety conditions of the two nuclear reactors in the country, the degree of risk that the workers and nearby residents are exposed to, and the way that nuclear waste is handled. As mentioned in the Introduction, the Israeli public prefers that nuclear matters remain taboo. Hence, as long as there is no direct nuclear threat to Israel, it is doubtful that there will be any change in the ambiguity policy. If another country in the region were to acquire nuclear ability, however, then that would alter the balance of forces in the Middle East.

ISRAEL'S STRATEGY IS to prevent other Middle Eastern countries from drawing level with it in terms of military strength. For decades, Israel's technological advantage over its neighbors has grown, and this was especially true in the past decade. The benefits of globalization are more marked in Israel than in the other countries of the region, because it is a democracy, with open channels of communication to the rest of the world and a free economy. In an equation of power in which only conventional weapons are counted, Israel may have an advantage, but that is not certain; when the nuclear option is factored in, Israel's forces far out-weigh those of its potential enemies. Israel is not interested in losing its nuclear monopoly and having to rely on a balance of terror.

In Israel's eyes—and this has been true of each and every one of its governments over the years, since nuclear capability was attained in the late 1960s—the idea of nuclear weapons in the hands of an enemy is to-tally unacceptable, because that would immediately wipe out Israel's de-terrent power. This power was clearly illustrated in the decision of President Sadat of Egypt to limit the aims of the 1973 war, and also in the first Gulf War, in 1991, when Saddam Hussein held back from firing missiles with chemical warheads at Israel. This inflexible stance may spring from the deep anxiety that afflicts the Jewish people in general and the Israelis in particular, as we have stressed throughout this book, or it may be founded on a rational analysis of reality. But in practice, it is the principle itself that is important not its origin. There is no chance at all that Israel will reconcile itself to living with a strategic threat posed by the ayatollahs' regime in Iran, for example, which regularly calls for the destruction of the Jewish state. Indeed, by 2005 Israel had already de-cided that it was not prepared to come to terms with such a change in the status quo.

Beyond the question of Israel's existence, a nuclear Iran would dra-matically affect American interests. On the one hand, those elements struggling against American interests would be strengthened: the rebels in Iraq, Baathist Syria, international terror groups like al-Qaida, and lo-cal terror organizations like Hezbollah and Hamas, as well as the funda-mentalist parties and other groups that have declared war on the Western way of life. On the other hand, those forces that support Amer-ican interests would be weakened: the Egyptian regime, the Jordanian monarchy, the Saudi Arabian dynasty, and the Gulf emirates. An Iranian nuclear option would bolster the regime of the mullahs in Teheran, and diminish the chances that it will be supplanted by more moderate ele-ments. At least three Muslim states in the region—Turkey, Saudi Arabia, and Egypt—would feel compelled to enter the nuclear race themselves in order to stay in the power game at all, something that could set the Middle East sliding down a slippery slope to uncontrollable chaos.

And turning eastward, in the direction of Pakistan and Afghanistan, and the Muslim Central Asian republics of the former Soviet Union, there too the situation could take a similar course. Since the dismantling of the Soviet Empire, Iran has extended its strategic interests in areas in Central Asia and the Caucasus, where there is a vacuum of power, by taking advantage of ethnic, religious, and language ties. Iran builds schools in Central Asian countries, sends mullahs to teach in mosques, distributes religious literature, and negotiates a wide range of bilateral cooperation. In the future, under the protection of a nuclear umbrella, extremist Shiite Iran would be able to foist its ideology on vast populations and ward off American influence.

Is Israel capable of acting on its own against Iran? It would prefer a diplomatic solution leading to the cancellation of the Iranian nuclear program, or at least to freezing it for a lengthy period. Most Israeli experts believe that the right combination of carrots and sticks would ultimately bring Iran around.

But what will happen if negotiations fail and Iran persists? Clearly Israel would prefer American military intervention, but the prevalent opinion among Israeli experts in early 2005 was that the United States would be very hesitant about using the force necessary to get Iran to give up on its nuclear aspirations.

Ever since the suspicion surfaced that Iran was busy making weapons-grade uranium, Israeli political and military leaders started declaring repeatedly that if and when Iran reached the point of no return, Israel would not hesitate to take military action against it.

Before a military operation could be launched against Iran there must be sufficient intelligence. Since the end of 2003, Western intelligence agencies, especially those of Israel and the United States, increased their efforts to gather information about Iran's nuclear activities. This does not mean that the results are good. Historical experience shows that locating nuclear activity being carried by parties who are not interested in having it exposed is a complicated matter. Almost all the countries that have engaged in the development of nuclear capability managed to pull the wool over the eyes of the intelligence agencies that were trying to keep tabs on them. France, China, Israel, South Africa, India, Pakistan,

Libya, Iraq, and many others were all suspects, but the smoking gun was never found and eventually, when most of them carried out test explosions, the world was taken by surprise. Iran started importing advanced-type centrifuge parts in the mid-'90s, and used them to build an installation for producing enriched uranium, but the world found out about it only in 2003. Western agencies never identified in time the smuggling network run by Abdul Qadeer Khan from Pakistan, or Libya's nuclear plans. Their assessments of the development of weapons of mass destruction in Iraq turned out to be way off the mark, this time, though, in the direction of exaggeration.

The United States operates spy satellites over Iran, as well as spy planes and drones dispatched from Iraq and Afghanistan, and also sends in agents from those countries. Israel also has two spy satellites.[4] Non-Israeli sources have said that Israeli intelligence uses the Kurdish territory in northern Iraq to put agents into Iran, and to gather data.[5]

Israel and the United States share intelligence about Iran, and their reactions to its moves are coordinated. It can be assumed that the two countries have accumulated some useful material on the defenses at those nuclear sites in Iran that have been identified, especially the centrifuge installation at Natanz and the 40-megawatt reactor under construction at Arak.[6]

The installation at Natanz was ready for use as of mid-2004, but its operation was frozen under an agreement Iran signed with the European Union in November 2004. In mid-2005, the centrifuges installation was still frozen, and the debate was far from over. The reactor is due to be completed in 2009, and after a year or two it will be possible to extract plutonium from the spent uranium.

It is doubtful that attacks on Natanz and Arak sites, however successful they might be, would eradicate Iran's nuclear plans because Iran has no doubt dispersed other subterranean uranium enrichment plants across the country. If one were hit, another could be activated. This was apparently one of the lessons Iran learned from the bombing of Iraq's Osirak reactor by the Israeli Air Force in 1981. Iran is a large country with some rough terrain and remote regions where military and scientific activity can be easily concealed.

Israel is unlikely to ask the United States to approve on any attack on

Iran, unless its planes have to fly over Iraq while U.S. forces are still there. There is no operational coordination between the two countries, although there is agreement in principle on the way in which Israel may rightfully respond to the threat of weapons of mass destruction. This agreement was framed in a document drawn up in 1998 and signed by President Bill Clinton and Prime Minister Benjamin Netanyahu. It states that the United States is "very concerned" by the nonconventional threats in the Middle East (without mentioning Iraq or Iran, although it was clear at the time that they were the subject of the statement) and that it understands that Israel needs defensive capabilities in the face of the threats. This is apparently the first written agreement between the two countries that refers to nonconventional threats against Israel and the manner in which it may respond to them. The agreement provides for a permanent apparatus for joint discussion on nonconventional threats in the Middle East. This machinery is separate from the working groups that have been meeting twice a year since the 1980s in the framework of the "strategic dialogue" between the two countries. On April 14, 2004, at the end of a series of discussions by the nonconventional threats panel, President George Bush and Israeli Prime Minister Ariel Sharon exchanged letters. Sharon released a section of one of these letters for publication, including the following American statement: "Israel has the right to defend itself with its own forces." This statement was understood as a direct message to Teheran that the United States recognized Israel's right to use its defensive capacity in the event that Iran develops nuclear weaponry.

The destruction of Iraq's reactor in 1981 was a historical precedent: For the first time, a regional power with nuclear capability had gone on the offensive to prevent a neighbor with considerable military power from developing nuclear weaponry. For the seven years prior to the attack, Israel had tried in various ways to stop Iraq from acquiring the installations and materials that would enable it to build a bomb. Straight after the attack, Prime Minister Menachem Begin made the following declaration: "Israel will not tolerate any nuclear weapons in the region"—a doctrine which is still in force today. The international reaction was largely negative. Then Secretary of State Alexander Haig called the operation "reckless," but after some time for reflection he issued a more balanced statement, which, on careful reading, turned out to be very important from Israel's point of view:

> The United States recognizes the gaps in Western military capabilities in the region, and the fundamental strategic value of Israel, the strongest and most stable friend and ally the United States has in the Mideast. Consequently, the two countries must work together to counter the full range of threats that the Western world faces in the region. While we may not always place the same emphasis on particular threats, we share a fundamental understanding that a strong, secure and vibrant Israel serves Western interests in the Middle East. We shall never deviate from that principle, for the success of our strategy depends thereupon.

Menachem Begin was satisfied at the "fundamental understanding" that Israel should be "strong, secure and vibrant"; that, after all, was why he had launched the operation.

Saddam Hussein kept his desire for revenge bottled up for exactly ten years until, in the Persian Gulf War in 1991, he unleashed barrages of Scud missiles at Israel. However, although he had chemical warheads at his disposal, he launched only the far less damaging conventional TNT ones in his attacks on Israel, so that the action would not be construed as an existential threat.[7] And indeed, because the missiles never endangered Israel's existence, Yitzhak Shamir, the prime minister at the time and an avowed hawk, nonetheless refrained from ordering the military to respond, in spite of warnings from other hawks in the political and defense establishments that total abstention from retaliation would undermine Israel's deterrence.

IF ISRAEL DECIDES to launch an operation aimed at destroying the Iranian nuclear program, the man in charge of the preparatory work will be the head of the Mossad, Major General Meir Dagan. Prime Minister Ariel Sharon assigned him the mission in November 2003. Until then, the responsibility for preventing the ayatollahs' regime in Teheran from making a bomb was divided among several governmental bodies and intelligence agencies, and was coordinated by the National Security Council, which was headed at the time of Dagan's appointment by Ephraim Halevy, his predecessor as director of the Mossad.

A military hero and political right-winger, Dagan is a natural leader, equipped with a cunning way of thinking. The best time to carry out operations is during periods of quiet, when the enemy isn't ready—this is the motto that he taught his subordinates, which they frequently quote. Several defense experts used the word "creative" to describe Dagan's ideas. Others called them "delusional." A current Mossad operative said that Dagan is one of the most resolute people he has ever come across. "Dagan is a quintessential operations contractor," reserves Major General Amram Mitzna has been quoted as saying. "Once given a mission he is simply unstoppable."

Dagan is a short man, whose stomach goes before him, certainly no James Bond, more reminiscent of a George Smiley, John Le Carre's anti-hero. Once his cellular phone was stolen from his car, and the media made a feast of it. "Search Under Way for Mossad Chief's Phone," screamed one front-page headline in a popular tabloid. The efforts of friends and admirers to create the image of a Bionic Man for Dagan never succeeded. Israel of the early 21st century has had its fill of heroic myths and its media takes delight in slaughtering sacred cows.

Dagan took over the Mossad when its morale was at one of its lowest ebbs, after a series of highly publicized failures. The worst blunder took place in Amman, Jordan, in 1997, when an attempt to assassinate the political chief of Hamas, Khaled Meshal, went wrong.[8] The head of the Mossad at the time, Danny Yatom, planned the operation and Prime Minister Netanyahu approved it. Eight years later, the Mossad had not yet recovered from the damage caused by the failure.

The Mossad also made errors gathering information on the weapons of mass destruction, especially in the three countries of the "outer circle": Iraq, Libya, and Iran, which have no common border with Israel but are close enough to threaten a fatal strike. The failure to identify Libya's nuclear program—which was uncovered in 2003—also had an embarrassing side. Not only did the Mossad not pick up the nuclear activity going on in Libya, but the spy agencies of the United States and Britain withheld information from it on the contacts those countries were maintaining with Gadhafi prior to his declaration that he was ready to abandon his nuclear aspirations. The chairman of the Knesset's Foreign Affairs and Defense Committee, Yuval Steinitz, called the Libyan fiasco "one of the gravest failures of Israeli intelligence."

Like the CIA, the Mossad invested a great deal of effort, money, and manpower in gathering information on the Iraqi arena, but in the end Israel didn't have the slightest idea whether Saddam Hussein's forces had a nonconventional capacity, and whether he planned to use them against Israel. Both the Mossad and military intelligence were severely rebuked by Steinitz's committee, because on the eve of the invasion of Iraq, they had greatly exaggerated Iraq's ability to attack Israel with missiles and weapons of mass destruction.

Under Dagan, the Mossad took on a different form and began focusing on two missions: the war on terror, and thwarting Iran's nuclear plans, which Dagan described as "the gravest existential threat to Israel since the founding of the state."

Before Dagan, the Mossad's function was to gather information of all kinds from all over the world, be it security-related, military, political, economic or industrial. Dagan narrowed the focus. Instead of trying to cover many targets, he decided, it would be better to deploy against Iran and against terror with all available resources. He stressed the operational side over research, and channeled most resources to special operations. Israel needed a force that could be activated anywhere on the globe, he said in a lecture to division heads of the Mossad. If an al-Qaida base were discovered in East Asia where terrorists were developing weapons of mass destruction, a dirty bomb, or chemical or biological materials that were meant to be used against Israel, the Mossad would have elite units, its own A teams, mobile and adequately equipped, whose task would be to eliminate it. If the prime minister approved a pinpoint operation against a nuclear installation in Iraq, Dagan said, the Mossad would have a unit trained to carry it out.

In order to prepare the organization for its new missions, since September 2003 the Mossad has almost completely ceased dealing with classical intelligence evaluation, and instead become a headquarters training field operatives for special missions. Some two hundred employees were retired, mostly desk jockeys who dealt with gathering and analyzing information. Some field stations abroad were closed, and others restaffed. Seven division heads were replaced. Intelligence-gathering units were made smaller, and operational units expanded. In 2004 the Mossad recruited three times as many agents as it had in previous years, and the pattern is reminiscent of the days of Isser Harel, who was licensed by Ben-Gurion to kidnap and kill, and Zvi Zamir, who was ordered by Golda Meir to hunt down and kill the terrorists who had murdered members of the Israeli team at the Munich Olympics in 1972.[9] The reorganization Dagan carried out in the Mossad was the most extensive since its founder, Isser Harel, was forced to resign following the affair of the German scientists.

Two appearances by Dagan before the Knesset Foreign Affairs and Defense Committee, at the end of 2003 (the first by a Mossad director in eighteen years) and early in 2005, made it clear that American and Israeli intelligence services saw eye to eye on the Iranian threat. In January 2005, he said that Iran was close to completing the construction of its centrifuge installation at Natanz, something that he defined as especially worrisome, and it was capable of producing enriched uranium in amounts that would enable it to make a bomb. Iran, he declared, was "close to the point of no return." At both of his briefings, Dagan told the committee that an Iranian bomb would be a threat not only to Israel, but to Europe too.

On the question of the means of delivery, Dagan said that Iran was developing surface-to-surface missiles with ranges of from 1,400 to 2,000 kilometers (870 to 1,240 miles), covering the whole of Israel and large parts of Europe, and had devoted resources to acquiring bombers that could carry nuclear bombs long distances. It was also assisting the fundamentalist terror groups Hezbollah, Hamas, and Islamic Jihad. It was supplying Hezbollah, the Lebanese Shiite organization, with short-range rockets. Knesset member Steinitz, chairman of the Foreign Affairs and Defense Committee and a political hawk, responded thus: "The moment that Iran becomes a nuclear power, a black curtain will come down over Israel, the Middle East, and the whole world."

Dagan did not give the committee details on the means used by the

Mossad to gather information in Iran and on operational plans. But IDF spokesmen have hinted more than once that Israel was planning a military operation. Israel's minister of defense, Shaul Mofaz, speaking in his mother tongue, Persian,[10] in a broadcast to Iran on Israel's state-run radio station, Kol Yisrael, said: "If there will be a need to destroy Iran's nuclear capability, the necessary steps will not harm Iranian civilians." The previous chief of staff, Lieutenant General Moshe Ya'alon, speaking on the same subject, said: "We do not only rely on others." His successor, Lieutenant General Dan Halutz, put it like this. "We'll rely on others until we have to rely on ourselves."

Israel's options for military action were varied, and different units of the air, naval, and land forces have trained to carry them out. A land operation, even when combined with air or naval transport, would be very complex and dangerous. An air attack would be far less risky. Iran's air defense system is not highly developed and it is doubtful that it could stop bombers from reaching the reactor under construction at Arak or the tunnels at Natanz housing the centrifuges. The distance from Israel to Bushehr, where in mid-2005, Russia completed construction of a 1,000-megawatt reactor, and to Esfahan, where the centrifuges are located, is some 930 miles. The Israeli Air Force has F-151 aircraft with a range of 2,765 miles, and F-16s, which with enlarged fuel tanks can fly 1,300 miles.[11] Also, the distance to the heavy-water reactor that is being constructed in Arak, in the Khondaub region, in central Iran, is within range of Israeli aircraft.

In order to destroy the tunnels at Natanz, special ordnance would be required, capable of penetrating deep into the earth, the kind that the U.S. used to bomb the caves at Tora Bora in Afghanistan. In September 2004, international and Israeli media quoted sources in the Pentagon and "security sources in Jerusalem" as saying that the United States was about to sell Israel five hundred BLU-109 guided bombs, so-called bunker busters that weigh a ton and can penetrate thirty feet of earth or concrete. In the U.S. Air Force they are guided either by laser beams or satellites.

According to sources in the Pentagon, the supply of these bombs to Israel was meant to maintain Israel's qualitative advantage and to advance American strategic and tactical interests. Reuters quoted sources in Jerusalem as saying: "This is not the sort of ordnance needed for the

Palestinian front. Bunker busters could serve Israel against Iran, or possibly Syria."

It is doubtful that Iran has the ability to respond directly to an Israeli attack. It is possible that Teheran would activate the Hezbollah, whose forces are deployed in South Lebanon with batteries of short-range missiles and Katyusha rockets, and which could severely disrupt life in northern Israel. Iran could also get Palestinian militia fighters to carry out terror attacks in Israel. From Israel's point of view, neither of these threats would be existential.

WHETHER THERE IS a military confrontation between Israel and Iran, or it is averted; whether the regime of the mullahs in Teheran remains in place, or more moderate Iranians supplant it; whether Iran gets its nuclear bomb, or is forced to give up its program in exchange for economic assistance—in the end Israel and the Muslim world will have to solve the disputes between them through negotiation.

When David Ben-Gurion first unveiled the reactor that he had built at Dimona in the emotional speech he made from the Knesset podium on December 21, 1960, he uttered only one sentence that referred to Israel's neighbors. He offered them "comprehensive and absolute disarmament in Israel and the neighboring Arab countries, with mutual supervision." At that time, the construction of the reactor had not been completed and the nuclear option was a distant dream. Nevertheless, the understanding that "absolute disarmament" was necessary was a fundamental principle of Israeli policy. This has not changed in forty-five years since, although it is possible that Iran's efforts to achieve nuclear capability will make the fulfillment of this principle more difficult than ever, tougher even than the hardest issues between Israel and the Palestinians.

Israel will come to negotiations on arms control and regional disarmament with a doctrine conceived by the late Shalhevet Freier. Freier was a wise and creative man who formulated his ideas clearly and sharply. He acquired experience in disarmament matters in the Pugwash organization, the prestigious club set up by renowned scientists and politicians in 1957, at the height of the Cold War, in order to reduce the danger of nuclear war.[12] In the 1970s and '80s, Freier served as a member of the Pugwash ruling council, where he was in touch with statesmen and diplomats from countries with which Israel had no relations at the time.[13]

The foundation of the disarmament doctrine conceived by Freier was composed of three principles:

1. Israel opposes the proliferation of nuclear weapons, as it has from the very beginning. Its own acquisition of nuclear capability was a defensive imperative that will fall away when peace is achieved.
2. Israel will give up its nuclear option only when it is proven beyond doubt that peace is an absolute and established fact and it is clear that it no longer needs the ultimate deterrent.
3. The nuclear demilitarization of the Middle East will be implemented through a regional pact established by negotiations between Israel and each of the states in the region, and not through joining the Non-Proliferation Treaty.

Egypt has demanded that Israel agree to disarmament becoming a stage in the peace process. First sign the NPT and give up the option of using nuclear weapons, the Egyptians said to Israel, and only then can regional peace be attained. Freier called this demand a booby trap. The states that signed the Non-Proliferation Treaty did so not out of purely moral motives but because it served their interests. Some states even went so far as to sign the treaty only in order to exploit it as a cover for developing a nuclear infrastructure, ostensibly for peaceful purposes, but which they intended to use for the development of weapons.

The experience that he accumulated during decades of representing Israel in international bodies led Freier to the conclusion that the country must not compete in that arena. In organizations like the International Atomic Energy Agency, the U.N.'s nuclear watchdog, Israel had no chance of success against the numerous votes of Muslim countries in Asia and Africa that customarily present an anti-Israel viewpoint in international organizations and together assemble an automatic majority against her. It was worthwhile participating in such organizations, Freier believed, but never expect in advance to accept their decisions.

The situation is different in the multilateral working group for re-

gional security that was set up in accordance with the peace treaty between Israel and Egypt, because its decisions are reached by consensus.
This, in Freier's opinion, was the only place where Israel should negotiate disarmament issues. Indeed, such negotiations must be carried out directly with each one of the confrontation countries, he wrote. Israel
should sign a regional disarmament pact only after it has studied the intentions of the Arab leadership in depth, in each state separately, and is
convinced that they really intend to maintain a lasting peace. The test
would be based on confidence-building steps taken over a prolonged period. There must be no shortcuts, he advised. They would only entail existential threats, whereas if the process were to be carried out stage by
stage, the risks would be cancelled out.[14]

The supervision of the disarmament process, Freier wrote, must be
conducted by a mutual apparatus set up by the states involved; Israel
should reject inspection by international bodies whose policies are determined by the balance of political considerations. The entire process
would be carried out over decades, and would consist of five stages:

Stage A: The signing of comprehensive and complete peace treaties
with each of the states of the region, including those without a common border with Israel: Iran, Iraq, and Libya. "As long as a country
is firmly committed to the destruction of Israel," Freier argued, "Israel can not ignore it." At this stage there is no discussion yet of
arms control or disarmament.

Stage B: As the peace is taking root, confidence-building measures
are decided upon and carried out over a period of time, and the intentions of the leaders of the region and their ability to carry out
their commitments are tested.

Stage C: A process of regional cooperation is instituted, with the
building of regional economic institutions and joint apparatuses for
the solution of environmental and water-shortage problems.

Stage D: When it is clear that mutual trust has been built, and the
sense of threat has been removed, negotiations on arms control and
disarmament begin. First, conventional arms control will be dis-

cussed, and only after that is over will nonconventional disarmament be discussed.

Stage E: An agreement on the establishment of a nuclear-weapons-free zone will be signed. It will be the last of the agreements on arms control.

The man who was responsible for physically importing the nuts and bolts of the nuclear option into Israel compiled this plan for getting rid of it. This was the humanist side of Shalhevet Freier's philosophy, and I believe that in this respect he represented his partners in the conception and implementation of Israel's nuclear vision. They never left a written doctrine, but it is possible that among the still-classified Ben-Gurion manuscripts, there are ideas and plans for the fate of the nuclear option in an era of peace that will yet be discovered.

Freier's disarmament plan was not composed as an exercise in theory. It was his values-driven answer to the moral dilemma that plagued someone who had been involved in the building of the bomb. One might wonder how it was that after Hiroshima and Nagasaki most of those involved in the creation of those bombs became stubborn fighters against the manufacture and proliferation of nuclear weapons, while in Israel, no strong opposition ever arose to the nuclear capability that Israel had developed. The answer lies in the fact that the creators of Israel's nuclear option had been exposed to the tragedy of the Holocaust and were aware of the urgent necessity to produce a means of immunizing the Jewish people against its ever happening again (and the same applies to the intellectuals in the Jewish world, including Israel, who never condemned Israel's nuclear program). But the basic assumption of the scientists, politicians, and managers behind the nuclear project was that when the menace had been stamped out, the immunization would no longer be necessary, and it could be discarded.

Shalhevet Freier and his colleagues were no less humanistic than Albert Einstein and Bertrand Russell, Leo Szilard and Glenn Seaborg, Robert Oppenheimer and Enrico Fermi, the men who launched and led the scientists' uprising against nuclear weapons. In November 1954, five months before he died, Einstein declared: "I made one great mistake in my life, when I signed that letter to President Roosevelt recommending that atom bombs be made, but there was some justification—the danger that the Germans would make them."

Freier might also have made one great mistake in his life when he helped Israel to obtain the nuclear option, but he too had a certain justification—the danger that Israel's neighbors would destroy the Jewish state.

NOTES

AUTHOR'S NOTE

1. HCJ 680/88; *Meir Schnitzer and Two Others v. the Chief Military Censor.*

INTRODUCTION

1. In 2004, Straw declared that Arab and Islamic states were threatening Israel's existence and denying its right to exist, and this "placed Israel in a different security category from any other country in the world." When a journalist asked Blair what the conditions were for making the Middle East a nuclear-free zone, the prime minister answered that Israel would have to be convinced that the countries surrounding it no longer wish it ill.

1. A DREADFUL JOURNEY

1. All quotations from Ben-Gurion in this chapter are from his diaries, unless otherwise stated.
2. Eisenhower's headquarters was located in the main office of the I. G. Farben concern, the manufacturers of Zyklon B gas used to kill millions of Jews in the death camps of Eastern Europe.
3. He apparently named himself after Yosef Ben-Gurion, who was described in the book *The Wars of the Jews* by the historian Flavius Josephus. At the time of the Jewish rebellion against the Romans, Yosef Ben-Gurion was leader of the Jewish government along with the high priest Hanan. He was a moderate leader who dealt with security matters but struggled against the Zealots. The Zealots grew in strength, assassinated Ben-Gurion, and took over the government. This ultimately led to the destruction of the Second Temple in 70 A.D. Josephus showers praise on Yosef Ben-Gurion, calling him "a man of many virtues . . . favoring the rule of the people, and full of the spirit of the love of freedom, more than all the other Jews."
4. At Sukkot, the Feast of Tabernacles, in the fall of 1906 in Jaffa, Ben-Gurion was elected to the central committee of Poalei Zion, the Workers of Zion party. That was his first official political post. A few weeks later, he was present when the party's platform committee met in an ancient Arab caravansary in Ramleh, on the main road from Jerusalem to Jaffa, and set a revolutionary goal for those times, the establishment of a "Hebrew state." Days later, the second party conference formulated the goal as follows:

"The party aspires to political independence for the Jewish people in this country."

The Workers of Zion party evolved in 1919 into Ahdut Ha'avodah (Labor Unity); in 1930 into Mapai (the Workers Party of Eretz Yisrael); in 1965, Ma'arakh (Alignment); and in 1968 into Mifleget Ha'avodah, the Labor Party of today.

5. Yehuda Leib Magnes (1877–1948) was an American Reform rabbi who early in the 20th century rebelled against the anti-Zionism of the Reform movement in the United States. He was one of the founders of the American Jewish Committee. A pacifist thinker, he opposed British imperialism and supported the Russian Revolution. In 1922 he moved to Palestine and preached Jewish-Arab understanding.

6. The Arab Revolt broke out spontaneously on April 15, 1936, when Arabs stopped a truck on a road in Samaria and shot the Jews who were traveling in it. Two were killed and one wounded. Two days later, members of the Haganah killed two Arabs. In Tel Aviv, angry Jews beat up Arabs. On April 19, an Arab mob rioted in the streets of Jaffa, murdering sixteen Jews. A few days later, the "Arab High Committee," led by al-Husayni, was set up and took responsibility for the conduct of the struggle. It demanded that the British government stop Jewish migration to Palestine and that the sale of land to Jews be banned. The Jewish leadership girded for defense, and Ben-Gurion ordered a policy of restraint so the Arabs would have to confront the British authorities. The Arab committee declared a general strike that lasted six months. Armed Arab gangs carried out terror attacks on the roads and at Jewish settlements. When the revolt affected key arteries and governmental installations, the British government ordered the army to use force to suppress it. In September, the army used heavy weapons, tanks, and planes against the rebels and by late October 1936, the first phase of the revolt lost its momentum and died out.

   The second phase began in September 1937, shortly after the Peel Commission recommended the partition of Palestine between Jews and Arabs. The Zionist leadership agreed to the partition plan, but the Palestinian leadership rejected it and encouraged Palestinian militias to resume the revolt. Although the British authorities in Jerusalem retaliated by banning the Arab High Committee, in London the government surrendered to the committee's demands. In the summer of 1939, the British government published a White Paper that limited Jewish immigration to Palestine and restricted the purchase of land by Jews, and the revolt ended. Now the Zionists responded with fury, but because of Hitler's attack on Poland on September 1, 1939, the subject of Jewish immigration and settlement in Palestine was rendered all but moot for the next six years.

7. Since the First Zionist Congress in 1897, these gatherings had been in the nature of a parliament of the Jewish people. The delegates convened usually once every two years in a European city. They were elected by Jewish communities across the globe, according to a regional-proportional system. The

right to vote was given to each Jew who registered and made a donation, known as "the Zionist shekel." The congresses elected the Zionist executive, which served as a kind of government of the Jews of the world.

8. *Haganah* means "defense" in Hebrew, and was used as the name for an underground military organization set up by the Zionist movement in Palestine to protect the Jewish community and carry out military operations against the British mandatory government and expedite its departure.

9. Japan would surrender in two months time, on September 2.

10. The Sonneborn Institute millionaires paid for the purchase of the ferryboat *Exodus*, which was used in 1947 to carry 4,500 refugees, who were survivors of the Holocaust, from southern France to Palestine. However, the British seized the ship at sea and sent the refugees back to Europe. The affair had a profound effect on world public opinion and the British were compelled to abstain from sending illegal immigrants back to Europe. Instead they were transported to detention camps in Cyprus.

2. THE A TEAM

1. The Institute was financed by Israel Sieff, one of the founders of the British retail chain Marks & Spencer. Sieff was a close friend of Weizmann and served as his secretary at the Conference of Versailles after World War I. Israel's younger son, Daniel, died tragically in 1933 at the age of eighteen. Daniel's brother was Lord Marcus Joseph Sieff, who died in 2001 at the age of eighty-seven.

2. The Negev is the southern part of the State of Israel, covering about 60 percent of the area of the country. Most of it is sparsely populated desert. The phosphate deposits that contain uranium are south of the city of Beersheba, in the Oron Valley and Wadi Zin. The phosphates are mined by the Negev Phosphates Chemicals Co. on the Plain of Rotem, near the Dimona reactor.

3. Natural uranium, U-238, contains 0.72 percent of U-235, the fissile isotope of uranium. Isotopes are forms of an element having different atomic weights, because of the number of neutrons in each nucleus. For example, in its natural, simple form, a hydrogen nucleus contains one proton and no neutrons, but there are also hydrogen nuclei that contain a neutron. This hydrogen isotope is known as deuterium.

4. Ephraim Katchalsky-Katzir was the first Israeli elected to the American Academy of Sciences. In the 1970s he served a term as president of the State of Israel. Aharon Katchalsky-Katzir was murdered in a terror attack at Ben-Gurion Airport outside Tel Aviv in May 1985, carried out by members of the Japanese Red Army terrorist organization who were collaborating with Palestinian terrorists.

5. The five scientists were chairman Bergmann; Israel Dostrovsky of the Weizmann Institute; Giulio (Yoel) Racah and Shaul K. Cohen of the Hebrew University; and Franz Ollendorf of the Technion.

6. De Shalit helped solve the mystery surrounding a message that Werner

Heisenberg, a leader of Germany's nuclear fission research during World War II, passed to his Danish counterpart Niels Bohr when they met in Copenhagen in 1941. The mystery occupied historians and physicists for over fifty years and was the subject of a drama, *Copenhagen*, by British playwright Michael Frayn. In the early 1960s, after a visit by Bohr to the Weizmann Institute, de Shalit said that Bohr had revealed Heisenberg's 1941 message: "You know that we are going to win this war and we will be building a new high-tech Europe, based on the discoveries in quantum physics and nuclear energy. Why don't you join us." In February 2002, the Bohr family published documents written by Niels and his wife about the meeting with Heisenberg; they proved that de Shalit's account was accurate.

7. PWR stands for Pressurized Water Reactor, the kind used in most of the nuclear power stations in the world. In contrast to the "swimming pool" type, in PWRs it is possible to irradiate 200-300 uranium rods simultaneously, and to extract plutonium from them.

3. A FRENCH WINDOW OPENS

1. Thomas was interviewed in Paris in 2001, at the age of ninety. It was the first time he had spoken for the record on the French-Israeli nuclear connection. In his book, *How Israel Was Saved: Secrets of the Suez War* (*Comment Israel fut sauvé: les secrets de l'expédition de Suez*, 1978), he details the establishment of the special security relationship between France and Israel, but avoids discussing nuclear cooperation.

2. SDECE, the French intelligence agency at the time, was formally known as the Service de la Documentation Extérieure et du Contre-Espionnage.

3. The battle of Verdun was the longest battle between France and Germany in World War I. It began in February 1916, and ended on December 18. There were a million casualties on both sides. The battle is famous for having ended without giving either side a tactical or strategic advantage.

4. AN UNPRECEDENTED DEAL

1. Neeman served as president of Tel Aviv University from 1971 to 1975.

2. Renowned physicist Frédéric Joliot-Curie, whose wife, Irène, was the daughter of Pierre and Marie Curie, and a Nobel laureate like her husband, was high commissioner of the French Atomic Energy Commission in the years 1945–51. An ardent communist, he was dismissed from his post in 1950 and replaced by Francis Perrin, who years later would approve of the nuclear deal with Israel. The sacking of Joliot-Curie did not dispel American suspicions that classified nuclear information would reach the Soviet Union through France.

3. Production of weapons-grade plutonium began in 1949, at the Le Bouchet experimental laboratory, and later at the nuclear reactors erected at Saclay, near Paris. Large-scale production of plutonium in France began in 1956,

when a reactor near Marcoule attained criticality. (A reactor goes critical by setting in motion the fission chain reaction in the fuel rods that are dumped inside the heavy water pool.) This was a 38-megawatt reactor with a production capacity of twelve kilograms of plutonium a year.

4. Qalqilya is in the northern part of the West Bank, in the Samaria region. In the 1950s the West Bank was controlled by Jordan. It was conquered by Israel in 1967. In 1995, as part of the second Oslo accord, Israel withdrew from parts of the West Bank, including the city of Qalqilya, and handed over civilian control to the Palestinian Authority.

5. In a tête-à-tête with Mollet, Ben-Gurion said he aimed to take control of all Sinai and to annex it to Israel, in order to exploit the oil, which he said was to be found there. At the meeting with the French delegation that opened the Sèvres conference, Ben-Gurion expounded upon his vision for a comprehensive settlement in the Middle East, based on the following principles: internationalization of the Suez Canal, disbanding the Kingdom of Jordan and dividing it between Iraq and Israel, British patronage over Iraq and the Arabian peninsula, and French patronage over Syria and Lebanon (where Christian rule would be assured). The French listened to the plan politely, and Dayan wrote in his diary that the plan "might be seen as fantastic, even naive." Ben-Gurion would occasionally let himself get carried away with his visionary ideas when meeting with world leaders.

6. The First Kingdom of Israel existed from approximately 1000 until 586 BCE; the Second from 536 BCE until 70 CE, the year in which the Second Temple and Jerusalem were destroyed by the Romans, and Israel became a Roman province. When the modern state of Israel was established, marginal messianic groups advocated the establishment of the Third Kingdom of Israel. Ben-Gurion had never identified with messianic ideas, and always took pains to stress his secular world outlook. Biographers of Ben-Gurion surmise that it was the tension that had built up before the British and the French invasion, as well as the flu that had afflicted him during the first days in November, that caused his bizarre messianic outbreak.

7. The reasons and circumstances for using the expression "Third Kingdom" at the victory address to IDF troops at Sharm el-Sheikh are not mentioned in any of Ben-Gurion's published writings and memoirs, or in Dayan's diary.

5. FIRST NUCLEAR ACCIDENT

1. November 9, 1938, the night of anti-Jewish riots and burning of four hundred synagogues in Nazi Germany and Austria. Ninety-one Jews were killed, hundreds injured, and an estimated 20,000 were sent to concentration camps. It is also referred to as Crystal Night, Night of Broken Glass, or Pogromnacht.

2. Heading the organization that absorbed young immigrants in agricultural educational institutions in Palestine was Henrietta Szold, who was born in

Baltimore and is famous for founding the American Zionist women's organization Hadassah. Most of the literature on the migration of Jews to the Land of Israel erroneously ascribes the founding of Aliyat Hanoar to Szold.

3. Ernest Bevin, the British foreign minister in the government that the Labour Party formed after the 1945 elections, set a strict policy against immigration of Jewish refugees from Europe to Palestine. Convinced that Britain should maintain its strategic position in the Middle East, Bevin wanted to cooperate with the region's Arab regimes. Ben-Gurion called his policy "Bevin's ugly war against the Jews" and in October 1945 directed a united uprising of Jewish underground organizations in Palestine against the British administration. Bevin blamed the United States for the situation. He said that President Truman's insistence on Jewish immigration to Palestine was dictated by domestic American politics. The United States wanted displaced Jews to emigrate to Palestine, said Bevin, "because they did not want too many of them in New York." George Lenczowski, in his book *American Presidents and the Middle East*, wrote that Truman considered Bevin's speech undiplomatic and "almost hostile."

4. Before 1951, the functions of the Mossad were performed by the Foreign Ministry's "Political Department."

5. In recognition of his contributions to Israel's war effort, Ratner was given the defense establishment's highest award, the Israel Security Prize, in 1959.

6. Avner Cohen, in *Israel and the Bomb*, writes that Sadeh told him that at this meeting Ratner told Sadeh he had been chosen as a candidate for Israel's most secret enterprise—the nuclear project. Cohen reports that Sadeh did not remember if Ratner had used the words "nuclear bomb" or "nuclear device" but that Sadeh was sure Ratner had used one of these phrases. A person who spoke with Sadeh very soon after the 1994 meeting says Ratner had spoken in detail about the project.

7. Mapam was the second-largest party in the Knesset in the early years of the state. It aligned itself with the Labor Party in the years 1969–84. Today it is part of the left-wing Meretz-Yahad.

8. Polonium-210 is a highly toxic and radioactive material and must be handled with great care. A milligram of plutonium-210 emits as much alpha radiation as about 5 grams of radium.

9. A critical reactor is one that operates at constant power, emits thermal energy, and produces a chain reaction.

10. Pierre Péan's *Les deux bombes* was published in 1981.

11. This is the structure of Dimona according to Mordechai Vanunu's disclosures and Pierre Péan's investigation. Over the years more institutes have been built, and today there are nine. There is no Institute 7.

12. Jonathan Pollard, the American Jewish naval intelligence analyst who was sentenced to life imprisonment for spying for Israel, was controlled by LEKEM.

13. Within ten years, the body designated for defense research and development underwent three metamorphoses: HEMED, the IDF's Scientific

Corps, 1949–52; EMET, the Defense Ministry's Division for Research and Planning, 1952–58; and RAFAEL, the Authority for Weapons Development, in 1958 and since.

14. Soustelle wrote a book about the history of Zionism, *The Long March of Israel from Theodor Herzl to the Present Day* (1969).

6. A NUCLEAR COMPLEX GROWS IN THE DESERT

1. Harel was interviewed in the summer of 2002, a few months before his death. It was the first interview he ever gave about the nuclear project.

2. In the 1959 elections, Ben-Gurion's Mapai party won 47 seats (out of 120 in the Knesset). Another 5 were won by Arab parties affiliated with Mapai. Despite this, negotiations for a coalition government were drawn out. One reason was internal struggles in Mapai.

3. "For five years I was commander of the air force, and for three of them they tried to get rid of me," Tolkowsky said in a 1997 interview.

4. Mapai (or the Labor Party) led the pre-state Jewish community and the State of Israel from the mid-1930s until May 1977, when the center-right won a general election for the first time and Menachem Begin formed the government.

5. In 1962, a dollar equaled three Israeli liras and 250 million liras were worth $83 million.

6. In 1960, with a dollar worth 1.8 lira, $80 million was worth 144 million lira.

7. Senator Robert Taft of Ohio was the son of President William Howard Taft and was considered the most outspoken critic of Roosevelt's New Deal policies. In the years during which his influence over the Republican Party was strong, 1939–53, he was known in the media as "Mr. Republican."

8. Robert Hannegan, of Irish descent, was a close adviser to President Truman, and served as national chairman of the Democratic party, and postmaster general in the first Truman administration. He died of a heart disease in 1949, age forty-six.

9. Moshe Sassoon later served as senior deputy to the director general of the Foreign Ministry and as Israel's second ambassador to Egypt.

10. Feinberg owned the Coca-Cola franchise in Israel and the Jerusalem Hilton Hotel. In the 1970s, when his bank, American Bank & Trust Company, had been suspected of mismanagement and two of its officers were convicted of fraud, the Israeli Bank Leumi purchased it to save it from collapse.

11. The United Jewish Appeal was founded in the U.S. in 1939, in response to the November 1938 Kristallnacht pogrom in Nazi Germany. It combined the fundraising efforts of the United Palestine Appeal and the Joint Distribution Committee. The UJA provides financial support for Jews throughout the world. After World War II it helped hundreds of thousands of displaced Jews resettle in Israel, the States, and elsewhere.

12. According to publications of the International Atomic Energy agency, eight kilos of plutonium are needed to build one bomb, but it seems that the

agency published an exaggerated amount intentionally, in order to deter those with impure intentions. In 1994 the U.S. Department of Energy reduced that estimate to four kilograms. To build one "very small" one-kiloton nuclear bomb, the equivalent of a thousand tons of TNT and which causes substantial damage over a one-kilometer radius, one kilogram of plutonium is enough, but advanced technology is needed.

13. One bomb, called "Little Boy," was made using uranium 235, and dropped on Hiroshima. Of the two bombs made of plutonium, one was used in the July 1945 trial at the Trinity site in New Mexico, and the other "Fat Boy" was dropped on Nagasaki. The "Little Boy" employed the cannon method, in which conventional explosives push one mass of uranium into another. The resulting critical mass was bombarded with neutrons. In "Fat Boy" the implosion method was used, discussed later in this chapter.

14. Julius and Ethel Rosenberg, an American Jewish couple, were arrested in 1950 and convicted of passing the formula for the critical mass in a plutonium bomb to the Soviet Union. They were executed for espionage in 1953.

15. Reactors moderated by heavy water, used for the production of plutonium from natural uranium, have been built in India, Pakistan, Israel, and North Korea.

16. According to former Dimona technician Mordechai Vanunu, Israel has developed the ability to process and enrich uranium in a facility erected for this purpose in Dimona.

17. The Norsk Hydro plant was built in 1934 in Rjukan, in Norway's Telemark region. Immediately after the German conquest it was handed over to the scientists charged by Hitler with building an atomic bomb. The plant became famous from the Hollywood film, *The Heroes of Telemark* (1965), starring Kirk Douglas, which depicted the real-life attempt by the Norwegian underground to sabotage it in November 1943.

18. In the acquisition agreement, the Indian government vowed that it would use the heavy water only for peaceful purposes, but no machinery for inspection was set. This is paragraph 9 of the agreement, the only one that deals with the use that India would make of the heavy water: "The heavy water sold hereunder shall be for use only in India by its Government in connection with research and use of atomic energy for peaceful purposes, and shall be retained by the Government, or by other parties authorized by the Government, and not resold or otherwise distributed."

7. DIMONA IS UNCOVERED

1. In 1954, security personnel in the U.S. Embassy in Tel Aviv had discovered a microphone concealed in the ambassador's office. In 1956, listening devices were found in two telephones in the private residence of the American military attaché.

2. Polonium, known also as radium F, is a radioactive material found in small quantities in uranium ore.

3. In the post–World War II period, when only two countries possessed atomic bombs, the nuclear weapons proliferation question was referred to as the "third country" problem. After Britain made its bomb, it became the "fourth country" problem, and since France joined the nuclear weapons club in 1960, the "nth country" problem.

4. In his book, *I Found Israel's Atom Bomb Factory*, Kittredge claimed that together with a colleague from the American Embassy in Tel Aviv he was the first to identify the reactor in Dimona.

5. Israeli radar picked up a U-2 incursion on March 10, 1959. Two Super Mysteres scrambled to intercept the spy plane, but could not climb to 70,000 feet.

6. Ukrainian-born Kistiakowsky had studied in Berlin and was on the faculty of Harvard University. In the Manhattan Project, he was on the team that created the first atom bomb that was tested in New Mexico on July 16, 1945. Colleagues said that after the test the impulsive Kistiakowsky hugged project leader Robert Oppenheimer and yelled out in triumph. In 1976, his diary of the eighteen-month period during which he advised the White House was published. The passages involving nuclear matters, including the Israeli project, were excluded.

7. In the late 1950s, Canada supplied India with a research reactor and enriched uranium, and trained Indian scientists and technicians. The two countries agreed that the reactor would be used for peaceful purposes only. India upgraded it and used it to produce plutonium.

8. DE GAULLE THROWS A MONKEY WRENCH IN THE WORKS

1. A paratroop unit was organized in Corsica to fly to Paris on May 24, 1958, and seize control of the centers of government. The operation was code-named Resurrection.

2. On April 11, 1958, a few days before the end of his term as the last prime minister of the Fourth Republic, Félix Gaillard signed the orders to carry out an atomic bomb test. Two months later, on June 17, de Gaulle convened the Defense Council of France and it was decided that the test would be held early in 1959.

3. De Gaulle tried to have the clauses of the NATO charter amended, so that the United States would no longer be in command of the alliance. When he failed, he declared in a speech at the French military college (École Militaire) on November 3, 1959, that he would establish an independent strategic force: "what we must achieve during the coming years is a force capable of acting exclusively on our behalf, a force which for the sake of convenience we shall call 'force de frappé,' which can deployed anywhere at any time. It goes without saying that the basis for this force will be atomic armament—whether we manufacture it or buy it—but it will belong to us."

4. The shortage of weapons-grade plutonium lasted until 1966, when the

French Defense Ministry appropriated plutonium from civilian projects for its own use. The problem was solved in the 1970s, when reactors for the production of plutonium for military use went into operation at Marcoule.

5. According to Abel Thomas, Couve de Murville initiated the embargo "because he was an anti-Semite" but other Frenchmen who knew the minister cast doubt on this.

6. In early 1962, when the OAS openly rebelled, liberal circles in France claimed that the Mossad had trained a secret unit of Jews that carried out acts of terror against Muslims in Oran and supported the extremist nationalists struggling against the granting of independence to Algeria, among them General Raoul Salan and Jean Suisini. The Israeli Embassy in Paris denied the allegations, which appeared in *Le Figaro*, January 5–6 and January 10, 1962.

7. The group scattered poison in prison camps where the Allies were holding suspected members of the SS, but to no substantial effect.

9. THE DECEPTION THAT WORKED

1. Each one of the sides formulated the replies differently, but the essential matters are presented similarly in both formulations.

2. In the 1950s, the United States' economy was already dependent on oil from the Middle East. In 1955, 58 percent of the United States' oil came from the Middle East, compared to 16 percent in 1944.

3. Senator John F. Kennedy, quoted in *Near East Report*, March 17, 1958.

4. In October 1957, Eisenhower's secretary of state John Foster Dulles told the Israeli ambassador in Washington, Abba Eban, "Our great problem . . . was that we were tagged as supporters of Israel and Zionism, while the Soviet Union claimed to be against them. This was a liability for us to carry in the Arab world. The way to escape it was to make the Arabs see that the Soviet Union was a greater danger than Israel."

5. Israeli scholar Abraham Ben-Zvi has analzyed the turning point in the attitude of the United States toward Israel that came in the middle of 1958. See his *Decade of Transition: Eisenhower, Kennedy, and the Origins of the American-Israeli Alliance* (1998).

6. Israel needed antiaircraft missiles for protection against the MiG warplanes that the Soviet Union was supplying to Egypt. Its first request to buy U.S.-made Hawk missiles was rejected by President Eisenhower at the beginning of 1960. During John Kennedy's visit to Israel in May 1960, six months before he was elected president, the senator was asked to act to supply Israel with the missiles. In August 1962, following heavy Israeli pressure, Kennedy approved the sale of the Hawks and sent Mike Feldman to Jerusalem to bring the message to Ben-Gurion.

7. A generation later, in the 1990s, Ben-Gurion's grandson Alon Ben-Gurion was the manager of the Waldorf-Astoria.

8. Cyrus L. Sulzberger, the *New York Times* columnist, reported that Ben-

Gurion had also told him of his astonishment at Kennedy's words, saying "Why should he say such a thing to a foreigner?"

10. A MOSSAD CONSPIRACY

1. The elections for the 5th Knesset were held on August 15, 1961. Ben-Gurion's Mapai party lost some 12 percent of its strength and it dropped from 47 seats to 42 in the 120-member house. Mapai's satellite Arab parties dropped one seat.

2. The Inshas reactor runs on 10-percent-enriched uranium fuel. At Inshas a number of other research facilities are located: a small French-supplied "hot cell" complex for plutonium extraction research; a pilot nuclear fuel factory, completed in 1987, used to process natural uranium mined in Egypt; and the Middle East's first industrial electronic accelerator.

3. In 1945, von Braun had organized the surrender of his missile factory to the Americans, and was taken prisoner with some five hundred scientists and technicians who worked there. He was taken to the United States, recruited into the military, and worked for fifteen years developing missiles and rockets. In 1960 he moved to NASA, became director of the Marshall Space Flight Center in Alabama, and worked at developing the Saturn V booster rockets, which were used to send astronauts to the moon. He died of cancer in 1977 in Alexandria, Virginia.

4. The Federal Republic of Germany and Israel established diplomatic relations in 1965. Before that Israel's interests were represented by a mission known as the commercial delegation, located in Cologne, near Bonn, then the capital city.

5. This hotel, known as the oldest in Europe, is a historical landmark in the annals of Zionism. In August 1897, when the First Zionist Congress convened in Basel, Theodor Herzl, the man who first envisioned a Jewish state, was photographed posing on the balcony of his room in the hotel, leaning on the railing and gazing at the Rhine River. This photograph has become identified with the Zionist vision, and in one of the hotel's rooms a museum commemorating the event has been established.

6. Ben-Gurion did not know that the United States and Britain had provided practical support for the Iraqi revolution, and that the CIA had given the rebels intelligence and arms. At that time, strategic coordination and intelligence cooperation between the United States and Israel were minimal. It was just after the revolution that Saddam Hussein was elected leader of the Ba'ath party.

7. It was at this meeting that Amit persuaded Gehlen to provide backing for the claim that an Israel spy who had been apprehended in Egypt, Wolfgang Lotz, was a German citizen, thereby saving him from the hangman's noose. Lotz had been sent to Egypt by military intelligence when Amit headed it. He was the source of the complete list of German scientists working in Egypt, and later he supplied the information that disproved Otto Joklik's

story. Egypt's security services discovered Lotz in the winter of 1965. Under interrogation, Lotz confessed to spying for Israel, but to improve his chances of avoiding execution he adamantly insisted he was a German citizen, although in fact he was an Israeli. Gehlen agreed to help Israel and to tell the Egyptians that Lotz was really a German, and in the end the court sentenced him to life imprisonment. He served three years and in a 1968 prisoner exchange was released and returned to Israel. Gehlen had a Nazi past, and had served as espionage chief on the eastern front during World War II. Straight after the war he was recruited by the CIA, where he served before becoming head of West Germany's intelligence service.

11. THE HEIR

1. At that time, the intention was to return 80,000–150,000 refugees to Israeli territory. This number was based on the Johnson plan documents and on reports by Feldman on his talks with the Israeli government in the summer of 1962.

2. Israeli crews were sent to the United States to train in the operation of Hawk missiles early in 1963. The Israeli Air Force took delivery of the first battery of Hawks in March 1965. On March 21, 1969, a battery operated by the IAF in the Sinai shot down a MiG 21, the world's first kill ever by the Hawk system. Since then, the Hawks sold to Israel have downed thirty-six warplanes and helicopters.

3. Meir told the president that if Israel would take in even "a very small number of Arabs," its existence would be in danger, because the Arab states were planning to "bring Arabs back and to make an Algeria out of Israel." This uncompromising position of Israel's practically wiped out the Johnson plan, and Kennedy dropped it. Prior to this, Syria had said the plan was unacceptable for the opposite reasons, and Egypt and Jordan had also voiced objections to it. In late January 1963, Secretary of State Rusk officially notified Ben-Gurion that the plan "cannot be implemented" and that the administration had no intention of trying "to push it further on the relevant parties."

4. Under the British Mandate (1919-1948), the high commissioner was the supreme governmental authority in Palestine, deriving his power directly from the monarch.

5. Ben-Gurion said that the Hebrew people preceded Abraham. He also said that only a small fraction of the Hebrew people—around 600 individuals—were in exile in Egypt and that the Bible unfairly belittles the great achievements of Ancient Egypt. *Ben-Gurion Looks at the Bible*, David Ben-Gurion; Jonathan David Publishers, New York 1972.

6. The Greater Israel movement was set up after the 1967 war. Among the founders were intellectuals and writers, including Nobel literature laureate Shmuel Yosef Agnon, Haim Hazaz, and Yehuda Burla, by whose writings many Israelis had been educated, as well as political and military figures who until then had been known for their moderation; some were members of

kibbutzim, and some were close to Ben-Gurion's party. The group bestowed legitimacy on the messianic settlement movement on the West Bank.

7. Leibowitz's condemnation of the continued occupation of the West Bank attracted a great deal of public and media attention. On one television broadcast, he caused an uproar by calling the soldiers serving in the conquered territories "Judeo-Nazis." He encouraged soldiers to refuse to serve in the territories as conscientious objectors. The decision to award him the Israel Security Prize—the country's highest honor—in 1992 engendered a stormy dispute, and in the end he waived the prize. His positions had considerable influence on young Israelis, which only swelled after his death in 1994.

8. The U.S. Navy's operational unit in the Mediterranean Sea, which comprised some forty vessels, including an aircraft carrier and 175 warplanes, as well as a battalion of Marines equipped with amphibious vehicles.

9. On July 23, 1963, Robert Komer, a senior official of the National Security Council, wrote in a memo to President Kennedy that the State Department considered that granting a public guarantee to Israel was not an appropriate solution, because it would "undermine our even-handed Middle East policy, thus reducing our leverage on the Arabs to reduce Arab-Israeli tension." At the same time it would give Israel "a blank check to be obstreperous in its Arab policy, confident that our guarantee would protect it from any adverse consequences of its actions."

12. CLEANING THE STABLES

1. The gates of the United States were gradually closed to migrants from Eastern Europe after Congress enacted the Emergency Quota Act in March 1921, which set immigration limits according to country of origin. In 1924 the National Origins Act was passed, setting an annual ceiling of 150,000 immigrants. Only 30 percent of them could be from Eastern or Southern Europe. These laws were in force in the 1930s and most of the '40s.

2. Descriptions of the Johnson family's history and religious faith are based on documents and tapes in the Lyndon B. Johnson Presidential Library, Austin, Texas.

3. "Behold the days are coming, saith the Lord, that I will raise to David a branch of righteousness; a King shall reign and prosper, and execute judgment and righteousness in the earth. In his days Judah will be saved, and Israel will dwell safely; now this is his name by which he will be called: the Lord our righteousness." (Jeremiah 23:5,6)

4. America's Bible Belt traditionally refers to the Protestant South, where born-again Christianity flourishes and Scripture is revered by many as the ultimate authority for daily life and faith.

5. Alice Glass was the mistress of Charles Marsh, and then his wife. Biographers of Johnson, among them Robert Caro, have said that in the late 1930s and early '40s, she had a romantic relationship with Johnson too. Glass was married five times, and died in December 1976.

6. Some sections of the story of Johnson's involvement in "Operation Texas" are based on research by James M. Smallwood, professor of history at Oklahoma State University.

7. According to a document issued by the French Dassault Aviation Group in September 1962, Israel learned that the group was developing a medium-range missile for the French army, the MD-600. Based on the characteristics of the MD-600, Dassault developed for Israel the first version of the Jericho missile. The blueprints that were prepared at Dassault for the archetype of the Jericho 1 show a two-stage all-weather ballistic missile, designed to carry a 750-kilogram warhead and to be launched from permanent launching pads to a distance of up to 500 kilometers, with a target-precision range of 1 kilometer. The agreement for the manufacture of the missile was signed in Tel Aviv in April 1963 (almost one year before Eshkol met Johnson in Washington). Dassault sources revealed that after 1965, Israel assembled the missile in a local plant. Israel has never admitted the existence of the Jericho missiles, but U.S. intelligence sources published assessments that Israel independently developed the second generation of the Jericho missile, the long-range Jericho 2. According to the American assessments and other foreign publications, the Jericho 2 has a range of 1,500 kilometers and carries a 1,000-kilogram payload.

8. At a summit conference in Cairo in January 1964 that was intended to respond to Israel's plan to divert water from the Jordan River for irrigation in the Negev desert, leaders of the Arab states decided to form a Unified Arab Command and to establish the Palestine Liberation Organization. At a second summit, in Alexandria in September, the Arab leaders declared the goal of eliminating Israel. The second summit actually unified the armies of Egypt, Syria, and the Hashemite Kingdom of Jordan.

9. The nickname was bestowed upon him by Henry Cabot Lodge Jr., the American ambassador in South Vietnam, who said that "arguing with Komer was like having a flamethrower aimed at the seat of one's pants."

10. Sharett died five months later, at the age of seventy-one. His relations with Ben-Gurion were never repaired.

11. Ever since 1908, and indeed to this very day, the Zionist movement has claimed that when the first Zionists came to redeem the Promised Land, it was empty of inhabitants. Ruppin was one of the few who dared to say as early as the 1920s that the land was populated by Palestinians. This position led him to the conclusion that a binational state should be established in the Land of Israel. In 1925 he was among the founders of Brit Shalom, and he headed it until 1929, but after the Arab riots started that same year, Ruppin changed his mind and began advocating a single Jewish state.

12. In the beginning of the '60s, RAFAEL developed and tested the prototype of the sea-to-sea missile "Luz," which later was known as the "Gabriel" missile. All testing results were disappointing. At that time Israel Aircraft Industries (IAI) suffered from a dramatic reduction in orders that threatened its very existence. Following the Egyptian missile launching in July 1962,

production of the sea-to-sea missiles was transferred from RAFAEL to IAI. In mid-1965, as part of a reorganization, Eshkol and Dinstein moved RAFAEL's missile R&D units to the IAI.

13. "WE HAVE THE OPTION"

1. One important goal was not achieved: No. 2, "Populating the Negev and developing it." As for No. 9, "Striving for a stable peace with our Arab neighbors," there was much striving, but peace was elusive.

2. The years of the great expansion were 1957–65. In 1966, economic activity slowed down, mostly as a result of a government policy restricting the flow of resources. After the Six-Day War, the economy began growing again.

3. The area of the State of Israel within the borders of the United Nations Partition Plan of 1947 was some 6,200 square miles. The area within the armistice agreement of 1949 (the "Green Line") was 8,000 square miles. To-day, with East Jerusalem and the Golan Heights, which Israel annexed after the Six-Day War, but not including the West Bank and the Gaza Strip, the area is 8,550 square miles, or slightly larger than New Jersey.

4. Television had not yet managed to penetrate the obstacles that Ben-Gurion placed in its way. He claimed that the medium was shallow and the country didn't need it. Television broadcasts began in 1967, first on an experimental basis.

5. In Chapter 4 we mentioned the Soviet Union's responsible policy during the Suez war. It is also worth noting its responsible conduct on the issue of nuclear proliferation. The policies on this matter adopted by France, and to a lesser degree, West Germany, were a lot less responsible than those of the Soviet Union.

6. According to Michael Oren's study, the main cause of the confrontation in 1967 was Arab opposition to Israel's efforts to divert the waters of the Jordan River in its territory in order to irrigate the Negev. The escalation began when Syria planned to block most of Israel's water sources. In his analysis, the National Water Carrier, from the Sea of Galilee to the Negev, worried the Egyptians far more than the Dimona reactor, because they feared that it would make it possible to settle millions of Jews in the desert, on Israel's border with Egypt. This never happened. The Negev is as empty today too, despite the fact that in the 1950s and '60s Ben-Gurion had made populating it an important national priority.

7. Israel placed its first order for the Dassault-made, mach-2 Mirage III fight-ers in 1959. Prime Minister Ben-Gurion's authority was at its peak and the France-Israel love affair was still blooming. Between April 1962 and July 1964, the IAF deployed 76 Mirage III fighters in three squadrons. The "Shahak" (heavens), as the Mirage was called in Israel, was the first IAF fighter equipped with air-to-air missiles.

8. Only after the war did it become known how bad the condition of the Egyptian army was on the eve of hostilities. Much of the armor and artillery

was out of commission, the reinforcements rushed back to Egypt from the Yemen arena were not battle-ready, and the battle orders were confused. Many units were never told what their roles in the war were supposed to be.

9. In his autobiography, *The Story of My Life*, Moshe Dayan, whom public opinion had forced Eshkol to make defense minister on the eve of the war, wrote that he decided not to consult Ben-Gurion on the conduct of the war. "He was living in a world that had passed away," Dayan wrote. "He admires de Gaulle, exaggerates Nasser's strength, and does not know how to appreciate fully the power latent in the IDF."

10. A situation assessment of the U.S. National Security Council dated September 1, 1966, reads: "Israel retains qualitative superiority over any of the various combinations of Arab states with which it could be expected to come into direct conflict."

11. McNamara was interviewed for the Lyndon B. Johnson Library's Oral History Collection in 1993.

12. The first five were the United States, the Soviet Union, Great Britain, China, and France.

13. Before the Six-Day War, RAFAEL supplied thirty Shafrir 2 missiles to the Israeli Air Force. Not one of them downed an enemy plane. On June 6, a Shafrir 2 hit a Tupolev 16 (Soviet-made) heavy bomber of the Iraqi air force that had entered Israeli airspace, but the plane was also struck by antiaircraft fire, and the hit was not credited to the missile. On June 15, after the fighting was over, a Shafrir downed a MiG-21 flying south of the Suez Canal. After the war, the missile was improved and since 1969, the IAF has used it to shoot down some two hundred enemy aircraft. The Argentinean air force was equipped with Shafrirs, but in the Falklands war it never managed to use it to down any Royal Air Force planes.

14. A SECRET COMPROMISE

1. In the 1960s, Bloch was asked to assist Israel's nuclear program by solving theoretical questions connected to his research into the magnetism of the atom. In 1952 he won the Nobel Prize in physics (together with Edward Purcell) for his discoveries in the measurement of nuclear magnetic resonance, on which MRI medical instruments are based.

2. Teller would later recount: "Einstein took the letter from Szilard, signed it and said: 'This is the first time we would get energy directly from the atomic nucleus rather than from the sun, which got it from the atomic nucleus.' He handed the letter back to Szilard. The rest is known to everybody. I had played my essential role as Szilard's chauffeur."

3. In the early 1950s, at Columbia University, Gershon Goldhaber worked on the development of the basic particle accelerator, the cyclotron, and in Berkeley in the 1960s he worked on the Bevatron, the world's most powerful accelerator at that time.

4. In April 1954, Teller, testifying at hearings conducted by the Atomic Energy

Commission on the security clearance of Robert J. Oppenheimer, said, ". . . I feel I would prefer to see the vital interests of this country in hands that I understand better and therefore trust more." In the wake of this testimony Oppenheimer lost his clearance as an adviser to the AEC. In 1962, Teller received the Enrico Fermi Award from the U.S. government for his contribution to nuclear physics. A year later Oppenheimer received the award, and at the presentation ceremony the two men shook hands in an apparent reconciliation, but Oppenheimer never recovered from the damage caused by Teller's testimony and never forgave him.

5. One of Teller's ideas, which he discussed with Neeman and Sadeh, was to use nuclear blasts to dig a canal between the Mediterranean and the Dead Sea, and to exploit the difference in elevations to produce electricity. This proposal was an example of Teller's thinking, as expressed in his Operation Plowshares initiative in the 1950s, in which he advocated the use of nuclear explosions to carry out large engineering projects, such as constructing deep-water harbors, or diverting the course of rivers, or crushing ores deep below the surface of the earth. In the United States and the Soviet Union, experiments were carried out in these applications, but they did not yield practicable results. Teller was actually preceded in these ideas by the father of the Indian nuclear program, Homi Jehangir Bhabha, who had also proposed using atomic explosions for the excavation of canals. Ben-Gurion was enthusiastic about such ideas and would frequently refer to them.

6. There is no certainty that Rabin's interpretation is correct. On several occasions Clifford contended that Truman had decided to recognize the independence of the State of Israel out of conviction and humanitarian considerations, and not for domestic political advantage. In his autobiography, *Counsel to the President*, Clifford wrote that he had recommended recognition of Israel because of Jewish-American commitment to liberal political and economic policies.

7. President Johnson described the attack on the *Liberty* as a critical moment in his life. The first message received from the ship identified the attacking planes as Soviet, and the president faced a fateful dilemma: whether to order his forces to attack Soviet ships in the Mediterranean. But before he reached a decision, the White House was told the planes were Israeli.

8. A similar opinion was expressed by other administration figures, among them Secretary of State Rusk and the chairman of the Joint Chiefs of Staff, Thomas H. Moorer.

9. In the last year of Kennedy's presidency, American aid to Israel totaled $40 million. In 1965, Johnson's second year in the White House, this figure rose by some 80 percent, reaching $71 million. The following year there was yet another increase of 80 percent, and aid totaled $130 million. In that year, military aid was greater than the total military aid between 1948 and 1965. Kennedy had approved the supply of only defensive weapons; five batteries of Hawk antiaircraft missiles. Johnson approved the supply of offensive weapons; tanks, Skyhawk and Phantom aircraft, and artillery.

15. THE SADAT-KISSINGER AXIS

1. In the 1973 war, the author of this book served as a military correspondent for the public radio station Kol Israel ("The Voice of Israel"), and from October 7 was attached to the forward command post of the division commanded by Adan.

2. Three days later, on October 12, Dayan once again offered his resignation to Meir, and she once again refused to accept it. At that time, the first allegations were being aired within the political establishment to the effect that it was Dayan who was responsible for the failures that occurred at the beginning of the war.

3. After the 1973 war, Katzir made at least one more statement about the nuclear option. On December 2, 1974, he said, "It has always been our intention to develop a nuclear potential . . . We now have that potential." See Steve Weissman and Herbert Krosney, *The Islamic Bomb*, p. 105.

4. In the 1973 war, Israel lost 2,688 soldiers, about three and a half times as many as in the 1967 war. The number of fallen was the equivalent to the United States losing 240,000 soldiers. The accepted figure for fatal casualties in the Arab armies in 1973 is 19,000. American intelligence estimated that in the 1967 war 61,000 Arab soldiers were killed.

5. On October 7, for example, the Israeli Air Force attacked twenty missile batteries on the Golan Heights, and only one was knocked out. Nine Israeli Phantom aircraft were shot down during these attacks. In retrospect, it transpired that the tactics employed had been erroneous. The plans called for assaults by large formations, some 100 planes at a time, on targets selected on the basis of aerial photography. Planning an assault of this strength took ten to twelve hours after the photographs were developed, and this gave the Syrians time to move the missile batteries to new positions, which had been prepared in advance. It took a few days for the IAF command to learn the lessons and change the tactics. Foursomes of planes were sent in to attack the batteries just after the aerial photos were taken. In order to reduce their vulnerability, the batteries at the edges of the missile deployment were attacked first, and only afterward the batteries at the center. As of October 10, this new tactic began gradually swinging the war in Israel's favor. The Israeli Air Force lost 102 planes in the war; 44 airmen were killed and 53 taken prisoner.

6. In mid-September, Sadat expelled thousands of Soviet advisers from Egypt, in order to cut the Gordian knot of ties with the Soviet Union and draw nearer to the American sphere of influence. But the Nixon administration responded to his initiative unenthusiastically and did not take up the challenges involved.

7. In the early 1970s, it was accepted in Israel that Egypt would not go to war until the latter had the ability to establish aerial superiority, and that Syria would not go to war on its own. Despite the fact that Sadat began preparing for the war at the start of 1973, Israeli intelligence estimated that there

would be no war before 1975. In September 1973, military intelligence (AMAN) had gathered information indicating the explicit intention of Egypt and Syria to go to war. Late in September, King Hussein of Jordan initiated a secret meeting, held in a Mossad facility near Tel Aviv, with Prime Minister Meir, at which he warned her that the Syrians were entering an offensive deployment. Nevertheless, AMAN ruled out any possibility that war would break out. On October 4, AMAN discovered that the families of Soviet advisers in Egypt were being evacuated, and the head of the Mossad was warned by a senior agent in Egypt that a coordinated surprise attack was about to take place. On October 5, AMAN was still insisting that there was a "low probability" of war breaking out. American intelligence was also remiss, as State Department intelligence chief Ray Cline explained in an internal memo: "Our difficulty was partly that we were brainwashed by the Israelis, who brainwashed themselves."

8. This version is from the transcript of Kissinger's conversation with Meir. In his book *Crisis*, Kissinger refrains from including this exchange and claims that the conversation with Meir was about establishing the cease-fire.

9. The Defense Condition scale runs from 5 to 1, with 5 being a normal state of readiness and 1 meaning maximum readiness.

10. For example, in the most widely circulated paper in the country, *Yediot Aharonot*, on September 24, 2004.

11. At their meeting in Washington right after the war, Meir claimed that Kissinger had prevented Israel from achieving the surrender of the Third Army. He replied: "You gave me good military reports but you didn't tell me what you intended. I had no reason to think twelve more hours, twenty-four more hours, were decisive. We made a ceasefire agreement, with direct negotiation, which was always your position . . . Then you took on the Third Army after the ceasefire . . . Had I known about it, I would have done different things in Moscow, like delaying submission of the resolution." Kissinger's statements from the protocol of the meeting with Meir in Washington contradict the transcript of their phone conversation. He is therefore attacking Meir without justification.

12. An earlier version of the play, titled *Golda*, was staged on Broadway in 1977. Anne Bancroft played the title role. In that version, Dimona and the bomb were never mentioned.

13. Evidently, research shows, Meir meant the fourth day of the war, October 9, following the failure of Adan's armored division counterattack.

16. TWO SCENARIOS: WAR (WITH IRAN) OR PEACE

1. In terms of the Jewish population of Israel, the increase was 25 percent.

2. The committee issued its report in the summer of 1980, stating that it was possible that the flash "was of natural origin possibly resulting from the coincidence of two or more natural phenomena." Moreover, the report said that the signal picked up by the satellite "was probably not from a nu-

clear explosion. Although we cannot rule out that this signal was of nuclear origin."

3. See Hersh, *The Samson Option*, pp. 271–72. By this time, the United States already estimated that Israel had achieved nuclear capability, but there was no certainty as to the level of development that had been reached. Only after the demise of South Africa's apartheid regime, in 1993, did the then prime minister F. W. de Klerk announce that South Africa had produced a nuclear bomb. The democratic regime dismantled the bomb and did away with the nuclear program.

4. Ofek 5 and Eros 1, whose photographic ability at night and in bad weather is limited. In mid-2004, the launch of Ofek 6 failed, but plans exist for Ofek 7.

5. Israel has had military links with the heads of the Kurdish autonomous region in northern Iraq since the 1960s. In 2004, reports were published in the United States that Israel was training Kurdish commando forces, and running agents in Kurdish areas in Syria and Iran. The Israeli Embassy in Washington denied the reports. There are some 4 million Kurds in Iran, 9 percent of the population, most of them concentrated in the Zagros mountains, near Iran's western border with Iraq and Turkey.

6. Iran learned from Pakistan's success and so provided for two parallel systems for the manufacture of fissile material. One is for the extraction of plutonium by means of a heavy-water reactor, and the other for the enrichment of uranium by centrifuges. Both systems give them the option of making nuclear bombs, and the purpose of the duality is to ensure that if there are hitches in one, the process will not be held up.

7. Iraq launched thirty-nine missiles at Israel during the war. Half of them caused some damage. Most of them were aimed at central Tel Aviv, where the military headquarters and the Defense Ministry are located, but they missed their target. On the thirty-second day of the Persian Gulf War, a Saturday, two Scuds fell in the desert in southern Israel. They had apparently been aimed at the Dimona reactor. The media brouhaha over the Scud attacks was tremendous, and the panic they sowed in Israel was not inconsiderable, although they caused few casualties: two killed and a few dozen wounded.

8. On September 25, 1997, Mossad agents injected poison into the back of Meshal's neck while he was walking down a main street in Amman. Meshal was taken to a hospital, and King Hussein of Jordan threatened to break off ties with Israel. Prime Minister Benjamin Netanyahu was forced to have the antidote to the poison supplied to the hospital where Meshal lay dying, as well as to free the founder of Hamas, Sheikh Ahmed Yassin, from an Israeli prison. Meshal was saved, and he was expelled from Jordan and relocated to Damascus. In 2004, Israel assassinated Yassin by means of a rocket fired from a helicopter gunship. It may well have been Dagan who recommended the elimination of Meshal, since at the time he was serving as Netanyahu's counterterrorism adviser.

9. Prime Minister Meir gave the order immediately after the eleven athletes and officials of the Israeli team were killed. Agents searched for them for years, and several died of unnatural causes. In one case, in Lillehammer, Norway, Mossad agents killed a Moroccan waiter whom they incorrectly identified as a terrorist.

10. Mofaz was born in Iran and came to Israel with his family at the age of nine. He was the second top-echelon Israeli to speak to the Iranians in their own language. Mofaz was preceded by the president, Moshe Katzav. The current chief of the General Staff, Dan Halutz, is also of Iranian origin.

11. In October 1985, the Israeli Air Force attacked the headquarters of the Palestine Liberation Organization in Tunis, 1,600 miles from Israel. It was an act of retaliation for the murder of three Israelis on a yacht in Cyprus. The aircraft were refueled in the air over the Mediterranean.

12. The Pugwash organization played a behind-the-scenes role in the preparation of the international conventions and agreements on armament limitations, among them the Partial Test Ban Treaty of 1963, which Israel joined, the Non-Proliferation Treaty of 1968, which Israel has not ratified, as well as pacts that limit the development of biological and chemical weapons.

13. During its break in relations with Israel, the Soviet Union chose to deal with Freier for contacts with the Israeli government. In 1970, Freier had established a connection with the head of the KGB, General Yevgeni Primakov, a connection that gradually strengthened over the next fifteen years. The two reached an understanding on how the Soviet Union would vote in the council of the IAEA when Israel's nuclear plans were discussed. In the aftermath of the October 1973 war, Freier conveyed information to Egypt through the Soviets.

14. The peace treaty between Israel and Jordan says the sides are interested in establishing a Middle East that is free of weapons of mass destruction, both conventional and nonconventional, within the context of a comprehensive, lasting, stable peace, characterized by readiness to dispense with the use of force, by conciliation, and by goodwill.

BIBLIOGRAPHY

BOOKS, ARTICLES, AND INTERVIEWS

Acheson, Dean. *Present at the Creation: My Years in the State Department.* New York: Norton, 1969.

Barnaby, Frank. *The Invisible Bomb: The Nuclear Arms Race in the Middle East.* London: I. B. Tauris, 1989.

Bar-Zohar, Michael. *Ben-Gurion: A Political Biography.* 3 vols. Tel Aviv: Am Oved, 1977 (in Hebrew).

Bass, Warren. *Support Any Friend: Kennedy's Middle East and the Making of the U.S.-Israel Alliance.* Oxford: Oxford University Press, 2003.

Ben-Zvi, Abraham. *Decade of Transition: Eisenhower, Kennedy, and the Origins of the American-Israeli Alliance.* New York: Columbia University Press, 1998.

———. *John F. Kennedy and the Politics of Arms Sales to Israel.* London: Frank Cass & Co., 2002.

Black, Ian. *Israel's Secret Wars: A History of Israel's Intelligence Services.* New York: Grove Press, 1991.

Blumberg, Stanley A., and Louis G. Panos. *Edward Teller: Giant in the Golden Age of Physics.* New York: Scribner, 1990.

Bregman, Ahron. *A History of Israel.* London: Palgrave Macmillan, 2002.

Bundy, McGeorge. *Danger and Survival: Choices About the Bomb in the First Fifty Years.* New York: Random House, 1988.

Burrows, William E., and Robert Windrem. *Critical Mass: The Dangerous Race for Superweapons in a Fragmenting World.* New York: Simon & Schuster, 1994

Campbell, Kurt M., Robert J. Einhorn, and Mitchell B. Reiss. *The Nuclear Tipping Point: Why States Reconsider Their Nuclear Choices.* Washington, D.C.: Brookings Institution Press, 2004

Caro, Robert. *The Years of Lyndon Johnson.* Vol. 1, *The Path to Power.* New York: Knopf, 1982.

Clifford, Clark. *Counsel to the President: A Memoir.* New York: Random House, 1991.

Cockburn, Andrew, & Leslie Cockburn. *Dangerous Liaison: The Inside Story of the U.S.-Israeli Covert Relationship.* New York: HarperCollins, 1991.

Cohen, Avner. *Israel and the Bomb.* New York: Columbia University Press, 1998.

Cohen, Yoel. *The Whistleblower of Dimona: Israel, Vanunu, and the Bomb.* New York: Holmes & Meier, 2003.

Collins, Larry, and Dominique Lapierre. *O Jerusalem!* New York: Simon & Schuster, 1988.

Dallek, Robert. *An Unfinished Life: John F. Kennedy, 1917–1963*. New York: Random House, 2003.

Dayan, Moshe. *The Story of My Life*. Jerusalem: Edanim & Dvir, 1976 (in Hebrew).

De Gaulle, Charles. *Memoirs of Hope: Renewal and Endeavor*. Translated by Terence Kilmartin. New York: Simon & Schuster, 1971.

Eban, Abba. *Personal Witness: Israel Through My Eyes*. New York: Putnam, 1992.

Eldar, Mike. *The People in the Shadow*. Tel Aviv: Israeli Ministry of Defense, 1997 (in Hebrew).

Evron, Joseph. *A Rainy Day*. Tel Aviv: Ot-Paz, 1968 (in Hebrew).

Evron, Yair. *Israel's Nuclear Dilemma*. Ithaca, N.Y.: Cornell University Press, 1994.

Feldman, Shai. *Israeli Nuclear Deterrence: A Strategy for the 1980s*. New York: Columbia University Press, 1982.

Forland, Astrid. "Norway's Nuclear Odyssey: From Optimistic Proponent to Nonproliferator." *Nonproliferation Review* 4 (Winter 1997): 1–16.

Frankel, Max. *High Noon in the Cold War: Kennedy, Khrushchev, and the Cuban Missile Crisis*. New York: Ballantine, 2004.

Freedman, Lawrence. *Evolution of Nuclear Strategy*. New York: St. Martin's Press, 1983.

Freier, Shalhevet. "A Nuclear-Weapon-Free Zone in the Middle East and Effective Verification." *Disarmament: A Periodic Review by the United Nations* 16,3 (1993): 66–91.

Gardner Feldman, Lily. *The Special Relationship Between West Germany and Israel*. Boston: Allen & Unwin, 1984.

Golan, Mati. *Peres*. Tel Aviv: Shoken, 1982 (in Hebrew).

Goldschmidt, Bertrand. *The Atomic Adventure: Its Political and Technical Aspects*. New York: Pergamon, 1964.

———. *Atomic Rivals: A Candid Memoir of Rivalries Among the Allies over the Bomb*. Translated by Georges M. Temmer. New Brunswick, N.J.: Rutgers University Press, 1990.

———. "The Supplies of Norwegian Heavy Water to France and the Early Development of Atomic Energy." *IFS Info*. (Norwegian Institute for Defense Studies, Oslo) 4 (1995): 24–26.

Goldstein, Yossi. *Levi Eshkol: Biography*. Jerusalem: Keter, 2004 (in Hebrew).

Heikal [Haikal], Muhammad Hasanayn. *Autumn of Fury: The Assassination of Sadat*. New York: Random House, 1983.

Hersh, Seymour. *The Samson Option: Israel's Nuclear Arsenal and American Foreign Policy*. New York: Random House, 1991.

Kerr, Malcolm H. *The Arab Cold War: Gamal A'bd al-Nasir and His Rivals, 1958–70*. Oxford: Oxford University Press, 1971.

Kimche, Jon, and David Kimche. *The Secret Roads: The "Illegal" Migration of a People, 1938–1948*. London: Secker & Warburg, 1954.

Kissinger, Henry A. *Crisis: The Anatomy of Two Major Foreign Policy Crises*. New York: Simon & Schuster, 2003.

————. *Nuclear Weapons and Foreign Policy.* New York: Harper & Bros., 1957.

Kittredge, George W. *I Found Israel's Atom Bomb Factory.* Rockport, Maine: Schooner Bay Printing, 2000.

Lenczowski, George. *American Presidents and the Middle East.* Durham, N.C.: Duke University Press, 1990.

Mardor, Munya M. *Rafael.* Tel Aviv: Israel Ministry of Defense, 1981 (in Hebrew).

————. *Strictly Illegal.* London: R. Hale, 1964.

McKinzie, Richard D. Interview with Abraham Feinberg, August 23, 1973. Truman Presidential Library, Independence, Missouri.

Meir, Golda. *My Life.* New York: Putnam, 1975.

Meron, Dan, ed. *Shalhevet Freier's Work and Political Doctrine.* Remembrance booklet. Tel Aviv: Israel Atomic Energy Commission, 1995 (in Hebrew).

Milhollin, Gary. "Heavy Water Cheaters." *Foreign Policy* 69 (Winter 1987–1988): 100–19.

————. "Who Controls the Israeli Bomb?" *Arbeiderbladet* (Oslo), January 21, 1987 (in Norwegian).

Nakdimon, Shelomoh. *First Strike: The Exclusive Story of How Israel Foiled Iraq's Attempt to Get the Bomb.* New York: Summit Books, 1987.

Oren, Michael B. *Six Days of War: June 1967 and the Making of the Modern Middle East.* Oxford: Oxford University Press, 2002.

Péan, Pierre. *Les deux bombes.* Paris: Fayard, 1981.

Peres, Shimon. *Battling for Peace: Memoirs.* Edited by David Landau. London: Weidenfeld & Nicolson, 1995.

Pick, Pinhas. "The Hagana Military Network in Jerusalem, 1946–1948." In *Jerusalem in 1948.* Jerusalem: Yad Ben-Zvi, 1984 (in Hebrew).

Rabin, Yitzhak. *The Rabin Memoirs.* Boston: Little, Brown, 1979.

Rabinovitch, Itamar. *The Brink of Peace: The Israeli-Syrian Negotiations.* Princeton, N.J.: Princeton University Press, 1999.

Randers, Gunnar. *Atomkraften: Verdens hap eller undergang. [Atomic Energy: The World's Hope or Its Demise?]* Oslo: J. W. Cappelens forlag, 1947 (in Norwegian).

Reinharz, Jehuda. *Chaim Weizmann: The Making of a Zionist Leader.* Oxford: Oxford University Press, 1985.

Rose, Norman. *Chaim Weizmann: A Biography.* New York: Viking, 1986.

Roth, Philip. *The Plot Against America.* New York: Houghton Mifflin, 2004.

Sachar, Howard M. *The History of the Jews in America.* New York: Knopf, 1992.

Sadeh, Dror. *Nucleus of Truth.* Tel Aviv: Privately published, 2003 (in Hebrew).

Sereni, Ada. *Ships with No Flag.* Tel Aviv: An Oved, 1973 (in Hebrew).

Shalom, Zaki. *Between Dimona and Washington: The Development of Israel's Nuclear Option, 1960–1968.* Beersheba: Ben-Gurion Research Institute, Ben-Gurion University Press, 2004 (in Hebrew).

Shlaim, Avi. *The Iron Wall: Israel and the Arab World.* London: Norton, 2001.

Slater, Leonard. *The Pledge.* New York: Simon & Schuster, 1970.

Steinberg, Gerald M. "Parameters of Stable Deterrence in a Proliferated Middle

East: Lessons from the 1991 Gulf War." *Nonproliferation Review* 7, 3 (Fall–Winter 2000): 43–60.

Stewart, Steven. *The Spymasters of Israel.* New York: Ballantine, 1982

Teveth, Shabtai. *Ben Gurion: The Burning Ground, 1886–1948.* London: Hale, 1988.

Thomas, Abel. *Comment Israel fut sauvé: Les secrets de l'expédition de Suez.* Paris: Albin Michel, 1978.

Weisgal, Meyer. . . . *So Far: An Autobiography.* New York: Random House, 1971.

Weissman, Steve, and Herbert Krosney. *The Islamic Bomb: The Nuclear Threat to Israel and the Middle East.* New York: Times Books, 1981.

Weitz, Yechiam. "Ben-Gurions Weg zum 'Anderen Deutschland' [Ben-Gurion's Path to 'the Other Germany'] 1952–1963." *Vierteljahrshefte für Zeitgeschichte* 48, 2 (April 2000): 255–80.

Weizmann, Vera, and David Tutaev. *The Impossible Takes Longer: The Memoirs of Vera Weizmann.* New York: Harper & Row, 1967.

Woodward, Bob. *Plan of Attack.* New York: Simon & Schuster, 2004.

Yaniv, Avner. *Deterrence Without the Bomb: The Politics of Israeli Strategy.* Lexington, Mass.: Lexington Books, 1987.

Zameret, Zvi, and Hana Yablonka, eds. *The Second Decade, 1958–1968.* Jerusalem: Yad Ben-Zvi, 2000 (in Hebrew).

ONLINE RESOURCES

Federation of American Scientists. "[Israeli] Nuclear Weapons." http//www.fas. org/nuke/guide/israel/nuke.

Ford, Peter Scott. "Israel's Attack on Osiraq: A Model for Future Preventive Strikes?" Thesis, Naval Postgraduate School, Monterey, Calif., 2004.; http: // www.fas.org/man/eprint/ford.pdf.

Joint Congressional Inquiry into Intelligence Community Activities Before and After the Terrorist Attacks of September 11, 2001. http://www.gpoaccess. gov/serialset/creports/911.html.

Norris, Robert S. et al. "Israeli Nuclear Forces, 2002." *Bulletin of Atomic Scientists* 58 (September–October 2002). http://www.thebulletin.org/article_nn.php? art_ofn=s002norris.

Nuclear Threat Initiative. "Country Overviews: Israel." http://www.nti.org/e_ research/e1_israel_1.html.

Nuclear Weapon Archive. "Israel's Nuclear Weapons Program." http://nuclear weaponarchive.org/Israel/Index.html.

"Photos Reveal Israeli Nuclear Capacity." *Middle East Intelligence Bulletin*, Sept. 5, 2000. http://www.meib.org.articles/0009_me3.htm.

Smallwood, James M. "Operation Texas: Lyndon B. Johnson's Attempt to Save Jews from the German Nazi Holocaust." http://www.texancultures.utsa.edu/ hiddenhistory/Pages1/SmallwoodLBJ.htm.

Wisconsin Project on Nuclear Arms Control. "Israel's Nuclear Weapon Capability: An Overview." *The Risk Report*, 2, 4 (July–August 1996). http://www.wisconsinproject.org/countries/israel/nuke.html.

ARCHIVES

Archives Nationales Françaises, Paris, France
Ben-Gurion Diaries and Personal Papers, Ben-Gurion Herritage Institute and Research Center, Sdeh Boker, Israel.
Dwight D. Eisenhower Presidential Library, Abilene, Ks., U.S.A.
Haganah Archive, Tel Aviv, Israel
Israel Defense Forces Archive, Tel Aviv, Israel
Israel Intelligence Archive, Herzliya, Israel
Israel State Archive, Jerusalem, Israel
John F. Kennedy Library, Boston, Mass., USA
Levi Eshkol Papers, Eshkol Center, Jerusalem, Israel
Lyndon B. Johnson Library, Austin, Texas, U.S.A.
Moshe Sharett Israel Labor Party Archives, Beit Berl College, Israel
National Archives, Washington, D.C., U.S.A.
National Archives (Riksarkivet), Oslo, Norway
National Security Files, Washington, D.C. U.S.A.
Public Records Office, London, United Kingdom
Weizmann Institute of Science Archives, Rehovot, Israel

NEWS

Al-Ahram (Cairo)
BBC News
CNN News
Daily Express (London)
Der Spiegel (Hamburg)
Ha'aretz (Tel Aviv)
Israeli Air Force Journal
Jane's Defence Industry
Jane's Defence Weekly
Jerusalem Report
Le Figaro (Paris)
Le Monde (Paris)
Los Angeles Times
Near East Report
New York Times
Sunday Times (London)
Washington Post

INDEX

Abbas, Mahmoud, 339
Abramov, Zalman, 230
Adan, Avraham "Bren," 325
Adenauer, Konrad, 206
Agranat, Shimon, 324
Algeria:
    and Egypt, 60–61, 64–66, 74–75, 93
    and France, 58, 60–61, 65–66, 72,
        75–76, 87, 91, 104, 168, 169–70,
        172–73, 184
    nuclear tests in, 154, 198
Algerian National Liberation Front
    (FLN), 60–61, 65, 66, 169
al-Qaida, 340, 346
Alvarez, Luis, 343
Amer, Abd al-Hakim, 279, 282
Amit, Meir, 202, 209, 210, 212–13, 224,
    326–28
Anderson, Robert B., 158–59
Arab League, establishment of, 21
Arab Revolt (1936), 18, 20
Arabs:
    attacks feared by Jews, 10, 16–17, 25,
        26, 34, 36, 39, 55, 58, 62–65,
        202–5, 208, 211, 214–15, 254,
        271–72, 293–95, 346, 359
    as avowed enemy of Israel, 19–20,
        187, 189, 200, 211, 228, 252–53
    conflicts with Jews, 19–20, 26,
        82–90, 94–95; see also specific wars
    equilibrium with, 337–42
    France and Israel against, 58, 62,
        69–73, 77, 82–90, 91, 184
    Hitler supported by, 21
    "Islamic bomb" development, 46,
        231, 274, 353–56
    in Palestine, 15, 16, 19, 20, 216, 219,
        275

political alliances of, 37, 63, 183,
    211, 256, 272, 275, 329
Soviet support of, 91, 93–94, 126,
    151, 182, 247, 293–94, 298–99,
    329
and space race, 200–207
and U.S., 94, 180, 186, 194, 216,
    219, 238, 253, 295–96, 299,
    329–31
Arafat, Yasser, 339
Assad, Hafez al-, 275
Atlee, Clement, 84
Atomic Energy Act (1954), 52
Atomic Energy Commission, France
    (CEA), 79, 81, 106, 109, 115,
    165, 168
Atomic Energy Commission, Israel:
    and Dimona, 120, 122, 146, 150,
        166, 175, 187–88
    and EMET, 43, 47, 50
    founding of, 112
    and nuclear accident, 103–4
    nuclear studies, 78, 100–101, 103
    and RAFAEL, 114, 266
    reorganization of, 263, 266
    and Sadah's studies, 100, 176–77
Atomic Energy Commission, U.S., 53,
    78, 141, 147, 152, 155–56, 190,
    192
Auschwitz death camp, 143

Badeau, John S., 214, 222
Baghdad Pact (1955), 183
Balfour Declaration (1917), 15, 18,
    21–22
Barak, Ehud, 3
Barbour, Walworth, 220, 221–23, 224,
    232, 233, 273, 294

Barlev, Haim, 125, 285, 325
Bar-Zohar, Michael, 14, 51, 64, 192, 194, 211, 225
Begin, Menachem, 121, 211, 338, 349, 350
Ben Bella, Ahmed, 60, 86
Ben-Gal, Joseph, 207, 208
Ben-Gurion, David:
  anxieties of, 20, 55–56, 64, 72–73, 86, 87, 94, 119, 211–12, 323
  and Arab-Jewish conflicts, 16, 19–20, 22, 63–64, 77, 83, 84–86, 88, 89–90
  birth and background of, 13, 14–15
  and Britain, 23–24, 84, 227
  as defense minister, 42, 51, 53, 57, 236
  and Egyptian missiles, 204–6, 208–10
  and elections, 119, 199, 261
  and French connection, 11, 59, 68–69, 72, 78, 81, 95, 173–74
  and fund-raising, 135–37
  and Germany, 8–10, 206, 208–11
  and the Holocaust, 7–8, 15–16, 28, 29, 111
  influence of, 277–78, 281
  isolation of, 209, 210–12, 225–26, 259–60
  and Lavon Affair, 50–51, 119, 225–26, 227, 258–59, 261
  leadership traits of, 16, 19, 126, 211, 225–26, 227, 234, 259–60, 269, 278
  leave taken by, 49, 259
  and media stories, 157, 163, 231
  military preparedness sought by, 20, 25, 26, 37, 51, 229
  name of, 14
  and nuclear option, see nuclear capability
  and opposition, 199, 209, 215, 259–60, 266–67, 278
  personal traits of, 14–15, 19, 22–23, 211–12, 226, 234, 252

  as prime minister, 10, 24, 30, 56, 57, 103, 227, 269
  and RAFAEL, 113–14, 240–41
  and Rafi party, 260–61, 278, 281
  and refugees, 11, 217
  resignation of, 223–28
  and rockets, 196–99, 229
  and security, 117–18, 120–21, 229, 234
  and Six-Day War, 277–78
  speeches by, 27–28, 149, 161–62, 166, 200, 241, 250, 276, 355
  and U.S. as ally, 23–24, 183–87
  and U.S. hegemony, 178–79, 220–22, 224–25, 232
  U.S. visits by, 10, 25–27, 163–64, 187, 190, 192–95, 201, 302
  weapons sought by, 57, 58, 60, 62, 66, 229
  and Zionism, 13–14, 15, 17, 23, 25, 27, 184
Ben-Gurion, Paula Monbaz, 25, 30, 51, 223
Ben-Gurion, Yosef, 361n3
Ben-Gurionists, 31, 263
Ben-Natan, Arthur, 99
Bergen-Belsen concentration camp, 7–8, 28
Bergmann, Ernst, 107
  and AEC, 42–43, 190, 234–35, 263
  and Ben-Gurion, 32, 34, 35, 37–38, 45, 95, 176, 240–41, 262, 263
  birth and background of, 31–32, 33
  and Dimona, 111, 112, 114, 148, 149, 155, 159, 166, 175, 190–91, 235, 236
  and EMET, 42–43, 47, 101–2
  and IDF, 35, 38
  and nuclear capability, 32, 34, 37–38, 45–46, 50, 53–55, 78–79, 100–101, 108, 114, 141–45, 152–53, 155, 157, 159, 166, 231, 234–35, 263
  personal traits of, 45, 176
  and RAFAEL, 125, 126, 175, 176, 199, 204, 240, 263

reputation as scientist, 33, 46, 47, 263

and research institute, 32–35, 39, 42, 45–50, 52, 78, 101–2, 103, 108, 240

resignation of, 263

and Weizmann, 32–35, 240, 263

Berlin, Sir Isaiah, 22

Bevin, Ernest, 99

Bidault, Georges, 12

Billotte, Pierre, 64, 65

Blair, Tony, 1

Bloomfield, Louis and Bernard, 136

Bohr, Niels, 143, 288, 364n6

Bonen, Zeev, 199–200

Bourgès-Maunoury, Maurice, 57, 58, 61–62, 65, 66, 67–71, 77–78, 79, 84, 86, 89, 90–91

Brandeis, Louis D., 25

Braun, Wernher von, 203

Brezhnev, Leonid I., 332–34

Britain:
    and Arab world, 83, 183
    and arms embargo, 36, 68
    and Balfour Declaration, 15, 18, 21–22
    and "Black Sabbath," 133–34
    blockades by, 11, 40, 132, 280
    breakup of Empire, 15, 26
    conflicting promises of, 17–18, 20–22, 23, 84
    intelligence activity in, 150–52, 155, 217, 351
    Jews in armed services of, 20–21, 30, 36, 101, 111, 227
    and Middle East conflicts, 77, 82–85, 87–89
    and nuclear power, 38, 80, 145, 152, 161, 344
    Palestine as mandate of, 10–11, 17–18, 20–23, 132–34
    refugee quotas set by, 11–12, 21, 132–33, 280
    and Suez Canal, 71, 82–85, 87–89, 92, 95
    and Sykes-Picot treaty, 18
    and U.S. relations, 218, 255
    and Zionism, 20–22, 23–24, 25, 184

Brit Shalom, 16–17, 230, 288

Bronfman, Samuel, 136

Buber, Martin, 16, 230

Buchenwald concentration camp, 12, 58

Bulganin, Nikolay, 88

Bundy, McGeorge, 186, 191, 210

Bush, George W., 3, 331, 339, 349

Camp David (1978), 296, 335, 338

Camus, Albert, 12, 59

Canada, 80, 136, 161

Carter, Jimmy, 296, 335, 338, 342

Chamberlain, Neville, 278

China, 94, 181, 315, 342, 344

Churchill, Winston, 20–21, 84

Chuvakhin, Sergei, 282

CIA (Central Intelligence Agency), U.S., 151–56, 164–66, 209–10, 269, 287, 292–93, 296, 303, 317, 329

Clausewitz, Carl von, 330

Clifford, Clark, 299–301, 305, 308, 309, 312, 313

Clinton, Bill, 3, 194, 331, 349

Cold War:
    arms race in, 253–54, 273–74, 294, 296, 299
    balance of power in, 151, 181, 182–83, 197, 253–54, 272, 281–82
    and Cuban missile crisis, 219–20, 233, 272, 281
    détente in, 315
    nuclear threat in, 116, 220, 234, 273, 290, 302, 334, 355
    space race in, 197–98, 200–207, 292
    U.S. focus in, 37, 86, 93, 233–34, 299, 315

Committee for Nuclear Demilitarization of the Middle East, 229–31

concentration camps, 7–8, 12, 28, 58, 62–63, 132, 143, 247, 284

Couve de Murville, Maurice, 171, 173–74
Croach, Jesse, 190–91
Cuban missile crisis, 219–20, 233, 272, 281
Czechoslovakia, 39, 61, 63, 70

Dachau concentration camp, 8, 28, 247
Dagan, Meir, 350–51, 352, 353
Dassault Industries, 273, 296
Dayan, Moshe:
    and Arab-Jewish conflicts, 63, 64, 72, 77–79, 83, 84–85, 87, 88–89
    and Ben-Gurion's resignation, 224
    early years of, 44
    and French weaponry, 57, 62, 67, 69, 70, 72
    and Israeli intelligence, 75
    and nuclear capability, 79, 80, 90, 91, 126, 234, 284
    and political conflict, 119, 120, 260–61, 281
    and Six-Day War, 278, 281, 284
    and U.S. relations, 234, 236, 237, 238
    and Yom Kippur War, 323–28
D-Day (June 1944), 12, 58, 62
Debré, Michel, 168
de Gaulle, Charles, 125
    and Algeria, 65, 168, 169–70, 172–73, 184
    and Free French forces, 11, 12, 58
    and nuclear capability, 168, 170–74, 176
    political strategy of, 169–71, 172, 184, 296
    as president, 91, 168–71
Dimona nuclear project:
    acceptance of, 228–29, 248, 316–19
    administration of, 114–15, 175
    capacity of, 109, 214
    construction of, 91, 108–12, 118, 129, 146, 147–48, 155, 162, 169, 174, 191, 221, 222, 269
    cost of, 115, 126–29, 135–37, 160, 186
    defense of, 216, 276–77
    design of, 109–10, 140
    as deterrent in the basement, 221–22, 229, 235–39, 250–52, 269, 318, 332, 341
    evolution of, 80–81, 268–70
    and foreign intelligence probes, 117–18, 150–61, 164–66, 276, 342
    French experts in, 113, 115, 118, 229
    heavy water for, 141–45, 152, 161
    inspection of, 159, 174, 178–79, 181, 185–95, 201, 220–22, 224–25, 228, 232–35, 237, 239–40, 273, 283, 296, 317–18, 342
    and nuclear option, 225, 228, 235–39, 277, 286–89, 303, 342
    opposition to, 122–27, 128, 129, 173, 177, 229–31
    planning of, 114–15, 118
    and plutonium production, 171, 174, 269, 277
    political control of, 263–67
    public awareness of, 122, 146–50, 161–62, 164, 166, 180, 200, 201–2, 219, 274, 276, 316, 355
    secrecy of, 95, 100, 110–11, 113, 114, 117–18, 120–22, 128, 162, 166, 175, 176, 189, 240, 303, 317, 342, 345
    and Six-Day War, 276–79, 282–83
    as "textile factory," 27, 105, 157
    U.S. substitute for, 222, 235–39, 248
    Vanunu's leaks about, 109, 110, 140, 166, 188, 269, 344–45
Dinstein, Zvi, 232, 239, 250, 259, 261–62, 264, 265, 294
Dobrynin, Anatoly, 253–54, 333
Dostrovsky, Israel, 37–38, 45, 53, 79, 140, 174, 175, 266
Duckett, Carl, 293, 296, 303
Dulles, Allen, 155–56, 158, 159
Dulles, John Foster, 36, 89, 93, 117, 118, 183–84

Eban, Abba, 123, 234, 298–99
Eden, Anthony, 21, 83–84, 87, 92

Egypt:
  and Algeria, 60–61, 64–66, 74–75, 93
  in Arab unions, 63, 93, 183, 211,
    217, 256, 272, 275, 329
  and Camp David, 296, 335, 338
  economic problems of, 322
  equilibrium with, 337–38, 338, 356
  French-Israeli joint operations
    against, 69–73, 77, 82–90, 91
  German aid to, 203–11, 213, 214–15
  Israeli intelligence in, 50–51, 127,
    203, 208, 214, 331
  Israel threatened by, 58, 63, 205,
    214–15, 228, 252–53, 275, 311;
    see also specific wars
  missiles in, 202–10, 213, 248, 253,
    311
  nuclear capability of, 127, 197, 200,
    202, 205, 214, 248, 253, 273, 274,
    311
  Revolution Day celebrations in, 196,
    197, 200, 202
  and Sinai, see Sinai peninsula
  and Soviet Union, 70, 93–94, 202,
    253, 272–73, 274, 295, 314–15,
    322
  in space race, 200–207, 253
  and Suez Canal, 50–51, 70–71,
    82–88, 92–95, 297, 299, 314–15,
    319, 322–24, 328–29
  and Tiran Straits, 63, 71, 277
  and U.S. interests, 220, 254–55,
    295–96, 329–31, 346
  weapons sold to, 36, 61, 63, 70, 71,
    94, 293–94
  Yemen offensive of, 217–18, 271,
    272, 279
Eichmann, Adolf, 81, 206, 223, 271
Einstein, Albert, 96, 97, 116, 142,
  288–89, 358–59
Eisenhower, Dwight D., 9–10, 52, 70,
  83, 86, 89, 93, 156, 183
Eisenhower administration:
  and Dimona project, 158–61,
    163–64, 178–79, 186, 238

  and Middle East, 37, 86, 87, 94, 100,
    180, 182, 183, 219, 232, 258, 295,
    319
Eisenhower Doctrine, 94, 182
Elazar, David "Dado," 323–24, 327, 336
Elgozy, Georges, 59–60
Eliot, Theodore L., 316–18
Elon, Amos, 231
Ely, Paul, 63, 72
EMET, 42–43, 44–47, 48, 49–51,
  101–2, 107, 113–14
Erdos, Paul, 288
Eretz Yisrael (Land of Israel):
  Arab attacks in, 19–20
  building of, 9, 10, 17, 23, 40, 259
  immigration to, 9, 13, 25, 132
  independent Jewish state in, 15, 16,
    21, 23, 24
  settlers of, 16, 25, 26, 111, 133, 259,
    339
Erhard, Ludwig, 249, 256
Eshkol, Levi, 195
  and Ben-Gurion, 210, 223, 224, 227,
    259–61, 266–67
  death of, 293, 314
  and Dimona, 120, 128, 235–39,
    263–64
  and Johnson, 194, 234, 244, 252–55,
    261, 262, 294–95, 296–97, 298
  and Kennedy's letter, 224, 232–39
  and Lavon Affair, 226, 227, 258–59
  and nuclear capability, 250–52, 256,
    257, 261, 262–65, 273, 274–75, 293
  personal traits of, 234, 238, 265
  political career of, 227, 260, 281
  as prime minister, 176, 226–28, 238,
    258–65, 271, 281
  reorganization by, 176, 261–67
  and Six-Day War, 276–77, 281, 285
  U.S. visit by, 251–55, 256
  weapons sought by, 237–38, 247–49,
    250, 294, 297, 298

Farley, Philip J., 188, 190, 193, 302
Faure, Edgar, 59, 65

Feinberg, Abraham, 129–37, 185, 186, 249, 308–9
Feldman, Myer "Mike," 185–86, 192, 205, 216–17, 218, 249–51
Fermi, Enrico, 48, 358
Finney, John W., 157, 314
Fortas, Abe, 249
France:
    and Algeria, 58, 60–61, 65–66, 72, 75–76, 87, 91, 104, 168, 169–70, 172–73, 184
    and arms embargoes, 36, 60, 65, 68, 171–76, 296
    capitulation to Nazis by, 12, 62–63, 68, 92
    intelligence activities of, 66, 74–75, 93
    and Israel against Arabs, 58, 62, 69–73, 77, 82–90, 91, 184
    and NATO, 169
    nuclear capability of, 67–68, 76, 79–80, 91, 92, 106, 109, 138, 139, 154, 169, 170–72, 181, 198, 342–43, 344, 369n3
    nuclear reactor supplied by, 46, 78–82, 86, 89–92, 95, 153, 161, 165, 200, 229, 239, 269
    and Suez Canal, 71, 80, 82–90, 92, 95, 169
    support for Jews from, 11–12, 62–63, 68–70, 79, 100, 115, 119, 139, 142, 143, 149, 161, 169, 170–74, 229, 239
    and Sykes-Picot treaty, 18
    Syria as mandate of, 18
    Vichy regime in, 12, 92
    and Vietnam, 79–80
    wartime resistance in, 11, 12, 58, 59
    weapons sought from, 57–58, 60, 61–62, 64–72
    weapons supplied by, 11, 66–72, 74, 213–14
Frankfurter, Felix, 25
Free French movement, 11, 12, 58, 62
Freier, Shalhevet, 49, 107

    birth and background of, 97–98
    and nuclear capability, 81, 90, 92, 99–100, 115–16, 169, 343, 355–58
    personal traits of, 96–97, 111, 358
    and refugees, 98, 132, 133

Gadhafi, Mu'ammar, 340, 352
Gates, Thomas S., 158, 159
Gazit, Mordechai, 188–90, 193, 251, 302
Gehlen, Reinhard, 213
Georges-Picot, François, 18
Gerhardsen, Einar, 142–44
Germany:
    atomic research in, 289, 316, 359
    Mossad activity in, 206–8, 212–13, 353
    reparations from, 206, 270
    technical help to Egypt from, 203–11, 213, 214–15
    weapons to Israel from, 209, 223, 225, 249–50, 255–56, 258, 320–21
    and World War II, 15, 59, 62, 68, 245, 289
Gibson, William, 335
Gilbert, Pierre, 77
Glass, Alice, 245
Goercke, Paul-Jens, family of, 207
Golda's Balcony (Gibson), 335
Goldberg, Arthur, 308–9
Goldhaber, Shulamith and Gershon, 290
Goldschmidt, Bertrand Leopold, 172
Gomberg, Henry Jacob, 146–50, 153, 155–56, 160, 166–67
Gromyko, Andrei, 117
Gruen, David, see Ben-Gurion, David
Guillaumat, Pierre, 79
Gulf War (1991), 346, 350

Haakon VII, king of Norway, 143
Hadari, Ze'ev "Venya," 111–12
Haganah, 26, 35–36, 38, 41, 42, 44, 98–99, 132, 186, 227, 246

Haifa Flying Club, 101
Haig, Alexander, 349
Haikal, Muhammad Hasanin, 200–201, 214, 274, 275
Halevy, Ephraim, 351
Hall, Lawrence B., 155
Hammarskjöld, Dag, 142, 216
Hancock, Patrick Francis, 151
Hannegan, Robert, 131
Harel, Isser, 75, 78, 80–81, 326
    and Dimona, 117–18, 119
    and Egyptian missiles, 203, 204, 205–6, 208, 210
    and Mossad, 72, 208, 212, 353
    and political conflict, 119, 210, 212
    political influence of, 81, 102, 212
Harman, Avraham "Abe," 156, 161, 217, 251
Harriman, Averell W., 234, 256, 301
Harrison, Earl G., 25
Heisenberg, Werner, 288, 363–64n6
Helms, Richard, 283, 293
HEMED, 35, 37–38, 42, 50, 112
Hersh, Seymour M., 343
Herter, Christian A., 156, 158–60
Herzl, Theodor, 371n5
Herzog, Jacob, 250
Hiroshima, atomic bomb on, 28, 51, 119, 288, 358, 368n13
Hitler, Adolf, 12, 21, 62, 72, 88, 130, 183, 245, 254, 287, 288, 289
Hod, Motti, 310, 311
Hofstadter, Robert, 167
Holocaust:
    concentration camps, 7–8, 12, 28, 58, 62–63, 132, 143, 247, 284
    fears of another, 41, 64, 232, 254, 271, 358
    German reparations for, 206, 270
    horror of, 28, 29, 223, 247, 284
    Jewish sacrifice of, 15, 29, 133, 143–44
    Kristallnacht, 97, 367n11
    lessons learned from, 10, 12, 23, 28–29, 34, 58, 62–63, 116, 133, 143–44, 181, 232, 247, 287, 358

    public awareness of, 15–16, 37, 111, 271
    survivors of, 60, 97, 111, 132, 187, 245–46, 271
Horowitz, Jules, 172
Hull, Cordell, 131
Hungary, revolt in, 86, 88, 93
Husayni, Haj Amin al-, 19, 21
Hussein, king of Jordan, 82–83, 184, 211, 217, 256, 379n7
Hussein, Saddam, 340, 341, 346, 350, 352
Hussein ibn Ali, Sharif of Mecca, 18

India, 141, 161, 164, 181, 295, 316
International Atomic Energy Agency (IAEA), 144–45, 159, 178–79, 252, 356
Iran, 217, 321, 341, 346–48, 350–55
Iraq, 83, 279
    coups in, 37, 93, 183, 211
    nuclear reactor of, 282, 341, 349–50, 351
    and terrorism, 340, 341, 346
Ismail, Muhammad Hafez, 329
Israel:
    Arab threats against, see Arabs
    army founded by, 20, 26–27, 32, 35–36
    austerity in, 59, 78, 104
    building of, 13, 17, 337
    and Camp David, 296, 335, 338
    censorship in, 157, 176, 208, 223, 230–32, 250, 262, 270, 327
    conformist society in, 121, 230, 345
    disarmament doctrine of, 355–58
    existence of, 65, 89, 92, 94, 185, 187, 208, 211, 217, 219, 221, 239, 271, 324, 326, 330, 332, 338–39, 346, 355, 359
    and France against Arabs, 58, 62, 69–73, 77, 82–90, 91, 184
    French arms to, 57–58, 60–62, 66–72, 74, 213–14
    German arms to, 209, 223, 225, 249–50, 255–56, 258, 320–21

Israel (*continued*)
    independence of, 10, 16, 18, 20, 24,
        236, 238
    intelligence activities in, 61, 66, 73,
        74–77, 93, 98–99, 103, 169, 203,
        247, 272, 275, 277, 331, 347–48,
        351–53
    map, 4
    military preparedness of, 51, 133,
        199–200, 249, 271–72, 330
    "not the first to introduce nuclear
        weapons," 250–52, 256, 257, 275,
        296, 298, 306, 309–11, 314
    nuclear option of, *see* nuclear capa-
        bility
    policy of ambiguity in, 201, 248,
        250–52, 281, 298, 303, 306, 309,
        342–45
    refugees to, *see* Jews
    security of borders, 58, 208, 257,
        270–71, 272, 275, 278, 297, 322,
        329, 339
    and September 11 attacks, 340–41
    socialism in, 46, 103
    strategic value of, 94, 182, 183–84,
        350
    survival of, 36, 44, 61, 62, 64, 67,
        119, 187, 189–90, 202, 211, 222,
        234–36, 247, 254, 271, 291, 302,
        310, 326, 349, 359
    technological superiority of, 33, 95,
        189, 241, 270, 283, 345–46
    territories of, 84–85, 87, 88, 89, 182,
        216, 227, 275, 284, 320, 323, 329,
        331, 333, 338–39
    Third Commonwealth of, 325–26,
        327
    as U.S. ally, *see* United States
    wars with Arabs *see specific wars*
    weapons sought by, 57–62, 64–72,
        209, 237–38, 249–50, 251, 254,
        255–58, 284, 294, 297, 298–99,
        303–13, 315–19
Israel Aircraft Industries (IAI), 204–5,
    262

Israel Defense Forces (IDF), 30, 72
    formation of, 35
    and French intelligence, 75
    and nuclear capability, 38, 256
    research and development in, 38, 45,
        47–48, 101–2
    and Six-Day War, 276, 284
    weapons for, 36, 37, 39, 44, 56, 57
    and Yom Kippur War, 323
Israeli Air Force, 36, 68, 153, 283, 294,
    303, 314–15, 328, 348, 354

Jarring, Gunnar, 319
Jerusalem, 19, 339
Jews:
    Arab attacks feared by, *see* Arabs
    and Balfour Declaration, 15, 18,
        21–22
    Diaspora of, 14, 135
    extermination of, 29, 41
    and Holocaust, *see* Holocaust
    homeland of, *see* Eretz Yisrael; Israel
    intercessors for, 135
    military training for, 10, 16, 20, 25,
        26, 223, 225
    in Norway, 143–44
    in Palestine, *see* Palestine
    refugees, 9–12, 14, 21, 25, 40–42, 86,
        97, 98, 102, 132, 242, 245–46, 280
Johnson, Joseph E., 216
Johnson, Lyndon B., 242–58, 298
    and elections, 181, 245, 255, 297, 308
    and Eshkol, 194, 234, 244, 252–55,
        261, 262, 294–95, 296–97, 298
    and Jewish-American community,
        246–47, 255, 308–9, 313
    and Jewish refugees, 245–46
    religious roots of, 243–44, 254, 257
    and U.S.-Arab relations, 295, 299
Johnson, Sam Ealy Sr., 243
Johnson administration:
    commitment to Israel's security, 243,
        247–50, 258, 261, 294, 295, 298,
        301–14, 319
    and Dimona, 247–48, 254–55, 287

and nuclear capability, 302–13, 317
and Six-Day War, 279, 282, 283, 285
Johnson plan, 216–17, 219
Joklik, Otto, 205–6, 207, 208, 210
Jordan:
    in Arab unions, 63, 256
    and balance of power, 217, 256–58, 338, 346
    and British mandate, 18, 84
    instability in, 37, 93, 183, 184, 211
    Israel threatened by, 58, 63, 82–86
    and Six-Day War, 275, 278

KAMAG (Negev Nuclear Research Center), 114, 175
Katchalsky, Aharon (Katzir), 42, 125, 280
Katchalsky, Ephraim (Katzir), 42, 124, 125, 188, 190, 192, 230, 266, 280, 327–28, 336
Kaufman, Ed, 135
Keightley, Sir Charles, 82–83
Kennedy, John F., 146, 164, 179–81, 184–86, 295
    assassination of, 240, 242
    and Ben-Gurion, 192–95, 211, 220–22, 224, 302
    letter of demands from, 221–22, 224–25, 232–35, 238–39, 248
Kennedy, Joseph P. Sr., 186
Kennedy administration, 163, 179–82
    and Cuban missile crisis, 219–20, 233
    and Dimona, 186–95, 221–22, 224–25, 228, 232–39
    and Israel-U.S. relations, 218–22, 258, 319
    and Johnson plan, 216–17, 219
    nonproliferation focus of, 164, 180–81, 185–87, 193, 219, 222, 233–35, 248, 251, 273, 302
Khrushchev, Nikita, 211
Kissinger, Henry A., 315, 316–19, 324, 328, 329–30, 332–35, 338, 342
Kistiakowsky, George, 158
Kleinwachter, Hans, 203, 207
Knesset, 208–9, 211

and elections, 103, 199
and nuclear capability, 120–21, 161–62, 166, 179, 200, 232, 250, 251, 276, 284
Koenig, Marie-Pierre, 58, 60
Kol Yisrael, 27, 162, 270, 354
Komer, Robert, 186, 249, 255, 256–57, 301
Kosygin, Aleksey, 282
Krug, Heinz, 207

LaCoutour, Jean, 170
Laskov, Haim, 126–27
Lavon, Pinhas, 49–51, 225, 258
Lavon Affair, 50–51, 119, 214, 225–26, 227, 258–59, 261
Lawrence, T. E., 18
Lebanon, 18, 37, 93, 183, 184, 338, 339, 341, 353
Leibowitz, Yeshayahu, 230
Leinsdorf, Erich, 245
Liberty, 303–4
Libya, 202, 340, 348, 351–52
Lipkin, Harry J. "Zvi," 111, 112, 175
Lipsky, Louis, 25
Livermore National Laboratory, California, 174, 290, 320
Livneh, Eliezer, 230
Lloyd, Selwyn, 84
Lodge, Henry Cabot Jr., 93
Lotz, Wolfgang, 371n7

Magnes, Yehuda Leib, 16, 288
Malraux, André, 59
Mangin, Louis, 57, 70, 71
Manhattan Project, 51–52, 109, 116, 137, 172, 288, 291, 369n6
Maquis, 11, 12, 58, 62
Mardor, Gonnie, 31, 47, 49, 265, 280, 286
Mardor, Lenka, 30–31, 39, 265
Mardor, Meir "Munya," 52, 98
    birth and background of, 41
    and Defense Ministry, 30–31, 36, 38–42, 81, 113, 282

Mardor, Meir "Munya" (*continued*)
   and Dimona, 111, 123, 128, 175
   and EMET, 42–43, 44–47, 49–50,
      51, 101–2, 107
   and *Patria*, 40–42, 280
   and political conflict, 261–63,
      264–66
   and RAFAEL, 113–14, 123–27, 175,
      196–99, 202, 204–5, 240, 262–63,
      264–66, 268, 279–80, 284, 285,
      286
   and refugees, 10–11, 40–42, 111,
      132, 133, 280
   and Six-Day War, 284, 285
   and Zionism, 38–39, 41
Mardor, Rami, 30, 47, 202, 265, 280,
      290–91
Marsh, Charles Edward, 245
Marshall, George C., 300
Massu, Jacques, 168
McCone, John A., 157, 158, 159
McMahon, Sir Henry, 17–18
McNamara, Robert S., 249, 279, 294,
      299
Meir, Golda, 108, 217, 298, 314
   and Arab-Jewish conflicts, 78, 89
   and Ben-Gurion, 81, 206, 209, 210,
      223–24, 225, 228, 259
   and Dimona, 117, 120, 178, 187,
      228–29, 319, 335–36
   and Egyptian missiles, 205, 208
   as foreign minister, 69, 72, 77, 81,
      100, 171
   and French connection, 171, 173
   and Germany, 206, 208, 223, 225
   and Kennedy administration,
      218–20, 228, 233, 234, 258
   memoirs of, 227, 323, 336
   and Nixon, 194, 315–16, 318
   and political conflict, 119, 120
   and RAFAEL, 196, 262
   suicidal thoughts of, 322–23, 336
   and Yom Kippur War, 323–26
Mendelsohn, Erich, 33
Mendès-France, Pierre, 80

Meshal, Khaled, 351
Messerschmitt, Willy E., 203–4
Middle East:
   Arab-Jewish conflicts in, *see specific
      wars*
   arms embargoes in, 36, 56, 60, 65,
      68, 171–76, 296
   balance of power in, 36–37, 63,
      93–95, 173, 181, 182–84, 194,
      198, 200–207, 210, 216–20, 231,
      238, 247–49, 251, 253–54, 258,
      274–75, 276, 303–4, 308, 346–49
   colonial era ended in, 92
   disarmament in, 355–58
   Eisenhower Doctrine in, 94, 182
   Israel "not first to introduce nuclear
      weapons into," 250–52, 256, 257,
      275, 296, 298, 306, 309–11, 314
   map, 5
   nuclear options in, *see* nuclear
      capability
   oil in, 21, 38, 180, 218
   peace sought for, 185, 216–17, 244,
      296, 319, 329–31, 335, 337–39,
      341, 357
   political instability in, 37, 93, 183,
      184, 211
   terrorism in, 338–39, 340–41
Mofaz, Shaul, 354
Mollet, Guy, 65, 66, 68–69, 72, 79, 85,
      89, 90–91, 92
Montor, Henry, 26
Morgenthau, Henry Jr., 136
Mossad:
   and Algeria, 66, 72, 75, 173
   early years of, 11
   and Egyptian-German connection,
      206–10, 212–13, 215
   in Europe, 99, 206–8, 212–13, 353
   fear of, 110
   and Gomberg, 166
   and Iran, 350–54
   left out of the loop, 75, 119
   and political conflict, 212, 351
   roles of, 173, 351–53

Moulin, Jean, 12
Munich Olympics (1972), 353
Mussolini, Benito, 72

Nagasaki, atomic bomb on, 28, 51, 119,
    288, 358, 368n13
Naguib, Muhammad, 217
Nahal Soreq reactor, 53–56, 107, 140,
    146, 147, 149, 153, 162, 191, 202,
    266
Nahmias, Joseph, 57–58, 61, 77
Nasser, Gamal Abdel, 62, 67, 331
    and Algeria, 61, 64–65, 91
    as avowed enemy of Israel, 92, 200,
        201, 228, 252–53, 295
    death of, 322
    and nuclear option, 196, 197,
        200–201, 202, 214, 253, 281, 283
    political strategy of, 63, 197, 200,
        210, 253, 271–77, 283, 295, 319
    and Six-Day War, see Six-Day War
    and Soviet Union, 94, 201, 272
    and Suez Canal, 70–71, 82, 83, 85,
        92–95, 297, 319
    and U.S., 94, 182–83, 184, 220, 253,
        295, 329
    Yemen offensive of, 217–18, 272
NATO, 144, 169, 213, 235
Navon, Yitzhak, 7, 64, 210, 224, 225
Nazis:
    Arabs as allies of, 21
    causing sympathy to Jews, 62–63, 65,
        271
    French capitulation to, 12, 62–63,
        68, 92
    French resistance to, 11, 12, 58, 59
    and Holocaust, 7–8, 12, 28, 58, 111,
        132, 271, 284
    and Jewish property, 227
    Norway occupied by, 142, 143–44
    revenge sought against, 176
Neeman, Yuval, 37–38, 137, 151
    and Ben-Gurion, 38, 47, 76, 224, 225
    and French connection, 74–77, 79
    and RAFAEL, 174–75

and Teller, 290, 291–92, 320
Negev Nuclear Research Center, see Di-
    mona nuclear project
Netanyahu, Benjamin, 3, 349, 351
Neumann, John von, 288
Nitze, Paul H., 308
Nixon, Richard M.:
    and elections, 181, 297–98
    and Israel's survival, 308, 318–19,
        324
    and Meir, 194, 315–16, 318
Nixon administration:
    and Middle East peace, 319
    and nuclear capability, 317–18, 342
    and Watergate, 330
    and Yom Kippur War, 332–35
Non-Aligned Movement, 197
Norway, 141–45, 152, 161
Novy, James, 245–46
nuclear capability:
    administration of, 114–15, 175
    and arms race, 253–54, 273–74
    atomic bombs, 28, 51, 119, 288
    atoms for peaceful purposes, 45, 52,
        53, 91, 100, 144, 161–64, 179,
        193, 201, 358
    and balance of power, 151, 189,
        202–5, 210, 231, 238, 276
    Ben-Gurion's quest for, 13, 20, 23,
        24, 28, 34, 37–38, 47, 50, 51–52,
        55, 76, 78, 79, 89–90, 94, 95, 100,
        108, 119, 120–22, 127–29,
        141–42, 222, 228, 247, 269, 290,
        332, 342
    budgeting for, 113, 126–29, 135–37
    deterrent advantage in, 28, 34, 55,
        68, 79, 111, 119, 125, 126,
        127–28, 181, 187, 189–90,
        221–22, 235–39, 253, 269, 271,
        281, 302, 311, 321, 330, 332, 341,
        346, 356
    at Dimona, see Dimona nuclear pro-
        ject
    evolution of, 52–55, 80–81, 85–86,
        89, 95, 268–70, 316, 342

nuclear capability *(continued)*
  French aid with, 46, 78–82, 86,
      89–92, 95, 142, 153, 156, 161,
      165, 171–72, 174, 200, 269
  French embargo on, 171–76
  and heavy water, 78, 106, 141–45,
      152, 161
  inspections of, 54, 164, 186–95, 220–
      222, 232–35, 237, 239–40,
      317–18
  international control of, 152, 163
  Israel as "not first to introduce,"
      250–52, 256, 257, 275, 296, 298,
      306, 309–11, 314
  Israel's attainment of, 268–69, 277,
      279–80, 320, 337
  Israel's policy of ambiguity in, 201,
      248, 250–52, 281, 298, 303, 306,
      309, 342–45
  and lab accident, 103–4
  media stories about, 156–57, 158,
      162, 198, 269, 270, 274, 314,
      320–21, 328, 344
  missiles, 196–200, 202–5, 229,
      273–74, 296, 311, 314, 328
  moral element of, 116, 291
  at Nahal Soreq, *see* Nahal Soreq
      reactor
  nonproliferation of, 163–64, 180–81,
      185–87, 193, 219, 222, 233–35,
      248, 273, 291, 302, 305, 313, 316,
      318, 342, 356
  Norway's aid with, 141–45, 152
  "nth countries" with, 150, 152, 269,
      281, 302, 310, 316
  opponents of, 48, 49–50, 55, 78–79,
      199, 230–32
  and phosphates, 38, 45
  plutonium production in, 53–55, 79,
      86, 91, 106, 121, 139, 140–41,
      147, 155, 163, 171, 189, 190, 193,
      214, 269, 277
  political control of, 263–67
  and RAFAEL, *see* RAFAEL
  scientific infrastructure for, 46,
      137–42
  and Six-Day War, 276–79, 281–83,
      284–85
  submarines, 320–21
  swimming-pool reactor, 53, 78
  Teller as adviser on, 289–93
  training for, 92, 148–49, 172, 174, 202
  and uranium, 38, 53, 54, 78, 91,
      137–40
  and weaponry, 156, 158, 160, 162,
      163, 174, 189, 200, 289–90
  and Yom Kippur War, 324–28

Ollendorf, Franz, 230
Oppenheimer, Robert, 52, 108, 290,
      291, 358
Organisation de l'Armée Secrète (OAS),
      170
Oslo accords (1993), 331
Oz, Amos, 336

Pakistan, 181, 340, 347, 348
Palestine:
  Arab-Jewish cohabitation in, 16–17,
      230, 331, 338
  Arab-Jewish conflicts in, 16–17,
      19–20, 26, 94, 275
  Arab population in, 15, 16, 19, 20,
      216, 219, 275
  and Balfour Declaration, 15, 18
  British departure from, 98–99
  as British mandate, 10–11, 17–18,
      20–23, 132–34
  as independent state, 331, 339
  Jewish community in, 9, 10, 12, 14,
      20, 21, 26, 32, 132–33
  Jewish homeland in, 18, 20–22
  Jewish immigration to, 8–12, 14,
      18–19, 21, 25, 40, 97
  partition of, 21, 25, 134–35, 362n6
  refugee problem in, 186, 216–17,
      219, 247
  and settlements, 331, 338
Palestine Liberation Organization
      (PLO), 338

Palestinian Authority, 338–39

Patria, 40–42, 102, 280

Pauli, Wolfgang, 48, 108

Péan, Pierre, 109, 110–11, 269

Peleg, David, 177

Peres, Shimon:
  and Arab-Jewish conflicts, 63, 77–79,
    84–85, 89, 281
  and Ben-Gurion's resignation, 224,
    225
  birth and early years of, 43–44
  and Dimona, 111, 112, 117–18,
    122–23, 124, 125, 128–29, 175,
    187, 194, 228, 236
  and Egyptian missiles, 204–5, 209,
    210
  and EMET, 43, 44, 45, 49
  and French connection, 57,
    59–60, 61–62, 64–72, 75, 77,
    79–81, 85–86, 89–92, 173, 174,
    213–14
  and Germany, 209, 212, 223
  and nuclear capability, 52, 79–81,
    85–86, 90–92, 100, 108, 114, 115,
    120, 126–27, 128, 151, 195, 234,
    238, 250–51, 255, 257, 343
  political career of, 43, 44, 120, 260,
    261, 281
  and political conflict, 119, 120, 129,
    151, 260–61, 263
  and RAFAEL, 196, 199, 213

Perrin, Francis, 90–91, 106, 168, 171

Pilz, Wolfgang, 204, 213

Pincher, Chapman, 157

Pineau, Christian, 65, 66–67, 68, 70,
  71–72, 77–78, 84, 85–86, 90

Placzek, George, 288

Pojidaev, Dimitri, 282

Pomerantz, Venya (Hadari), 111–12

Prat, Emmanuel "Mannes," 111,
  112–13, 114, 128, 151, 175, 176,
  187, 191, 192, 263–64

Pugwash Council, 96, 116, 355–56

Quisling, Vidkun, 143

Rabi, Isidore Isaac, 48, 52

Rabin, Yitzhak:
  and Ben-Gurion's resignation, 224,
    227
  and Clifford, 299–301, 308, 313
  and Clinton, 194
  death of, 304, 338
  memoirs of, 300, 306, 312–13, 318
  and military preparedness, 271–72,
    275, 276, 303–13, 314, 318
  and nuclear capability, 198, 256, 261,
    301–13, 317
  as U.S. ambassador, 297–98,
    299–314
  and U.S. draft memorandum, 304–7
  and Warnke, 300–314, 317

Racah, Giulio (Yoel), 48

RAFAEL, 113–14, 175, 188, 240–41
  and Egyptian missiles, 202, 204–5,
    213
  and Israeli rockets, 196–99
  and nuclear capability, 149, 268–69,
    279–80, 286
  and production, 114, 122–27, 174,
    199–200, 264
  and reorganization, 176, 261,
    262–63, 264–66
  and research, 114, 204, 263, 264
  and Six-Day War, 279, 284, 285

Randers, Gunnar, 142–45

Ratner, Yevgeni "Jenka," 100–102, 126,
  199, 268, 279–80

Reichardt, Charles, 155

Reid, Ogden, 147, 149, 157, 163–64,
  178, 201, 221

Reston, James, 231

Rodfa, Munir, 283

Rofeh, Hava, 104–5

Rogers, William P., 315, 319

Ronn, Moshe, 231

Roosevelt, Franklin D., 24, 131, 289, 358

Rosenberg, Julius and Ethel, 368n14

Rostow, Walt, 294

Rothschild family, 137

Ruina, Jack, 343

Rumsfeld, Donald, 1–2
Ruppin, Arthur, 259
Rusk, Dean, 179, 201, 217, 249, 254, 294, 298–99, 305, 309, 312, 313
Russell, Bertrand, 96, 116, 358

Saclay Centre, France, 106–7, 112, 171
Sadat, Anwar al-, 182, 295–96, 322–23, 328 31, 332, 335, 338, 346
Sadeh, Dror, 100, 102–7, 168, 171–72, 173, 176–77, 291–92
Sadeh, Haya, 100, 102, 103, 115, 291, 292
Saint-Gobain Nucléaire, 92, 174
Salam, Abdus, 47
Salan, Raoul, 370n6
Sapir, Pinhas, 120, 225, 262
Sassoon, Moshe, 133–34
Saudi Arabia, 184, 217, 218, 279, 340, 346
Scherrer, Paul, 48
Schiff, Ze'ev, 230–31, 262, 281, 343–44
Schlenk, Wilhelm, 31
Seaborg, Glenn, 358
Seaburn, Eugene T., 155
September 11 attacks, 340–41
Sèvres Protocol, 84–86, 90, 95
Shalev, Avner, 336
Shalit, Amos de, 53, 104
    and Dimona, 111, 264
    nuclear option opposed by, 48, 49, 54–55, 76, 78–79, 108, 124, 199
    and research institute, 102, 103, 151
Shamir, Yitzhak, 350
Shapira, Danni, 283
Shapira, Haim Moshe, 277–78
Sharett, Moshe, 49, 51, 53, 69, 119, 226, 259
Sharon, Ariel, 3, 325, 332, 349, 350
Shazar, Zalman, 224, 258
Shpruch, Tamar, 7, 9, 10, 29
Shubinski, Yitzhak, 59
Sieff family, 137
Sieff Research Institute, 32, 33, 142
Silver, Abba Hillel, 24, 25, 131

Sinai peninsula, 38, 71, 84, 86–87, 88, 89, 182, 232, 272, 275–76, 323, 328, 329, 331
Six-Day War (1967), 230, 253
    Arab unions in, 278–79
    Egyptian attack in, 282
    Egypt's entry into Sinai, 272, 275–76
    and French arms embargo, 296
    Israeli conquest in, 284, 285, 293, 295, 331
    Nasser's preliminary activities to, 272–76
    and nuclear option, 276–79, 281–83, 284–85
    Teller's admiration for, 291, 293
    "Waiting" period before, 271, 275–84, 285, 332
Slavin, Chaim, 27
Smith, Walter Bedell, 9
Sonneborn, Rudolf S., 26, 136
Sonneborn Institute, 27, 136
Soustelle, Jacques, 66, 115, 169–70, 171
South Africa, 181, 342, 343
Soviet Union:
    atomic research in, 172
    and Cold War, 37, 219–20, 233, 272, 281–82, 290, 315
    collapse of, 340, 347
    détente with, 315
    Jews emigrating from, 339–40
    Middle East interests of, 21, 37, 61, 63, 70, 72, 87, 88–89, 91, 93–94, 126, 151, 182–83, 184, 201, 202, 217, 219, 247, 253, 256, 272–73, 274, 293–94, 295, 298–99, 322, 329, 347
    and nuclear secrets, 80, 179, 344
    nuclear threats from, 12, 88–90, 92–93, 116, 219–20, 232, 233, 334–35
    pogroms in, 19
    and Suez, 83, 86, 87, 88–89, 93, 116
    and War of Attrition, 314–15
    and Yom Kippur War, 322, 329–30, 332–34

Staebler, Ulysses, 190–91
Stein, Gabriel, 230
Steinitz, Yuval, 352, 353
Strauss, Franz Josef, 205, 223
Strauss, Lewis L., 53–54
Straw, Jack, 1
Suez Canal, 50–51, 70–71, 80, 82–90,
        92–95, 116, 169, 182, 201, 226,
        232, 297, 299, 314–15, 319,
        322–24, 328–29, 331
Suisini, Jean, 370n6
Susanna operation, 50
Sykes-Picot treaty (1916), 18
Syria, 18, 58
    in Arab unions, 63, 183, 211, 217,
        256, 272, 275, 329
    coups in, 275
    and Israel's borders, 272, 275
    and peace negotiations, 338, 339
    Soviet weapons to, 293–94
    and U.S. interests, 295, 340–41, 346
    and Yom Kippur War, 322–23, 326,
        328, 329
Szilard, Leo, 288, 358
Szold, Henrietta, 365–66n2

Tal, Yisrael, 326
Talbot, Phillips, 186, 222
Talmi, Igal, 175, 264
Taylor, Theodore, 109, 344
Teller, Edward, 52, 174, 287–93
    birth and background of, 287–88
    and CIA, 287, 292–93, 296, 303, 317
    and Einstein's letter, 288–89
    and Holocaust, 287
    and Manhattan Project, 288, 291
    as nuclear adviser to Israel, 289–93
    nuclear research of, 289, 320
    and Star Wars, 291–92
Terboven, Josef, 143
terrorism, war on, 340–41, 346, 352–55
Thiry, Jean, 172
Thomas, Abel, 12, 57, 58, 61–62, 64,
        65–68, 70, 72, 77, 79, 80, 88, 89,
        90–91, 92

Thomas, Pierre, 12–13, 58, 62
Tiran Straits, 63, 71, 277
Tolkowsky, Dan, 125–26, 151
Truman, Harry S., 24–25, 131–32, 134,
        135, 300–301
Tsur, Zvi, 196, 204, 209, 224, 234, 238
Tzur, Jacob, 57, 61, 68–69, 70, 77, 81, 100

Unified Arab Command, 256
United Arab Emirates, 183, 346
United Arab Republic (UAR), 183, 189,
        193–94, 248, 253, 272
United Nations, 52, 53, 88–89, 134,
        142, 276, 277, 356, 375n3
United Palestine Appeal, 26, 130
United States:
    and Arab world, 94, 180, 186, 194,
        216, 219, 238, 253, 295–96, 299,
        329–31
    and arms embargo, 36, 68, 182
    atomic energy policies of, 52–55,
        163, 344
    and Cold War, see Cold War
    and control of nuclear power, 80,
        119–20, 141, 144, 150, 152,
        160–61, 163–64, 178–82, 220,
        224–25, 232–39
    hegemony of, 68, 79, 144, 178–79,
        182, 220–22, 224–25, 232–39,
        299, 305–13
    inspections by, 54, 164, 186–95,
        220–22, 232–35, 237, 239–40,
        317–18
    intelligence activity of, 146, 150–61,
        164–66, 209–10, 269, 283, 303,
        342, 344, 347–48, 351, 353
    Israel as ally to, 2–3, 181, 182–87,
        216, 218–22, 236, 239, 250–58,
        294, 298–99, 300–313
    and Israeli survival, 94, 218–19,
        235–36, 341, 349
    Jewish community in, 23, 24, 25–27,
        37, 130–31, 135–36, 181, 185–86,
        194, 217, 242–43, 246–47, 255,
        256–57, 298, 301, 308–9, 316, 340

United States: (*continued*)
  reactor from,   Nahal Soreq reactor
  and Suez, 83, 86, 87, 88, 89, 93–95, 329
  and Zionism, 24, 26–27, 130–31,
    184, 185
United Workers Party (Mapam), 103,
  231
Urbach, Ephraim, 230
U Thant, 276

Vanunu, Mordechai, 109, 110, 140, 145,
  166, 188, 269, 344–45
Vietnam, 79–80, 253, 255, 297, 299,
  315, 334
von Braun, Wernher, 203
Vorontsov, Yuli, 299

War of Attrition (1968), 297, 298, 299,
  314–15, 319
War of Independence (1948–49), 20, 29,
  30, 36, 39, 44, 63, 140, 260, 282
Warnke, Paul C., 181, 194, 247,
  299–314, 317, 343, 344
Weisgal, Meyer, 25, 26, 34, 35, 48,
  49–50, 151
Weisskopf, Victor, 48, 52
Weizman, Ezer, 125, 126, 278
Weizmann, Chaim, 26, 142, 263, 288
  and Balfour Declaration, 21–22
  diplomacy favored over force, 22,
    23–24, 33
  and partition, 134–35
  personal traits of, 22–23
  as president, 24
  and World Zionist Organization, 21,
    23, 24, 32
Weizmann, Vera, 32, 33, 35
Weizmann Institute, Rehovot, 24, 32
  and Bergmann, 33–34, 35, 45, 78, 240
  and EMET, 49–50
  nuclear conference in, 107–8
  nuclear research division of, 52,
    101–2, 106, 149

pure research in, 48, 50, 188
security research in, 33–34, 37, 102
and Sieff Institute, 33, 142
Wigner, Eugene Paul, 154, 287–88
Wilson, Harold, 279
Wise, Stephen S., 24, 25
Wolfson, Isaac, 137
Wolfson, Yehuda, 103, 104
World War I, 17–18
World War II, 25, 33, 58, 59, 62, 68
  atomic bombs ending, 28, 51, 119,
    288, 358
  onset of, 15, 20, 245, 288, 289
  Zionism in, 184
World Zionist Organization, 21, 23, 24,
  32

Yaari, Meir, 231–32
Yariv, Aharon, 277
Yatom, Danny, 351
Yemen, 217–18, 271, 272, 279
Yom Kippur war (1973), 285, 322–35,
  337–38, 346

Zacks, Samuel, 136
Zamir, Zvi, 353
Ze'evi, Rehavam, 336
Zionism, 38–39, 41, 44
  and Biltmore program, 25
  and British promises, 20–22, 23–24
  French sympathy for, 12, 115
  goals of, 13–17, 19, 40, 337
  idealism in, 20–21, 260
  and Jewish homeland, 23, 25, 259, 339
  leadership of, 22, 259
  and Mossad, 11
  myths of, 16
  and partition, 134
  in U.S., 24, 26–27, 130–31, 185
  U.S. sponsorship sought for, 23–27,
    184
Zippe, Gernot, 137
Zorea, Meir, 125